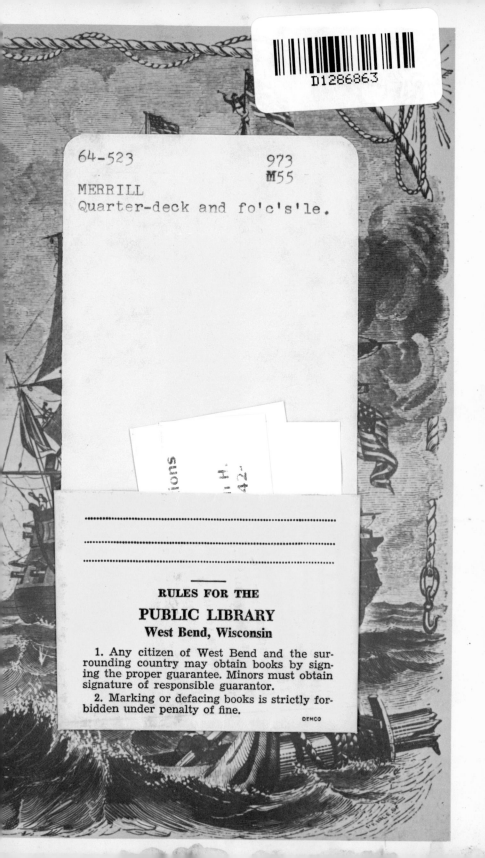

Quarter-Deck
and Fo'c's'le

Quarter-Deck and Fo'c's'le

THE EXCITING STORY OF THE NAVY

Edited by JAMES M. MERRILL

RAND McNALLY & COMPANY

Chicago   New York   San Francisco

Rand McNally wishes to thank the following sources who have kindly given permission for use of the photographs appearing in this book: U.S. Naval Photographic Center and the National Archives for all official U.S. Navy photographs appearing on pages 33, 53 (*bottom*), 59, 65, 69, 127, 149, 201, 221, 255 (*bottom*), 259 (*bottom*), 277, 289, 291, 299, 329, 361, 367, 405, 421, 423, 425, 431, 455, and 485; The Peabody Museum of Salem, pages 53 (*top* and *left*), 67 (*top*), 85 (*top*), 95, and 159 (*top*); New York Historical Society, endpieces, pages 47 (*top*), 159 (*bottom*), 255 (*top*), 259 (*top*), and 293; Chicago Historical Society, page 85 (*bottom*); New York Public Library, page 103; and the Library of Congress, page 115.

For my children, Eugenia and James,
that they may give thanks for all those who
laid down their lives in the service of our country

NOW HEAR THIS

Quarter-Deck and Fo'c's'le contains edited letters, essays, eye-witness accounts, ballads, journals, logbooks, and war diaries, written by officers and men who, themselves, served in the United States Navy from the Revolution up to the present.

No other branch of the armed forces functions with such pomp. Drill and discipline are what the petty officers demand at Annapolis, bawling orders from the corners of their mouths as the middies parade to the beat of the drum. Spit-and-polish survives in an age of space projectiles and nuclear weapons. It is less than twenty years, after all, since officers of the Pacific fleet, protecting the marines on Iwo Jima, dressed for dinner in ties and starched khaki shirts while American dive bombers screamed down on the Japanese defenders.

To this day it is a harrowing thing to hear the United States Navy sound General Quarters on a destroyer; a marvelous spectacle to see the men muster on a battle cruiser in the harbor of some Pacific outpost—Guam, say, or Midway—or some steamy port among the archipelagoes. There on the quarter-deck they form in their white uniforms, as they have for almost two centuries. When the barked commands have died away, the work has stopped, and all is silent, then the pure silvery notes of the night bugle ring out across the harbor—infinitely sad, infinitely old, infinitely poignant.

The purpose of this book is to let the sailors of the United States Navy tell their story. These writers put on a surprisingly good show. The reader will get a sense of continuity and of the ultimate brotherhood of Jones and Halsey, of Porter and Perry, of Rodgers, Hull, and Decatur. He will meet Seaman Cross, Gunner Evans, Lieutenant Cushing, and many more interesting and significant American bluejackets for the first time. Midshipman Fanning describes the duel between the *Bonhomme Richard* and the *Serapis;* Seaman Shaw tells of gunboat action in Tripoli Harbor; Purser's Steward Wales details the events of the *Somers* mutiny; Seaman Diggins chronicles Farragut's run past the Confederate forts at

New Orleans; Captain Sigsbee reports the explosion of the *Maine;* Commander Taussig writes of destroyer attacks on German U-Boats; a naval officer's widow recounts the tragedy of the airship *Akron;* Radioman Barker preserves the drama of Japanese air strikes; the skipper of the *Triton* logs the nuclear submarine's circumnavigation of the globe.

I do not suggest that this anthology is a history of the United States Navy. The private letter, the diary, the contemporary journal, the official report are too subjective, too slanted. Yet their very bias preserves the qualities that schoolbooks rarely, if ever, achieve—the writer's involvement makes the past real, vivid, interesting. They underscore that millions of seamen and petty officers no less than admirals and cabinet officials contribute to the heritage of the United States Navy.

I do not suggest, either, that these are the best possible selections—too much is available, too much is lost—but they do sample the many phases of naval activity and were composed by all kinds and types of personnel. I have omitted materials written by marines, merchant mariners, coast guardsmen, news correspondents, although, occasionally I include accounts by civilians attached to the Navy. For clarity I have abridged certain selections, canceling out superfluous words, phrases, and paragraphs, careful not to tamper with fact or interpretation. To preserve the spice of the fo'c's'le, the mispelled words and faulty grammar remain. The brief notes accompanying each selection are intended to provide background only.

I am appreciative of the assistance given me by the Mershon Center on Education in National Security and a Haynes Foundation Summer Grant through the auspices of Whittier College. Battle stars for help up and beyond the call of duty go to Dr. John H. Kemble, Pomona College; Dr. Brainerd Dyer, University of California, Los Angeles; Dr. David B. Tyler, Wagner College; Dr. Robert E. Johnson, University of Alabama; Drs. Albert W. Upton and Benjamin Whitten and Mrs. Ann D. Chandler, all of Whittier College. Thanks go to Mrs. John Simmons, who typed my manuscript as expertly as any Yeoman 1/c. My wife, Ann, has earned another hash-mark (Women's Reserve) for her patience, blue-penciling, and courageous handling of our children during her tour of duty on this volume.

JAMES M. MERRILL

Whittier, California

TABLE OF CONTENTS

I: Beat to Quarters
1776 - 1815

II: Attention All Hands
1815 - 1861

III: Stand to the Guns
1861 - 1898

IV: Commence Firing
1898 - 1918

V: This Is Not a Drill
1918 - 1945

VI: Ahead Full
1960

LIST OF PHOTOGRAPHS

LIST OF PHOTOGRAPHS

The United States Navy is the surest guarantor of peace which this country possesses.

THEODORE ROOSEVELT
3 December 1906

Quarter-Deck
and Fo'c's'le

The beginning of our navy, as navies now rank, was so singularly small that I am of the opinion it has no precedent in history. Was it proof of madness in the first corps of sea officers to have, at so critical a period, launched out on the ocean with only two armed merchant ships, two armed brigantines, and one armed sloop, to make war against such a power as Great Britain?

JOHN PAUL JONES

CHAPTER I

Beat to Quarters

1776 -1815

D URING the American Revolution, the Continental Navy provided the backbone of the naval fighting force; the privateers and ships of the states were auxiliaries. The Navy manned its warships and converted merchantmen with crews recruited from trading vessels, fishing craft, whalers, and the Army. At its maximum strength in the fall of 1776, it counted twenty-seven ships in commission—a pitiful contingent to pit against the British Goliath. This disparity was heightened by the superior average size of the Royal Navy's men-of-war and their heavier cannon. To venture out against such odds required men of high courage.

Hopelessly inadequate but buttressed by France, who opened her ports and sent her ships to American waters, the Continental Navy was vital to final victory. The sea arm fed munitions to the American Army, supported military operations ashore, and raided and destroyed commerce in British home waters.

I

THE ACTION WAS WARM, CLOSE,
AND OBSTINATE

Captain John Paul Jones in the Continental frigate Ranger, *18,
sailed from France in April, 1778 to scourge the shores of England,
Scotland, and Ireland. Jones relates to the American representatives
at the Court of France how on the 24th he attacked the British ship-
of-war* Drake, *off the Irish coast.*

BREST, May 27, 1778.

GENTLEMEN, I now fulfil the promise made in my last, by
giving you an account of my late expedition.

I sailed from Brest 10th of April. My plan was extensive. I therefore did not, at the beginning, wish to encumber myself with prisoners.
On the 14th I took a brigantine between Scylla and Cape Clear,
bound from Ostend with a cargo of flaxseed for Ireland, sunk her,
and proceeded into St. George's Channel. On the 17th I took the
ship *Lord Chatham,* bound from London to Dublin, with a cargo
consisting of porter and a variety of merchandize, and almost within
sight of her port; the ship I manned and ordered for Brest. Towards
the evening of the day following, the weather had a promising appearance, and the winds being favorable, I stood over from the Isle
of Man, with an intention to make a descent at Whitehaven. At 10
o'clock, I was off the harbor with a party of volunteers, and had
everything in readiness to land, but, before eleven, the wind greatly
increased, and shifted so as to blow directly upon the shore; the sea
increased of course, and it became impossible to effect a landing.

21

This obliged me to carry all possible sail, so as to clear the land, and to await a more favorable opportunity.

On the 18th, in Glenbue Bay, on the south coast of Scotland, I met with a revenue wherry; it being the common practice of these vessels to board merchant ships, and the *Ranger* then having no external appearance of war, it was expected that this rover would have come alongside. I was, however, mistaken, for, though the men were at their quarters, yet this vessel outsailed the *Ranger,* and got clear, in spite of a severe cannonade.

The next morning, off the Mull of Galloway, I found myself so near a Scotch coasting schooner, loaded with barley, that I could not avoid sinking her.

Understanding that 10 or 12 sail of merchant ships, besides a tender brigantine with a number of impressed men on board, were at anchor in Loughryan in Scotland, I thought this an enterprise worthy attention, but the wind shifted in a hard squall so as to blow directly in, with an appearance of bad weather; I was therefore obliged to abandon my project.

Seeing a cutter off the lee-bow steering for the Clyde, I gave chase in hopes of cutting her off; but finding my endeavors ineffectual, I pursued no farther than the rock of Ailsa. In the evening I fell in with a sloop from Dublin, which I sunk to prevent intelligence.

The next day, the 21st, being near Carrickfergus, a fishing boat came off, which I detained. I saw a ship at anchor in the road, which I was informed by the fisherman, was the British ship-of-war *Drake,* of 20 guns. I determined to attack her in the night. My plan was to over-lay her cable, and to fall upon her bow, so as to have all her decks open, and exposed to our musketry, &c.; at the same time it was my intention to have secured the enemy by graplings, so that, had they cut their cables, they would not thereby have attained an advantage.

The wind was high, and unfortunately the anchor was not let go so soon as the order was given; so that the *Ranger* was brought up on the enemy's quarter, at the distance of half a cable's length. We had made no warlike appearance, of course had given no alarm; this determined me to cut immediately, which might appear as if the cable had parted, and at the same time enabling me, after making a tack out of the Lough, to return with the same prospect of advantage which I had at the first. I was, however, prevented from returning; as I with difficulty weathered the lighthouse on the lee side of the Lough, and as the gale increased.

The weather now became so very stormy and severe, and the sea so high, that I was obliged to take shelter under the south shore of Scotland. The 22d introduced fair weather; though the three kingdoms as far as the eye could reach were covered with snow. I now resolved once more to attempt Whitehaven; but the wind became very light, so that the ship could not in proper time approach so near as I had intended. At midnight I left the ship, with two boats and thirty-one volunteers. When we reached the outer pier, the day began to dawn. I would not however abandon my enterprise; but despatched one boat under the direction of Mr. Hill and Lieutenant Wallingsford, with the necessary combustibles, to set fire to the shipping on the north side of the harbor, while I went with the other party to attempt the south side. I was successful in scaling the walls, and spiking up all the cannon in the first fort. Finding the sentinels shut up in the guard house, secured them without their being hurt. Having fixed sentinels, I now took with me one man only (Mr. Green), and spiked all the cannon on the southern fort; distant from the other a quarter of a mile.

On my return from this business, I naturally expected to see the fire of the ships on the north side, as well as to find my own party with everything in readiness to set fire to the shipping in the south. Instead of this, I found the boat under the direction of Mr. Hill and Mr. Wallingsford returned, and the party in some confusion, their light having burnt out at the instant when it became necessary. By the strangest fatality my own party were in the same situation, the candles being all burnt out. The day too came on apace; yet I would by no means retreat while any hopes of success remained. Having again placed sentinels, a light was obtained at a house disjoined from the town; and fire was kindled in the steerage of a large ship, which was surrounded by at least an hundred and fifty others, chiefly from two to four hundred tons burthen, and laying side by side aground, unsurrounded by the water. There were, besides, from seventy to an hundred large ships in the north arm of the harbor, aground, clear of the water, and divided from the rest only by a stone pier of a ship's height. I should have kindled fires in other places if the time had permitted. As it did not, our care was to prevent the one kindled from being easily extinguished.

23

After some search a barrel of tar was found, and poured into the flames, which now ascended from all the hatchways. The inhabitants began to appear in thousands; and individuals ran hastily towards us. I stood between them and the ship on fire, with a pistol in my hand, and ordered them to retire, which they did with precipitation. The flames had already caught the rigging, and began to ascend the mainmast—the sun was a full hour's march above the horizon; and as sleep no longer ruled the world, it was time to retire. We re-embarked without opposition, having released a number of prisoners, as our boats could not carry them. . . .

When we had rowed a considerable distance from the shore, the English began to run in vast numbers to their forts. Their disappointment may easily be imagined, when they found at least thirty heavy cannon rendered useless. At length, however, they began to fire; having, as I apprehend, either brought down ship's guns, or used one or two cannon which lay on the beach at the foot of the walls dismounted, and which had not been spiked. They fired with no direction; and the shot falling short of the boats, instead of doing us any damage, afforded some diversion, which my people could not help showing, by discharging their pistols, &c., in return of the salute. Had it been possible to have landed a few hours sooner, my success would have been complete. Not a single ship, out of more than two hundred, could possibly have escaped, and all the world would not have been able to save the town. What was done, however, is sufficient to show that not all their boasted navy can protect their own coasts; and that the scenes of distress which they have occasioned in America may be soon brought home to their own door. One of my people was missing, and must, I fear, have fallen into the enemies' hands after our departure. I was pleased that in this business we neither killed nor wounded any person. I brought off three prisoners as a sample. . . .

On the morning of the 24th I was again off Carrickfergus, and would have gone in had I not seen the *Drake* preparing to come out. It was very moderate, and the *Drake's* boat was sent out to reconnoitre the *Ranger*. As the boat advanced I kept the ship's stern directly towards her; and though they had a spy glass in the boat, they came on within hail, and alongside. When the officer came on the quarterdeck, he was greatly surprised to find himself a prisoner; although an express had arrived from Whitehaven the night before. I now understood, what I had before imagined, that the *Drake* came out in consequence of this information with volunteers, against the *Ranger.* The officer told me, also, they had taken up the *Ranger's* anchor. The *Drake* was attended by five small vessels full of people, who were led by curiosity to see an engagement. But when they saw the *Drake's* boat at the *Ranger's* stern they wisely put back.

Alarm smokes now appeared in great abundance, extending along on both sides of the channel. The tide was unfavorable, so that the *Drake* worked out but slowly. This obliged me to run down several times, and to lay with courses up and main-topsail to the mast. At length the *Drake* weathered the point, and having led her out to about mid-channel, I suffered her to come within hail. The *Drake* hoisted English colors, and, at the same instant, the American stars were displayed on board the *Ranger.* I expected that preface had been now at an end, but the enemy soon after hailed, demanding what ship it was? I directed the master to answer, 'the American Continental ship *Ranger;* that we waited for them, and desired that they would come on; the sun was now little more than an hour from setting, it was therefore time to begin.'

The *Drake* being astern of the *Ranger,* I ordered the helm up and gave the first broadside. The action was warm, close, and obstinate. It lasted an hour and four minutes, when the enemy called for quarter; her fore and main-topsail yards being both cut away, and down on the cap; the top-gallant yard and mizen-gaff both hanging up and down along the mast; the second ensign which they had hoisted shot away, and hanging on the quarter-gallery in the water; the jib shot away, and hanging in the water; her sails and rigging entirely cut to pieces; her masts and yard all wounded, and her hull also very much galled. I lost only Lieutenant Wallingsford and one seaman, John Dougall, killed, and six wounded; among whom are the gunner, Mr. Falls, and Mr. Powers, midshipman, who lost his arm. One of the wounded, Nathaniel Wills, is since dead; the rest will recover. The loss of the enemy in killed and wounded was far greater. . . .

The night and almost the whole day after the action being moderate, greatly facilitated the refitting of both ships. A large brigantine was so near the *Drake* in the afternoon that I was obliged to bring her to. She belonged to Whitehaven, and was bound for Norway.

I had thought of returning by the south channel; but, the wind shifting, I determined to pass by the north, and round the west coast of Ireland. This brought me once more off Belfast Lough, on the evening after the engagement. It was now time to release the honest fishermen, whom I took up here on the 21st, and as the poor fellows had lost their boat, she having sunk in the late stormy weather, I was happy in having it in my power to give them the necessary sum to purchase everything new which they had lost. I gave them also a good boat to transport themselves ashore; and sent with them two infirm men, on whom I bestowed the last guinea in my possession, to defray their travelling expenses to their proper home in Dublin. They took with them one of the *Drake's* sails, which would sufficiently explain what had happened to the volunteers. The grateful fishermen were in raptures; and expressed their joy in three huzzas as they passed the *Ranger's* quarter.

I again met with contrary winds in the mouth of the North Channel, but nothing remarkable happened, till on the morning of the 5th current, Ushant then bearing S.E. by S., distance fifteen leagues, when seeing a sail to leeward steering for the Channel, the wind being favorable for Brest and the distance trifling, I resolved to give chase, having the *Drake* in tow. I informed them of my intentions, and ordered them to cast off. They cut the hawser. The *Ranger* in the chase went lasking between N.N.E. and N.N.W. It lasted an hour and ten minutes, when the chase was hailed and proved a Swede. I immediately hauled by the wind to the southward.

After cutting the hawser, the *Drake* went from the wind for some time, then hauled close by the wind, steering from S.S.E. to S.S.W. as the wind permitted, so that when the *Ranger* spoke the chase the *Drake* was scarcely perceptible. . . . Towards noon it became very squally, the wind backed from the S.W. to the W. The *Ranger* had come up with the *Drake,* and was nearly abreast of her, though considerably to the leeward when the wind shifted. The *Drake* was however kept by the wind, though, as I afterwards understood, they knew the *Ranger,* and saw the signal which she had hoisted.

After various evolutions and signals in the night, I gave chase to a sail which appeared bearing S.S.W. the next morning at a great distance. The chase discovered no intention to speak with the *Ranger;* she was, however, at length brought to, and proved to be the *Drake.*

I immediately put Lieut. Simpson under suspension and arrest, for disobedience of my orders, dated the 26th ult., a copy whereof is here inclosed. On the 8th, both ships anchored safe in this Road, the *Ranger* having been absent only twenty-eight days. Could I suppose that my letters of the 9th and 16th current, (the first advising you of my arrival, and giving reference to the events of my expedition; the last advising you of my draft in favor of Monsieur Bersolle, for 24,000 livres, and assigning reasons for that demand), had not made due appearance, I would hereafter, as I do now, inclose copies.

Three posts have already arrived here from Paris, since Compte d'Orvilliers showed me the answer which he received from the minister, to the letter which inclosed mine to you. Yet you remain silent. M. Bersolle has this moment informed me of the fate of my bills; the more extraordinary, as I have not yet made use of your letter of credit of the 10th of January last, whereby I then seemed entitled to call for half the amount of my last draft, and I did not expect to be thought extravagant, when, on the 16th current, I doubled that demand. Could this indignity be kept secret I should disregard it; and, although it is already public in Brest and in the fleet, as it affects only my private credit, I will not complain. I cannot, however, be silent when I find the public credit involved in the same disgrace. I conceive this might have been prevented. To make me completely wretched, Monsieur Bersolle has told me that he now stops his hand, not only of the necessary articles to refit the ship, but also of the daily provisions. I know not where to find to-morrow's dinner for the great number of mouths which depend upon me for food. Are then the continental ships-of-war to depend on the sale of their prizes for a daily dinner for their men? *'Publish it not in Gath!'*

My officers as well as men want clothes, to cover their nakedness and the prizes are precluded from being sold before farther orders arrive from the minister. I will ask you gentlemen, if I have deserved all this? Whoever calls himself an American ought to be protected here. I am unwilling to think that you have intentionally involved me in this sad dilemma, at a time when I ought to expect some enjoyment.

Therefore I have, as formerly, the honor to be, with due esteem and respect, gentlemen, yours, &c.

[JNO. P. JONES.][1]

THE AMERICAN PLENIPOTENTIARIES AT THE COURT OF FRANCE.

II

SINK AND BE DAMNED!

Like many American seamen, John Kilby, serving on a privateer, was captured and clamped into a British prison, from which he was exchanged. He joined John Paul Jones in France and fought again.

Midshipman Nathaniel Fanning, captain of the maintop on board Jones' Bonhomme Richard, 32, picks up the narrative to describe the duel with the English frigate Serapis, 50.

On the 15th day of November, 1776, we on the *Sturdy Beggar* fell in with a double-decked brig, *Glasgow,* bound to St. Johns, Newfoundland, loaded with King's naval stores. We engaged her and after one and one-quarter hours action, captured her. On the first day of December, same year, we fell in with the ship the *Smyrna,* galley of eighteen guns, bound to London, and after an action of three-quarters of an hour, captured her. The invoice of her cargo was eighty-thousand pounds sterling. We were then in the Bay of Biscay. Prize-master George Sampel, an Irishman, was put on board with a sufficient number of hands to work the ship. I was one of the hands put on board, the *Sturdy Beggar* being still in company with us. . . . On the 9th day of the same month (December) and year (1776), we were captured by the *Resolution,* seventy-four guns. The brig *Sturdy Beggar* being then in sight, the man-of-war gave chase after the Rebel, as they so called her. The little brig hauled her wind and out-sailed the seventy-four. . . . On the 13th day of the same month and year, we had an uncommon gale of wind which lasted nearly fifty hours. The seventy-four lost her main-yard, and it was with great difficulty that the ship could be saved. In the same gale, the *Sturdy Beggar* was foundered and every soul lost. On the 22nd day of December, 1776, we arrived in Spithead, England, where to our great mortification we found our other prize, the brig, *Glasgow,* laying in port, all prisoners together. . . . We were carried up to Hazel Hospital for trial and condemnation (a mock-trial, to be sure). After calling over all our names, the Judge rises up and pronounced sentence in these words, "You are all condemned for piracy and high treason on His Majesty's high seas." (Here permit me to say I wish to know who gave him the high seas). So it was that we were all marched up to Fortune's Jail, formerly Queen Anne's Hospital, under a strong guard of soldiers, and locked up by nine o'clock at night in the cold sweating walls with about three hundred more brave Americans. . . . Our crew lay in this place twenty-two months. . . . During this time we were on Rebels' allowance, which is two-thirds of what is allowed to prisoners of war. . . . We had nine ounces (per man, per diem) of the worst kind of beef.

The whole bullock was cut up, bone and all, with a butcher's cleaver, then weighed out together and tied up in messes for either four or six, just as we chose to have it, and then it was boiled all together in one large copper, in nothing but clear water. At twelve o'clock, one man from each mess attended at a window and received our allowance of beef and one pint of the soup, as they called it. We had bread served once every three days, and four ounces of salt per week. This we got every day, Saturdays excepted. For on that day . . . we had nine ounces of cheese and a small wooden platter of burgoo. Upon that allowance we all lived during the time of our imprisonment. For me to inform you how many plans we laid to extricate ourselves from that unpleasant place, will astonish you. . . . Although there were forever, both night and day, soldiers keeping guard in every part of the jail, it being three or four stories high, we would cut holes through the ceiling, go up in the garret and then cut a hole in the chimney. . . . We would then go down the chimney by cords taken from our hammocks, and first dig under the foundation of the wall and then, with the pockets cut out of our clothes, haul up the dirt and store it away. This was done until we had gotten outside of the pickets. Then we would draw lots to determine how many and who should go and take their chances for liberty once more. This was done in many parts of the house that we were confined in. If detected and brought back, they were put in the black hole, a dungeon, for forty days and nights, put on bread and water, and also put on the list of the last Rebels that were committed (and the last to be exchanged).

Although the penalty was so great, many made the attempt and some actually succeeded in getting away. Captain Cortney, Commander of the *Oliver Cromwell* of Philadelphia, and one hundred men laid a plan to make their escape. It was to mount the pickets, kill the sentinels, and run off in the open day. The watchword was given and they did make the attempt. The whole guard fired on them as they ran by. Some were killed. Cortney fell but actually got away. Many were taken up and brought in again, then condemned to the Black Hole. The pavements of the lower floors were all laid with bricks. Some managed to take up the bricks, and dig down until they got below the wall, then dig outside the pickets. This was all done by concealing the dirt in some parts of the prison and by drawing lots as before. At this time ten men, all officers, made their escape. . . . A like plan was laid, when many more got off nearly as before. A Mr. Greenleaf, a printer by trade, of Philadelphia, by some means procured ladies clothes and actually marched out of the gates in the day time as the turnkeys were often passing to and fro. We cut a hole through the ceiling up in the garret, went down a three story chimney and then by tunneling under ground, thirty more men went out. However, by bad judgment in the measurement of the ground, when they were to rise up, they fell short, for just at the dawn of day they broke ground directly in a very large hog sty.

The hogs made such a noise that the turnkeys gave the alarm and every soul was brought back. . . . A certain Captain Parsons, who did duty over us, openly told his guard that if any one of them would kill a Rebel, he would give them five guineas. A certain man by name, Patrick Spellman, a corporal, one of his guard, went into the guard house, brought out his musket, pointed it through the pickets, and fired through the yard, when about three or four hundred of us were walking to and fro. The ball went through the body of Bartholemew White of Philadelphia, a tailor by trade. . . . It will be nothing but right to say that there were some very friendly to us and I believe, to the American cause. Many proved it. Captain O'Kelly made us a donation of one hundred guineas, as did many other noted men. Captain O'Kelly did duty over us six months, and would frequently come into the prison and give us some comfort by saying, "Hold out. You will all be exchanged before long." Mr. Hartley, a member of the British Parliament, once came in and said the same words. Many other men of high standing did likewise. A few days before the exchange was known by any of us, ten men got out and every soul of them brought back, and put in the Black Hole. At last the day and hour of exchange were announced to us. A few moments before the exchange, we all went to the iron gates and called to our companions, then in the Black Hole, to wish them well. One of them, a Philadelphian, called his God to witness and bound it with a horrible oath, saying that he would be in the city of Nantes before us. I thought it only words said in the heat of passion. The agent called all of our names, and then read us these words: "You all now have received His Majesty's most gracious pardon." At that time there was a loud cry from many of our men: "Damn his Majesty and his pardon too."

The gates were opened and one hundred of us were marched out under a guard. We were accompanied by fine music. Some of our boys cried out "Give us Yankee Doodle!" and they certainly did play it for us all the way down through the town, where, from twenty to thirty thousand souls were looking at us, hundreds of whom cried out from the windows: "We wish you all well!" We were put on board the ship, *Milford* . . . sailed for France, and arrived in the port of Paim Boeuf. For the first time in nearly two and half years we were free. After staying in this port three days, we got a vessel and were conveyed up to the city of Nantes. The first men that met us on the wharf were the very men that we left in the Black Hole. They informed us that on the night we left, they broke out and went down where all the men-of-war lay, stole a barge belonging to the fleet, put to sea, and landed safe in France. . . . We were all quartered at a tavern, The Sign of the Three Sailors, where we were eight days.

Finding that it was necessary that we should seek employment, thirty-three of us determined to get with Captain John Paul Jones, Commander of the ship *Bonhomme Richard* of forty guns, which was lying in the port of L'Orient. . . . To get over from Nantes to L'Orient where the ship lay, it was necessary to send to Jones a letter informing him of our intentions. . . . He sent over two officers, his sailing-master Cuting Lunt and the gunner, James O'Connor. Thirty-three of us did enter and sign the ship's papers. . . . We arrived on the third day after setting off. On the day following we all received from Mr. Moylan, the Continental Agent, twenty French crowns as entrance money, and had permission to remain on shore that night. We thought proper to take what is commonly called "a man-of-wars' cruise. . . ."

We thought it would be imprudent to take all of our money with us and O'Connor advised us against keeping it with us on that night. We every man put in his hands nineteen crowns for safe-keeping until

31

the morning, and in the morning both O'Connor and money were all gone.

We all went on board of the ship *Bonhomme Richard.* The first sight that was presented to our view was thirteen men stripped and tied upon the larboard side of the quarter-deck. The boatswain's mate commenced at the first nearest the gangway and gave him one dozen lashes with a cat-o'nine-tails. He went on until he came to the coxswain, Robertson. (These men were the crew of the captain's barge.) When the Boatswain's mate came to Robertson, the first lieutenant said: "As he is a bit of an officer, give him two dozen. . . ." They had carried the Captain on shore, and so soon as Jones was out of sight, they all left the barge and got drunk. When Jones came down to go on board, not a man was to be found. Jones had to hire a fishing boat to carry him on board. . . . After they were thus whipped, Captain Jones addressed us: "Well gentlemen and my lads I well know where you have all been for a long time. I know you are true to your country, and as my ship has got a severe name, if any of you should want any liberty that is not allowed by the rules of the ship, you are to come into my cabin and let me know. . . ." The marines, both officers and soldiers, were French and Irish brigands. The whole ship's crew amounted to about four hundred men. . . .

We hove short a peak, loosed fore topsail, weighed anchor and sailed on a cruise in company with the *Alliance,* a frigate of thirty-six guns, commanded by Captain Peter Landais, a Frenchman; the *Pallas,* a frigate of thirty-two guns, commanded by Captain Cottineau, a Frenchman; a frigate of thirty-six guns, said to belong to the Ladies of Honour of France, commanded by a Frenchman with a French crew, which boat never was under the command of Jones, the Commodore of the squadron, but had a commission that is called a "Roving Commission"; the brig, *Le Vengeance* of twelve guns, a French commander and crew; a lugger of ten guns, a French captain and crew; all in the service of Congress, the frigate said to belong to the Ladies of Honour excepted, and under the command of the Honorable John Paul Jones, which fleet was fitted out by that good man Dr. Benjamin Franklin, then in Paris, Commissioner for the United States of North America.

As we were beating down to the island of Groix, a man fell off the main top sail yard on the quarterdeck. As he fell, he struck the

Right: John Paul Jones, commander of the frigate *Bonhomme Richard* when it engaged the British frigate *Serapis* (below).

cock of Jones' hat, but did no injury to Jones. He was killed and buried on the island of Groix. We again sailed and continued our cruise. For several weeks nothing happened, after which the frigate said to belong to the Ladies of Honour left us. . . . We continued our cruise, captured, sunk, and destroyed many ships. At length, we appeared off Leeth Roads, Scotland. We were still going up the coast. Every officer was dressed in full British uniform and not a French soldier was to be seen on our deck.

A pilot came on board. Jones asked him what was the news on the coast. "Why," said he, "very great and bad news! That rebel, Paul Jones, is expected to land every day." Jones asked him then what they thought of the rebel Jones, saying he wished he could come across him. "What!" said he, "he is the greatest rebel and pirate that ever was and ought to be hanged." Jones then asked him if he knew who he was talking to, and observed, "I am Paul Jones." The poor pilot dropped on his knees and begged for his life. Jones said "Get up! I won't hurt a hair of your head, but you are my prisoner."

On going up the Roads, the commander of the fort at the entrance of the place sent out an express, (supposing us to be a British fleet) requesting a few barrels of powder. Jones sent him one barrel of powder with a request that he keep up good lights as the night was very dark and the weather squally. Lights were kept up. While beating up together with the rest of the fleet, an eighteen gun English cutter was close along side of us, and even got foul of us three or four times. All of this time, all of our officers were in full English uniform. In the morning the cutter was two miles ahead and many large ships were sailing athwart us. At last we were compelled to take charge of one of them. She was manned with three men, and we left the crew on board to make them believe that we were an English fleet. Under the pretext of helping them safe into port, we put on board of her a man by the name of Walker as prize-master. As soon as we got out of reach of cannon shot, Walker uphelmed and ran his prize on shore. This gave alarm, but we still kept on until we arrived abreast of the town where we intended to land. The object was to demand a contribution of two hundred and fifty thousand pounds sterling and it was to be delivered in two hours or the town was to be laid in ashes. We were fully able to carry out our threat for we had with us every kind of combustible.

Our boats were all manned and ready to set off, but just then the cutter ahead of us fired three signal guns and the forts from Edinburgh and elsewhere all commenced firing. But though their fire was ineffectual yet on account of the increasing gale, we were obliged to abandon the enterprise. We hoisted in all the boats, up-helmed, and put before the wind and shortly left the land. The gale continued to increase and that night we bent and lost three new foresails from the foreyards. Boatswain's mate, James Garrett, either got drunk or was much alarmed at the dreadful night, so that he did not attend to his duty. First Lieutenant Dale went on the fore-castle and rattaned him well, which I thought very right. We then shaped our course for England. On our way, we fell in with many vessels, which we either sunk, burned or destroyed, at the same time keeping fast all of their crews as prisoners.

On the 23rd day of September 1779, we spied a fleet of ships. We gave chase at six o'clock. A signal was given for the *Pallas* to haul her wind and take charge of the small ship of war, the *Countess of Scarborough,* of twenty-six guns. Another signal was for the *Alliance* to come under our lee and for the brig and lugger to keep under our stern. The *Pallas* obeyed. The *Alliance,* a fast sailing ship, came up along side. Jones both by signal and verbally directed Landais: the *Bonhomme Richard* will lay the large ship along side, and the *Alliance* will come under the enemy's stern and rake her. Contrary to orders, the *Alliance* hauled her wind and went in pur-suit of the small ship and commenced firing at long shot. The enemy engaged. The *Pallas* got up and ran along side the small ship and after a small action captured her. The *Alliance* hove to at this time. The *Bonhomme Richard* was still bearing down on the large ship, which was then protecting a large fleet of merchant ships. To protect that valuable convoy, he (the enemy) hove to, hauled up his canvass and prepared for action. Side lanthorns were up throughout the enemy's ship and every man at quarters was plain to be seen. We were then a very small distance from them and you may be sure that our ship was well prepared for action. While we were bearing down upon the enemy, she hailed us: "Hoie! the ship a-hoie!" Our Captain, with a large trumpet in his hands, made no answer. The enemy again cried: "The ship a-hoie!" Jones in a loud voice said: "I can't tell what you say." The enemy again replied: "Tell me what ship that is directly or I will sink you." Jones answered: "Sink and be damned!" Both ships were within fifty yards of each other and at the words, "sink and be damned," I fully believe no man living could tell which ship fired first. . . .[2]

[*Fanning*] . . . At this first fire, three of our starboard lower-deck guns burst, and killed most of the men stationed at them. As soon as Captain Jones heard this, he gave orders not to fire the other three eighteen pounders mounted upon that deck. Soon we perceived the enemy, busy running out their guns between decks, which convinced us the *Serapis* was a two decker, and more than our match. She had by this time got under our stern, which we could not prevent. She raked us with whole broadsides, and showers of musketry. Several of her eighteen pound shot having gone through and through our ship made a dreadful havoc among our crew. The wind was now very light, and our ship not under proper command, and the *Serapis* outsailing us by *two feet to one;* which advantage the enemy discovered, and improved it, by keeping under our stern, and raking us fore and aft. All this time our tops kept up an incessant and well-directed fire into the enemies' tops which did great execution. The *Serapis* continued to take a position, either under our stern, or athwart our bow; gauled us in such a manner that our men fell in all parts of the ship by *scores.* The ship commander, to extricate us from this scene of bloody carnage; for, had it lasted one-half an hour longer, the enemy would have slain nearly all our officers and men; ordered the sailing master, *a true blooded Yankee,* whose name was Stacy, to lay the enemies' ship on board; and as the *Serapis* passed across our fore foot, our helm was put hard a-weather, the main and mizzen topsails, then braced aback, were filled away, a fresh flaw of wind swelling them which shot our ship quick ahead, and she ran her jib boom between the enemies' starboard mizzen shrouds and mizzen vang. Jones cried out, "Well done, my brave lads, we have got her now; throw on board the grappling-irons, and stand by for boarding": which was done, and the enemy soon cut away the chains. More were thrown on board.

As we now hauled the enemies' ship snug alongside of ours, her jib-stay was cut away aloft and fell upon our ship's poop, where Jones assisted Mr. Stacy in making fast the end of the enemies' jib-stay to our mizzen-mast. The former checked the latter for swearing, saying, "Mr. Stacy, it is no time for swearing now, you may by the next moment be in eternity; but let us do our duty." A strong current was now setting in towards Scarborough, the wind ceased to blow, and the sea became as smooth as glass. The enemy finding that they could not easily extricate themselves from us let go one of their anchors, expecting that if they could cut us adrift, the current would set us away out of their reach. The action had now lasted about forty minutes, and the fire from our tops having been kept up without intermission, with musketry, blunderbusses, cowhorns, swivels, and pistols, directed into their tops, these last became silent, except one man in her foretop, who would peep out from behind the head of the enemies' foremast and fire into our tops. I ordered the marines to reserve their next fire, and the moment they got sight of him to level their pieces at him and fire. They did, and we saw this skulking tar, fall out of the top upon the enemies' forecastle. Our ensign-staff was shot away, and both that and the thirteen stripes fell into the sea in the beginning of the action. . . . Both ships now lying head and stern, and so near together that our heaviest cannon amidships, as well as those of the enemy, could not be of any use, as they could neither be spunged nor loaded. The enemy leaped on board of our ship, and some of them had got upon the fore part of our quarter-deck; several were killed, and the rest driven back on board of their own ship, some of our men followed them, and were killed. Other attempts to board were made by both parties in quick succession, [but] many were slain upon the two ships' gangways. . . . At this time the enemy's fleet was discernible by moonlight in shore of us, but could not perceive any of our squadron except the brig *Vengeance,* and the small tender, which lay astern of us, neither of whom dared to come to our assistance.

It had now got to be about forty-eight minutes since the action began. The enemy's tops being entirely silenced, the men in ours had nothing to do but to direct their whole fire down upon the enemy's decks and forecastle; this we did, and with so much success that in about twenty-five minutes we had cleared her decks so that not a man on board the *Serapis* was to be seen. However, they still kept up a constant fire, with two eighteen pounders upon the lower gun-deck, and two nine pounders upon her upper gun-deck. Her four guns annoyed us very much and did our ship considerable damage. About this time the enemy's light sails, which were filled onto the *Serapis's* cranes over her quarterdeck sails caught fire; this communicated itself to her rigging and thence to ours; thus were both ships on fire. The firing on both sides ceased till it was extinguished by the contending parties, after which the action was renewed again. By this time, the topmen in our tops had taken possession of the enemy's tops. . . . We transported from our own into the enemy's tops, stink pots, flasks, hand grenadoes, &c., which we threw in among the enemy whenever they made their appearance. The battle had now continued about three hours, and as we had possession of the *Serapis's* top, which commanded her quarterdeck, we were well assured that the enemy could not hold out much longer, and were momently expecting that they would strike to us, when the following farcical piece was acted on board our ship:

A report was at this time, circulated among our crew between decks, that Captain Jones and all his officers were slain; the gunners were now the commanders of our ship; that the ship had four of five feet of water in her hold; that she was sinking: they advised the gunner to go upon deck, together with the carpenter, and master at arms, and beg of the enemy quarters. These three men mounted the quarterdeck, and bawled out as loud as they could, "Quarters, quarters, for God's sake, quarters! our ship is a-sink-in!" and immediately got upon the ship's poop with a view of hauling down our colours. Hearing this in the top, I told my men that the enemy had struck and was crying out for quarters, for I actually thought that the voices of these men sounded as if on board of the enemy; but in this I was soon undeceived. The three poltroons, finding the ensign, and ensign-staff gone, they proceeded upon the quarterdeck, and were in the act of hauling down our pendant, still bawling for "quarters!" when I heard our commodore say, in a loud voice, "what d---d rascals are them—shoot them—kill them! . . ." He had just discharged his pistols at the enemy. The carpenter, and the master-at-arms, hearing Jones's voice, skulked below, and the gunner was attempting to do the same, when Jones threw both of his pistols at his head, one of which struck him in the head, fractured his skull, and knocked him down, at the foot of the gangway ladder, where he lay till the battle was over.

Both ships now took fire again; and on board of our ship it set our main top on fire. The water which we had in a tub, in the tops, was expended without extinguishing the fire. We next had recourse to our clothes, by pulling off our coats and jackets, and throwing them upon the fire, and stamping upon them, which smothered it. Both crews were busily employed in stopping the flames, and the firing on both sides ceased. The enemy now demanded if we had struck, as they had heard the three poltroons halloo for quarters. "If you have," said they, "why don't you haul down your pendant"; as they saw our ensign was gone. "Ay, ay," said Jones, "we'll do that when we can fight no longer, but we shall see yours come down the first; for you must know, that Yankees do not haul down their colours till they are fairly beaten." The combat now recommenced again with fury; and continued for a few minutes, then the cry of fire was again heard. The firing ceased, and both crews were once more employed in extinguishing it, which was soon affected, when the battle was renewed with what cannon we could manage: hand grenadoes, stink pots, &c., but principally with lances and boarding pikes. With these the combatants killed each other through the ship's port holes, which were pretty large.

At three quarters past 11 P.M. the *Alliance* frigate hove in sight, approached within pistol shot of our stern, and began a heavy and well-directed fire into us, as well as the enemy. (The moon at this time retired behind a dark cloud). It was in vain that our officers hailed her. . . . The *Alliance* kept a position either ahead of us or under our stern, and made havoc and confusion on board of our ship; and she did not cease firing entirely, till the signal of recognisance was displayed. . . . This had the desired effect. And at thirty-five minutes past 12 at night, a single hand grenado having been thrown by one of our men out of the main top of the enemy, struck on one side of the combings of her upper hatchway, and rebounding from that, fell between decks, where it communicated to a quantity of loose powder scattered about the enemy's cannon; and made a dreadful explosion, and blew up about twenty of the enemy. This closed the scene, and the enemy now bawled out "Quarters, quarters, quarters, for God's sake!" It was, however, some time before the enemy's colours were struck. The captain of the *Serapis* gave repeated orders for his crew to ascend the quarterdeck and haul down the English flag, but no one would stir. . . . The captain of the *Serapis* therefore ascended the quarterdeck, and hauled down the very flag which he had nailed to the flagstaff. . . . Captain Jones ordered Richard Dale, his first lieutenant, to select out of our crew a number of men, and take possession of the prize. . . .

Thus ended this ever memorable battle. The officers, headed by the captain of the *Serapis,* now came on board of our ship; the latter (Captain Parsons) enquired for Captain Jones, to whom he was introduced by our purser. They met, and the former accosted the latter, in presenting his sword: "It is with the greatest reluctance that I am now obliged to resign you this, for it is painful to me, more particularly at this time, when compelled to deliver up my sword to a man, who may be said to fight *with a halter around his neck!"* Jones, after receiving his sword, made this reply: "Sir, you have fought like a hero, and I make no doubt but your sovereign will reward you in a most ample manner for it." Captain Parsons then asked Jones what countrymen his crew principally consisted of; the latter said, "Americans." "Very well," said the former, "it has been *diamond cut diamond* with us. . . ." The two captains now withdrew into the cabin, and there drank a glass or two of wine together. Both ships were now separated from each other, and were mere wrecks; the *Serapis's* three masts having nothing to support them, fell overboard with all the sails, tops, yards, rigging, &c., making a hideous noise in the water. . . .

We were now much alarmed on board of our ship having two more enemies to encounter, almost as formidable as those we had just conquered, fire and water. Our pumps had been kept going without any intermission for about two hours, and still the water in the ship's hold increased fast. The ship had received several shot in her bottom so low, that it was impossible to find means to stop them up, so that it was reduced to a certainty that she must sink in a short time. . . .

The fire had now penetrated to within the thickness of a pine board to the bulk head of the magazine of powder. We well knew that one or two things must happen; either the ship would burn down to the water's edge and then sink, or she would sink first. In this dilemna Jones ordered the signal of the distress to be hung out, with the *Alliance, Pallais* and *Vengeance* observing, sent their boats to our assistance. The powder was ordered to be got out of our magazine, and that no man should quit the *Good Man Richard* till every cask of powder was safe on board of the boats then alongside. The English officers were much frightened at this, as the fire was at that moment in and about the powder room, and we expected every moment to be blown into the air. The English officers assisted us in getting up the powder; and Captain Jones encouraged them by telling

40

them that he would not abandon his own ship till every cask of powder was out of her. This piece of service being accomplished in a few minutes, after which Jones and the English officers embarked on board of the boats, and went on board of the *Serapis,* first leaving orders with his officers to abandon the *Good Man Richard* after we had got all the wounded men and English prisoners out of her and put them on board of the squadron. . . .

The *Pallais* had captured the *Countess of Scarborough,* after a brisk action, which two ships now joined the squadron. The *Serapis* having been pierced with several shot between wind and water was thought to be sinking; the assistance of the crews of the different ships was demanded on board of the *Serapis;* the chain pumps were kept constantly going, and the cranks double manned. . . .

But to return to the *Good Man Richard,* where we were busily employed in getting out the wounded. The alarm was given that the English prisoners, about fifty, who had been let out of confinement after the battle, had taken possession of our ship and were running her on shore; they were at this time absolutely masters of the quarter-deck, spar-deck and forecastle, and had got the ship before the wind, and her yards squared by the braces, steering directly in for the land. Another battle ensued, but we having the greater part of the arms suitable for a close fight, and although they out-numbered us, soon over-powered them, and again became masters of the ship. . . .

I now took a full view of the mangled carcasses of the slain on board of our ship; especially between decks, where the bloody scene was enough to appal the stoutest heart. To see the dead lying in heaps—to hear the groans of the wounded and dying—the entrails of the dead scattered promiscuously around, the blood (*American too*) *over one's shoes,* was enough to move pity from the most hardened and *callous breast.* And although my spirit was somewhat dampened at this shocking sight, yet when I came to reflect that we were *conquerors,* and over those who wished to bind America in chains of everlasting slavery; my spirits revived, and I thought perhaps that some faithful historian would at some future period enrol me among the heroes and deliverers of my country. . . .

I think this battle, and every circumstance attending it minutely considered, may be ranked with propriety, the most bloody, the hardest fought, and the greatest scene of carnage on both sides, ever fought between two ships of war of any nation under heaven. . . .[3]

The contest was bloody, both decks ran with gore,
And the sea seemed to blaze, while the cannon did roar;
"Fight on, my brave boys," then Paul Jones he cried,
"And soon we will humble this bold Englishman's pride."

"Stand firm to your quarters—your duty don't shun,
The first one that shrinks, through the body I'll run;
Though their force is superior, yet they shall know,
What true, brave American seamen can do."

The battle rolled on, till bold Pearson cried:
"Have you yet struck your colors? then come alongside!"
But so far from thinking that the battle was won,
Brave Paul Jones replied, "I've not yet begun!"

We fought them eight glasses, eight glasses so hot,
Till seventy bold seamen lay dead on the spot.
And ninety brave seamen lay stretched in their gore,
While the pieces of cannon most fiercely did roar.

The *Alliance* bore down, and the *Richard* did rake,
Which caused the bold hearts of our seamen to ache;
Our shot flew so hot that they could not stand us long,
And the undaunted Union of Britain came down.

To us they did strike and their colors hauled down;
The fame of Paul Jones to the world shall be known;
His name shall rank with the gallant and brave,
Who fought like a hero for our freedom to save.
Hurrah! Hurrah! Our country for ever, Hurrah![4]

III

PUBLIUS PLEADS FOR A NAVY

During the years of peace which followed the Revolution, Americans were intent upon union and, in 1787, framed the Constitution.

*To urge states to ratify this document, Alexander Hamilton, under a
pseudonym, argues in the* Federalist Papers *for a national navy as
an instrument of diplomacy and protector of commerce.*

. . . A further resource for influencing the conduct of European
nations toward us, in this respect, would arise from the establishment
of a federal navy. There can be no doubt that the continuance of the
Union under an efficient government would put it in our power, at
a period not very distant, to create a navy which, if it could not vie
with those of the great maritime powers, would at least be of respectable weight if thrown into the scale of either of two contending parties.
This would be more peculiarly the case in relation to operations in the
West Indies. A few ships of the line, sent opportunely to the reinforce-
ment of either side, would often be sufficient to decide the fate of a
campaign, on the event of which interests of the greatest magnitude
were suspended. Our position is, in this respect, a most commanding
one. . . . A price would be set not only upon our friendship, but
upon our neutrality. By a steady adherence to the Union, we may
hope, erelong, to become the arbiter of Europe in America, and to
be able to incline the balance of European competitions in this part
of the world as our interest may dictate. . . .

To this great national object, a NAVY, union will contribute in
various ways. Every institution will grow and flourish in proportion
to the quantity and extent of the means concentrated towards its
formation and support. A navy of the United States, as it would
embrace the resources of all, is an object far less remote than a navy
of any single State or partial confederacy, which would only embrace
the resources of a single part. It happens, indeed, that different portions of confederated America possess each some peculiar advantage
for this essential establishment. The more southern States furnish in
greater abundance certain kinds of naval stores—tar, pitch, and turpentine. Their wood for the construction of ships is also of a more
solid and lasting texture. The difference in the duration of the ships of
which the navy might be composed, if chiefly constructed of Southern
wood, would be of signal importance, either in view of naval strength
or of national economy. Some of the Southern and of the Middle
States yield a greater plenty of iron, and of better quality. Seamen
must chiefly be drawn from the Northern hive. The necessity of
naval protection to external or maritime commerce does not require

a particular elucidation, no more than the conduciveness of that species of commerce to the prosperity of the navy. . . .[5]

During the French Revolution in the mid-1790's, privateers swarmed the Mediterranean and the Caribbean, and cruised off the coast of the United States, plundering shipping despite American neutrality. Conditions became intolerable. Although no formal declaration of war existed, American ships were ordered to seize French privateers and men-of-war. The three years of hostilities on the high seas welded the United States Navy into a unified organization whose ships captured or destroyed eighty-four vessels, most of them privateers.

IV

BRAVE YANKEE BOYS

The old naval ballad, "Brave Yankee Boys," is a succinct introduction to the victory of the Constellation, 36, *commanded by Thomas Truxtun, over* L'Insurgente, 36, 9 February 1799, a few leagues southwest of the Island of Nevis in the West Indies.*

'Twas on the 9th of February at Montserat we lay,
And there we spy'd the *L'Insurgente* at the break of day:
    We rais'd the orange and the blue,
    To see if they our signal knew,
    The *Constellation* and the crew
        Of our brave Yankee boys.

Then all hands were call'd to quarters while we pursu'd the chase,
With well prim'd guns, our tompions out, and well splic'd
    the main brace,
    Then soon to France we did draw nigh,
    Compell'd to fight, they were, or fly,
    These words were pass'd "Conquer or Die,"
        My brave Yankee boys.

Loud our cannons thunder'd, with peals tremendous roar,
And death upon our bullets wings that drench'd their decks in gore.
    The blood did from their scuppers run,
    Their chief exclaim'd, "We are undone,"
    Their flag they struck, the battle was won,
        By brave Yankee boys.

Then to St. Kitts we steered, we brought her safe in port,
The grand salute was fired and answered from the Fort;
    Now sitting round the flowing bowl,
    With hearty glee each jovial soul,
    Drink as you fought without control,
        My brave Yankee boys.

Now here's a health to Truxtun who did not fear the sight
And all those Yankee sailors who for their country fight,
    John Adams in full bumpers toast,
    George Washington, Columbia's boast,
    And now to the girls that we love most,
        My brave Yankee boys.[6]

. . . on the 9th . . . at Noon . . . discovered a large Ship to the Southward, on which I bore down. She hoisted American Colours and I made our private Signal for the Day, as well as that of the British, but finding she answered neither, must confess that I immediately suspected her to be an Enemy, and in a short Time after found that my Suspicions were well founded, for she hoisted the french national Colours, and fired a Gun to Windward (which is a Signal of an Enemy). I continued bearing down on her, and at ¼ past 3 PM. she hailed me several Times, and as soon as I got in a Position for every Shot to do Execution I answered by commencing a close and successful Engagement, which lasted until about half after 4 PM, when she struck her Colours to the United States Ship, *Constellation,* and I immediately took possession of her; she proves to be the celebrated french national Frigate, *Insurgente* of 40 Guns, and 400 Men, lately out from France, commanded by Monsieur Barreaut, and is esteemed one of the fastest sailing Ships in the french Navy. I have been much shattered in my Rigging and Sails, and my fore top Mast rendered from Wounds useless; you may depend the Enemy is not less so; I intend to get into Bassateer Roads, Saint Christophers if possible, with my Prize, but the Wind being adverse and blowing hard, I much doubt, in the crippled State of both Ships (without a Change) whether I shall effect it, and if not I must make a Port to Leeward. The high State of our Discipline, with the gallant Conduct of all my Officers, and Men, would have enabled me to have compelled a more formidable Enemy to have yielded, had the Fortune of War thrown one in my Way; as it is, I hope the President and my Country will for the present be content, with a very fine Frigate being added to our infant Navy, and that too with the Loss of only one Man killed, and three wounded. . . .

THOMAS TRUXTUN.[7]

John Rodgers, first lieutenant, was sent with midshipman Porter and eleven men, to take possession of the prize, and superintend the removal of her crew to the *Constellation*. The wind blew high, and occasioned so much delay in removing the crew, that night set in leaving one hundred and seventy-three prisoners on board the *Insurgente*, to be guarded by lieutenant Rodgers, and his small party.

. . . The *Insurgente* resembled a slaughter house; her decks not having been cleared of the dead or dying; her spars, sails, and rigging, cut to pieces, and lying on deck. Navigating her in this situation, in a gale of wind, by two officers and eleven men, who were at the same time charged with the duty of guarding one hundred and seventy-three prisoners, without handcuffs or shackles, and the hatches all uncovered, was a service not to be envied by the boldest man living.

Lieutenant Rodgers immediately secured all the small arms; ordered the prisoners into the lower hold of the ship, and placed at each hatchway a sentinel, armed with a blunderbuss, cutlass, and brace of pistols, with orders to fire, if any one of the prisoners should attempt to come upon deck. . . . In this situation, he was placed for three nights and three days, during which time, neither he nor midshipman Porter could take the slightest repose, being compelled to be constantly on the watch, to prevent the prisoners from rising upon them, and re-taking the ship, which their numbers would have enabled them to do, with ease, but for the precautions taken, and the vigilance practiced by lieutenant Rodgers and his party. One moment's intermission would have lost the ship, as the prisoners had manifested a disposition to re-take her, and were incessantly upon

Huzza for our Navy!

Another 15 minutes Job.

Being the 8th Naval Victory in which John Bull has been obliged to douce his flag, to the invincible skill of *American Tars.*

CHARLESTON, SUNDY MORNING, SEPT. 19th, 1813.

We have the satisfaction of announcing to the public that the United States sloop of war ARGUS is in the offing, with the British sloop of war BARBADOES her prize in company, taken after a desperate engagement of 15 minutes, carried by boarding.

Capt. Allen, of the Argus, has just come up, and we have conversed with a midshipman who states that she was taken off Halifax, but it was deemed expedient to proceed to this place for the purpose of escaping the British blockading squadrons. He also states that the captain, R. P. Davies, of the Barbadoes was killed, and the vessel was commanded the most part of the action by the 1st Lieut. Savage.

British loss, 97 killed and wounded. American loss, 12 killed and wounded.

The Argus rates 16 and carries 20 guns, the Barbadoes rates 28 and carries 32 guns. She had previously captured, Aug. 22, the James Madison of 14 guns.

☞ *This is the second Engagement in which Captain ALLEN has signalised himself, as he was 1st Lieu't. of the U. States, was in the Engagement with the Macedonian, took Command of her and brought her into port.*

Published Worth, Tuesday, 28th September, 1813.

10th Wed'y 29th Sept. This proved to be a gross imposition on the Public.

the watch for a favorable moment to accomplish their purposes. She was, under these circumstances, safely conducted into St. Kitts, at which place the *Constellation* had previously arrived. . . .

Clerk of the Navy Goldsborough.[8]

After the Quasi-War with France, the American Navy was weakened by Jeffersonian economy and neutralism. Yet incidents arose which demanded naval protection. For years the African states of Morocco, Tunis, Algiers, and Tripoli had fostered pirates who preyed upon commerce in the Mediterranean. Only payment of tribute or the presence of a powerful navy gave safety. In May, 1801 the Bashaw of Tripoli, dissatisfied with the annual tribute of some $80,000, declared war against the United States.

V

BEANS, BARLEY, AND GOAT'S MEAT

The United States frigate Philadelphia, *36, blockading off Tripoli smashed into an uncharted reef, 1 November 1803, while chasing a craft. Enemy gunboats and shore batteries opened fire. At sunset after a resistance of four hours, Captain William Bainbridge surrendered the* Philadelphia. *The Tripolitans, employing vessels and lighters, got the frigate off the rocks, recovered her guns, took her triumphantly into the harbor, and held the Americans captive for an exorbitant ransom. Seaman Elijah Shaw recounts his experiences.*

. . . We cruised off Tripoli and commenced operations by throwing shells into the city, and by occasionally firing guns at the fort—our shots generally being returned, but without any damage to us.

Ship number four having no carpenter, I was called upon one day to go on board and make some slight repairs. Lieut. Somers accompanied me. The vessel at the time was lying twenty miles from the city, and some distance from the rest of the squadron. After the repairs were made, our commander proposed, if volunteers could be raised, to run in and exchange a few shots with the Turks. There were but eighteen on board, including the Commander, all of whom readily volunteered. . . . We run in near the battery, though not within reach of their guns, and lay off and on for some time, for the purpose of decoying them out; and soon had the pleasure of seeing two boats push out towards us. Each of these boats carried 36 men and two 32 pounders. They ventured about four miles from the battery; we opened our gun. I say *gun,* for we had only men enough to work one gun at a time—a 32 pounder. We had two of that class, and when one became hot we used the other.

The boats of the enemy were very low, and we had to take as close aim as we would for a duck. Ninety-two shots were fired without effect; but the ninety-third struck one of the boats between wind and water, and she immediately sunk. The other then steered for the harbor. We followed her, crowding all the sail we could. We gained upon her rapidly; and when within pistol shot we received orders to fire. The fire did tolerable execution. I had taken deliberate aim at the Tripolitan captain; but unfortunately my musket exploded, injuring my left hand to such an extent as to render the thumb and one finger useless, and breaking the first joint of one of the fingers on my right hand.

By this time the boats were along side, and we had orders to board. I jumped upon the bulwarks of the enemy's boat, receiving a blow from a cutlass, on the back part of my ankle, just above the quarters of my shoe, which severed the main cord. I sprang on the deck, but striking my other foot on one of the ring bolts, broke my ankle directly above the joint. Sprawling upon deck, unable to rise, I discovered the Turk from whom I had received the first injury, sitting between me and the bulwarks. He was wounded in one of his legs, and was also unable to rise. He made a pass at my head with his cutlass, cutting through my hat and a silk handkerchief, leaving a gash some two inches long in my head. I recovered, and made a thrust at him. He parried the blow, breaking about two inches from the end of my cutlass, and making another hole through my hat. Thinking of my pistols, I drew one of them with my left hand. . . . I took as good aim as I could, and was fortunate enough to give the fellow the entire contents of the pistol—one ball and three buck shot. He immediately expired.

The rest of the enemy were by this time killed, with the exception of seven, who had jumped overboard. We took our prize in tow, not being prepared to risk a brush with a number of gun-boats which had put out from the battery. . . . The next day I was taken on board the Philadelphia, and my wounds dressed. My messmates gave me three cheers as I reached the deck, and "spliced the main brace," in other words, treated me to an extra glass of grog. There was but one of our men wounded besides myself. He received a blow in his right hand, by which he lost the use of it.

Not long after the skirmish we gave chase to a Greek vessel loaded with provisions for the enemy. After pursuing her without being able to intercept her, our commander ordered the ship to be put about. While in the act of doing so, she ran upon a reef of rocks; and every attempt to get her off proved fruitless. We were out of reach of the batteries; but immediately one hundred or more gun-boats and galleys put out from the shore, and completely surrounded us. As our vessel careened badly, the guns on one side pointing into the air, and those on the other into the water, the Commodore saw that resistance was useless, and surrendered at once.

. . . On board the Philadelphia were a little over three hundred souls. We were forced on board the Turkish gun-boats, taken ashore, and confined in prison. We were stripped of our clothing, and each man supplied with a frock reaching the hip, and petticoat-trowsers reaching an inch below the knee. We were ironed down to the stone floor, twelve men in a room, our feet about twelve inches apart, and our hands fastened to an iron passing across our breasts, so that we could not turn our bodies on either side.

Each morning our irons were loosed, and we taken out into the yard. . . . We were permitted to remain in the yard about an hour, during which time our daily allowance of food was served. This consisted of a biscuit of ground beans and barley, unsifted, and weighing about five ounces, three ounces of goat's meat, and one gill of sweet oil. We soaked our biscuits in water, and then ate them with the oil—making one scanty meal answer for three. This was our manner of living for the nineteen months and seven days we remained prisoners. It should be added that we always had as much water as we wished, and that, too, of a superior quality. At the expiration of the hour, the Turks would march us back to the prison, iron us down, and allow us to remain in that situation until sundown, when we were again granted an airing of fifteen minutes, after which we would retire to our night's rest, if rest it could be called.

After being confined for about two weeks, we were put to work, some at carrying bags of sand, and others drawing stone, for the completion of the wall around the city. . . .

From forty to fifty men constituted a team for each cart. These were awkward, clumsy vehicles. The weight of the stone ranged from two to four tons, some of them being sixteen feet in length and two feet square, and were hoisted underneath the axletree by means of a jack-screw. . . . The distance we drew them was about three quarters of a mile. We drew two loads each day. A guard of twelve Turks, armed with muskets, and six drivers provided with whips, accompanied each cart. These whips were cruel instruments. They were about the size of our heavy raw-hides, the tip end being split about eight inches, and three half-hitch knots taken in each strand. The Turkish drivers seemed to take great pleasure in the severe treatment of the "Christian dogs" . . . and when they thought we did not draw hard enough, they applied their whips with an unsparing hand.

The road was a complete bed of quick sands in which the wheels would settle at least a foot. We worked bare-headed and bare-footed; and the climate being very warm, our necks and feet were burnt to a perfect blister. . . .

The first view we had of our ship, was one morning while loading stone on a height of ground overlooking the harbor. We learned that she had been got off a few days after we left her—She was then lying within half a mile of the battery, and was manned by a large number of Turks, whose colors floated aloft . . . the sight called forth tears and the most poignant reflections. . . .[9]

VI

THE *PHILADELPHIA* BURNS

The loss of the Philadelphia *left the* Constitution, *44, the only American frigate in the Mediterranean. Commodore Edward Preble decided to destroy the* Philadelphia *at her moorings and discussed the*

*plan with Lieutenant Stephen Decatur, who volunteered for the
duty. Five officers and sixty-two men prepared a captured Tripolitan
ketch, renamed the* Intrepid, *and, with the brig* Siren, 16, *to cover
the retreat, sailed toward Tripoli Harbor. A gale set in. For six days
the expedition tossed about. Finally on 16 February 1804 the weather
moderated. Decatur's letter to Preble gives the results of this expedition.*

. . . At 7 o'clock I entered the harbour with the *Intrepid, Syren*
having gained her station without the Harbour, laid her along side
the *Philadelphia,* boarded, and after a short contest carried her. I
immediately fired her in the Store Rooms, Gun Room Cockpit & Birth
Deck and remained on board until the flames had issued from the
Spar Deck hatch ways & Ports, and before I got from alongside the
fire had communicated to the rigging and tops. . . .

The noise occasioned by boarding . . . gave a general alarm on
shore, and on board their cruisers. . . . They commenced a fire on
us from all their Batteries on shore, but with no other effect than one
shot passing thro' our Top Gallt Sail.

The Frigate was moored within half Gun shot of the Bashaw's
Castle, and of their principal Battery; two of their Cruisers lay within
two cables length on the starboard quarter and their Gun Boats within half Gun shot on the starboard bow she had all her Guns mounted
and loaded which as they became hot went off as she lay with her
Broadside to the town, I have no doubt but some damage has been
done by them. Before I got out of the harbour, her cables had burnt
off, and she drifted in under the Castle where she was consumed.
I can form no judgment as to the number of Men that were on board
of her; there were about 20 killed—A large boat full got off, and
many leapt into the Sea. We have made one prisoner, and I fear
from the number of bad wounds he has recd. will not recover, altho' every assistance & comfort has been given him—

I boarded with sixty men & Officers, leaving a guard on board the
Ketch for her defence; and it is the greatest pleasure I inform you,
I had not a man killed in this affair, and but one slightly wounded—
Every support that could be given I recd. from my Officers . . . permit me also, Sir, to speak of the brave fellows I have the honor to
command, whose coolness and intrepidity was such, as I trust will
ever characterise the American Tars. . . .[10]

Above: The United States frigate *Philadelphia* being fired on by enemy gunboats in Tripoli Harbor. *Right:* Stephen Decatur, the brave lieutenant, who, in order to keep the ship out of enemy hands, burned the *Philadelphia*. *Below:* Commemorative "Liverpool Jug" celebrating the sinking of the *Philadelphia* and the capture of the *Macedonian* by Commodore Stephen Decatur. This jug was mass produced in Liverpool, England, to recapture trade in the American market after the War of 1812.

VII

BLOODBLISTERS

Still imprisoned ashore, Seaman Shaw resumes his narrative.

We heard the guns and explosion from our prison, but did not know the cause. We supposed that an attack had been made on the city, and that some vessel had been blown up. The next morning we were let out as usual to receive our breakfast, dinner and supper at one and the same meal, and could perceive by the increased harshness used towards us, that something had gone wrong with the Turks.

About 9 o'clock the next morning, we were brought out and seized up to be burnt! Shirts made of coarse hemp cloth, and well saturated with melted brimstone, had been provided for each man. These shirts were so stiff, that they would readily stand up when placed on the ground. We were kept seized up until 4 o'clock, expecting every moment that fire would be applied to our combustible garments. But our lives were saved by the Commander (Preble). He threatened that if we were killed, he would not spare a life in the city, that all, high and low, old and young, should feel the retributive vengeance of the Americans. We were released, and conducted back to prison again.

During the remainder of our captivity, it was easy to see that we were treated with more rigor than before the destruction of the Philadelphia. A few days after, as I was drawing hard at the cart, one of the drivers gave me a blow over the shoulder. In the rage of the moment, I gave him a blow with my fist under his ear, that brought him upon the sand. He got up, and rubbing his head, muttered some threat that I did not understand. The next night, I had a very *striking* translation of the Turks threat. After being ironed down, I received one hundred and eighty-two lashes on the bottom of my feet! The next morning, there were bloodblisters on my feet as large as the palm of my hand; in this condition I was obliged to resume my work in the hot sand, bare-footed! On another occasion, one of my comrades received three hundred lashes for the same offense. So much for Turkish mercy!

VIII

I SAY, SAM JONES, I LEAVE YOU MY BLUE JACKET

Commodore Preble, continuing a close blockade of Tripoli, conceived the idea of sending a fireship loaded with explosives into the harbor to destroy enemy shipping and shatter the castle. Commanded by Lieutenant Richard Somers, seamen stowed one hundred barrels of powder, one hundred and fifty fixed shells, and slow-burning fuses on board the Intrepid. *Midshipman Charles Ridgely recalls the action. No sailor on the* Intrepid *could tell the story, for none survived.*

. . . Two nights successively did the *Intrepid* move; but, owing to baffling winds, nothing could be accomplished. These failures, and an unusual movement in the harbor after dark on the third night, led Somers to believe that the suspicions of the enemy had been excited, and that they were on the look out. It was the general impression that their powder was nearly exhausted; and as so large a quantity, as was on board the ketch, if captured, would greatly protract the contest, before setting off, he addressed his crew telling them "that no man need accompany him, who had not come to the resolution to blow himself up, rather than be captured; and that such was fully his own determination!" Three cheers was the only reply. The gallant crew rose, as a single man . . . while each stepped forth, and begged as a *favor,* that he might be permitted to *apply the match!* It was a glorious moment, and made an impression on the hearts of all witnessing it, never to be forgotten.

All then took leave of every officer, and of every man, in the most cheerful manner, with a shake of the hand, as if they already knew that their fate was doomed; and one and another, as they passed over the side to take their post on board the ketch, might be heard to cry out, "I say, Sam Jones, I leave you my blue jacket and duck trowsers, stowed away in my bag;" and, "Bill Curtis, you may have the tarpaulin hat, and Geurnsey frock, and them petticoat trowsers I got in Malta—and mind, boys, when you get home, give a good account of us! . . ."

It was about nine o'clock on the night of the 4th of Sept., 1804.

The *Nautilus* had been ordered to follow the *Intrepid* closely in, to pick up and bring out her boat's crew, in case they should succeed in the exploit. Though it was very dark, we never lost sight of her, as I had been directed . . . to keep constant watch of her with a night glass.

At the end of an hour, about 10 o'clock, P. M., while I was engaged in this duty, the awful explosion took place. For a moment, the flash illumined the whole heavens around, while the terrific concussion shook every thing. Then all was hushed. . . . On board the *Nautilus,* the silence of death seemed to pervade the entire crew . . . and one feeling, alone, had possession of our souls—the preservation of Somers and his crew!

As moment after moment passed by, without bringing the preconcerted signal from the boat, the anxiety on board became intense; and the men, with lighted lanterns, hung themselves over the sides of the vessel, till their heads almost touched the water—a dark night—with the hope of discovering something which would give assurance of its safety. Still, no boat came, no signal was given; the unwelcome conclusion was forced upon us, that the fearful alternative—of blowing themselves up, rather than be captured had been put in execution. . . . Still, we lingered on the spot till broad day-light—though we lingered in vain. . . . Such was the end of the noble fellows.[11]

IX

MY GOD, IS IT POSSIBLE?

The war with Tripoli ended in 1805. The treaty involved no payment for peace or provision for future tribute, but required a $60,000 ransom for the release of the Philadelphia's *imprisoned crew.*

Two years later anger in the United States toward Great Britain became white hot when, in June, 1807, the British man-of-war Leopard, *50, impressed seamen from the American frigate* Chesapeake, *38, Captain James Barron. Third Lieutenant William Henry Allen was on board the* Chesapeake *when she was chased, halted, and fired upon near Cape Henry.*

. . . At 3 P.M. she hailed and informed the Commodore, she had a letter for him. The Commodore answered "we will heave to, and you can send your boat on board . . ." observed the English ship making preparations for battle. The English boat left the ship with an answer to the letter . . . most of our officers were below some *abed* and asleep, when there was a confused rumor of going to quarters. I immediately ran to mine on the gun deck, looked out one of the ports and saw the English ship abeam of us, training her guns upon us. Our officers on the gun deck used every exertion to clear the guns, which at this moment was in the following state: in the first division of 5 guns was the armourers forge & billows standing, on two of the guns a pile of boards, on the two others a carpenters work bench; in the 2nd division, cable lying on deck, nine sick men hanging in their hammocks over and about the guns, with their bags between them; in the 3 division, a screen was up, a table standing, chairs, a locker, and a harness cask; the guns secured, not a match, spunge, or powder horn at one of them. . . . The drum and fife attempted to beat to Quarters, but were stopped by order of the Commodore. In the confused state were we, when the first gun was fired from the Leopard she hailing us at the same time, the Commodore answering from the gangway, "I do not hear what you say," In one minute she gave us a broadside, I then heard some one sing out to fire, but heard no official orders, at this moment it was impossible to do so; not a powder horn or match at the guns, in about 15 or 20 minutes one of the Lieuts was fortunate enough to get a horn of powder, primed his guns and endeavored to fire them with the Loggerheads, but they were not enough; he then took a coal of fire between his fingers and fired one gun at the enemy, when the Commodore sang out from above, *"stop firing we have struck."* during this time the Leopard kept up a constant fire upon us, with round grape, Langrage, cannister, and Musquetry. She immediately sent an officer on board, mustered our crew and took from them 4 men said to have deserted the English frigate Melampus, the commodore sent a note to the English captain desiring him to take possession of the ship, this he absolutely refused to do and made sail leaving us with 4 feet water in the hold, 23 shot through our hull, the Bowsprit cap shot away, our foremast disabled . . . and with great regret I mention, 3 men killed & 20 wounded 12 of them severely.

In narrating to you the circumstances that led to the disgracefull surrender of this ship, I have not digress'd from the subject to give vent to my wounded feelings—Oh! that some one of their murderous balls had deprived me of the power of recollection the moment our colours were struck. Nothing could equal so horrible a scene as it was, to see so many brave men standing to their Quarters among the blood of their butchered and wounded country men and hear their cries without the means of avenging them; and when we would have done it, to have our colours struck, yes in 3 minutes every gun would have been at work—My god is it possible. My country's flag disgraced. You cannot appreciate you cannot *conceive* of my feelings at this moment. . . . I feel—Yes—I proudly feel, I would have willingly given my trifling life an offering for the honor of my country—Yes— give us a *Commander* give us *a man* to lead us to glory and there is not an officer in this ship that will not immolate himself to serve his country. . . .[12]

The United States was little prepared for the War of 1812. The Navy had in commission seven frigates, two corvettes, and seven sloops of war, brigs, and schooners. The British marshaled seven times that number in the western Atlantic. Yet, officered by men still in early middle age, who had served under Truxtun and Preble in the French and Tripolitan wars, the United States Navy maintained high standards of professional efficiency. American frigate victories at sea and squadron successes on the lakes sustained the nation's morale throughout the war.

X

BRAVE HULL IS QUITE THE DANDY

The Constitution, *44, Captain Isaac Hull, sailed out of Boston on 2 August 1812 bent on raiding enemy commerce and, southeast of Halifax on the 19th, met the British frigate* Guerrière, *38. The first decisive naval action of the war, this battle was of importance not*

Right: "Brave Hull is Quite the Dandy." Captain Isaac Hull, commanded the United States frigate *Constitution* in daring raids on enemy shipping and in its famous battle with the British frigate *Guerrière,* (*below*). This was the first decisive naval battle of the War of 1812 and gave the Americans a victory badly needed after disappointment over military campaigns on the lake frontier.

only to the Navy but to the entire country, which had experienced
disappointment over the military campaign on the lake frontier.

. . . with the *Constitution* under my command, a sail was discovered from the mast head . . . but at such a distance we could not tell what she was. All sail was instantly made in the chase, and soon found we came up with her. At 3 P. M. could plainly see that she was a ship on the starboard tack under easy sail, close on a wind; at ½ past 3 P. M. made her out to be a frigate; continued the chase until we were within about three miles, when I ordered the light sails to be taken in, the courses hauled up, and the ship cleared for action. At this time the chase had backed his maintop-sail, waiting for us to come down. As soon as the *Constitution* was ready for action, I bore down with intention to bring him to close action immediately; but on our coming within gun-shot she gave us a broadside and fired away, and wore, giving us a broadside on the other tack, but without effect; her shot falling short.

She continued wearing and manoeuvering for about three quarters of an hour, to get a raking position, but finding she could not, she bore up, and run under her topsails and gib, with the wind on her quarter. I immediately made sail to bring the ship up with her, and five minutes before 6 P.M. being along side within half pistol-shot, we commenced a heavy fire from all our guns, double shotted with round and grape, and so well directed were they, and so warmly kept up, that in 15 minutes his mizen mast went by the board, his main yard in the slings and the hull, rigging, and sail very much torn to pieces. The fire was kept up with equal warmth for 15 minutes longer, when his mainmast and foremast went, taking with them every spar, excepting the bowsprit. On seeing this we ceased firing, so that in thirty minutes after, we got fairly along side the enemy; she surrendered, and had not a spar standing, and her hull below and above water so shattered, that a few more broadsides must have carried her down.

After informing you that so fine a ship as the *Guerrière,* commanded by an able and experienced officer, had been totally dismasted, and otherwise cut to pieces so as to make her not worth towing into port, in the short space of thirty minutes, you can have no doubt of the gallantry and good conduct of the officers and ship's company I have the honor to command; it only remains therefore for me to assure you, that they all fought with great bravery; and it gives me a great pleasure to say, that from the smallest boy in the ship to the oldest seaman, not a look of fear was seen. They all went into action, giving three cheers, and requested to be laid close along side the enemy. . . .

ISAAC HULL[13]

Yankee doodle, keep it up,
Yankee doodle dandy,
For riddling British ships I'm sure,
Brave HULL is quite the dandy.

XI

THE SHANNON AFFAIR

In June, 1813 the American frigate Chesapeake, *38, Captain James Lawrence, set sail from Boston with a raw crew to search out enemy commerce and riddle his line of water communication from Canada. With a fair wind the* Chesapeake *trailed Captain P. B. V. Broke and his crack frigate* Shannon, *38, for some miles off shore. To reconstruct the action, Lieutenant George Budd's report, the Court of Inquiry's findings, and Midshipman Barry's report are quoted.*

Halifax, June 15, 1813

,Sir,

The unfortunate death of Captain James Lawrence and Lieutenant Augustus C. Ludlow, has rendered it my duty to inform you of the capture of the late U. States frigate *Chesapeake.*

. . . About 15 minutes before 6 P. M. the action commenced within pistol shot. The first broadside did great execution on both sides, damaged our rigging, killed among others Mr. White, the sailing master, and wounded Captain Lawrence. In about 12 minutes, after the commencement of the action, we fell on board of the enemy, and immediately after, one of our armchests on the quarter deck was blown up by a hand grenade thrown from the enemy's ship. In a few minutes one of the Captain's Aides came on the gun deck to inform me that the boarders were called. I immediately called the boarders away and proceeded to the spar deck, where I found that the enemy had succeeded in boarding us and had gained possession of our quarter deck. I immediately gave orders to haul on board the foretack, the purpose of shooting the ship clear of the other, and then made an attempt to regain the quarter deck. I again made an effort to collect the boarders, but in the mean time the enemy had gained complete possession of the ship. On my being carried down to the cock-pit, I there found Captain Lawrence and Lieutenant Ludlow both mortally wounded; the former had been carried below previously to the ship's being boarded; the latter was wounded in attempting to repel the boarders. . . .

I enclose to you a return of the killed and wounded, by which you will perceive that every officer, upon whom the charge of the ship would devolve, was either killed or wounded previously to her capture. . . .

GEORGE BUDD[14]

Report.

The court are unanimously of opinion, that the *Chesapeake* was gallantly carried into action by her late brave commander; and that the fire of the *Chesapeake* was much superior to that of the *Shannon*. The *Shannon* being much cut in her spars and rigging, and receiving many shot in and below the water line was reduced almost to a sink-ing condition, after only a few minutes of cannonading from the *Chesapeake;* while the *Chesapeake* was comparatively uninjured. And the court have no doubt, if the *Chesapeake* had not accidentally fallen on board the *Shannon,* and the *Shannon's* anchor got foul in the after quarter port of the *Chesapeake,* the *Shannon* must have soon surrendered or sunk.

It appears to the court, that as the ships were getting foul, Capt. Lawrence ordered the boarders to be called; but the bugle man, Wm. Brown, had deserted his quarters, and when discovered and ordered to call, was unable, from fright, to sound his horn; that midshipmen went below immediately to pass the word for the boarders; but not being called in the way they had been usually exercised, few came upon the upper deck; confusion prevailed; a greater part of the men deserted their quarters and ran below . . . when the *Shannon* got foul of the *Chesapeake*, Capt. Lawrence, his 1st Lieutenant, the sailing master, and lieutenant of marines were all killed or mortally wounded, and thereby the upper deck of the *Chesapeake* was left without any commanding officer, and with only one or two young midshipmen . . . previously to the ships getting foul, many of the *Chesapeake's* spar deck division had been killed and wounded, that these being left without a commissioned officer, or even a warrant officer, except one or two inexperienced midshipmen, and not being supported by the boarders from the gun deck, almost universally deserted their quarters. And the enemy, availing himself of this defenceless state of the *Chesapeake's* upper deck, boarded and obtained possession of the ship with very little opposition.

. . . The court are unanimously of opinion, that the capture of the late United States frigate *Chesapeake* was occasioned by the following causes: the almost unexampled early fall of Capt. Lawrence, and all the principal officers; the bugle-man's desertion of his quarters, and inability to sound his horn . . . the failure of the boarders on both decks to rally on the spar deck, after the enemy had boarded. . . .

The court cannot, however, perceive in this almost unexampled concurrence of disastrous circumstances that the national flag has suffered any dishonour from the capture of the United States frigate *Chesapeake*, by the superior force of the British frigate *Shannon*, of 52 carriage guns, and 396 men. Nor do this court apprehend that the result of the engagement will in the least discourage our brave seamen from meeting the enemy hereafter on equal terms. . . .

This court respectfully beg leave to superadd, that unbiased by any illiberal feelings towards the enemy, they feel it their duty to state, that the conduct of the enemy after boarding and carrying the *Chesapeake*, was a most unwarrantable abuse of power after success.

The court is aware that in carrying a ship by boarding the full extent of the command of an officer cannot be readily exercised; and that improper violence may unavoidably ensue. When this happens in the moment of contention, a magnanimous conquered foe will not complain. But the fact has been clearly established before this court, that the enemy met with little opposition on the upper deck, and none on the gun-deck. Yet after they had carried the ship, they fired from the gun-deck down the hatchway upon the berth-deck and killed and wounded several of the *Chesapeake's* crew, who . . . were un-armed and incapable of making any opposition; that some balls were fired even into the cockpit: and what excites the utmost abhorrence, this outrage was committed in the presence of a British officer stand-ing at the hatchway.

W. BAINBRIDGE, *President*.[15]

Washington City, July 30, 1813

Sir,

After the enemy had complete possession of the ship midshipmen Randolph and Flushman were ordered from the fore and main-top. In coming from the shrouds lieutenant Falkner (the British officer) said to his men, *kill those damned rascals*. Immediately, several muskets were discharged at them, but without effect. My station was in the mizen-top. I was looking on deck when I saw one of the *Chesapeake's* men crawling along, attempting to get below with one of his legs off. *One of the enemy stepped up to him with his cutlass, and immediately put an end to his existence.* Lieutenant Falkner looked up in the mizen-top; pointed at me, said to his men, "go up three of you and throw that damned Yankee overboard." They immediately rushed up, seizing me by the collar; "now," said they, "you damned Yankee, you shall swim for it," attempting to throw me overboard; but I got within the rigging, when one of them kicked me in the breast, which was the cause of my falling; being stunned by the fall, I lay some time senseless, and *when I came to, I was cut over the head with a cutlass.*

Eleven of our midshipmen were confined in a small place, nine feet by six, with an old sail to lie on, and a guard at the door, until a day before our arrival at Halifax; and likewise eleven of us upon five rations, and some days only one meal. Our clothes were taken on board of the Shannon; lieutenant Wallis, the commanding officer on board, would not let us take our clothes below with us, but pledged his word as an officer, we should receive our clothes. But we discovered next morning *that their midshipmen had on our clothes and side arms.* We were conversing together respecting our clothes—one of their midshipmen overheard our conversation, and made a report to the lieutenant commanding. He then sent word to us, that if we said any thing more about the clothes, he would put us in the fore hold with the men. We expected to receive our clothes when we arrived in port, but I assure you, sir, nothing was ever restored.[16]

James Lawrence (right)
commanded the brig *Ches-
apeake* (below) when she
was captured by the British
frigate *Shannon*.

XII

CAPTAIN ALLEN PASSED A RESTLESS NIGHT

The humiliating defeat of the Chesapeake *was followed by the loss of the brig* Argus, *16, Captain William Henry Allen, which sailed from New York in June, 1813. For a month Allen raided the English and Irish Channels and seized nineteen prizes before, on 14 August, the British brig-of-war* Pelican, *18, intercepted him off Ireland. A portion of the* Argus' *cruise is noted by her surgeon.*

. . . August the 11th Wednesday at sea . . . Bristol Channel

After a chase of 4 hours Captured a large Ship the *Mariner*—laden with Sugar &c Bound to Bristol. Crowded all sail after another to leeward—12 Sail in sight in that direction—A Brig & Cutter to windward—after a long chase captured the other named the *Betsy* laden with Sugar—at the same time captured a Pilot Boat Cutter *Jane*—Soon after, a Brig and a Cutter Sloop from Poole to Liverpool with Clay. Sent in the Prisoners in the Brig. Sent in the *Betsy* a prize—Burnt the *Mariner*—Sunk the Cutter Sloop.

10 oClk P M captured another Cutter Sloop the *Dinah & Betty* from Cork with cattle. Killed and got on board 2 head—Burnt her.

August 12th Thursday at sea   off the Saltees Ireland

Captured a new Brig called the *Ann* from Cardigan to London with Slate and Welsh Woolens. Sunk her   Brought too a Portuguese Brig bound to Cork—Sent the Prisoners from the 2 last prizes on board of her. Gave chace to two large Ships and a Brig to leeward—Allowed the Brig to Pass us and continued the chase after the large vessels—All showing English colors. One ship showing 18 ports and the other 16 apparently preparing for action. Brought them too and sent Mr. Allen on board the largest the Captain of which refused to come on board us; and before our boat had returned they both made sail keeping close to each other. Made sail and engaged them both. The large one struck after receiving 2 broadsides—chased the other close in and she escaped among the rocks. The large one proved a Scotch Ship the *Defiance* mounting 14 long nines 21 men—from Greenock to Newfoundland.

66

August 13th Friday   idem

At 2 oClk A. M. captured a large Brig the *Baltic* laden with sugar bound to Dublin—at 5 a Sloop laden with deal boards—at 6 burnt the *Defiance* and the *Baltic*—threw overboard the cargo of the Sloop and sent her away with the Prisoners at 9 P M—fired a gun and brought too a large Brig the *Belford*—which had nearly ran aboard of us—She proved to be from Dublin bound to London laden with linen wine &c worth 100,000£—Took out of her a box of Plate and burnt her.

August 14th Saturday   St George's Channel

Early this morning came to action with a large English Brig She captured us after an action of 45 minutes She proved to be the *Pelican.*

August 15th   Sunday   at sea

The following list comprehends the number of killed and wounded on board of our vessel.

Mr. Wm W Edwards   Midshipman.   Killed by shot in the head.

Mr. Richd Delphy   Midshipman.   Do   Had both legs nearly shot off at the knees—he survived the action about 3 hours

Joshua Jones   Seaman—Killed.

Geo Gardiner   Seaman—His thigh taken off by a round shot close to his body. He lived about ½ an hour.

Jno Finlay   Seaman—His head was shot off at the close of the action.

Wm Moulton   Seaman   Killed.

The following were wounded

Wm H Allen Esq—Commander—His left knee shattered by a cannon shot. Amputation of the thigh was performed about 2 hours after the action—An anodyne was previously administered—An anodyne at night.

Lieut Watson—1st—Part of the Scalp on the upper part of the head torn off by a grape shot—the bone denuded. It was dressed lightly and he returned and took command of the deck. Now on board the *Pelican.*

Mr Colin McCloud—Boatswain—Received a severe lacerated wound on the upper part of the thigh, a slight one on the face and a contusion on the right shoulder. Dressed simply with lint and roller Bandage. . . .

Owing to the disordered state of the vessel the wounded have wretched accomodation—I endeavoured to make their condition as comfortable as possible—Divided those of our people who remained on board, and were well, into watches—in different parts of the vessel. . . . Directed Lemonade & Tamarind water to be kept made and served to the Wounded. . . .

August 16th Monday   arrived at Plymouth

Capt Allen—Morn—No fever—has had some slight spasms in the stump—anodyne was occasionally administed—He has been for some time troubled with a dyspeptic complaint which is disagreeable in his present state. . . .

Eve—an exudation of the thinner parts of the blood now begins to appear thro' the dressings—stump as easy as can be expected. . . . Enjoined a light diet—Chicken broth, Panada &c—Administed a purg. but it was not retained. . . .

Joseph Jordan—Died this morning. . . .

Our wounded are in a distressed condition. The riotous behaviour of the captors is such that they have no rest whatever and are frequently trodden upon and bruisd by them.

Directed to day thin Chicken broth to be served out to them with their light Nourishment.

August 17th Tuesday   Plymouth

The wounded and sick Seamen were this morning carried to the hospital—Mr. Hudson attended them—I request'd him to enquire what accomodation he could find for the captain at the Town as the noise & tumult on board is very disagreeable.

Capt Allen—Stump in a good state—but little soreness—but has some fever this morning. . . .

This afternoon I obtained permission to go to town for the purpose of hiring private lodgings for the Captain. On return found him worse. Vomiting more frequent. Pulse weak and frequent—Skin cold—now & then troubled with Hiccup—Mind, at times, wandering—false vision. . . .

August 18th Wednesday

Capt Allen—Passed a very restless night—vomiting continues, altho' wine & occasional anodynes seemed to relieve it. This morning I dressed the Stump assisted by the Surgeon the *San Salvador* Flag Ship. Found the incision united but a little at the inner angle—Surface flabby Discharge thin, sanious—Whole appearance exhibiting a want of action in the parts.

On consultation with the Surgeon of the Flag Ship and, with Dr

British brig-of-war *Pelican*
capturing the brig *Argus*
(above), commanded by
William Henry Allen (right).

Magrath of the Mill Prison Hospital, it was agreed to have him removed thither. . . . The disagreeable condition of the vessel—his danger, and the eminent medical assistance at the Hospital concur in inducing us to adopt this plan.

11 A M Capt Nash of the *San Salvador*, sent his launch with a large cot slung in it.

12 M Arrived at the Hospital and found a neat & commodious apartment ready—on arrival he complained of languor & appeared somewhat fatigued—a glass of wine reviv'd him—vomiting continues. . . . Skin moist & cold.

9 P. M.—Pulse feeble, frequent, interrupted, skin covered with a clammy moisture—Vomiting continues unabated notwithstanding the use of anti Emetic remedies. He is extremely restless, desireing often to have his position altered. . . .

11 oClk P M. He died. . . .

August 21st Saturday—Mill Prison

Attended the funeral of Capt Allen with Mr Denison Mr Hudson & Mr Snelson as Mourners. . . .[17]

> Yankee sailors have a knack,
>   Haul away! yeo ho, boys,
> Of pulling down a British Jack,
>   'Gainst any odds you know boys.
> Come three to one, right sure am I,
>   If we can't beat 'em, sure we'll try,
> To make Columbia's colors fly,
>   Haul away! yeo ho, boys.
>
> Yankee sailors, when at sea,
>   Haul away! yeo ho, boys!
> Pipe all hands with merry glee,
>   While aloft they go boys!
> And when with pretty girls on shore,
>   Their cash is gone, and not before,
> They wisely go to sea for more,
>   Haul away! yeo ho, boys!
>
> Yankee sailors love their soil,
>   Haul away! yeo ho, boys!

And for glory, ne'er spare toil,
　　But flog its foes, you know boys!
Then while its standard owns a rag,
　　The world combin'd shall never brag,
They made us strike the Yankee flag,
　　Haul away! yeo ho, boys![18]

TEN DOLLARS REWARD

Deserted from the Rendezvous for the U. S. frigate Congress, No. 50, Fish Street, Boston, on the 21st inst. a yellow man, by the name of Garset Johnson, (seaman) aged 19 years, 5 feet 9 inches high, or thereabout, dressed in a blue jacket, yellow trowsers, and red flannel shirt. Whoever will apprehend said deserter and deliver him to the Rendezvous, or on board the U. S. frigate Congress, shall receive the above reward.

　　　　　　　　　　　　For John H. Elton
　　　　　　　　　　　　Rec'g Officer
　　　　　　　　　　　　C. O. CANNON.[19]

XIII

TO MAKE THE BEST OF EVERYTHING

Carpenter's Mate Samuel F. Holbrook enlisted in the United States Navy and reported on board gunboat No. 98 tied up to a New York wharf.

. . . No. 98, the gunboat, was in a very filthy condition, and among her crew were some of the Essex's 16 men, who were very quarrelsome and overbearing; supposing themselves to be entitled to more privileges than any of the others. The officers of the boat were also from among the Essex's 16.

We often came short of our rations, especially of the fresh beef; one pound per diem was sent on board for each man and boy; but the officers in the cabin usually kept two or three women, besides company from the shore to dine. . . .

71

A plentiful supply of rum was brought on board, without any restraint whatever; consequently the crew were continually drunk, and very quarrelsome.

The nights were hideous, both among officers and seamen. Scarcely a night passed without a fight.

I selected a berth near the cabin bulk-head, and close up in a corner, and as soon as I had taken my supper, crawled into it, to get out of the din. Among the men in the hold were several bad women, who usually mingled in the fights, and scarcely ever were without a pair of splendid black eyes. Many a night have I lain in my snug hiding place, and looked out on the drunken tumult before me, and bitterly lament the course I had taken, in entering the navy.

This sudden transition from a civilized life to a residence among brutes, was overwhelming to my feelings. I found that I had an important lesson before me, and that the earlier it was learned, the better: *to make the best of everything. . . .*

The mistakes and follies of the past may teach us to be more cautious for the future; but they should never be allowed to paralyze our energies, or surrender us to weak repining.

I knew that I should not remain long on board a gun boat; my habits were good; I used no intoxicating drinks; never had played a game of cards, nor was I ever found in bad company; and I had another cheering thought, that I might be promoted to the rank of carpenter, as I was now only carpenter's mate, and was resolved to do my duty faithfully, and leave the rest with God.

One night, about nine o'clock, we were alarmed by a terrible shouting from one of the other boats, who were hailing us, and at the same time, keeping up a brisk fire of musketry; we could just discern, through the darkness, a boat pulling rapidly towards the shore, and a gruff voice crying out, *"Blood for supper! Blood for supper!"* Lieut. Odenheimer hailed every gunboat, and ordered them to man their boats, and go in pursuit of the fugitives.

Our boat was instantly hauled alongside, and six men, of which I was one, and a midshipman, ordered into her; each man was armed with a loaded pistol and a cutlass.

We pulled directly for the runaway boat, that was now close under the Brooklyn shore; we followed them by their noise, and as soon as they saw that they were pursued, they struck off again for the New York side. It being very dark, we could just discern the boat a short distance ahead, but they succeeded in landing before we could get up with them. And now commenced the hunt.

Here were seven of us, that composed our boat's crew, and all armed to the teeth. We went directly to the "hook," the abode of infamy and wretchedness, where we supposed the deserters had gone; and here, in going from house to house, we were exposed to the insults of those who inhabited these dens. It was certain, that we should not find either sympathy or co-operation in the object of our pursuit, for deserters, thieves, murderers, and pickpockets all find an asylum in this pandemonium of wretchedness. The midshipman who had charge of our gang, was a blustering fellow, and I thought he would get us into a fight, which was, however, avoided.

We gave up the chase, and returned, unsuccessful, to our gunboat.

The small vessels comprising the Flying Squadron were purchased and lying at the Brooklyn Navy Yard. We were shifted from the steam-frigate to the Navy Yard to man these vessels; as they were all to undergo alterations, the crews could not live on board until after the repairs had been completed. We were put on board the old prize ship Alert. She was the first prize taken by the frigate *Essex,* and as she was old, was converted into a receiving ship.

When I first went on board this filthy tub my heart sunk. I thought the gunboat was the filthiest thing that floated, but as the saying goes, she was not a circumstance to the old Alert.

Order and discipline seldom prevail on board of a receiving ship. In some cases they are commanded by some old worn-out naval officer whose energy, if he ever had any, has entirely gone. Or perhaps the command is given to some dissipated fellow who does not know how to treat men. The seamen who are put on board these dismal abodes are constantly shifting; some probably do not remain twenty-four hours. So there is but little opportunity for establishing any permanent rules and regulations on board a receiving ship, whatever may be the disposition of the Commander.

These remarks are intended to apply only to the time of the late war with England. Since then I believe there has been much improvement in this class of ships. At the time I was on board the Alert she was commanded by a drunken tyrannical master's mate, and when I had reached the berth deck, with my bag and hammock, I walked aft to the place set apart for petty officers, and was just about laying them down when a fellow sung out to me:

"I say! look out for the lice there; there are some as big as cockroaches."

I thought if they were as large as that, I could easily catch them, so I left my dunnage and went on deck. . . .

There were about two hundred men and boys on board this ship, who had been recruited for the Flying Squadron.

The weather was very cold and stormy, and many of these poor fellows had sold every article of clothing except what they stood in, for rum. . . . The ration of a half pint of raw whiskey was served to each man at seven and a half o'clock in the morning, and scarcely a dozen out of the whole crew had a blanket or a bed. The government furnished them with a hammock, and many kept themselves too drunk to hang them up, and would lie down and sleep upon the wet deck; then followed severe colds, which often terminated in consumption, fever and death. But the half pint of raw whiskey in the morning gave them new life for a short time, and then they were down again. . . .

One morning a dead man was found on the berth deck, near the main hatch. The poor fellow had died during the night, probably from exposure, as he possessed neither bed nor clothing. It appeared that there was no one on whom the duty of taking proper care of the corpse devolved, so it lie there all that day, frozen stiff.

I ate but little, for my stomach fairly loathed everything I saw in the shape of food. As the weather continued very stormy, we were kept on board, and I had as much as I could do to watch my clothes bag. We spent about a week in this miserable manner. . . .

Perhaps the reader may think that in my description of the gunboat, and the receiving ship, Alert, that I have painted things in too high colors; but I assure you, that the half has not been told. I find myself at a loss for words that will give an adequate idea of scenes that I have witnessed, while in the United States Navy; but more particularly, during the war with England. It may be, that I was more sensitive than I should have been, and circumstances, which appeared so unpleasant, perhaps, to another would hardly have been noticed. . . .

The old Alert was now so crowded with fresh recruits, that it became necessary to ship some of us on board the Corvette John Adams. I was among the draft selected for her; we went on board early in the morning. The purser's steward had not arranged for our rations, so we had nothing to eat that day, until just at night, when we got some fresh beef, which I ate raw. The John Adams, soon after we joined her, was ordered to be fitted as a cartel for Bermuda, to bring home the crew of the U. S. frigate President, which had been captured by a British squadron off New York, and carried into that place. We were now divided round among the gunboats; myself and twelve others were put on board a gunboat which had been used as a tender for the frigate President, while she lay in the harbor of New York. This gunboat had been hauled up in a cove, and was full of rats and old rigging. A Negro was given us for a cook, and we were to live on board this craft, until the vessels composing the Flying Squadron were ready to receive their crews. . . .

The weather continued very cold, and we could do but little work in the yard. Our black cook had been detected in stealing from an officer, and was sent on board the boat in double irons, and there confined, which deprived us of his services, and himself, the use of his limbs; for in consequence of his confinement both feet were frozen, and the groans of the poor fellow were really distressing.

He was removed to the hospital, but lost both feet; they were amputated soon after he entered the doctor's list. Truly, *"The way of the transgressor is hard."* In consequence of a trifling theft, this man is a cripple for life. . . .

Our boat was leaky, and no one would take the trouble to pump her out. One night, just before we turned in, the water made its appearance over the platform, and when we come to examine the pump, it was found to be choked and entirely useless. We concluded to stay on board that night, and on the morrow to apply to the captain of the yard for other quarters. About twelve o'clock, one fellow got out of his hammock and found himself knee deep in water. He gave the alarm, all hands roused up, and before we could get all our clothes and bedding on deck, she heeled over and sunk. I made a jump and got on board another boat that lay alongside; and she was half full of water. The rest of the crew got off by means of the boat and some spars. In jumping on board the other boat, I fell on an iron belaying pin, and hurt myself severely. All this was in the night, it was dark and cold, but we made no noise.

By the sinking of this boat many lives were lost, as might be seen by the floating bodies around her next morning. And as the gunboat had been condemned before we went on board of her, we now considered her condemnation fully Rat-ified. The repairs on board the Firefly were now so far advanced that we, poor sunken fellows, had permission to take our hammocks and bags on board of her, and our meals on board the Cyane.

The command of the squadron devolved on Captain Wolcott Chauncey—he being the seignor captain among those of the Flying Squadron. And he was a Tartar sure enough, as the following little incident will show. Two young men, who were mechanics' apprentices, had shipped for the squadron, and had been at the Navy Yard but a few days, when, probably feeling a little homesick, took French leave one evening, and went over to the city. On the following morning, they were missed at muster, and their absence reported to Capt. Chauncey, who immediately sent a midshipman to find them. They were both found together, having met with some of their companions, and who had all been on a frolic. These young men were brought on board an old bomb ketch, and confined with double irons two days, and on the morning of the third, at nine o'clock, all hands were called along-side the ketch, to witness punishment. . . .

Here were about three hundred men, boys and marines, assembled round the old hulk to see these two young men nearly flayed alive, for going over to New York without leave. When all had assembled, the two prisoners were brought from their place of confinement, more dead than alive. The first was stripped and seized up.

On these occasions, every man and officer stands with hats off, and perfectly silent, in order to show the *supremacy* of a law that cuts a man's flesh to pieces.

Capt. Chauncey, standing on a slight elevation, and with a stentorian voice, addressed the crowd: *"Men! what the law allows you, you shall have, but by the eternal ———— if any one of you disobeys that law, I'll cut your back bone out.* Go on with him, boatswain's mate and do your duty, or by ——, you shall take his place."

The shrieks of the youngster were dreadful, calling upon God and all the holy angels to save him. After the first dozen, another boatswain's mate took the cat, and when he had received two dozen, he fainted, and hung by his wrists. The punishment was suspended for a few moments until he had revived sufficiently to stand on his feet; he then took four dozen more, making six in all, and when taken down he could not stand.

The other received seven dozen; he fainted, however, before he

had received the first, and received the greater portion of his punishment in that state. The flesh was fairly hanging in strips upon both
backs; it was a sickening sight. . . .

Notwithstanding my previous determination to make the best of
everything, and to become hardened to whatever might come along,
discontent seemed to return with additional force. I began to give a
gloomy look into the future. The idea of being captured, and then of
lingering in a British prison, and this horrid flogging, and the companions that I must pass the remainder of my servitude with. These
feelings seemed to work like an avalanche upon me; and there was
a possibility that in my present position, I might be flogged at the
gangway, too, as many a man has been, without knowing for what.

I was heartily disgusted with everything that belonged to a man-
of-war; and after a night's deliberation, came to a fixed determination, that I would desert, and get into some foreign country, and
there remain until I had accumulated something; and probably by
that time I should be forgotten, and could then return to my native
country. . . .

I obtained permission to go to New York, and managed to get
my clothes bag on shore, and deposited it with Jack Anderson's wife.
I crossed the ferry, and had no sooner stepped out of the ferry-boat,
than a strong feeling of self-reproach came over me. Mr. Barnwell
had given me liberty to be absent twenty-four hours; his treatment
to me had been like that of a kind father, and now to requite this
good feeling by desertion, seemed to be the heighth of ingratitude. All
this made me half determined to re-cross the ferry.

I thought if I could find a friend into whose ear I could pour
my trouble, and obtain from him some consoling advice, even that
would make me happy.

I went to the Bull's Head Inn, in the Bowery, the depot for
wagons that plied between New York and Boston, (as the water
communication was cut off by the British cruisers) and found that a
wagon would start next morning by daylight. I saw the driver, and
bargained with him to carry me to Boston, and for which I was to
give him my pea-jacket.

I did not awake the next morning until after the hour at which
the wagon was to start; so, I lost my passage; but such a night as I
passed cannot be described; what with horrid dreams and direful forebodings, I was nearly distracted. I spent the day in walking round

the wharves, as no wagon started until the next day. . . . I called on an elderly gentleman, to whom I told my story. He happened to be the friend I had been seeking, and he urged me by all means to abandon this rash alternative, and serve my time out honorably, and then I should have nothing to embitter my future life. . . . My conversation with this good old man caused me again to waver in my present intention.

On the afternoon of the second day of my absence from the brig, I met Wilson, who had just come over from the Navy Yard. Mr. Barnwell had enquired for me, and he had told him that I was sick, and at the house of a friend in New York. Mr. Barnwell sent him for me, with orders to have me brought over if I was able to stand.

Jack and I understood the whole affair, and I went with him to the Navy Yard, and quietly on board the brig, and resumed the job on which I had been at work, when I went ashore. Next morning, Mr. Barnwell came to me, and enquired about my health. . . .

In the afternoon, he called me on the quarter-deck, and said he, "I observe that you are a young man of good habits, and acquainted with your business; I have also observed that you are active and get quickly through any job you undertake, and shall appoint you carpenter of this brig; your official appointment I will hand you to-morrow; and that I feel a pleasure in doing this from what I have seen of you since your attachment to the Navy." He then gave me twenty dollars and liberty to go over to New York. All this seemed to me like a dream, and yet it was real; my trouble was over! I was now a warrant officer—out of the reach of the lash—had a comfortable state-room, and a boy to wait upon me. Truly, this was a metamorphosis. . . .[20]

XIV

WHAT A GLORIOUS DAY FOR MY COUNTRY

Under the command of Commodore Oliver Hazard Perry, the American force on Lake Erie consisted of two new 20-gun brigs, Lawrence *and* Niagara, *the brig* Caledonia, *3, and six schooners.*

*British Captain Robert Barclay commanded a squadron which in-
cluded the* Detroit, *19, the* Queen Charlotte, *17, also ship-rigged, the
brig* Hunter, *10, and the schooners* Lady Prevost, *13, and* Chippeway,
1, and the sloop Little Belt, *3. Perry's victory on 10 September 1813,
witnessed by Seaman David C. Bunnell, encouraged the American
army under William Henry Harrison to invade Canada, where it won
the decisive Battle of the Thames.*

. . . We returned to Put-in Bay, and the second day, (Friday)
was memorable and ever to be remembered tenth of September 1813.
The sun rose in all his glory—but before it set, many a brave tar on
both sides was doomed to a watery grave, and many a jovial soul
who had "led the merry dance on the light fantastic toe," the evening previous, never danced again—unless we have our frolics after
death.

The first intelligence we received of the approach of the enemy's
squadron, was from the man at the mast head—"Sail ho!"—An
officer of the deck replied, "Where away?" "Off Rattlesnake Island."
Before the officer had time to inquire what she looked like, the man
bawled out again—"Sail ho!—sail ho—six sail in sight sir." As if by
instinct, every soul at once exclaimed—"The enemy is in sight."—
All was bustle and hurry, but no confusion. The signal was made to
weigh the anchors, which was done with surprising alacrity. We had
sixty fathoms of cable out, and it was not more than fifteen minutes
before we had our sails set and anchors up. The wind was ahead,
and the enemy to the windward, but in fifteen minutes after we had
got fairly under way, the wind shifted to the opposite point of compass, which brought us to the windward.

Commodore Perry ordered his flag to be hoisted. We knew this
flag was on board, but none of us knew what the motto was, until
it was unfurled to the breeze—when we discovered the dying words
of the brave Lawrence—"DON'T GIVE UP THE SHIP!"

This flag was eighteen feet long and nine broad—painted blue—
the letters on it very large and white. When it was unfurled, the
whole squadron gave three cheers. . . .

All were busy in getting every thing in order for the battle—the
shot were got up from below—the guns well loaded and primed—
and all was in complete readiness. The drums beat to quarters, and
every man repaired to his station. The words "Silence—stand to your

quarters!" were given, and the signal to form a line. The wind was light, and our line was soon formed, when we bore down upon the enemy in perfect order.

There being only a light wind, we neared the enemy very slowly. . . . The word, *"silence"* was again given—we stood in awful impatience—not a word was spoken—not a sound heard, except now and then an order to trim a sail, and the boatswain's shrill whistle. It seemed like the awful silence that precedes an earthquake. . . . My pulse beat quick—all nature seemed wrapped in awful suspense. . . . At length there was a gun fired from the Detroit, and the action commenced. A gentle zephyr had wafted us near the enemy, and then died away. . . . Our all was at stake. America had never before had an opportunity since she became a nation, of meeting squadron to squadron.

No sooner had the first gun been fired from the Detroit, than they opened a tremendous fire from their whole line, of round, grape and canister shot. The Scorpion, Tigress and Aerial, having long guns, returned their fire with considerable effect. Our vessel (the Lawrence) carried 20 guns—ten on each side. . . . My comrades fell on all sides. One man who stood next to me, was most shockingly wounded —having both his legs shot off, and a number of the spikes from the bulwark drove into his body. He was carried below, and survived until he heard victory proclaimed—he then exclaimed, "I die in peace," and immediately expired.

The whole of the enemy's line kept up an incessant fire, and our impatience became almost insupportable, but our ever watchful Commodore knew what was best to be done, and ordered the long gun to be manned, and fired; it was done in an instant, and the shot reached the enemy. We kept up a fire with it for a few minutes, when an order from our commander put every man in motion— "Stand by"—a second intervened—"Fire." . . .

I paid attention to the gun which I had charge of, and loaded and fired as fast as possible, and at one time in a great hurry, shoved in a crowbar, and I found after the action was over that it did its duty on board the Detroit, by cutting away three shrouds of her main rigging.

At last my gun got so warm that it jumped entirely out of its carriage. Five of my men out of eight were either killed or wounded. I went to the next gun and found but one man left, but by the

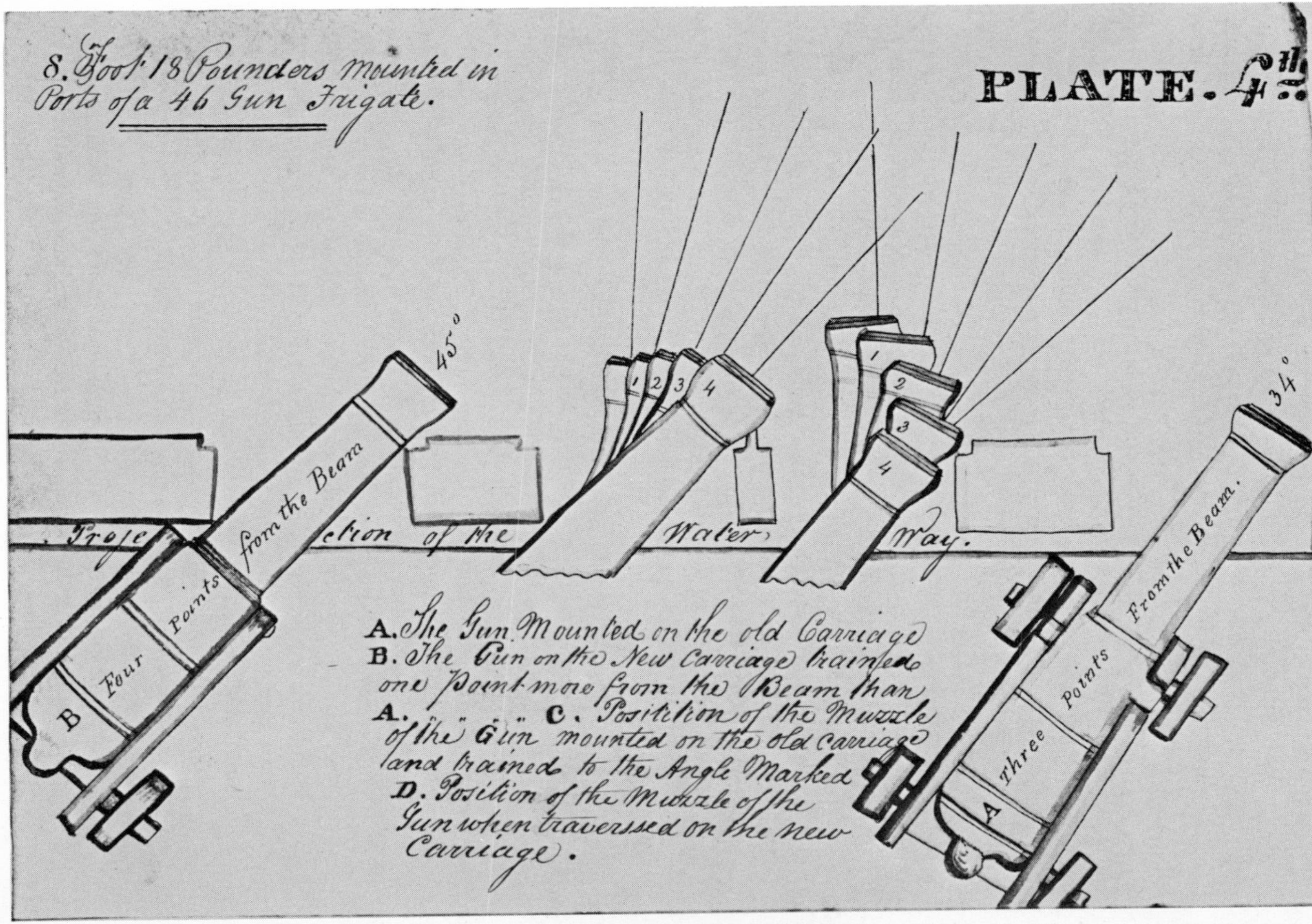

8 Foot 18 Pounders Mounted in
Ports of a 46 Gun Frigate.

34°

From the Beam.

Three points

A

May.

Water.

Direction of the

Fore Aft Beam

Four Points

B

45°

A. The Gun Mounted on the old Carriage
B. The Gun on the New Carriage trained on
Point more from the Beam than
A. "the" Gun. C. Position of the Muzzle
and trained on the old Carriage
and trained to the Angle Marked
D. Position of the Muzzle of the
Gun when traversed on the new
Carriage.

assistance of my three she was soon made to play again. I could now only hear an occasional gun fired from our vessel. I looked up to see if our flag was still flying, and with pleasure beheld, partly obscured by smoke, the star spangled banner yet waving, and heard Perry exclaim, "Man the boat."

I looked along the deck, and such a sight at any other time would have made me shudder. The deck was in a shocking predicament. Death had been very busy. It was one continued gore of blood and carnage—the dead and dying were strewed in every direction over it—for it was impossible to take the wounded below as fast as they fell. . . .

On board the Niagara, to which vessel Perry went in the height of the battle. . . . Perry made the signal to close with the enemy— we made sail and were soon in close contact with the British, and the action was renewed with great vigor. The only words I recollect of hearing Perry say were—"Take good aim my boys, don't waste your shot." The smoke was so dense that it was impossible to see the enemy —but we were so close that by firing on a level we could not miss— their vessel being so much higher out of the water than ours. The Lawrence struck her colors for a little time, and then hoisted them again.

I stooped down to get a shot, and accidentally put my hand on a small brass swivel, (it was nine inches long and would carry about a two pound ball;) it struck me in an instant that it would be a handsome present for "John Bull"—so I rammed it into my gun and let go—it was found after the action on board the Detroit. . . .

The action raged with fury on both sides for some time, when Perry, finding that our ammunition began to grow short, resolved to make one finishing blow. He ran down with the intention of board- ing, but the Queen Charlotte had run afoul of the Detroit, which rendered her useless, as she could not fire at us without killing their own men—while our shot took effect in both of them. Our flag was shot away, which produced three cheers from the enemy—but they were sadly mistaken—it was soon hoisted again. In short, after a bloody and well contested conflict of three hours and forty eight min- utes, the undaunted Union of Great Britain come down. . . .

We had peas boiling for dinner—our place for cooking was on deck, and during the action a shot had penetrated the boiler, and the peas were rolling all over the deck—we had several pigs loose on deck, and I actually saw one of them eating peas that had both his hind legs shot off. . . . A hardy old tar who acted in the station of "*Stopperman*," (when any of the rigging is partly shot away, they put a stopper on the place, to prevent it from going away entirely) discovering our *main stay* partly shot away, jumped and began to put a *stopper* on, and while in the act, another shot cut the stay away below him, which let him swing with great force against the mast— He gravely observed—"Damn you, if you must have it, take it."—A shot from the enemy struck one of our guns, within a quarter of an inch of the calibre; little pieces of metal flew in every direction, and wounded almost every man at the piece. . . .

The Sloop Little Belt attempted to make sail and steer for Malden —the Scorpion gave her chase, and fired a *"long tom"* at her: the first shot struck close to her stern—the next entered her starboard quarter, and went out at her larboard bow, and she surrendered. This made the victory complete. . . .

What a glorious day for my country. . . .[21]

> *U. S. Brig* Niagara, *off the Western Sisters*
> *Head of Lake Erie, Sept. 10, 1813—4 P.M.*

Dear Genl.

We have met the enemy and they are ours—two ships, two brigs, one schooner & one sloop.

> Yours with great respect
> and esteem
> O. H. PERRY[22]

Major Genl. Harrison

XV

WE HAVE BEEN UNFORTUNATE, BUT NOT DISGRACED

Of all the American commerce-destroying cruises made during the war, the most famous was that of the frigate Essex, *32, under Captain David Porter, whose official report follows.*

Essex Junior, July 3rd, 1814
At Sea

Sir,

   . . . I sailed from the Delaware on the 27th of October, 1812, and repaired (agreeably to instructions from Commodore Bainbridge) to Port Praya, Fernando de Noronho, and Cape Frio; and arrived at each place on the day appointed to meet him. On my passage from Port Praya to Fernando de Noronho, I captured his Britannic Majesty's packet Nocton; and after taking out about 71,000 pounds sterling in specie, sent her under command of Lieutenant Finch for America. I cruized off Rio de Janeiro, and about Cape Frio, until the 12th of January, 1813, hearing frequently of the Commodore, by vessels from Bahia. I here captured but one schooner, with hides and tallow—I sent her into Porto Rico. The Montague, the Admiral's ship, being in pursuit of me, my provisions now getting short, and finding it necessary to look out for a supply, to enable me to meet the Commodore by the first of April, off St. Helena, I proceeded to the island of St. Catharines (the last place of rendezvous on the coast of Brazil) as the most likely to supply my wants, and at the same time afford me that secrecy necessary to enable me to elude the British ships of war on the coast, and expected there. I here could procure only wood, water and rum, and a few bags of flour; and hearing of the Commodore's action with the Java, the capture of the Hornet by the Montague, and a considerable augmentation of the British force on the coast, and of several being in pursuit of me, I found it necessary to get to sea as soon as possible.

   I now, agreeably to the Commodore's plan, stretched to the southward, securing the coast so far as Rio de la Plata. I heard that Buenos Ayres was in a state of starvation, and could not supply our wants; and that the government of Montevideo was very inimical to us. The Commodore's instructions now left it completely discretionary with me what course to pursue, and I shaped my course for the Pacific; and after suffering greatly from short allowance of provisions, and heavy gales off Cape Horn, I arrived at Valparaiso on the 14th of March, 1813. I here took in as much jerked beef and other provisions as my ship would conveniently stow, and ran down the coast of Chili and Peru; in this track I fell in with a Peruvian corsair, which had on board twenty-four Americans as prisoners, the crews of two whale ships, which she had taken on the coast of Chili.

David Porter (below), commander of the United States frigate *Essex* which engaged the British frigate *Phoebe* and the sloop-of-war *Cherub* (above).

The captain informed me, that, as the allies of Great Britain, they would capture all they should meet with, in expectation of a war between Spain and the United States. I threw all his guns and ammunition into the sea, liberated the Americans, wrote a respectful letter to the viceroy, explaining the cause of my proceedings, which I delivered to her captain. I then proceeded for Lima and re-captured one of the vessels as she was entering the port. I proceeded for the Gallipagos Islands, where I cruized from the 17th of April, until the 3rd of October, 1813; during which time I touched only once on the coast of America, which was for the purpose of procuring a supply of fresh water.

While among this group, I captured the British ships, employed chiefly in the whale fishery: *Montezuma, Policy, Georgiana, Greenwich, Atlantic, Rose, Hector, Catharine, Seringapatam, Charlton, New Zealander, Sir A. Hammond.* . . .

The Rose and Charlton were given to the prisoners, the Hector, Catharine and Montezuma I sent to Valparaiso, where they were laid up; the Policy, Georgiana and New Zealander, I sent for America; the Greenwich I kept as a store ship, and the Atlantic, now called Essex Junior, I equipped with twenty guns, and gave command of her to lieutenant Downes.

Lieutenant Downes had conveyed the prizes to Valparaiso, and on his return brought me letters informing me, that the squadron under the command of commodore James Hillyar, consisting of the frigate Phoebe, of thirty-six guns, the Racoon and Cherub sloops of war, and a store-ship of twenty guns had sailed on the 6th of July for this sea. The Racoon and Cherub had been seeking me for some time on the coast of Brazil, and on their return from their cruize, joined the squadron sent in search of me to the Pacific. My ship, after being near a year at sea, required some repairs to put her into a state to meet them; which I determined to do, and bring them to action if I could meet them on nearly equal terms. I proceeded now in company with the remainder of my prizes, to the island of Nooaheevah or *Madison's* island, lying in the *Washington* group; here I caulked and completely overhauled my ship, made for her a new set of water casks, and took on board from my prizes provisions and stores for upwards of four months, and sailed for the coast of Chili on the 12th of December, 1813. Previous to sailing, I secured the Seringapatam, Greenwich and Sir Andrew Hammond under the guns

86

of a battery, which I erected for their protection, I left them under the charge of lieutenant Gamble of the marines, with twenty-one men, with orders to repair to Valparaiso, after a certain period.

I arrived on the coast of Chili on the 12th of January, 1814. . . .

I had completely broken up the British navigation in the Pacific; the vessels which had not been captured by me, were laid up and dare not venture out. I had afforded the most ample protection to our own vessels, which were on my arrival, very numerous and unprotected. The valuable whale fishery there is entirely destroyed, and the actual injury we have done them may be estimated at two and a half millions of dollars, independent of expenses of the vessels in search of me. They have furnished me amply with sails, cordage, cables, anchors, provisions, medicines and stores of every description; and the slops on board them have furnished clothing for the seamen. We had lived on the enemy since I had been in that sea, every prize having proved a well found storeship for me. . . .

For the unexampled time we had kept the sea, my crew had continued remarkably healthy. I had but one case of the scurvy, and had lost only [eight] men by death. . . .

I had done all the injury that could be done the British commerce in the Pacific, and still hoped to signalize my cruize by something more splendid before leaving that sea, I thought it not improbable that commodore Hillyar might have kept his arrival secret, and believing that he would seek me at Valparaiso as the most likely place to find me, I determined to cruize about that place, and should I fail of meeting him, hoped to be compensated by the capture of some merchant ships from England.

The Phoebe, agreeably to my expectations, came to seek me at Valparaiso, where I was anchored with the Essex, my armed prize the Essex Junior, under the command of lieutenant Downes, on the look out off the harbour; but, contrary to the course I thought he would pursue, commodore Hillyar brought with him the Cherub sloop of war, mounting 28 guns, a complement of 180; the force of the Phoebe, 53 guns, and a complement of 320 men. Both ships were sent into the Pacific, in company with the Racoon of 22 guns and a store ship of 20 guns, for the express purpose of seeking the Essex, and were prepared with flags bearing the motto, "God and country; British sailors' best rights—Traitors offend both." This was intended as a reply to my motto *"Free Trade and sailor's Rights,"* under the erroneous impression that my crew were chiefly Englishmen, or to counteract its effect on their own crews. The force of the Essex was 46 guns and her crew, which had been much reduced by prizes, amounted only to 255 men. The Essex Junior mounted twenty guns, with only 60 men on board. In reply to their motto, I wrote at my mizen, *"God, our Country and Liberty; Tyrants offend them."*

On getting their provisions on board, they went off the port for the purpose of blockading me, where they cruized for near six weeks; during which time I endeavoured to provoke a challenge, and frequently, but ineffectually, to bring the Phoebe alone to action, first with both my ships, and afterwards with my single ship. I was several times under way, and ascertained that I had greatly the advantage in point of sailing, and once succeeded in closing within a gunshot of the Phoebe, and commenced a fire on her, when she ran down for the Cherub, which was two and a half miles to leeward. . . . Commodore Hillyar seemed determined to avoid a contest with me on nearly equal terms, and from his extreme prudence in keeping both his ships ever after constantly within hail of each other, there were no hopes of any advantages to my country from a longer stay in port. I determined to put to sea the first opportunity which should offer; and I was the more strongly induced to do so, as I had gained certain intelligence that the Tagus, 38, and two other frigates, had sailed for that sea in pursuit of me; and I had reason to expect the arrival of the Racoon from N.W. coast of America where she had been sent for the purpose of destroying our fur establishment on the Columbia. A rendezvous was appointed for the Essex Junior, and every arrangement made for sailing, and I intended to let them chase me off, to give the Essex Junior an opportunity of escaping.

On the 28th March, the wind came on to blow fresh from the southward, when I parted my larboard cable and dragged my starboard anchor directly out to sea. Not a moment was to be lost in getting sail on the ship. The enemy were close in with the point forming the west side of the bay; but on opening them, I saw a prospect of passing windward, but on rounding the point a heavy squall struck the ship and carried away her main-top-mast, precipitating the men who were aloft into the sea, who were drowned. Both ships now gave chase, and I endeavoured in my disabled state to regain the port; but finding I could not recover the common anchorage, I ran close into a small bay, about three-quarters of a mile to leeward of the battery on the east side of the harbour, and let go my anchor within pistol shot of the shore, where I intended to repair my damages as soon as possible. The enemy continued to approach, and shewed an evident intention of attacking, *regardless of the neutrality of the place where I was anchored, and the caution observed in their approach to the attack of the crippled Essex was truly ridiculous, as was their display of their motto flags, and the number of jacks at all the mast-heads.*

I got my ship ready for action, and endeavoured to get a spring on my cable, but had not succeeded, when the enemy, at 54 minutes after 3 P.M. made his attack, the Phoebe placed herself under my stern, and the Cherub on my starboard bow; but the Cherub soon finding her situation a hot one, bore up and ran under my stern also; where both ships kept up a hot raking fire, I had got three long 12 pounders out of the stern ports, which were worked with so much bravery and skill, *that in half an hour we so disabled both as to compel them to haul off to repair damages.* In the course of this firing, I had, by the great exertions of Mr. Edward Barnewall, the acting sailing-master assisted by Mr. Linscott, the boatswain, succeeded in getting springs on our cable three different times; but the fire of the enemy was so excessive, that before we could get our broad-side to bear, they were shot away and rendered useless. My ship had received many injuries, and several had been killed and wounded—but my brave officers and men were no ways discouraged—all appeared determined to defend their ship to the last extremity, and to die in perference to a shameful surrender. *Our gaff, with the ensign and the motto flag at the mizen, had been shot away, but Free trade and Sailors' Rights, continued to fly at the fore. Our ensign was replaced by another—and to guard against a similar event, an ensign was made fast in the mizen-rigging, and several jacks were hoisted in different parts of the ship.* The enemy repaired his damages for a fresh attack; he now placed himself, with both his ships, on my starboard quarter, out of the reach of my carronades, and where my stern guns could not be brought to bear—he there kept up a most galling fire, which it was out of my power to return. My top-sail sheets and haulyards were all shot away, as well as the jib and fore-top-mast-stay-haulyards. The only rope not cut was the flying jib-haulyards— and that being the only sail I could set, I caused it to be hoisted, my cable to be cut, and ran down on both ships.

The firing on both sides was now tremendous; I had let fall my foretopsail and foresail, but the want of tacks and sheets rendered them almost useless—yet we were enabled for a short time to close with the enemy; and although our decks were now strewed with dead and our cockpit filled with wounded—although our ship had been several times on fire, and was rendered a perfect wreck, we were still encouraged to hope to save her, from the circumstance of the Cherub, from her crippled state, being compelled to haul off. She did not return to close action again, although she had it apparently in her power to do so, but kept up a distant firing with her long guns. The Phoebe, from our disabled state, was enabled however, by edging off, to choose the distance which best suited her long guns, and kept up a tremendous fire on us, which mowed down my brave companions by the dozen. Many of my guns had been rendered useless by the enemy's shot, and many of them had their whole crews destroyed— we manned them again from those which were disabled, and one gun in particular was three times manned—fifteen men were slain at it in the course of the action! but strange as it may appear, the captain of it escaped with only a slight wound. Finding that the enemy had it in his power to choose his distance, I now gave up all hopes of closing with him, and, as the wind for the moment, seemed to favour the design, I determined to endeavour to run her on shore, land my men and destroy her. We had approached the shore within musket shot, and I had no doubt of succeeding, when in an instant the wind shifted from the land and payed our head down on the Phoebe, where we were again exposed to a dreadful raking fire.

My ship was now totally unmanageable: yet as her head was toward the enemy, and he to the leeward of me, I still hoped to be able to board him. At this moment Lieut. Downes came on board to receive my orders, under the impression that I should soon be a prisoner. He could be of no use to me in the then wretched state of the Essex; and finding (from the enemy's putting his helm up) that my last attempt at boarding would not succeed, I directed him to return to his own ship, to be prepared for defending and destroying her in case of attack. . . .

The slaughter on board my ship had now become horrible, the enemy continued to rake us, and we were unable to bring a gun to bear. I directed a hawser to be bent to the sheet anchor, and the anchor to be cut from the bows to bring her head round: this succeeded. We again got our broadside to bear, and as the enemy was much crippled and unable to hold his own, I have no doubt he would have drifted out of gun shot before he discovered we had anchored, had not the hawser unfortunately parted. My ship had taken fire several times during the action, but alarmingly so forward and aft at this moment, the flames were bursting up each hatchway, and no hopes were entertained of saving her; our distance from the shore did not exceed three quarters of a mile, and I hoped many of my brave crew would be able to save themselves, should the ship blow up, as I was informed the fire was near the magazine, and the explosion of a large quantity of powder below served to increase the horror of our situation—our boats were destroyed by the enemy's shot; I directed those who could swim to jump overboard, and endeavour to gain the shore. Some reached it—some were taken by the enemy, and some perished in the attempt; but most preferred sharing with me the fate of the ship.

We, who remained, now turned our attention wholly to extinguishing the flames; and when we had succeeded went again to our guns, where the firing was kept up for some minutes, but the crew had by this time become so weakened, that they all declared to me the impossibility of making further resistance, and entreated me to surrender my ship to save the wounded, as all further attempt at opposition must prove ineffectual, almost every gun being disabled by the destruction of their crews. I now sent for the officers of divisions to consult them; but what was my surprize to find only acting Lieut. Stephen Decatur M'Knight remaining. . . .

I was informed that the cockpit, the steerage, the wardroom and the berth deck could contain no more wounded; that the wounded were killed while the surgeons were dressing them, and that unless something was speedily done to prevent it, the ship would soon sink from the number of shot holes in her bottom. And on sending for the carpenter he informed us that all his crew had been killed or wounded, and that he had once been over the side to stop the leaks when his slings had been shot away, and it was with difficulty he was saved from drowning. The enemy from the smoothness of the water, and the impossibility of our reaching him with our carronades, was enabled to take aim at us as at a target; his shot never missed our hull, and my ship was cut up in a manner which was perhaps, never before witnessed—in fine, I saw no hopes of saving her, and at 20 minutes after 6 P. M. gave the painful order to strike the colours.

91

75 men, including officers, were all that remained of my whole crew, capable of doing duty, and many of them severely wounded, some of whom have since died. The enemy still continued his fire, and my brave though unfortunate companions, were still falling about me. I directed an opposite gun to be fired, to shew them we intended no further resistance; but they did not desist; four men were killed at my side, and others in different parts of the ship. I now believed he intended to shew us no quarter, and that it would be well to die with my flag flying as struck, and was on the point of again hoisting it, when about ten minutes after hauling the colours down he ceased firing.

I cannot speak in sufficiently high terms of the conduct of those engaged for such an unparalleled length of time, under such circumstances, with me, in the arduous and unequal contest. Let it suffice to say that more bravery, skill, patriotism and zeal were never displayed on any occasion. . . .

We have been unfortunate, but not disgraced. The defence of the Essex had not been less honorable to her officers and crew, than the capture of an equal force, and I now consider my situation less unpleasant than that of commodore Hillyar, who, in violation of every principle of honour and generosity, and regardless of the rights of nations, attacked the Essex in her crippled state; within pistol shot of neutral shore; when for six weeks I had daily offered him fair and honorable combat, on terms greatly to his advantage. . . .

My loss has been dreadfully severe, 58 killed or have since died of their wounds; and among them lieutenant Cowell; 39 were severely wounded, 27 slightly, and 31 are missing; making in all 155, killed, wounded, and missing. . . .

The loss in killed and wounded has been great with the enemy. Both the Essex and Phoebe were in a sinking state, and it was with difficulty they could be kept afloat until they anchored in Valparaiso next morning. The battered state of the Essex, will, I believe, prevent her ever reaching England, and I also think it will be out of their power to repair the damages of the Phoebe so as to enable her to double Cape Horn. All the masts and yards of the Phoebe and Cherub are badly crippled, and their hulls much cut up. Nothing but the smoothness of the water saved both the Phoebe and Essex. . . .

Soon after my capture I entered into an agreement with commodore Hillyar to disarm my prize the Essex Junior, and proceed with the survivors of my officers and crew in her to the United States, taking with me all her officers and crew. He consented to grant her a passport to secure her from recapture. The ship was small and we knew we had much to suffer, yet we hoped soon to reach our country in safety, that we might again have it in our power to serve it. . . .

In justice to commodore Hillyar, I must observe, that, although I can never be reconciled to the manner of his attack on the Essex, or to his conduct before the action, he has, since our capture shewn the greatest humanity to my wounded, and has endeavoured as much as lay in his power to alleviate the distresses of war by the most generous and delicate deportment towards myself and officers and crew. . . .

By the arrival of the Tagus, a few days after my capture, I was informed that besides the ships which had arrived in the Pacific in pursuit of me, and those still expected, others were sent to cruize for me in the China Seas, off New Zealand, Timor and New Holland, and that another frigate was sent to the River la Plata.

To possess the Essex it has cost the British government near six millions of dollars, and yet, sir, her capture was owing entirely to accident; and if we consider the expedition with which naval contests are now decided, the action is a dishonour to them. Had they brought their ships boldly into action with a force so very superior, and having the choice of position, they should either have captured or destroyed us in a fourth the time they were about it. . . .

I sailed from Valparaiso on the 27th April, where the enemy were still patching up their ships.

Annexed is a list of the remains of my crew to be exchanged. I also send you a list of the prisoners I have taken during my cruize, amounting to 343.

I have the honor to be, &c.

D. PORTER.[23]

The honorable Secretary of the
navy of the United States,
Washington.

CHAPTER II
Attention All Hands
1815-1860

D URING the relatively peaceful period between the War of 1812 and the Civil War, the United States Navy policed the sea lanes, protecting a flourishing merchant marine and implementing national policies in distant waters, and explored and charted seas, rivers, and the far reaches of the Pacific Ocean. Slowly, iron and steam were replacing wood and sail, and rifled cannon were substituted for smoothbores.

I

TRUST IN COLD STEEL

Piracy extended through the Caribbean from the Bahama Islands to the coasts of Central and South America. Between 1815 and 1823, governments reported nearly 3,000 piratical attacks against merchant ships. To stamp out the criminals, the United States Navy established a West Indian Squadron. The work was arduous. Bluejackets scoured the intricate bays and lagoons, searched out buccaneer vessels and camps, capturing sixty-five craft, and, by 1825, had practically put an end to the scourge. A survivor's account of the boarded merchant ship Mary *and Midshipman W. F. Lynch's narrative complement each other.*

. . . At this moment a flash of light, perhaps a musket burning priming, proceeded from the vessel in pursuit, and we saw distinctly that her deck was covered with men. My heart almost failed me. I had never been in battle. Day at length dawned, and setting all her canvas, our pursuer gained alarmingly upon us. It was evident that she had followed us the whole night, being unwilling to attack us in the dark.

In a few minutes she fired a gun and came alongside. She was a pirate. Her boat was lowered, and about a dozen hideous-looking objects jumped in, with a commander at their head. The boat pushed off and was fast nearing us, as we arranged ourselves for giving her a broadside. Our whole stock of arms consisted of six muskets and an old swivel—a small revolving ship's cannon in use in the eighteenth and early nineteenth centuries—used as a signal gun, and a pair of pistols of my own, which I carried in my belt. The pirate boat's crew were armed with muskets, pistols, swords, cutlasses, and knives; and when she came within her own length of us we fired five of our muskets and the swivel into her.

Her fire was scarcely half given when she filled and went down, with all her crew. At this success we were inclined to rejoice, but looking over the pirate schooner we observed her deck still swarming with horrid-looking wretches. A second boat's crew pushed off, with their muskets pointed directly at us the whole time. When they came within the same distance as the other, we fired, but with little, if any effect. The pirates immediately returned the fire, and with horrid cries jumped aboard us. Two of our brave crew were lying dead upon the deck, and the rest of us expected nothing better. French, Spanish and English were spoken indiscriminately and all at once. The most horrid imprecations were uttered against us, and threats that fancy cannot imagine.

A wretch whose black, shaggy whiskers covered nearly his whole face and whose whole appearance was more that of a hell-hound than of a human being, approached me with a drawn cutlass in his hand. I drew one of my pistols and snapped it in his face, but it flashed in the pan, and before I could draw the other, the pirate struck me over the face with his cutlass and knocked me down. I was too much wounded to resist, and the blood ran in torrents from my forehead. In this situation the wretch seized me by the scalp, and thrusting his cutlass in my cravat cut it through completely. I felt the cold iron glide along my throat, and even now the very thought makes me shudder.

The worst idea I had ever formed of human cruelty seemed now realized, and I could see death staring me in the face. . . . I rose to my feet, and he pinioned my hands behind my back and led me forward to the foremast, where he tied me with my face to the stern of the vessel. The cords were drawn so tight around my arms and legs that my agony was excruciating. In this situation he left me.

On looking round, I found them all employed in plundering and ransacking everything we had. Over my left shoulder one of our sailors was strung up to the yard-arm, and apparently in the last agonies of death; while before me our gallant captain was on his knees and begging for his life. The wretches were endeavoring to extort from him the secret of our money; but for a while he was firm and dauntless. Provoked at his obstinacy, they extended his arms and cut them off at the elbows. At this human nature gave way, and the injured man confessed the spot where we had concealed our specie. In a few moments it was aboard their own vessel. To revenge themselves of our unhappy captain, when they had satisfied themselves that nothing else was hidden, they spread a bed of oakum on the deck, and after soaking it through with turpentine, tied the captain on it, filled his mouth with the same combustibles, and set the whole on fire . . . his agonies must have been unutterable, but they were soon over. . . .

On casting my eyes towards the schooner's stern, I discovered that our boatswain had been nailed to the deck through his feet, and the body spiked through to the tiller. He was writhing in his last agonies of crucifixion. Our fifth comrade was out of sight during all this tragedy; in a few minutes, however, he was brought upon the deck blindfolded. He was then conducted to the muzzle of the swivel and commanded to kneel. The swivel was then fired off, and his head was dreadfully wounded by the discharge. . . .

Seeing that the crew had been every one despatched, I began to think more of myself. My old enemy, who seemed to forget me, once more approached me, but shockingly besmeared with blood and brains. . . . He drew a stiletto from his side, placed its point upon my heart, and gave it a heavy thrust. I felt its point touch my skin; but the quilting of my bank bills prevented its further entrance. . . . At this moment a heavy flaw struck the schooner, and I heard one of the pirates say, "Voila un vaisseau!" They all retreated precipitately, and gaining their own vessel, were soon out of sight.

Helpless as I now was, I had the satisfaction of knowing that the pirates had been frightened by the appearance of a strange sail, but it was impossible for me to see it. Still tied to the foremast, I knew not what was my prospect of release. An hour or two had elapsed after they left me, and it was now noon. The sun played violently upon my head, and I felt a languor and debility that indicated approaching fever. . . .

The wretches had scuttled the schooner, and left me pinioned to go down with her. . . . I felt myself gradually dying away, and the last thing I remembered was the foaming noise of the waves. This was occasioned by a ship passing by me. I was taken in, restored to health, and am now a poor, ruined helpless man.[1]

[Midshipman Lynch recounts measures taken against the pirate menace.]

So intent were the pirates upon gratifying their rapacity, that the helm was abandoned, and, for a short time, they paid little attention to the management of the ship.

"Mr. Schumacker," said the quarter-master to the officer of the deck of a small Danish brig-of-war in the southern offing, "that ship to leeward is acting very queer."

"How so, Jansen?" said the lieutenant.

"Why, a little while ago," replied Jansen, "she was lying to, with her main top-sail to the mast; but now, she has drifted round, and is running before the wind with her head yards braced up."

"That is indeed strange," said the lieutenant. "Hand me the spyglass."

He looked steadily for some moments, and then calling a midshipman, said:

"Report to the captain, sir, that there is a very suspicious sail to leeward."

Before the captain made his appearance, the ship had again hauled by the wind, and was standing along the land. But when her previous movements were reported to him, and the fishing boat was now seen drifting from her, he ordered all sail to be made in chase. As soon as his intention was discovered, the ship packed on all sail. . . .

The chase continued for some time with little change of bearing; but as the ship approached the western extremity of the island, eddies of wind would whirl around the point, and take her sails aback. The pirates were, therefore, compelled to haul more from the land, which brought the courses of the two vessels to a nearer converging point. With an enemy's shore on one side (the alarm had now spread along the land), and a fast-closing and vindictive enemy on the other, the fate of the ruffians seemed inevitable.

The wind was blowing almost directly on shore, but the pirates persevered with a hardihood worthy of a better cause. As the first shot from the brig came crashing through her side, the ship flew up into the wind, and the next moment braced sharp on the other tack, she was standing to the eastward. By this manoeuvre, the brig was brought on the starboard quarter, and the pirates began to flatter themselves with the hope of escape, when, as they again approached the mouth of the harbor, they perceived several vessels, well manned, coming out to intercept them. The pirates now hauled more to the southward, bringing the brig on the starboard beam, and the vessels on the larboard quarter. But as shot after shot from the brig tore up the planking, or carried away a spar, it became more and more evident that the ship could not escape. At last, as the main top-mast fell over the side, the pirates, abandoning hope, put the helm up, and to the astonishment of thousands congregated on the roofs of the houses, and on the adjacent hills, steered before the wind, directly for the anchorage. In a short time, the desperate purpose was revealed. A thin, light smoke first arose; then it grew denser and blacker, and presently a red flame burst forth, which, wreathing around the rigging, and encircling the spars, the ship, in one sheet of fire, rapidly approached the harbor.

All was consternation among the shipping; and while the vessels that had started in pursuit, fled precipitately from the burning mass, the brig manned her boats, and attemped to board her. But men who had lighted their own funeral pyre were not to be subdued, and the boats fell back discomfited. The batteries of the town opened their fire, and cinders and burning fragments were scattered in every direction. Still the ship held her onward course, and was almost up with the shipping, when, most probably from the burning of the tiller-ropes, she broached to, and grounded on a shoal.

While the spectators gazed in wonder, and watched the figures of the wretched men as retreating step by step they reached at last the taffrail, the whole mass sprung suddenly into the air; a loud and deafening report succeeded, and the water and immediate shore were covered with brands and packages, and scorched and mutilated bodies. . . .

Our fleet here separated; the smaller vessels to cruise among the islands, while the ships repaired to Key West, preparatory to fitting out the boat-expeditions. Among others, I was a volunteer for this service, and at the expiration of a short time, found myself at that place, detailed for one of the barges. Our flotilla consisted of four boats—Gallinipper, Sand Fly, Gnat and Mosquito, under the command of Lieut Watson. They contained each, two officers, a coxswain, and sixteen men.

Burning for adventure, and happily ignorant of the trials which awaited us, we started on a pleasant day, and with sail and oar, plied eighty miles across, to the island of Cuba. We reached it in safety, and hearing that the pirates had selected and fortified a place difficult of access, our commander determined to attack.

That our approach might be as secret as possible, we concealed our boats in a narrow inlet during the day, but at early dusk, the oars were manned, and the order given to proceed. A little after midnight a breeze sprung up, and taking in the oars, with the exception of an officer and the steersman of each boat, every one slept as he best could, upon the three feet by ten inches of space allotted to him. Our watchful commander sought no repose, but when those who slept awoke, they found all sail taken in, and the boats lying quiet and motionless, near the mouth of a river, waiting for sufficient light to enter it.

It was the Sagua le Grand, the noted resort, the great stronghold of the pirates.

As the light increased, the time was spent in silent preparation. Presently from boat to boat, the order was passed to "close in"; and we gathered around that of our commander.

"My lads," he said, "this is no child's play we have undertaken. Whatever may be the force of the enemy, I am determined to attack him. Will you stand by me?"

A loud murmur of assent was the reply.

"Is your powder dry? Are your flints good—and your cutlasses well sharpened?"

He was told they were.

"Then muffle your oars and follow me; but make not the slightest noise, and wait until I give the word. *Then,* let your cry be *no quarter,* and he who first boards the enemy, shall be highly recompensed!"

At a signal we then fell into position, and our commander leading the way, we rounded the point, and rowed steadily but stealthily forward.

The river was broad at the entrance, but except in the channel, which was difficult to find and still more difficult to thread, it was very shallow. The headmost boat, sounding as she went, carefully proceeded, and regulating our motions by hers, we followed in the strictest silence. Not a word was allowed to be spoken, and concealed by the tangled brushwood, which beneath the overhanging trees lined the banks of the narrowing stream, an enemy, even at a short distance, might have mistaken the slight noise we made, for the gambols of the water-fowl which were disturbed at our approach.

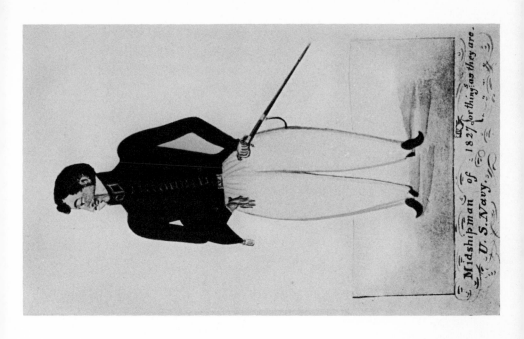

Midshipman of 1827, for things, as they are. U. S. Navy.

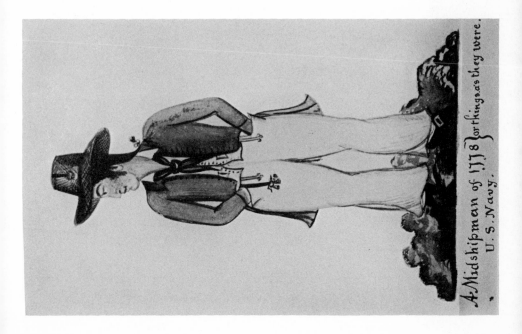

A Midshipman of 1778, or things, as they were. U. S. Navy.

After a space of time, we came to a wide lagoon, at the other side of which, half a mile distant, the pirates, as vigilant as we were cautious, were drawn up to receive us. Careened on a shelving beach, laid a merchant brig, the crew of which they had barbarously murdered. Along the shore were strewed bales and packages; and a hut and a few tents stood within the verge of a grove of lofty trees. On a projecting point, was a battery of several pieces of artillery, and on the other side of the brig, but a little farther out, was moored an armed schooner with her broadside towards us. Both the battery and the schooner were crowded with men.

As soon as we had pulled out into the lagoon, we formed our boats in a line abreast, and each man girded on his cutlass and stuck a pistol in his belt.

"Mr. V.," said our commander to the next in rank, "as the battery seems the most formidable, I will undertake it. Take the Sand Fly with you, and board the schooner. Lose no time with the musket, Sir, but lay her aboard on different points, and put your trust in cold steel. Now give way men, and *no quarter!*"

The boats bounded with a spring, and we were soon in the midst of a rattling hail of grape and canister, which made the water foam around us, our men cheering and shouting, as with rapid and furious stroke we bore down upon the enemy.

I was attached to one of the boats directed against the schooner. Besides the boom of the cannon fired from the schooner and the battery, the lake and the shores around rang with the incessant peal of musketry, and the hurling of the iron and lead around us was dreadful. . . . Ourselves upon the bow, the other boat farther astern, almost simultaneously, we laid the pirate aboard. To grapple the side, to spring on the bulwark and leap upon the deck, amid muskets, pikes, and brandished knives, was the work of an instant. With courage equal to our own, the pirates rushed forward to repel us, and a desperate hand to hand conflict ensued.

The musketry had now ceased, and a pistol shot was but occasionally heard, but the clash of steel was incessant, and the silent but deadly thrust became more frequent. The shout of an officer as he cut down the swarthy pirate was responded to by a wild cry of exultation from the men, and animated as by one spirit, we bounded forward with a cheer. A better cause and far more numerous force, could not have withstood our charge. The pirates gave way, slowly at first, but when our leader called out "push home, men! and no quarter!" and the cry "no quarter! no quarter!" was fiercely repeated, they turned, and springing to the side, leaped overboard, and endeavored to escape by swimming. Many of our men plunged after them sword in hand; others jumped to the boats, and pursuing, cut them down, while another portion, from the deck of the captured vessel, deliberately shot them as they struggled in the water.

On the part of those wretches, not a cry was raised—not a supplication uttered. When too hotly pursued, they turned to grapple where they could, and in silence they received the death wound, and in silence they sunk, their throats gurgling the water which was deeply crimsoned with their blood. Turning from the sickening sight, my eye rested for a moment upon the slimy and death-encumbered deck, when a shout on the shore reminded me of the battery.

Our boats had grounded some distance from the beach, but our men leaping out hastily formed, and advanced boldly to the attack. They were warmly received, and the contest was still undecided, when we carried the schooner. But, when those in the battery saw their fellow-pirates leap overboard, they took to flight. They were relentlessly pursued, and the scene which had been enacted upon the water, was repeated on the land. But few escaped; and destroying what we could not preserve, we gathered their booty, and bore our prize away in triumph. . . .[2]

II

QUALLAH BATTOO

The frigate Potomac, *44, Captain John Downes, hurried from New York via Cape Town to Quallah Battoo on the coast of Sumatra to chastise the natives who, under the leadership of the powerful local chief, Po Mahomet, had slaughtered many of the crew and plundered the merchantman* Friendship *of Salem in 1831. The* Potomac *anchored off Quallah Battoo in February, 1832 disguised as a Danish trading vessel. The schoolmaster and a petty officer set down the* Potomac's *retaliation.*

105

. . . At noon we hoisted the Danish national flag, and about two o'clock came to anchor off the town, after a passage of 55 days from the Cape of Good Hope. We came to in merchantman style, a few men being sent aloft, dressed in red and blue flannel shirts, and one top-sail being clewed up and furled at a time. We were all anxious to obtain a glimpse of the place, but no person was allowed to gratify his curiosity, for fear of disclosing our character to the natives. Not a single breeze fanned us. Every port being closed, the air that we breathed was close and stifled. The melted tar fell in drops upon the deck, and fairly broiled from the seams between the planks. We were obliged to preserve the strictest silence, and our situation remained uncomfortable in the extreme.

About four o'clock, Commodore Downes sent a party ashore for the purpose of reconnoitering the place. This party consisted of our first lieutenant, Mr. Shubrick; first lieutenant of marines, Mr. Edson; Lieutenants Pinkham, Hoff, and Ingersoll; acting Sailing-master Totten, and Passed Midshipman Tooley. They left the ship under pretence of contracting for a cargo of pepper. Mr. Shubrick went as captain of the ship, Mr. Edson as supercargo. The remainder in the capacity of common sailors to pull the boat, and they were dressed in a manner conformable to the different characters they assumed. They were obliged to smear their pantaloons with tar, and to stain their hands with rhubarb, that they might resemble old weather-beaten sailors. Their real design was to examine the relative position of the different forts, previous to making the intended attack. When all had approached within a few yards of the beach, they found it lined with a large body of men, exhibiting a warlike appearance, armed with javelins, creeses, cleavers, and sabres, and manifesting hostile intentions. They did not deem it prudent to land. Mr. Shubrick inquired for the rajah. They replied, "He no come down, he be one so great man." Mr. Edson next questioned them as to the price of pepper. They said, eight dollars per picul; but he finally succeeded in inducing them to lower the price to four dollars. A small number were invited to come down to them, and after a consultation was held, about half a dozen approached. Our officers finding that it was their intention to surround the boat, and apprehending some hostile design, pushed farther out to sea. The Malays then exclaimed, "What for you no come ashore?" An excuse was offered, and they were told that the next day the captain would come on shore and complete a bargain with them. They inquired with what cargo our ship was freighted and were informed that it was with opium. The gentlemen returned to the ship without ascertaining anything relative to the most advantageous method of assailing the forts.

During the absence of the party ashore, four Malay fishermen, attracted by the sight of an old clump of an Indiaman, as they supposed our ship to be, came alongside to sell their fish. Mr. Barry, who could converse a little in the Malay language, invited them on board. One came up with a couple of fish in his hand, but as soon as he reached the gangway, and saw our formidable battery and about 500 men thickly stowed together, he dropped his fish, hurried back to the boat, gave the alarm to his three companions . . . and began hastily to paddle off. Fearing they might give the alarm on shore, a mizzen-top-man instantly leaped through one of the ports into the boat, and seized them. They set up a yell and made some resistance, but a rope was instantly let down, and they, finding that they were about to be dragged into the ship, *nolens volens,* through one of the ports, thought it policy to submit. . . .

Our ship now presented a busy scene. It was determined to commence an attack upon the town the next morning. Muskets were cleaned, cartridge boxes buckled on, cutlasses examined and put in order. During the evening, the commodore sent for the officers commanding the several divisions, and gave them instructions to land, surround the town and forts, and demand indemnity for the outrage committed upon the *Friendship,* with the punishment of those concerned in the barbarous massacre of her crew; but to spare the women and children. . . .

At eight bells all hands were called. Those assigned to take part in the expedition were mustered, when Lieutenant Shubrick, the commander of the detachment, gave them special orders. No man was to utter a word after he had entered the boat; no one was to fire till the command was given; no man was to desert his ranks. Considerable time was occupied in getting the men into the boats. Several of the officers felt impatient at the delay and were fearful that they would be unable to effect a landing in season to surprise the enemy. At length the gallant band, to the number of 282 men, left the ship at two o'clock. . . .

[*Petty officer*] As the day began to break, we landed upon the soil of our enemy and formed in silence and good order, each division according to its number, and a 6-pounder bringing up the rear. The fusileers, a company of fine, stout and daring fellows, distributing themselves on each side of our line.

As we neared the lower fort the second division of musketeers and pikemen filed off to the left, and were soon lost amid the thick foliage which grows in wild luxuriance on every part of the island. In a few minutes after their departure the din of a hundred firearms was heard and assured us that the work of destruction and death had begun, and we hastened to join battle with the remaining foe.

The marine guard engaged the center fort, and after a short but desperate and bloody conflict in which one of the guard was killed, one dangerously wounded and several slightly wounded, it was taken, and all who had the semblance of a native, slaughtered.

The third division, (to which I was attached), the fusileers and the Betsy Bakers (so designated from the name of the little gun which they had christened "Betsy Baker") were left to charge the third and most formidable fort—our whole force amounting to 85 men. When we came within a few yards of the fort under a brisk fire of musketry and swivels from the enemy's batteries, we poured in a volley of leaden death.

We then charged the enemy in the rear, leaving the 6-pounder and fusileers to keep them employed on the opposite side, until we could make a break sufficient to carry the fort with our division, making terrible slaughter in the host that had the hardihood to oppose us. At a signal from the commander, the gun [Betsy Baker] proceeded to the bank of a creek, in the rear (under a brisk but impotent fire from the enemy's batteries, their guns being so disposed that to turn them was impossible) where they commenced a quick but steady cannonading upon the large proas or schooners in the creek; sweeping their decks fore and aft and killing great numbers of the renegades and doing considerable injury to their vessels—the largest of which succeeded in getting under way, and escaped by rounding the point in the creek.

In our second charge at the rear of the fort, one of our men was shot through the brain and immediately expired, and three others were slightly wounded; but we sprang with renewed vigor to the charge and revenged our fallen shipmates nobly. The massive gate which led to the enclosure around the fort was torn from its base, and the gun planted. But the flaming habitations of the fort which were throwing dark columns of fire to the sky and the almost furnace heat by which the gun crew were surrounded, forced them to evacuate, when the gun was instantly seized by a third of her stout crew and carried to the upper side of the fort, where they kept up a steady discharge of canister and grape shot for forty minutes, during which time the foe within the battlements fought most desperately. Our object was to compel the enemy to evacuate their stronghold and every stand of grape and canister had been expended without effecting this purpose.

Recourse was had to the boats, from which was obtained ten bags containing forty musket balls each; in three successive discharges we succeeded in dislodging them, but, from the heaviness of each charge, our gun was thrice dismounted and the carriage shivered to atoms which rendered her unfit for further service. But our aim had been accomplished and as the redskins attempted to escape, several of them were shot down by the fusileers.

At this instant the center fort blew up with a tremendous explosion and sent the helpless foe within its battlements to notify the shades of the coming of their kindred. The red glow of a hundred habitations shone in the morning sun, and the grand flag of our country was, in the space of two hours, waving in triumph o'er the ramparts of the conquered and the slain.

Thus fell before the brave seamen and marines of the *Potomac* the strong fortress of these heathen pirates which had, in the knowledge of the oldest inhabitants of the island, withstood the combined efforts of different tribes for a hundred years—presenting a striking example of the power of American arms, the bravery of Columbia's sons and the justice of their cause. . . .

On the following morning we got under way, stood within a mile of the shore, and at meridian commenced and kept up a steady cannonading upon the town and forts until a quarter past one p. m. In the evening a boat came alongside of us at 7 p. m., containing three natives bearing a flag of truce. They came on board and were conducted to the presence of Commodore Downes. When they had advanced within a short distance of him, they bowed with the utmost submission. They bore a message from the principal chiefs begging a cessation of hostilities and representing their situation as truly deplorable. During their stay on board, the good cheer of our officers was proffered and accepted by them, until the potent nectar of which they had tasted profusely began to operate—when they left us, bearing an answer from the Commodore to their chiefs, urging them to visit the ship that a negotiation might be had, and threatening them with vengeance more potent than they had so lately witnessed if they did not restore the spoils taken from the *Friendship*.[3]

III

THE KOSZTA INCIDENT

In July, 1853 Commander D. N. Ingraham of the St. Louis, *20, took the initiative in protecting Martin Koszta, a Hungarian who had taken out first United States citizenship papers. Koszta had been kidnapped by the Austrian Consul at Smyrna and detained under arrest on board the Austrian brig-of-war* Hussar, *16, in the harbor. The description of the events is from the diary of Passed Midshipman Ralph Chandler. After the incident, the United States government commended Ingraham for his prompt action and sustained the claim of Koszta.*

. . . on the morning of the twenty-fourth [of June] we let go the anchor in Smyrna harbor. . . . The first news that greeted our ears was a description of the horrible and barbarous manner in which the Austrian consul, assisted by the brig-of-war *Hussar*, had treated one Martin Koszta. . . . The facts of the case were laid before the captain. . . . Martin Koszta was one of the refugees that went to America with Kossuth, and while there filed a Declaration of Intention to become a citizen of the United States, and soon after left and came to Smyrna. Our consul refused to take him under protection as an American citizen, and for a few months he lived very quietly without being under the protection of any flag.

One evening while he was at one of the coffee houses . . . he was forcibly seized and thrown over the railing and then dragged some yards by a boat that was in waiting, sometimes under water and sometimes not, until the scoundrels thought themselves far enough from shore. They then took him into the boat and carried him to the *Hussar* where he was confined in chains on the lower deck. The brutal manner in which he was treated, together with his intention to become an American citizen, influenced Captain Ingraham. . . .

On our arrival, after the consul had seen the captain, a committee of citizens consisting of many English and Americans came on board . . . in behalf of the unfortunate Koszta, but . . . the captain could not take any immediate steps . . . but at once wrote to the minister at Constantinople. The minister proper was absent but Mr. Brown, the dragoman, was acting, and after two statements of the affair from Captain Ingraham his advice was to take the unfortunate prisoner at all hazards.

On July 2 . . . before breakfast the captain went on board the *Hussar* and demanded to see Koszta, but was told by the executive officer . . . that no such person was on board the brig. The contrary he knew, and therefore the captain informed the captain of the *Hussar* both verbally and in writing, that if Koszta was not delivered up by twelve meridian (it was then about 8:00 A. M.) he would take him by force. To which the Austrian captain replied, "I am a soldier, sir, as well as a sailor, and will obey the orders of my superior, the consul, come what may."

When Captain Ingraham came back and told what he had done there was no surprise expressed, but we all saw that unless the man was given up there would be bloodshed, and every man on board seemed anxious for a fight. The time was put off until 4:00 P.M. for his delivery into our hands and we had ample opportunity to get ready for action.

The Austrian force consisted of the brig *Hussar* of sixteen guns, the schooner *Artemisia* of twelve guns and a steamer of four guns. None of the guns of the Austrians were of as large calibre as ours, but their number exceeded ours by twelve guns. . . .

Our guns were loaded . . . the men armed with cutlasses and pistols, and the ship put in readiness for action. . . . We were all in a great state of excitement. . . .

The people on shore heard of our intention . . . and many of those men loudest in their advice to capture Koszta, now thought better of it and would rather a little diplomacy and forbearance were exercised. But it could not be. Either Koszta must be delivered into our hands or we would take him, and so matters stood at half past three when an express came from the shore stating that the Austrian consul . . . would negotiate. Agreements were entered into that Koszta should be delivered over to the French consul to be treated as a prisoner at large until the actions of the separate governments be known.

He was taken on shore, our boat following to see that everything was conducted properly, and so ended the Koszta excitement. . . .[4]

IV

THE HIGHEST SCHOLAR THAT RIDES

A celebrated diplomatic mission was Commodore Matthew C. Perry's visit to Japan. The extension of American whaling into Far Eastern waters and the rapidly increasing trade with the Orient compelled the United States to seek cordial relations with the island empire. On his first visit, Perry was instructed to place in sufficiently high hands a letter from President Fillmore addressed to the Japanese Emperor. John Rodgers Goldsborough made journal entries of this contact with the Japanese. Later, in March, 1854, Commodore Perry negotiated a treaty opening the ports of Hakodate and Shimoda to American shipping.

U. S. Ship Saratoga, Yeddo [Tokyo] Bay, Japan, July 1853.
July 8th, 1853. At daylight this morning in company with the steamers *Susquehanna* and *Mississippi* and Sloop of War *Plymouth*, we made the island of Niphon, coast of Japan, [and at] 1 P. M. the whole Squadron stood for the anchorage in Yeddo Bay. . . . Immediately upon the Squadron's anchoring a number of boats crowded with men continued hovering around the ships. They were all fantastically decorated with flags and banners containing Japanese characters. . . . They are propelled by from ten to twenty oars each and generally two or three men at each oar. . . . None of the boats were permitted to come alongside of any ship in the Squadron—though they all appeared quite anxious to go alongside the Flagship. Still none were permitted until fully convinced that a high officer was in one

of the boats—when he alone, with an interpreter who spoke Dutch, was allowed to come over the *Susquehanna's* side. The Commodore, however, would not see him, but directed the Flag Lieutenant to learn the object which brought him on board. Lieutenant Contee received this two-sworded mandarin, whose title we afterward ascertained to be "the highest scholar that rides," besides being the Governor of Ooragawa. He enquired the object of our visit, and was informed that we came on a peaceful and friendly mission, for the purpose of conveying a letter from the President of the United States to the Emperor of Japan, and that it could only be delivered to a high officer of state deputed by the Emperor to receive it. The "Scholar" said we must go to Naugasaki to deliver it. This was positively and peremptorily refused. . . . The following day "the highest scholar that rides" again visited the *Susquehanna*. He came on board, he said, to renew the request that we would go to Naugasaki. It was abruptly refused as at first, and the "scholar" was informed he must have a high officer with full powers to receive the letter, or the Commodore would land with his force and carry it himself. He begged for time to communicate with Yeddo. . . . He kindly and politely proffered us wood, water and provisions, which were declined. The conversation was concluded through interpreters who spoke the Dutch language, and was fully and plainly understood on both sides. . . .

Today about 2 P. M. "the highest scholar that rides" again visited the *Susquehanna*. He came on board to say that on Thursday next a person duly authorized by the Emperor of Japan would be prepared to receive the Commodore with his credentials, and that they were then engaged in erecting a house for his reception. . . .

Tuesday, July 12th. Two very long conferences have taken place today on board the *Susquehanna* between "the highest scholar that rides," accompanied by mandarins and interpreters, on the part of the Japanese Government, and Captain Adams and Lieutenant Contee on the part of Commodore Perry. . . . They came on board . . . to receive the letter for the Emperor of Japan, written by Commodore Perry, but it appeared upon investigations that they were not duly authorized or empowered to receive it, consequently we declined delivering it. . . . After a long palaver which amounted to nothing but a repetition of the past and present conversations . . . they asked for three hours to confer with some official on shore. It may be perhaps the Prince of Sagami . . . or it may be a person duly empowered by the Emperor. . . . At all events they left the *Susquehanna* about 1 P. M. for the shore, and returned to her again about 4 P. M. to say that a councillor of state with full powers from the Emperor would be prepared on shore to receive the Commodore on Thursday, the 14th, when and where an exchange of credentials would take place; and after being fully satisfied of the correctness of each other's powers, the original letter from the President of the United States to the Emperor of Japan would be received. He likewise exhibited a copy of the councillor's credentials with the imperial seals, which were examined and appeared to be perfectly correct. . . .

July 14th. This is the day appointed for the exchange of credentials between Commodore Perry and the accredited ambassador from the Emperor of Japan. Early in the morning the *Susquehanna* and *Mississippi* changed their berth to a position immediately opposite the place selected for the landing of our party, the *Plymouth* and *Saratoga* retaining their former positions. At 10 A. M. fifty men from each ship, all the marines of the Squadron, and about thirty officers, total number about 300, all well armed and equipped with two bands of music, the Commodore's broad pendant and a dozen American flags, the music playing "Yankee Doodle" and "Hail Columbia," landed on the shores of Japan. The Commodore was received by the "highest Scholar who rides," one or two chief mandarins and some 6 or 8,000 Japanese, of whom at least 1,000 were half-armed troops drawn up in military ranks on the beach, besides about an equal number on each of our flanks to cut off our retreat in case of hostility. But regardless of all intrigue or deception on their part, our little band marched up gaily with the national airs playing and colors flying, to the hall of audience situated about one hundred yards from the landing and near which they had mats and red cloth for us to walk on. Two great councillors of state received the Commodore, and their position and rank in the empire must have been very high, if I judge by the great respect shown them by the mandarins, who spoke to them only on their knees. The councillors of state were seated in lacquer chairs. They rose and bowed when the Commodore entered and then resumed their seats. The exchange of credentials now took place without much ceremony, one of the councillors handing Commodore Perry a receipt for his credentials. The letter of the President of the United States to the Emperor of Japan was now presented; it was enclosed in three beautiful gold-mounted rosewood boxes, and

Japanese conception of an American side-wheeler which visited Japan with Perry's Squadron in 1853.

carried before the Commodore by two of the handsomest boys belonging to the *Susquehanna,* as pages. The boxes were opened and the letters displayed, with three seals of solid gold impressed with the arms of the United States and attached to the letters by gold and silk cords; the two seals cost $1,000 each. The letter presented, the ambassadors were informed by Commodore Perry . . . that, as it would require time for consideration and reflection, he would expect an answer upon his return; that it was his intention to sail in three or four days for Lew Chew, China, and elsewhere; but that he would revisit Yeddo in April or May next, when he should expect the Emperor's reply to the President's letter. The interview then over, our little band marched down to the beach and reembarked for their respective ships. It was a great show, and a great day for America, for we are the first that have opened negotiations elsewhere than in Naugasaki, and the first to unfold our flag on these shores and lead an armed force. . . .[5]

American naval ships continued to patrol the seas. Life on board the men-of-war during the eighteen twenties, thirties, and forties was usually monotonous, occasionally exciting, always harsh.

V

THE SHAKEDOWN

A youthful seaman describes his first months in the United States Navy.

. . . I lost no time in hunting up a naval rendezvous. . . . I immediately made application to ship. . . . The articles of agreement were read over to me in a monotonous drawl; and I was asked, if I, of my own free will, did propose to sign them—a question which, in my ignorance, I considered highly superfluous, seeing that I had been at so much pains to obtain the chance so to do. At the tinkling of a small bell, I was requested to walk into an adjoining room, where a naval doctor examined into the stoutness of my frame and lungs, and the general soundness of my constitution. A report, in lead pencil, of the result, was placed in my hands, which I rendered up to the man of the drawl, who expressed his satisfaction; and in conclusion, asking me if I was fully aware of all the responsibilities I was about to take upon myself, and would swear to submit to the rules and regulations laid down for the government of the seamen in the United States Navy—questions which I did not presume to answer—told me to "touch the pen," while he very ingeniously wrote my name for me—a matter that I could have performed much more satisfactorily and legibly myself—and then said to me, with an expression of intense relief:

"There, my boy; now you belong to Uncle Sam. . . ."

Here I must explain the mode of "fitting out" green hands and drunken sailors, when they ship in the United States Navy. Each non-commissioned officer, seaman, landsman, or boy receives, on entering the navy, a sum of money amounting to three months' pay. This sum is designed to defray the expenses of a regular outfit of uniform, clothing, bedding, etc., which by the navy regulations, each man is compelled to have. The old man-of-war's men, who "have learnt a thing or two," when sober, generally take this advance-money into their own possession, and with it procure the necessary articles. Drunken sailors and green hands, whether men or boys, being unable to fit themselves out, are generally taken in hand by certain speculators in slop-clothing, who loaf about the rendezvous, where their cheatery is winked at. These thieves become security for the safe delivery on board of the new recruit, and then furnish him, in exchange for his three months' pay, with the articles of clothing enumerated in the navy regulations. . . . Unfortunately for poor "greeny," the *quality* of the clothing is not made matter of regulation. The slop-seller, while furnishing faithfully the *number,* made too in the fashion required, provides it of stuff which, it is safe to say, cannot be found anywhere else than in the establishments of these thieving outfitters. . . .

For instance, the blue cloth jacket and trowsers, which are only for *mustering* in on special occasions, are supposed to be made of very fine blue cloth. Those with which I was furnished were made of a species of rusty-looking serge, of which an old salt gave me a most faithful description, when he said it was "made of dogs' hair and oakum, and cost three pence an armfull," and added, "One might take a bull-dog by the neck and heels and fling him between any two threads of it." The white duck frocks and trowsers were made of yellow bagging, which, so coarse was its texture, would scarcely hold peas; and which was warranted not to last beyond the first washing. Instead of the "neat" black silk neckerchief and shining pumps, articles of dress in the excellence of which a true man-of-war's man greatly delights, the recruits are furnished a rusty bamboo rag, and shoes made of varnished brown paper, which vanish before the damp salt air as mist before the bright sun. And in place of the neat tarpaulin, hard as a brick, and almost as heavy, smooth and glossy, as though made of glass, the *crowning* glory of a man-of-war man's costume, was a miserable featherweight of lacquered straw, which imparted to the countenance beneath it a look of indescribable, almost unfathomable greenness, instead of that knowing, confident air peculiar to an old salt.

To complete the list, came the mattress, a coarse sack, loosely stuffed with a mixture of straw, shavings, and old rags—and the blankets, which would *not* serve as riddles for peas. The entire assortment was worth *nothing*. . . .

Arrived at New York, we were transferred at once on board the vessel for which we were destined, the C——, a seventy-four gun ship, which was then lying off the Navy Yard, taking in stores, and preparing for sea. Here a new scene of wonder opened to me. I had often, while at Philadelphia, boarded the large merchant vessels lying at the wharves, and had cause for surprise at the massive strength and solidity of all things about them, but here I found everything on so much greater a scale as to make all I had seen before dwindle down to Lilliputian dimensions. The hight from the water's edge to the top of the railing or bulwark, a distance of about thirty-five feet, gave me at once an idea of the vastness of the entire structure, which my mind had never conceived of. . . . Forward and aft stretched a long line of guns; amidship were placed two launches, boats capable each of carrying the loading of a moderate sized schooner, and containing at sea, four other boats, laid one within the other. Looking down the hatchway, I saw a long line of ladders, communicating with tier after tier of deck, until the lowest was lost in a darkness never illumined by the light of day. And overhead, the tapering masts seemed to lose themselves in the clouds, and the wilderness of rigging

which supported them to be an endless and undistinguishably confused mass of ropes.

But there was no time for surprise. "Come look alive there, don't
go to sleep," shouted in my ear by a coarse voice, startled me out of
my propriety nearly, and interrupted the strain of wonderment in
which I had become lost.

"Were you speaking to me, sir?" said I, politely and timidly, making a respectful bow at the same time, to a burly doublefisted sailor,
from whom the coarse voice seemed to have issued. A shout of
laughter from all within hearing greeted this green sally of mine, amidst
which I hastily made my descent to a lower deck. Here new scenes
awaited my ready eyes and ears. But there was no time to be aston-
ished. Everybody was busy. Men running hither and thither with loads
of rigging. Officers, in uniform of blue and gold, shouting orders
through tin speaking-trumpets; the cheering sound of the boatswain's
mate's pipes, and the regular tramp of the hundreds strung along, on
deck, at the tackle falls, hoisting in provisions; all united, made a
scene of noise and confusion in which it was impossible to stand still,
or to think, and I soon found it necessary to get some employment
myself, to avoid being knocked down and run over, in the rush of the
many conflicting crowds. I joined a division of about a hundred, who
were hoisting in barrels of beef and pork on deck, from a lighter
alongside. We had hold of one end of a rope, the other end of which
being made fast to a dozen barrels of provisions, the boatswain's
shrill whistle piped "go ahead," and we walked off with the fall, to
the merry notes of a fife. Landing the beef on deck, the barrels were
coopered, and then consigned by another set of men to their resting-
place in the hold.

A man-of-war is supposed to have on board, when ready for sea,
six months' supply of provisions and water, together with a sufficient
quantity of powder and shot, spare clothing, sails, and rigging, to
last the cruise of three years. To take in these supplies, and complete
the fitting of various portions of the rigging, for sea, was the work now
on hand, and at this we were kept early and late, rain or shine. All
hands were called up at four o'clock A. M., and the work continued
from that hour until six P.M., with intermission only for breakfast
and dinner. Not used to this kind of a life, the first wet weather completed what previous exposure had laid the foundation for, and I
woke up one morning gasping for breath, and scarcely able to stir.

119

I managed to tumble out of my hammock on to the deck, but could not lash it up. The "hurry up, hurry up, there" of the cross old boatswain's mate, although filling me with terror, was left unheeded, while I crawled between two guns, and laid myself down, crying and moaning with pain. Nearly all the hammocks were on deck, and mine not yet lashed up, when a kind old sailor, passing that way, heard me crying, and approached. He quickly saw what was the matter, and taking me up in his arms, like one would a baby, carried me into "sick bay." Returning directly with my hammock, he hung that up, lifted me into it, and bidding me not cry, but be of good cheer, hurried off to his work. I lay there unnoticed until nine o'clock, when the doctor made his regular round; after an examination of the symptoms, my disease was pronounced to be a violent pleurisy. Here I lay sick for many days. . . .

The sick bay was filled with sick men, many of them having upon them loathsome diseases, contracted in their debaucheries on shore. Several men died. While I was yet lying very low, the occupant of the hammock adjoining mine—(our beds touched)—died. . . .

To be sick on board ship seems to be the very height of earthly misery. The sick room on shore, surrounded as it is by every comfort, by all the appliances invented by art or suggested by love, which can make the sufferer's lot more bearable, is yet far from desirable. But to be bedridden on ship board is a horrible fate. Cooped up with dozens of others in a narrow space on one of the lower decks, badly ventilated, and reeking with all the odors peculiar to sick-rooms and ship's holds, annoyed constantly by the fretful complaint, the dull moan of pain, or the hollow cough, the invalid lies in his cot, hour after hour and day after day, thinking and thinking, until his brain is bewildered and his soul grows weary and faint. At stated intervals, a steward or loblolly boy makes the round of all the hammocks and cots, and supplies the wants of the sick. Twice a day, once at nine o'clock, A. M., and again at four, P. M., the dull monotony is invaded by the doctor's visit. At dark, or in bad weather, the portholes are closed, shutting out the last remnant of fresh air, and a dingy lantern, hung to the beams, sheds a faint light around its immediate proximity, by which the utter darkness of the outskirts is only made more clearly tangible. And there the sick man lies, his cot swinging with the motion of the vessel, the bilge-water rushing across the deck, the timbers creaking and groaning in concert with the moan of pain, until after an almost interminable night the bustle and noise overhead announce the advent of another day of misery. Really, it is surprising that anyone recovers in a "sick bay." For my part, as soon as I was once able to walk on deck, the doctor's steward saw my face no more. . . .[6]

VI

THE CAT

In his autobiography, Carpenter Samuel Holbrook describes the punishment of a culprit on board a frigate.

When we arrived, a messenger was dispatched to Arequipa, [Peru] to acquaint the merchants of our arrival, also to request them to be expeditious in getting their money on board. We expected to remain at least twenty days. The climate being exceedingly dry, it was concluded to paint ship.

As the paint department was under my charge, I was ordered to have verdigris enough mixed to paint the inside of the bulwarks on the spar-deck. I took a clean beef barrel, and put in a sufficient quantity of verdigris, and oil enough to mix it; but having no spirits of turpentine, as a substitute put in five gallons of whiskey. It was stirred up and well mixed to be ready for use on the following morning. At about eleven o'clock, I heard on the forward part of the gun-deck, a dreadful groaning with distressing efforts to vomit. There appeared to be much commotion among the men, I took no more notice of it and went to sleep again. Next morning I found out the cause of the trouble. These fellows who had been taken so suddenly ill, had seen me put the whiskey in the paint, and having a sufficient knowledge of chemistry to know that whiskey was one thing and verdigris another, and of course, after the heavier had settled, the lighter body would remain above, perfectly homogeneous. On the strength of this known fact, after the hammocks were piped down, and all was still, these "jolly Jack tars" stood around the paint barrel, anxiously waiting the time for nature to do her work, but being rather impatient, they concluded to taste, so in went one tin pot, and then another, and instead of tasting it, when the tin pot was once at the mouth, in consequence of its having oil with it, the good stuff was so slippery, that a good half pint went down each throat, before the pot was removed.

There must have been a great many at this banquet, for in the morning there was not a half a pint of whiskey left out of the five gallons. I made no complaint about it, but drew from the purser's steward five gallons more, and commenced using the paint. About the time we had got through painting, the money began to arrive from Arequipa; we could see the mules coming over the mountain paths, like a string of ants, it came in green hide sacks, each holding about $2,000 and each mule carrying two sacks, there were also cakes of virgin silver, each weighing $1,500. This money was stowed in the spirit room.

There are always men belonging to the hold called "holders," one of which is appointed captain, or, as he is called, "captain of the hold," and their duty is most generally below, getting out beef and pork, serving out water, keeping the cable tiers in order, &c. Then over them is placed an officer, sometimes a midshipman, who is called master-mate of the hold. On this officer devolves the sole charge of the spirit room, which is a part of the hold. No naked light is ever permitted here excepting when it is empty. It was here that the money was stowed. Six men were employed in packing away the sacks; three were in at the further end stowing and the others were passing the bags to them. Now they were all among the whiskey casks, and the smell of the good stuff had such a powerful effect upon their nerves, that by some means, best known to an old tar, they got a sip of this ever potent essence of life, death and mischief, and now they were all ripe for anything.

"I say, Jack," says Jim Innis, in a low voice, (the master's mate being on the gun-deck striking down the sacks,) "hand us in your knife here. These here dollars belong to the *bloody* Spaniards, and we might as well have a few as not, to pay us for our trouble in working here in this thundering hot hole."

A knife was passed in, and a sack cut, and all helped themselves. They stowed the dollars about their persons in the most ingenious manner, notwithstanding all this caution, they managed to get drunk, and fool-like, one fellow came up on the berth deck, and began to show his money.

It soon reached the master's mates ear, and soon it reached the first lieutenant. They were all brought on the half deck, a sentinel placed over them, when they were all searched, and Jim Innis was so drunk that he was brought legs and arms by four men, and when they laid him down, the dollars rolled from him in all directions. These fellows had, I think $192 between them, but the funniest of all was, that one of them positively declared to Mr. Maury that he had brought the dollars with him, and that they were the remains "of his last voyage's pay," but poor fellow, he little thought that the date of the dollar would betray him, for the dollars found on him were new, right from the mint, and dated 1820, and we left Boston in 1818. Notwithstanding these glaring facts, the fellow still persisted that he had brought the dollars with him. They were all put in double irons and under charge of a sentinel, were kept in confinement twenty days, then brought up for punishment. Five of them received seventy-five lashes each, but he who cut the bag was to receive a greater punishment, and according to the testimony of the others, this was Jim. . . . He was stripped and seized up, but his back presented an awful sight. He was with us in the Mediterranean during the Algerine war, was on board the Guerriere when she engaged the Algerine frigate, and during the action, the gun to which he belonged, burst, killing and wounding all the gun's crew. Jim was among the latter, he was sadly burnt from the neck to the hips, and even now, nearly four years after the accident, the flesh was quite tender.

Under these circumstances, Capt. Downes could not flog him on the back, therefore he must receive his punishment on what is usually denominated the seat of honor. In this case the culprit is not seized up the gangway, but is brought over a carronade in the following manner. Standing at the breech, he bends over towards the muzzle; his wrists are secured, one on each side the gun, to the forward axeltree, and his legs, to the gun tackle bolts in the carriage. His trowsers are then pulled down, thus presenting to the boatswain's mate, a prominent field for operation. And one lick with the cat here is worse than a dozen on the back. When all was ready, says the captain to him:

"Now sir, did you cut the bag?"

"Oh, no, sir, I did not."

"Well then, who did? Boatswain's mate go on with him."

And at the first lick, Jim sung out nobly, and fairly made the gun shake.

"Oh, now, my dear, good Capt. Downes, don't lick me any more, and I *will* tell you all."

"Well let us know who did it?"

"Oh, dear! just cast me loose, and then I'll tell you."

"Give it to him, boatswain's mate."

And obeying the order, put on a half dozen. The blood began to run and the flesh to quiver like jelly, and Jim's shrieks and cries fairly made the pigs look aft to see what was going on.

"Now, who cut the bag?"

Poor Jim had nothing more to say on that subject, but continued to beg most earnestly. He took the other half dozen and was let off. Now Jim was a short, chunky, funny sort of a fellow, and notwithstanding the pain he had, and was still suffering, after he was clear of the gun, he turned round among his shipmates, and with a half smile, dryly remarked:

"I've got off with four dozen less than them other beggars after all."

Besides the flogging, they were compelled to carry a 32 lb. shot, with 32 lbs. of chain attached to their legs, and a wooden yoke about the neck four feet long and nine inches broad, and on it was painted, in several places, in large letters, THIEF. . . .[7]

I fancy that those editors and legislators who sit in their cozy armchairs, in office or congressional hall, and talk wisely about the necessity of flogging for sailors, need only once to witness the infliction of the punishment they think so needful, and experience with their own breasts the feeling of dark humiliation which falls upon the soul at seeing the manhood being scourged out of a fellow creature, to alter their convictions as to the expediency of flogging. . . .

It may be asked here, what was the effect upon the rest of the ship's company. Of *visible* effect there was little. A man-of-war is not the place for too free an expression of opinion. The regulations of the service do not admit of freedom of speech. They contain such a word as *mutiny,* for which they provide "death, or such other punishment as a court-martial shall provide." And, as there can be no half-way-talk concerning so brutal a practice as flogging a human being—a creature created in the image of God—the consequence is an ominous silence. "A still tongue makes a wise head"—nowhere more so than in the service, where it is truly said: "You are allowed to *think* what you please, but you must not think aloud."[8]

VII

THE MUTINY

Dissatisfied with the haphazard method of training young officers, Commodore Matthew C. Perry urged sending groups of naval apprentices to sea on small ships where they could learn together. The brig Somers, 10, manned largely, but not exclusively, by apprentices, was an experiment in this line.

Returning to the United States from the African coast in 1842, the Somers, Commander Alexander Slidell MacKenzie, was the scene of an approach to mutiny. Apparently intent upon seizing the ship and converting her to piracy, young Acting Midshipman Philip Spencer, son of the Secretary of War, sought out a score or more of the crew to enlist them in his plot.

Possibly overestimating the seriousness of the affair, certainly aware of the risk of holding dangerous prisoners in irons, MacKenzie after consulting his officers hanged Spencer and two cohorts from the yardarm. When the Somers reached New York, the incident aroused nationwide controversy and, although exonerated by a naval court, MacKenzie's naval career was injuriously affected. One beneficial result of the Somers mutiny was that it discredited the best alternative to the establishment of a naval academy.

Purser's Steward J. W. Wales, First Lieutenant Guert Gansevoort, and MacKenzie gave testimony before the Court of Inquiry.

Wales: Spencer made the communication to me the evening of the 25th of November in the 2nd dog watch. I was standing forward by the bitts. Mr. Spencer came forward and after making a few remarks relative to the weather, desired me to get on the top of the booms with him, as he had something of great importance to communicate to me. I got up on the booms and he commenced the conversation by asking me these questions. "Did I fear death?" "Was I afraid of a dead person and dare I kill a person?" I was much surprised at these remarks and paused sometime to see if Mr. Spencer was in earnest, and I found he was very much in earnest. I told him I was not particularly anxious about dying quite yet, that I had no cause to fear a dead man, that should a man abuse me or insult me I thought I could muster sufficient courage to kill him if necessary.

Mr. Spencer remarked that he did not doubt my courage, that he knew it. He then asked if I could keep a secret. I told him I would; he then requested me to take an oath the purport of which was, that I should never communicate that conversation to anyone "so help me God." I took the oath as he directed and he then went on to state that he was leagued with about 20 of the Brigs company, to murder all her Officers, take the Brig, and commence pirating; he said he had the plan and stations of the men all drawn up, and he said it was then in his neckhandkerchief around his neck; he desired me to feel of it; I felt of the back part of his neckhandkerchief, and it made a noise as though there was paper inside, he then went on to state the manner he should proceed to take her.

The affray would commence some night when he had the mid-watch, some of those concerned with him would get in a scuffle on the forecastle, Mr. Spencer would then cause them to be brought to the mast, he would then call Mr. Rogers the Officer of the deck to pretend to settle the matter; as soon as Mr. Rogers had got to the gangway, they were to seize him and pitch him overboard; they would then have the vessel to themselves.

He would then proceed to station his men at the hatches to prevent any one coming on deck; the Keys of the arm chest, he said he could lay his hands on at any moment, he would then furnish his men with arms; this done, he (Mr. Spencer) was to proceed to the Cabin and murder the Commander with the least noise possible; this done he would go with some of his men to the Ward Room, and murder the Ward Room and Steerage Officers; he stated the Officers had no arms with the exception of the first Lieutenant, and all the arms he had was an old cutlass, which he should secure before the affray commenced; this accomplished he should come on deck, have the two after Guns slewed round so as to rake the deck, he would then have the whole crew called on deck, and would select from among them such as would suit his purposes. The remainder he should cause to be thrown overboard, this done he should proceed to clear the deck, by throwing overboard the launch and all the spare spars and rigging as they only tended to lumber up the deck, that should they stand in need of any spare spars or rigging they could easily supply themselves from the vessels they captured.

United States brig-of-war *Somers*.

This done the brig was to proceed to Cape St. Antonio or the Isle of Pines, one of these places, and there take on board one who was familiar with their intended business, and who was willing and ready to join them; this done they were to commence cruising for prises that whenever they would take a vessel they would murder all hands, as dead men told no tales he said; and, after taking from her that which would be of use to them, they would scuttle the vessel leaving no traces of her; should there happen to be females on board, he would have them taken to the Brig for the use of the Officers and men, using them as long as they saw fit, after that to make way with them. . . .

He then went on to state that the Commander had a large amount of money on board, that and what the Purser had, he said would make a pretty little sum to commence with. He then asked me what I thought of the project.

I thought it prudent to dissemble as much as possible in order to gather further intelligence of their movements; I told him I liked the plan and was favourable disposed towards it. My duty then called me away. Before I left Mr. Spencer we agreed to have another interview on the morrow, when he said he would show me the plan he had drawn up.

I then got off the booms, so did Mr. Spencer, he followed me as far aft as the gangway saying, "if I breathed a syllable of that which he had communicated to me, that I would be murdered; if he did not do it some of those concerned with him would; go where I might my life would not be worth a Straw" Mr. Spencer then went below. I Kept on deck about 15 Minutes after he went below. . . .

I then went to the Steerage door and found that the Wardroom lights were out, and that the Ward Room gentlemen had retired. I then thought I would let the matter rest till morning, turned in, and endeavoured to sleep but could not do it.

In the morning, as soon as I could get an opportunity, I got into the Ward Room and then made the matter known to the Purser, requesting him at the same time to get it to the Commander as soon as possible.

I did not then give him the full particulars, but condensed the matter as much as possible. I then went on deck, and told Mr. Gansevoort the first Lieutenant, that the Purser wished to see him immediately in the Ward Room. . . .

First Lieutenant Guert Gansevoort, USN: I immediately entered
the cabin and mentioned the circumstances. He (Commander Alexander Slidell MacKenzie, USN) received it with great coolness; said
that the vessel was in good discipline and expressed his doubts as to
the truth of the report. I asked him if I should see Mr. Wales myself
and get the information from him. He said no, he did not wish me
to do or to say anything about it. He assigned no reason at this time
for this, but ordered me to keep a strict lookout upon Mr. Spencer
and the crew generally. . . .

Commander MacKenzie: These various recollections, added to what
had been revealed to me, determined me to make sure at once of his
[Spencer's] person, though I had meditated, allowing Mr. Wales to
have another interview with him that evening for the purpose of
ascertaining more of his plans, as had been agreed upon between
them. If he was really in earnest, enough was already known. At evening quarters I ordered my clerk, O. H. Perry, doing the duty also
of midshipman and aide, all of the officers to lay aft on the quarter-
deck, excepting the midshipmen stationed on the forecastle. The master was ordered to take the wheel, and those of the crew stationed
abaft sent to the mainmast. I approached Mr. Spencer and said to
him, "I learn, Mr. Spencer, that you aspire to the command of the
Somers?" with a deferential, but unmoved and gently smiling expression, he replied, "Oh, no sir." "Did you not tell Mr. Wales, sir,
that you had a project to kill the commander, the officers and a
considerable portion of the crew of this vessel and convert her into
a pirate?" "I may have told him so, sir, but it was in joke." "You
admit then that you told him?" "Yes, sir, but in joke." "This, sir, is
joking on a forbidden subject; this joke may cost you your life. Be
pleased to remove your neck-handkerchief." It was removed and
opened, but nothing was found in it. I asked him what he had done
with the papers containing an account of his project which he had
told Mr. Wales was in the back of his neck-handkerchief. "It is a
paper containing my day's work, and I have destroyed it." "It is a
singular place in which to keep day's work." "It is a convenient one,"
he replied with an air of deference and blandness. I said to him,
"You must have been aware that you could only have compassed
your designs by passing over my dead body, and after that, the bodies
of all of the officers; you had given yourself, sir, a great deal to do;

it will be necessary for me to confine you, sir." I turned to Lieutenant Gansevoort and said, "Arrest Mr. Spencer, and put him in double irons." Mr. Gansevoort stepped forward and took his sword. He was ordered to sit down on the stern post, double ironed, and, an additional security, handcuffed. I directed Lieutenant Gansevoort to watch over his security, to order him to be put to instant death if he was detected speaking to or holding intelligence in any way with any of the crew. He was himself made aware of the nature of these orders. . . .

27 November: *Gansevoort:* I heard an unusual noise—a rushing on deck and I saw a body of men in each gangway rushing aft toward the quarterdeck. I said to the Commander, "God, I believe they are coming." I had one of Colt's pistols, which I immediately drew and cocked; the commander said his pistols were below. I jumped onto the trunk and ran forward to meet them. As I was going along I sang out to them not to come aft. I told them I would blow the first man's brains out who should put his foot on the quarterdeck. I held my pistol pointed at the tallest man I saw in the starboard gangway, and I think Mr. Rodgers sang out to me that he was sending the men aft to the mast rope. I then told them that they must have no such unusual movements on board the vessel; what they did they must do in their usual manner; they knew the state of the vessel and might get their brains blown out before they were aware of it. . . .

MacKenzie: I gave orders to make immediate preparations for hanging the three principal criminals at the main yard arms; all hands were now called to witness punishment. The after-guard and idlers of both watches were mustered on the quarter-deck at the whip intended for Mr. Spencer; the forecastle men and foretop men at that of Cromwell, to whose corruption they had been chiefly exposed; the maintop men of both watches at that intended for Small, who for a month or more had held the situation of captain of the maintop. The officers were stationed about the decks according to the watch-bill that I had made out the night before, and the petty officers were similarly distributed, with orders to cut down whoever should let go the whip with even one hand, or fail to haul on it when ordered. The ensign and pennant being bent on and ready for hoisting, I now put on my full uniform and proceeded to execute the most painful duty that has ever devolved upon an American commander—that of announcing to the criminals their fate. . . .

Findings of the Court of Inquiry
20 JANUARY 1843

. . . That Commander MacKenzie under these circumstances was not bound to risk the safety of his vessel, and jeopardize the lives of his crew, in order to secure to the guilty the forms of trial, and that the immediate execution of the prisoners was demanded by duty and justified by necessity. The court are further of opinion that throughout all of these painful occurrences so well calculated to disturb the judgment and try the energy of the bravest and most experienced officer, the conduct of Commander MacKenzie and his officers was prudent, calm, and firm, and he and they honorably performed their duty to the service and their country.

CHARLES STEWART,
President of the Court.[9]

VIII

THE DESERTION

Commander William Gibson, USN, describes to the editor of the Army and Navy Journal *the desertion from the Coast Survey vessel* Ewing, *which occurred in San Francisco Harbor, 1849, when he was a Passed Midshipman. Appended are several official letters written by the Commander-in-Chief, Pacific Squadron, explaining his actions.*

. . . On or about the 11th of September, 1849, I was a passed midshipman on board the U. S. schooner *Ewing,* Lieut. Comd'g McArthur, lying in the bay of San Francisco, about two miles off from the strange collection of frame shanties, tents, and ancient adobes, that then constituted the city of San Francisco. She was a coast survey vessel, officered and manned by and under the discipline of the Navy. Several cruising men-of-war and storeships of the squadron were in port, and the flag of Commodore T. Ap Catesby Jones flew

131

from the line of battle ship *Ohio*. On shore the gold excitement was at its wildest; the prices made the pay of the officers, let alone that of the men, ridiculous; bearded and sunburnt creatures, in roughly fantastic apparel, were daily coming in from the washings, their horny hands thrust into trowsers' pockets full of loose gold dust, that literally sprinkled the streets. The temptation was great; the crews would, if they could, have deserted nearly to a man. The extremest exercise of power conferred by naval law and the sharpest vigilance were necessary to prevent this; the muskets of the marines were kept loaded, the watch officers wore their pistols, and the officers in command of boats always backed into the landing, drawn revolver in hand. With these precautions the desertions had been few; the only flagrant case, which happened a short time previous to my affair, having been the pulling on shore, in broad daylight and under fire, of an extemporaneous crew in the *Ohio's* launch.

On the evening in question a number of Army officers and citizens from shore had dined on board the *Ewing*. Between nine and ten o'clock a boat was called away to land them. In place of the very young lad who usually did boat duty, I volunteered to take charge. I remembered afterwards that, by the light of the side lantern, I noticed a look and start of surprise in one or two of the boat's crew. Perhaps they apprehended a more difficult job than they had expected; perhaps it was true what they pleaded on their trial, that they had an especial liking for me, and (to quote the ghastly foregone conclusion in Keats' poem) were a little sorry for their "murdered man." It was a crew of five. The night was one of Egyptian darkness, and the ebb tide ran so strongly that it attracted attention. The log was hove from the *Ewing* and showed four knots. Receiving a caution from Rhind, our executive, not to be caught under the bows of the merchantmen that lay between us and the shore, I shoved off. Backing into a small wharf, where Sansom street now is, a pistol in each hand, I landed my passengers and started to return. When about half way to the nearest merchant vessel, some hundreds of yards from the shore, I put back my pistols and resumed the yoke ropes. In a few moments, the after oarsman, John Black, with a hoarse exclamation, threw his oar out of the rowlock and himself upon me. Struggling to my feet, I found myself clutched by several of the others. Their first effort semed to be to get possession of my pistols, but very soon one of them (Peter Black, I think) exclaimed: "Damn him, throw him overboard—that's the quickest way!" With this I found my arms free, and seized John Black by his neckerchief, dragging him overboard with me. Twisting it with one hand, I attempted to draw a pistol with the other, but the man was too heavy for me, the rest were striking at me with the oars, and, though an expert swimmer, I had to let go, wholly exhausted and half drowned. I swam off a little way, saw them help Black into the boat and settle into their places, and, with the question, "What will you give us to save your life?" they pulled off. Whether this was a real offer or a taunt, as I made no reply, I can never know. By this time my heavy clothes were saturated and I could just tread water, but I was so mortified and angry that I did not call for help until I heard the sound of their oars grow faint in the distance. Then I noticed that I was fast sweeping past the lights of the town, and for the first time realized in what deadly peril I was. I cried out that I was drowning, I heard shouts and excited noises of people on shore, then the sound of oars, felt myself swallowing a great deal of water, wondered why, and—I know no more.

There was a sense of strangulation—no suffering. Drowning is but a falling to sleep. Nor was there an instantaneous illumination of a whole life, like a landscape by a flash of lightning, of which I have read so much. All that I remember is, for one moment, a keen endeavor to realize the fact that I was to penetrate the mystery of Death, and I could not comprehend it. . . .

I was taken on shore insensible and apparently lifeless. For hours, according to the medical evidence, my condition was desperate. I came to momentary consciousness but to faint away again in convulsions, and it was not until four o'clock in the morning that I could utter the few words necessary to tell what had happened. That I sit here to write this, I owe, under Heaven, to Dr. Augustus Borvie, of Cal., then of the Navy, and to the other doctors, military and civil, who assisted him in his skilful efforts to restore me to life.

Boats from the *Ohio* and other vessels were promptly sent in pursuit; the *Ewing* proceeded up the bay; my brother and other Army officers started out on horseback. Gen. Persifer F. Smith, at Sonoma, ordered the 2d dragoons into the saddle to scour the mining regions. The whole community of San Francisco, gentle and rude alike, seemed eager to catch my assailants. A reward of $500 apiece was offered, and that and a description of the deserters was given to the people on board of a hulk lying at the junction of the Sacramento and San

Joaquin rivers, in time to effect their capture about thirty-six hours after their escape. When taken on board the *Ewing,* which had anchored in the night near by, and afterwards on board the flagship, the prisoners were allowed communication with no one. They repeatedly asked the sentinels: "Is Mr. Gibson dead?" and the stern silence which met the inquiry seems to have confirmed them in their natural belief that I was. When I entered the court room the effect was dramatic. I shall never forget how they sprang to their feet and stared at me as if I had been a ghost.

They were tried on board the sloop-of-war *Warren,* by a full court-martial, composed of thirteen members and two supernumeraries, and sentenced to death. The commodore had in the meantime shifted his flag to the frigate *Savannah,* and the *Ohio* had gone home. A number of distinguished officers were on that court—among the elder, the late Rear-Admiral L. M. Goldsborough—among the younger, the late Capt. Catesby Ap R. Jones, of the Confederacy. The sentence, according to military usage, was ordered to be carried into execution in twenty-four hours, but the time was afterwards extended one day. The poor fellows sent to see me, and I was naturally much affected, peculiarly so to find that they all united in exonerating the bow oarsman, a young Irishman about twenty years old. I went at once to the commodore to correct my evidence as to the participation of all, and pleaded for the lives of all, but more especially for this one. But the commodore was inexorable, and said whoever was not for me at such a time was against me.

At the last moment, upon the confession of the two Blacks, that they alone had planned the mutiny, the commodore commuted the sentence of three of them. But, in his eloquent address to the crews of the squadron, he repeated in stronger language what he had said to me, to the effect in substance: "that those who could look on at this cowardly, murderous assault on a young and delicate officer, he held in less respect than the bolder ringleaders, that he gave them their lives as an act of pure mercy, trusting to the sufficiency of the example." John Black was hung on board the *Ewing,* and Peter Black on board the *Savannah.*

The two Blacks bore purser's names, and told the clergymen who attended them their real ones, and I heard that one of them, John Black, was of a good family in Scotland. . . .

That the crews were in a state of incipient mutiny, so that these clergymen from shore were called upon to quiet them, is not true. With all respect to these gentlemen, I think that the hanging, deeply as I felt the awful fate of these unhappy men, and the address of Commodore Jones, were the proper and only sedatives. There were no more desertions. Contrary to the inference that one would draw from the communication in your columns, the discipline of that squadron was throughout magnificent. Never was the majesty of the law vindicated amid graver and more unmurmuring awe than at that execution. Commodore Thos. Ap Catesby Jones, as is well known, was a man of remarkable force and determination of character. And in no time of war were ever the devotion to duty, steady deportment and sleepless vigilance of officers more severely tried, and I do not like even the implication that any one of them trod the quarter-deck otherwise than proudly and self-reliant.[10]

The sentence of death under which Jonathan Biddy, William Hall and Henry Commerford stand condemned, is hereby commuted, and instead thereof each of the aforesaid, Biddy, Hall and Commerford, will receive one hundred lashes on the bare back, serve out the remainder of their term of enlistment without pay, and with a ball and chain on the leg, in solitary confinement, or at hard labor, or alternately both, at such navy yard or other place or places as the Secretary of the Navy may direct.

THOS. AP C. JONES
Commander in Chief,
Pacific Squadron

Flag Ship Savannah
Off San Francisco,
23d October, 1849.

The determination of the Commander in Chief to commute the sentence of death against Jonathan Biddy, William Hall and Henry Commerford, is not the result of any diminution of his abhorrence of the offense of which they were convicted by the Naval General Court Martial, nor from the slightest doubt of the justice of the sentence of the court. It was the province and duty of the court sitting in judgment on the accused to pronounce them guilty or not guilty, and the law fixes the penalty of the offence perpetrated, but to the reviewing power is left the exercise of clemency, when mercy can be shown without defeating the primitive ends of justice. It is a humane and merciful maxim, as just as it is charitable, that the life of man should never be taken when anything short of the taking of life would fully meet the ends of justice, and be sufficient punishment for the crime committed. Regarding these humane maxims as principles never to be lost sight of by the reviewing power when *finally* deciding the question of life or death of a fellow being, the *great* question arises whether the discipline of the Navy is so low, or the fidelity of its seamen so little to be relied on, as to forbid the exercise of mercy in the present instance. I cannot, *will not believe it.* What better proof have we than the fact that, since the law of April 23d 1800 was enacted, for the government of the Navy, now near half a century, this is the first instance with one exception when the sentence of death has ever been passed by a court martial for any other crime than *murder,* nor so far as my information goes, has there ever been more than one person condemned by the same court, or even in the same squadron. With this bright and honorable retrospect, may we not now, can we not now, exercise mercy, and by that mercy disarm the wicked?

I believe we may, and therefore I try the experiment, but let it be remembered that the clemency now shown, is not based upon any claim or *pretence* to it, on the ground that the offences upon which the accused were condemned to die, are not *worthy of death*—No—no such plea can be entered—no such claim can be admitted. *The Sentence of the Court was just, and in strict conformity to the law;* and in exercising the high prerogative of mercy, it is only with the sincere hope and confident expectation that the clemency shown will have a salutary effect in reclaiming the wicked and in confirming the penitent.

THOS. AP C. JONES,
Commander in Chief,
Pacific Squadron.

Flag Ship Savannah,
Off San Francisco,
23d October 1849

Conformable to the usage of the sea service, it is my painful duty to make some remarks upon the awful spectacle we have just witnessed. To see a fellow being, although he be no closer allied to us than by the common ties of humanity, calmly resign his life in the course of nature to the God who gave it, is, all times, a grave and a melancholy scene. But when such extreme penalties have to be inflicted on several persons at once, and the same time, and especially by and before those who like ourselves are wholly unaccustomed to such scenes, the like of which has never before occurred in the Navy of the United States, and I pray God in his mercy may never again occur, the effect is appalling, and must strike too deep on the heart and mind of every spectator, not to leave a salutary impression, which no length of time or diversity of circumstances can ever obliterate. . . .

The object of punishment is not vengeance, nor to return evil for evil. For the better security of persons and property the great human family have formed themselves into societies or organized bodies denominated governments—and these governments, representing the masses, have enacted laws, to restrain the wicked and to punish the guilty. . . .

The general features of the transaction upon which the charges of "Mutiny with intent to Kill" and "Desertion, with an attempt to Kill, and running away with a boat, the property of the United States" were founded and made the subject of trial before the Naval General Court Martial, which convened on board the U. S. Sloop of War *Warren* for that purpose on Monday, the 8th inst. are too well known in the squadron to make it necessary for me here to recite them, sufficient to say that the accused, whose lifeless bodies are now before us, were each and severally convicted after the most patient hearing of all testimony for as well as against them, and aided too, as they were, in their defence by the best and ablest counsel, whose efforts to save do justice alike to his head and his heart, were found guilty. . . .

I cannot dismiss you on this most solemn of all solemn occasions I have ever witnessed without once more (as I have already often done) admonishing you against the high crime of *Desertion,* a crime which even when unconnected with any other violation of the laws for the Government of the Navy, places the deserter's life in the power of any court martial by which he may be tried. . . .

If there yet remain any among you who meditate desertion, let them ponder well and count the cost before making the attempt; they may escape as some have, but they may be apprehended, tried, condemned and executed, as you now have the most appalling proof before your eyes. Remember that the line of moderate and mild sentences of courts martial for *desertion* has been severed by the sentence of the court by the examples before us . . . which will not be unheeded by future Courts Martial, or by those who have to execute their sentences, when *mercy* to the guilty would be cruelty to the innocent.

THOS. AP C. JONES,
*Commander in Chief,
Pacific Squadron.*[11]

Flag Ship Savannah
*Bay of San Francisco,
October 20th, 1849*

IX

THE NOOSE

Seaman Samuel Jackson, serving on the sloop St. Mary's *in Mexican waters, was charged, court-martialed, and hanged. Chaplain Fitch Taylor was with the unfortunate to the end.*

The court then proceeded to the trial of Samuel Jackson, Seaman of the U. S. Navy. . . .

Charges, and Specifications of Charges

Preferred by Commander John L. Saunders of the United States Navy against Samuel Jackson, a Seaman on board the U. S. Ship St. Mary's.

Charge 1st

Raising a weapon against his superior while in the execution of the duties of his office.

Specification. That about 3 A. M. on the 30th day of July 1846 Samuel Jackson a seaman on board the U. S. Ship St. Mary's did throw a belaying pin with intent to strike Benjamin Garrett a Boatswains Mate, on the same ship, during the said Garrett's watch on deck, and immediately after the said Garrett had reported said Jackson for abusive language to him while in the discharge of his duty.

Charge 2nd

Striking his superior officer while in the execution of the duties of his office.

Specification. That on the forenoon of the 14th day of August 1846 the said Samuel Jackson, Seaman as aforesaid, did coolly and deliberately and with malice aforethought, strike three times, with his fists and knock down, Lieutenant William Rogers Taylor, while the said Lieutenant Taylor was actually engaged in the duties of Executive Officer, on board the U. S. Ship St. Mary's.

Charge 3rd

Treating with contempt his Superior being in *the execution* of his office.

Specification. That the said Samuel Jackson, Seaman, did on the forenoon of the 14th day of August 1846 address the following language, or words to that effect, to acting Midshipman Thomas B. Childress, of the U. S. Navy, the said acting Midshipman Childress being in the execution of his office: to wit,

> *You need'nt pester yourself about it, Go Away. I can
> whip the whole of you, God damn you, if one comes
> at a time. You have me fast now and can hang me if
> you choose.*

and further that the said Samuel Jackson continued to curse and swear at the said actg Midn Childress during the whole of the time that the said actg Midn Childress was then and there engaged in the duties of his office.

Charge 4th

Uttering seditious and mutinous words.

Specification. That on the evening of the 13th day of August 1846, the said Samuel Jackson, Seaman, being then confined in irons did utter the following language, or words to this effect, to wit.

I wonder where all the Gentlemen were when the St. Mary's was fitted out. that not one—no, not one, could be found to go in her unless perhaps it may be one midshipman. A hell of a Captain, damn him! I hope if he does not suffer in this world he may in the next. I hope his family may suffer that his children may die—so that by cutting off the branches the trunk may wither with other similar language, the said Jackson knowing, all the time, that he was in the hearing of an officer and a marine.

139

. . . The Court closed its doors. The whole of the proceedings of the Court were then read over; after a short recess, the Court proceeded to deliberate on the charges and the testimony addressed to sustain them, on the prisoner's defence, and the evidence adduced in support of the same, and having maturely weighed and considered all the said evidence, the Court is of the opinion

That the Specification of the first charge *is not proved*

That the Specification of the second charge is proved and that the accused is *guilty* of the second charge.

That the Specification of the third charge is proved and that the accused is *guilty* of the third charge.

That the Specification of the fourth charge is proved and that the accused is *guilty* of the fourth charge.

The Court therefore, by a vote of Two thirds of all the members comprising said Court do sentence him, the aforesaid Samuel Jackson, Seaman, United States Navy, to be hanged by the neck until he be dead, at such time and place, as the Commander in Chief may direct.[12]

. . . Several courts-martial have occurred in the Home Squadron since the Cumberland has been the Flagship of this station. But only one where the penalties attached to the crime charged extend to the loss of life. This has lately occurred; and yesterday, the 13th of September, the sentence of the court was divulged to the fleet, with its approval by the Commander-in-chief, which, in view of its fearful consequences to the accused, has produced a deep sensation throughout the fleet.

The general order issued by the Commander-in-chief, and read on board the different ships of the squadron—all hands being mustered for hearing the document—stated—That a court martial having been held on board the St. Mary's, for the trial of S. Jackson and the Court, finding all these charges, save the first, to be proven, did sentence said S. J. to be executed. Therefore the Commander-in-chief directs, that said S. Jackson, seaman, be hanged by the neck, at the fore-yard-arm of the United States ship St. Mary's on Thursday, the seventeenth day of September, 1846, between the hours of 10 o'clock, A.M. and meridian. The general order then continues as follows:

"In order that a suitable impression may be made on the minds of all persons in the squadron, and that there may be nothing to divert their thoughts from so melancholy a spectacle, and that they may be duly impressed with the awful consequences which must ever follow such violations of law, as were committed by this unhappy man, it is directed that no work be done on that day; that when the preparatory signal is made for execution by the Cumberland, *a yellow flag* shall be displayed from the fore-royal-masthead of the St. Mary's, the officers and crews of every vessel of the squadron present shall be mustered on deck, and they shall be kept on deck until the yellow flag on board the St. Mary's is hauled down. . . .

"The fate of this unhappy man, it is hoped, will be a salutary influence, and impress on the minds of all present, the necessity of keeping a strict watch over their passions and tempers, at all times and in all situations. . . .

D. CONNER
Commanding Home Squadron."

Six bells now struck (11 o'clock). There was a stir over the decks, in answer to the preparatory signal now made from the Cumberland, to have all things in readiness of executing the sentence of the Court Martial. The prisoner knew not of the signal, but his quick ear detected the movement. And as the signal for the Cumberland fell to her decks, *the yellow flag* on board the St. Mary's was run up to the royal-mast-head.

All necessary preparations had been early made on the Saint Mary's for executing the sentence. A small platform had been arranged on the larboard side of the forecastle, a little above one of the guns and supported by a stanchion, one end of which rested in the muzzle of the gun. This gun was loaded. The clew-line was used as the whip-rope, by which the unfortunate man was to be run up to the larboard-arm of the fore-yard. And this line was so rove as to connect along the yard with a weight of round shot that was to descend by the fore-mast, and rouse the prisoner to the yard-arm. And this weight, for the time being, was held in its place near the main-top, by a line that led over the muzzle of the shotted gun. On firing the gun, the shot would cut the line, and the weight fall, bearing up the unfortunate man to the yard-arm.

And around the Saint Mary's on this beautiful sheet of water, lay the different ships and other vessels of the fleet, nine or ten in number, in full view of the transaction which was now so rapidly maturing to its finale. The yellow flag flying at the fore-royal-mast-head, all eyes from these different ships were gazing, with interest, for the succeeding signal of the Cumberland. The next signal would order the execution of the sentence of the court.

But, in the mean time, how was it with the prisoner, still awaiting in the agitation and fullness of his feelings, the summons, which the signal from the Flag Ship soon would lead to? A little before, he had put on his shoes, remarking that he would do it, though it was of little matter whether he did or not. And again, of his jacket, neatly folded upon his cot, he said, he did not know what he would need of it. The day was warm and bright, and the ships' crews were dressed in white. It was evident, however, that the hour was near at hand; and ere long, indeed, the sentry placed his hand upon the canvas and elevated one wing of the screen, as the First Lieut. of the St. Mary's entered, saying that he had come on the melancholy duty (naming the prisoner) to have him prepare for the execution of the sentence which had been pronounced upon him. The master-at-arms advanced—relieved the prisoner's wrists of the irons that embraced them—and then, the prisoner arose, and allowed his arms to be tied at the elbows, behind him. An ebullition of the prisoner's feelings burst forth. "Oh my God, that I should ever have been brought to this!" calling upon his Maker and his Saviour to be with him, and to extend him mercy and strength, in such a needed hour, and to receive him with pardon to himself.

It was soon over; and he preferred that his hands should be tied also, and that his slippers should be removed from his feet. He was now conducted to the main deck of the ship, near the capstan, all hands already having been piped to witness punishment, and were now mustered on the upper deck, with the officers in uniform on the quarter-deck. Captain Saunders, of the St. Mary's, advanced near to the prisoner, and read the death-warrant. . . .

As the Captain ended, the prisoner standing, pale, and hopeless, which gave interest to his finely chiselled face, added, in a respectful tone—

"I am ready, sir"; and then bursting into tears, he said,

"SHIPMATES! I warn you to take example from me, not to give way to your passions. By doing it, I have lost my life in this world—I fear I have lost my soul for eternity. I offer no extenuation for my offence. I freely forgive the Court which has pronounced the sentence of death against me—the Commodore, who approved the sentence; and all that may have any thing to do with it. I have but a few moments more to live, and I pray all to pray for me, for the few moments more that I have to live. . . ."

When the prisoner had ended his brief and unpremeditated admonition to his shipmates, he walked forward from the capstan to the mainmast, where he still stood with myself at his side, the master-at-arms attending him, while the First Lieutenant advanced to the forecastle, to see that all things were in readiness for ending the fearful tragedy. And while he was gone, the prisoner let his thoughts commune with his own soul and his God, making a single remark or two, and saying to me with other expressions, "I have a faint hope, now, that God will receive me. It is a faint hope." "And there—see! there"—directing my eye, rather, himself looking forward to the larboard fore-yard-arm, and seeing the preparations that had been made for the final scene, and on the forecastle, beneath the yellow flag which was now flying at the fore-royal-mast-head. But soon he turned his face to the mainmast, and knelt on a coil of rigging beside it, as I placed my hand upon his shoulder to support him, and buried my own face in my handerchief, as I leaned on the bits, while this man offered up another prayer in an audible tone, for his own soul . . . while old sailors and young ones with their wet eyes as seldom, if ever, their eyes were thus wet before. Nothing could surpass such a scene, on the deck of a man-of-war; while some near the mainmast and around it, wept audibly and aloud.

The First Lieutenant soon returned. The prisoner had risen . . . and . . . immediately ascended the deck of the forecastle.

As he approached the larboard side, his quick eye took in the scene, and he said to the First Lieutenant,

"Mr. K., I think that line should be overhauled a little more—there will not be drop enough to it."

"Yes, there will be, Jackson," returned the Lieutenant, "and, besides," continued the officer, *"the gun will kill you, Jackson. . . ."*

As he moved across the forecastle, and his eye ranged with a hurried glance down the larboard side of the ship, he said, as if catching the eyes of some, *"Good-bye, lads";* and then to the Master-at-arms beside him—*"Good-bye, Master-at-arms."*

He now stepped on to the platform. . . . The rope was placed over his head and adjusted to his neck. . . . I cast my eyes to the

Flag Ship. The fatal signal to execute the sentence of the court, was, that instant, being run up. I turned away my face, and two or three times paced across the forecastle deck. The cap was now drawn over the face of the prisoner. As I drew near him the words came from his lips, in earnestness of entreaty:

"Oh God—have mercy on my soul!"

"Oh Christ—have mercy on my soul!"

"O Jesus, into thy hands I commit my spirit!"

It was while one of the last two sentences was dwelling on the lips of this unfortunate man, that the officer, leaning over the fore-castle deck, said, in rather a suppressed voice, "FIRE!" At the same moment, the platform on which the prisoner stood, rose—the prisoner himself bounded a few feet in the air as the loud report of the cannon echoed over the waters; and, as if no space had intervened, the now senseless but one moment before praying man, was hanging, at the fore-yard-arm of the Saint Mary's! No muscle moved—no limb contracted. The concussion of the gun had indeed killed him; and there he hung the spectacle for a fleet to look upon, as evidence that a broken law will have its penalty.[13]

X

THE BURIAL

On board the Portsmouth *in the Pacific, 1845, Yeoman Joseph T. Downey, USN, offers a picture of the tragic death of his friend, Jack Whelean, and his burial at sea.*

. . . On 5th Sept. at 5 in the evening we hove up our anchor in the Port of Oahu and with a fine fair wind stood out to sea; after we were fairly underway and time for conversation was gained, some of the Old Growls were bitter in their complaints of the folly of sailing on Friday, and prognosticated bad weather and a long passage, if nothing worse. And sure enough, seemingly as if in fulfillment of part of their sayings, hardly had the Pilot left us when the wind died away stark calm, and for the whole night we lay rolling and tumbling like a log on the Ocean. Next morning however we caught a good breeze, and though for the first few days everything promised fair, it soon left us and we had nothing but a succession of calms or light head winds.

The passage we were now making rarely occupies vessels of even ordinary Sailing capabilities over 15 or 20 days, and we had hoped to make it much sooner, but in this we were disappointed as day after day rolled by and we still made no perceptible progress, the "Old Croakers" found plenty of food to growl on. Wherever you went about decks, and saw a group collected together, among them you would find one of these old fellows, who upon the least chance would declaim loudly against the hazard we ran of sailing on the unlucky day, and prognosticating that the long passage would not be the only misfortune that would happen to us. But few however of their young shipmates paid much heed to them and merely listened to the yarns they would spin about what had happened to vessels whose Masters had dared to sail on the forbidden day in times long past. But strange as it may seem, as if to confirm their superstition and put to shame all unbelievers, an accident and a serious one too, did happen.

Among our Crew we had but few old men (a sailor is called old at 35 or 40) but prominent among these few was Jack Whelean, a native of Philadelphia, a thorough sailor, and as jovial a messmate as ever ate a scouse. . . . Somewhere near the hour of 1 A. M. on the 24th of Sept. I was aroused from my sleep by hearing a cry, or groan from some person seemingly in great agony. . . .

As I opened the door the first object that met my gaze was my poor friend Jack stretched out upon the floor, surrounded by a pool of blood that seemed to stream forth from all parts of his body—his head was badly cut, his left eye closed altogether, while from the appearance of his legs I at once thought they were both crushed to pieces. I soon learned that he had fallen from the fore yard (where he had gone on duty) upon the Forecastle. It seems that after rigging out the Steering Sail Boom, some part of the running gear had got jammed, and in endeavoring to jerk it clear, he had lost his balance and fallen the whole distance (about 40 feet), striking upon his left knee, shattering that leg to a mass of jelly, breaking his right leg, and cutting his head deeply.

Our surgeons were immediately in attendance, but it was almost impossible to ascertain at once the extent of the injury sustained. He was a very lusty man, and in falling from such a height it was but reasonable to suppose he must have jarred his whole system. Amputation was suggested, but such was his corpulency that upon consultation, they decided that it was more than probable that he would die under the operation, and he could *but* lose his life. At all events, of the two evils they chose the least. The weather was cool and favorable, and by arranging the limbs in the best possible manner there was a chance (if he was not inwardly injured) of his recovery, but still he would be a cripple for life. This plan was accordingly adopted, and his leg was placed in a fracture case, the broken parts arranged with care, and nature left to do her own work.

Two or more of his messmates, as duty would allow, were constantly with him, and go where you would about decks the first question that greeted the ear would be, how is Jack? Is there any chance for him? And sorrow, deep heartfelt sorrow, prevailed among all. The Old Prophets, though they were as much shocked as any one, would however point at it as a fulfillment of their auguries, and became if possible more strongly convinced than ever in the doctrine of fatality.

On the morning of the accident, group after group would collect around the [Sick] Bay, all anxious to catch a glimpse at the sufferer or eager to assume the post of watcher by his side . . . From his continued insanity the surgeon pronounced that a concussion of the brain had been added to his other misfortunes, and that he could not long survive. The Bell, which hung under the Forecastle immediately above his head, was muffled, and the mournful sound emitted by it served to remind every one of the sad occurrence and its expected consequences and cast a deep gloom over every countenance. Orders were passed in a low tone, footsteps that always seemed unusually heavy, now seemed to fall noiselessly upon the ear, and all conversation in the neighborhood of the Bay was carried on in Whispers. . . . Soon after 8 A. M. on the 25th he sank into a stupor from which he never aroused, but continued breathing heavily until 5 P. M. when he quietly breathed his last. . . .

Early on the morning of the 26th the Body, after being sewed up in a Hammock and having a 64 Pound shot lashed at the feet, was removed to the Quarter Deck and covered with a Jack. At noon the call of "All Hands Bury the dead" summoned us on deck, where the crew were all assembled neatly in Blue. The Main Topsail **was**

146

thrown aback, the colors half masted, and the body being lain upon a plank in the Lee Gangway, our Captain began the beautiful and impressive service of the Episcopal Church. Solemnity was stamped on the countenance of every one, and at the words "we commit his body to the deep" the Jack was withdrawn, the inner end of the Plank raised, the body slid off, a sullen plunge was heard, and the waters closed over the remains of poor Whelean.

During the whole of the ceremony a large Bird was seen hovering round the Ship and shortly after we had filed away, he was joined by a second, though from whence he came was a mystery. The two continued for some seconds to circle round the spot, and then majestically rose out of sight. . . . As soon as the Hands were piped down, the gloom which had remained as long as the body was on board suddenly flew away, the usual noise and bustle commenced, and though the Sad fate of Jack was often mentioned, it was always spoken of as one of the things that have been. . . .[14]

XI

MEXICO

Although the Mexican War, 1846–1848, was primarily military, the United States Navy played an important part. Almost unopposed, ships secured sea communications, supported troop landings, and maintained an effective blockade. This war was the Army's show, although the Navy was essential in establishing control of California.

The following official dispatches by Commodore David Conner, Captain J. A. Aulick, Commodore Matthew C. Perry, Lieutenant David D. Porter, and Commander Thomas O. Selfridge are concerned with the successful, large-scale amphibious operation at Sacrificios, three miles south of Veracruz and the landings at Tobasco and Muleje.

United States Ship Raritan,
Off Sacrificios, March 10, 1847.
Sir: In my last despatch . . . I informed the department of the arrival of Major General Scott at Anton Lizardo. Most of the trans-

ports with troops, and the material of the army, having arrived about the same time, a speedy disembarkation was resolved upon; it being important that we should effect a landing before a norther should come on, as this would delay us two or three days.

After a joint reconnoissance, made by the general and myself, in the steamer "Petrita," the beach due west from Sacrificios . . . was selected as the most suitable for the purpose. The anchorage near this place being extremely contracted, it became necessary, in order to avoid crowding it with an undue number of vessels, to transfer most of the troops to the vessels of war, for transportation to Sacrificios.

Accordingly, on the morning of the 9th at daylight, all necessary preparations, such as launching and numbering the boats, detailing officers, &c., having been previously made, this transfer was commenced. The frigates received on board between twenty-five and twenty-eight hundred men, with their arms and accoutrements; and the sloops and smaller vessels numbers in proportion. This part of the movement was completed very successfully about 11 o'clock a. m., and a few minutes thereafter, the squadron under my command, accompanied by the commanding general, in the steamship Massachusetts, and such of the transports as had been selected for the purpose, got under way.

The weather was very fine—indeed we could not have been more favored in this particular than we were. We had a fresh and yet gentle breeze from the southeast, and a perfectly smooth sea.

The passage to Sacrificios occupied us between two and three hours. Each ship came in, and anchored without the slightest disorder or confusion in the small space allotted to her, the harbor being very much crowded, notwithstanding the number of transports we had left behind. The disembarkation commenced on the instant. Whilst we were transferring the troops from the ships to the surf-boats, (sixty-five in number,) I directed the steamers "Spitfire" and "Vixen," and the five gun-boats, to form in a line parallel with and close into the beach, to cover the landing. This order was promptly executed, and these small vessels, from the lightness of their draughts, were enabled to take positions within good grape range of the shore.

As the boats severally received their complements of troops, they assembled in a line abreast, between the fleet and the gun-boats; and, when all were ready, they pulled in together under the guidance of a number of the officers of the squadron who had been detailed for this

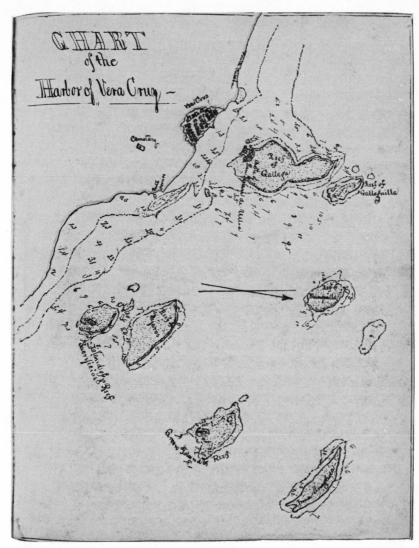

Map of Vera Cruz drawn during Mexican War.

purpose. General Worth commanded this, the first line of the army, and had the satisfaction of forming his command on the beach and neighbouring heights just before sunset. Four thousand five hundred men were thus thrown on shore almost simultaneously. No enemy appeared to offer us the slightest opposition. The first line being landed, the boats, in successive trips, relieved the men-of-war and transports of their remaining troops, by 10 o'clock, p. m.

The whole army, (save a few straggling companies,) consisting of upwards of ten thousand men, were thus safely deposited on shore, without the slightest accident of any kind. . . .

The general-in-chief landed this morning, and the army put itself in motion at an early hour, to form its lines around the city. There has been some distant firing of shot and shells from the town and castle upon the troops as they advanced, but without result.

I am still of the opinion . . . as to the inability of the enemy to hold out for any length of time. The castle has, at most, but four or five weeks' provisions, and the town about enough for the same time.

I am, very respectfully, &c.

D. CONNER,
Commanding home squadron.

Hon. John Y. Mason
Secretary of the Navy, Washington.

U. S. Ship Potomac, Off Sacrificios, March 25, 1847
Sir: In compliance with your letter this moment received, calling for a report of my proceedings in command of the detachment on shore yesterday, I have the honor to state, that the battery of three 8-inch Paixhan guns, and three long 32 pounders, landed from the squadron, was turned over to me at 10 o'clock, a. m., by the accomplished engineer officer who constructed it, (Captain R. E. Lee,) who, as well as Lieutenants Smith of the engineers, and Williams, aid to General Scott, remained in the battery throughout the fire. The enemy having but a few minutes before discovered our position, commenced the attack upon us. I immediately ordered the guns to be unmasked, and the firing commenced on the enemy's batteries, which was steadily and deliberately continued until about half-past two, p. m., when our last charge of ammunition, of which we had only about fifty rounds to each gun, was expended. By this time our sand-bag breastworks and traverses were much dilapidated by the shot of the enemy and the concussion of our own heavy pieces. I now directed the embrasures to

be closed up with sand bags (for the suggestion of which I must thank Captain Lee,) and everybody to seek the best shelter from shot that the work afforded, until the ammunition we expected should arrive.

At 4 o'clock, Captain Mayo with a fresh supply of ammunition, and a relief party of officers and men arrived. I then relinquished the command to him, agreeably to your order, and returned to my ship. Our loss was four men killed, and one officer and five men wounded, one of the latter mortally, (since dead,) the others slightly. When it is considered that we had the concentrated and very active fire of five of the enemy's batteries upon us, at a distance of less than eight hundred yards, besides occasional shells from the castle of "San Juan de Ulloa," it is a matter of surprise that our loss is so small. It affords me great satisfaction to add that every officer and man in the battery behaved with the utmost coolness, activity, and cheerfulness.

Commander A. S. Mackenzie, who had superintended the duty of placing the guns in battery, promptly tendered his services to me and took charge of one of the 32-pounders, which he managed with great skill, and I doubt not with great effect upon the enemy's works. In the course of the firing, the flag on one of the enemy's forts was brought down by a shot from a gun fired by Lieutenant Baldwin. It was, however, quickly again displayed from the same flagstaff. It is due to Midshipman Allen McLane that I should not omit to mention that a call for volunteers to cut away some brushwood which obstructed the view to a battery on which we wished to direct our fire, he sprang through an embrasure followed by two men, (Wm. Cavenaugh, seaman, the name of the other I have not been able to ascertain,) and amidst a shower of balls, quickly removed the obstruction, for which gallantry I complimented him on the spot. I am, however, sure that any other officer present would have been happy of an opportunity to have done the same. . . .

I am, very respectfully, your obedient servant,

J. A. AULICK, *Captain.*

To Commodore M. C. Perry,
Commanding home squadron, off Sacrificios.

United States Flag-Ship Mississippi,
Off Tobasco river, June 24, 1847.

Sir: Having . . . informed the department of my intention no longer to delay the attack upon the enemy's forces concentrated near the city of Tobasco, I anchored on the 13th off the bar of the river with a detachment of the squadron, consisting of the Mississippi, Albany, Raritan, John Adams, Decatur, Germantown, Stromboli, Vesuvius, Washington, and the steamers Scorpion, Spitfire, Scourge, and Vixen; the Etna and Bonita being stationed in the river.

On the 14th, the flotilla having crossed the bar, the barges and surf-boats containing seven pieces of artillery, and as many officers, seamen, and marines as could [be] spared from each of the vessels at anchor outside, with a detachment of forty seamen and marines from the Potomac, were then towed by the steamers across the bar, and joining the vessels at Frontera, the whole force was formed into line and proceeded up the river. . . .

When on the following day . . . information was obtained from an Indian that the enemy had thrown up breastworks in the thick chapparel lining the banks of the river at three different points, where they had posted in ambush armed parties in considerable force.

From all the positions indicated by the Indian the vessels and boats were fired upon, but the fire of the enemy was immediately silenced by our great guns and musketry. At the second position one of the seamen of the Vesuvius was severely wounded, and at the third, Lieutenant Wm. May received an escopet ball in his arm, and three men were slightly wounded. Lieutenant May at the time of receiving his wound was engaged in co-operation with Lieutenant James Alden in sounding and examining the obstructions placed by the enemy in the channel directly opposite to the breastwork.

Considering it doubtful whether the steamers could pass the obstructions without inconvenient delay, and being anxious to reach the main body of the enemy, I ordered their commanders to use every effort to ascend the river, and determined myself not to wait the experiment, but to land with the infantry and artillery, having previously made all the arrangements for landing, and forming the line of march. The barges and surf-boats were manned and formed opposite to the point selected for the landing, called "the seven palm trees," and near to the third entrenchment of the enemy, which had been a moment before raked by the great guns of the flotilla.

Everything being in readiness, I took the lead with my boat, accompanied by Captain Mayo—a volunteer, and acting as adjutant general—in another boat, and giving the order "to go ahead," the whole force, with three hearty cheers, pushed for the shore, landed and formed in separate columns on the bank, under the direction of Captain Mayo. In the space of ten minutes every officer and man was on shore and in position, with seven pieces of artillery, which were taken from the boats and hauled up a bank of twenty feet in height and nearly perpendicular, by the main strength of the officers and men attached to them. Boats were then sent for the three pieces belonging to the bomb vessels, and in twenty-five minutes the entire column of more than eleven hundred strong, with ten pieces of artillery, was in motion towards the city. Its march, however, was very much retarded by the difficulty of moving through the high prairie grass and the occasional thickets of chapparel; yet in opposition to all obstacles which presented themselves, and the excessive heat of the day, the column moved steadily on, preceded by the pioneers, and driving back with its artillery and advanced guard the outposts of the enemy entrenched by breastworks.

Meanwhile, the steamers had succeeded in crossing the obstructions in the channel, and proceeded gallantly up in face of the fire of the main battery of six guns and a body of infantry lining the entrenchments; and after exchanging a few shots with but slight injury to us, the enemy retired hastily from their defences, a measure undoubtedly precipitated by the proximity of our advancing column. At a little after four in the afternoon, I entered the city with the entire force of infantry and artillery, and took quiet possession of the public quarters. . . .

From the best information I have been able to obtain from several sources the enemy's force in action, on the 16th, may be estimated at fourteen hundred strong, and their loss about thirty killed, which, compared with the force under my command, and considering the advantages of his fortified position, may render the smallness of our loss remarkable.

I am sir, with great respect, your obedient servant,

M. C. PERRY,
Commanding Home Squadron

The Hon. J. Y. Mason,
Secretary of the Navy.

U. S. Steamer Spitfire, [off Tobasco], June 26, 1847
Sir: Agreeably to your order that I should furnish you with a report of the skirmish between a detachment of seamen from this vessel

and a party of Mexicans, yesterday evening, I have to state that after the exercise of small arms and field artillery in the plaza, I marched my men back of the Spanish consul's house, intending to take them through the different streets, for the purpose of giving confidence to the inhabitants. At the back of the consul's house, my attention was very much attracted by the facilities with which an enemy of ordinary capacity could approach directly to the plaza without fear of detection, as no sentries could perceive them, and followed the path, seeking the marks of those persons who fired on the sentries the night previous.

We had sufficient evidence that this path had been used by the Mexicans; we tracked them to a house not a musket-shot from the square, where they had evidently left their horses, which we supposed to have been twelve or fourteen, by the appearances. This path brought us into the main street, and I was about to return to the plaza, when muskets were fired by an officer and three men whom I had sent in advance to give the alarm, if necessary. I went to the spot, and found that they had fired on the mounted picket guard of the Mexicans, who immediately retreated. Here, it appears, the Mexicans had rendezvoused for some days, (judging from their fires being still lighted, and the marks of soldiers,) and after reconnoitring the place, I marched about again with the intention of returning to the plaza, not thinking it prudent to go any farther. We had not returned twenty yards before we were attacked, in the rear, by a large body of men, (I should say over a hundred, judging from their heavy fire,) and I ordered the men immediately to attack them, which they did with great spirit, and followed them up from bush to bush and house to house. At this time I had with me only twenty men and four officers; but our carbineers, consisting of twenty-five men, came up when they heard the firing, and took position on the right side of the road, where they kept up a galling fire upon every man who showed himself until the fire of the Mexicans ceased entirely. . . .

The damage we did the enemy I am unable to state, as I only saw two men fall myself, not knowing what force the enemy might be in. I made no search, but marched my men into town, bringing in the wounded; one severely hurt, and one other slightly. These are the facts connected with the case. No men could have behaved better than the officers and seamen, while under a heavy fire, and opposed to an invisible enemy, who was shooting at them from every bush. . . .

Much to my surprise, the Mexicans behaved with great spirit, and yielded their ground apparently with great reluctance. This convinces me that they were in much greater force than I had at first estimated.

I do not think any danger whatever is to be apprehended from an attack on the town from the class of men we encountered. They were what is termed regulars; but their firing was so bad that it was completely thrown away. I have since learned, that they retreated that night to the nearest village.

Very respectfully, your obedient servant,

D. D. PORTER,
Lieutenant Commanding.

Commander G. J. Van Brunt,
  Governor of Tobasco.

U. S. Ship Dale,
Harbor of La Paz, Lower California, October 10, 1847.
Sir: I have the honor to report that, after arriving off San José with the Congress, September 19, and Captain Lavallette having informed me that no news of importance had been received there, I proceeded, in obedience to my instructions, to this place, where I arrived September 23. I found the Lexington here, and immediately directed Lieutenant Commanding Benley to prepare for sea and proceed to Monterey.

Upon the representation of Lieutenant Colonel Burton, that disaffection to our authority existed at Loreto and Muleje, and that munitions of war had been landed at this latter place from Guaymas, I prepared this ship for sea, sailed from hence on the 26th ultimo, and anchored at Loreto on the evening of the 28th. I found all quiet there, but learned that arms and ammunition had been received at Muleje from Guaymas, and two hundred men had been landed there from Mexico. I arrived at Muleje on the afternoon of the 30th. As we approached the anchorage no one was seen but two persons, mounted and armed, whom I took for scouts. Hoping some one might come off, from whom information could be obtained of the condition of things on shore, I ran in under English colors, with a signal for a pilot.

After a lapse of time, no one coming off, I hauled down the English colors and hoisted the American, and sent Lieutenant T. A. M.

Craven on shore with a white flag, under cover of our guns, to gather intelligence of the state of affairs. He was met by a person with a white flag, who informed him that the place was in possession of Mexican forces; that troops had been landed there from Mexico; that they disclaimed the jurisdiction of the United States, and concluded by a threat to fire upon us if we attempted to enter the creek. On Lieutenant Craven's return, I despatched him with four boats and fifty men, to cut out a small schooner lying about half a mile up the creek, having sprung one broadside to a position to cover the boats and command the valley on either side of the creek. The schooner was brought out, after some delay produced by her having been scuttled and lying partially aground. During the operation, a large number of persons came down on the right bank of the creek, the majority on foot, within range of our battery, and nearly within musket range of the cutting-out party, but offered no opposition to our proceedings. I had given orders not to fire unless fired upon from the shore.

The vessel proved to be the schooner Magdalen, owned by Jesus Mandana, of Guaymas. She was stripped of everything moveable but her cables and anchors. I subsequently burnt her at sea, after taking from her all articles of value, as she was very old and retarded our sailing.

On the morning of October 1st, I again sent Lieutenant Craven on shore, with a white flag, directing him to ask to see the alcalde, and inquire if he had received a proclamation from the United States military commander of Lower California. Also, to offer four propositions to him:

1st. To preserve a strict neutrality during the war pending between the United States and Mexico.

2d. To surrender all arms, ammunition, &c., belonging to the Mexicans.

3d. To deliver up the sails, rigging, &c., of the Mexican schooner Magdalen.

4th. To abstain from all intercourse with Mexico.

The officer who came to meet Lieutenant Craven informed him the alcalde was not in power, but that he would mention to him what he had desired, and that my propositions, to which I had given three hours for a reply, would be answered in an hour.

While waiting for an answer, I warped the ship nearer in shore, and sprung her broadside, to command the creek and valley on both sides to a distance of two miles. The marine and small-arm men were prepared for landing, and the launch armed with a nine-pound gunnade. After I had made the necessary arrangements for an attack, I held a council of the lieutenants, who gave their opinions in writing, advising an attack if the terms I had proposed were not complied with. At 1 p. m., I received the papers . . . from the alcalde and Mexican military commandant. The tone, language and import of the latter's communication were so grossly insulting that I immediately determined on offensive operations, and accordingly ordered Lieutenant Craven on shore with the marines and two companies of small-arm men, consisting of about twenty-five men each, in four boats. Passed Midshipman Duncan, in the launch, with eight men, was to proceed up the creek, taking a light boat in tow, while the musketeers advanced on foot; the other boats remaining under cover of our guns.

At 2 p. m., just as the boats were entering the creek, I opened a fire from the ship's battery with round shot and shell, which was continued at intervals until 3½ p. m., when our shore party were nearly between us and the enemy. The shot and shell drove the enemy from their coverts, caused a precipitate flight up the valley, and dislodged them from a commanding eminence they had occupied on the right of the creek, one and a half or two miles from the ship.

Lieutenant Craven landed on the right bank of the creek, advanced up that side of the valley, and gained the hill from which we had driven the enemy by our shot and shell. While the small-arm men were going up the valley, the launch pulled up the creek unmolested, till she arrived at a point about two miles from the ship, when a fire was opened upon her from the bushes, buildings, and neighboring heights, which was returned with so much effect as to cause our opponents to make a rapid retreat. From the hill the small-arm men were fired at from several ambuscades, and from a place on the adjoining high ground; but a few well directed volleys from our side started them from their lurking places, and drove them up the stream. Leaving a small force on the hill, Lieutenant Craven, with the remainder of his men, descended to the road along the right bank of the creek, where he was joined by the launch. They were again assailed from the opposite shore from the jungle and hills beyond; but a few well directed fires started them out, and, as previously, put them to flight. After advancing half a mile further, where a bridge crosses the stream, and finding the enemy had abandoned the village and fled up the valley, or to the hills—the launch being frequently aground, in consequence of a receding tide, the men much exhausted by the heat, (the thermometer being above 90°,) and the day drawing to a close—Lieutenant Craven ordered a return to the ship, where the whole party arrived at 5 p. m., without the loss of a man, and having but two slightly wounded.

At 4 p. m., having lost sight of our men from the ship, and apprehensive it was the enemy's design to draw them into an ambuscade further up the valley, I directed the signal of recall to be made.

A small sloop was found high up the creek, but being rotten she was abandoned, after an unsuccessful attempt to set her on fire.

The town or village of Muleje, and the valley, to the extent of three miles on both sides of the creek, had been deserted by the enemy, and was in our possession. We could have destroyed the crops, and reduced to ashes every building within that distance; but believing the force assembled there was principally from Guaymas, and knowing the wishes of our government towards the inhabitance of the Californias, I have directed Lieutenant Craven not to burn the town, nor to permit property of any description to be injured. Only one building was burnt, and from that some one had fired upon our party. . . .

Permit me to observe, sir, that in making the attack on Muleje, I was actuated solely by motives of duty. The flag had been insulted, and I felt it was imperative on me, in order to sustain its honor, to resent in the most summary manner the insult. . . .

Hoping that my proceedings may meet your approbation, I am, sir, very respectfully, your obedient servant,

THOS. O. SELFRIDGE,
Commander U. S. Navy.

To Commodore W. Branford Shubrick,
Comdg. U. S. naval forces in the Pacific ocean.[15]

XII

ICEBERGS AND CORAL REEFS

The decades from 1840 to 1860 also witnessed a series of naval explorations and scientific expeditions. Undertaken by a special act

The sloop *Vincennes* in Antarctic waters with the Wilkes Expedition.

Drawings of four types of seamen who boarded captured vessels.
From the manuscript diary of Edward Yorke McCauley.

*of Congress for the purpose of gaining navigational and other infor-
mation which would aid and promote commerce, the Wilkes Expedition into the Antarctic and Pacific, 1838–42, is the best known of
these ventures. Commanded by Lieutenant Charles Wilkes, USN, the
sloops* Vincennes *and* Peacock, *the brig* Porpoise, *and two small
schooners spent several months in antarctic waters, meeting hardships
and dangers, skirted the southern ice barriers, and discovered a broad
sector of the Antarctic Continent. They surveyed some 280 Pacific islands and explored the Oregon coast. The Pacific Ocean was crossed
three times during nearly four years of arduous sailing ship service.
Charles Erskine was a member of the Wilkes Expedition.*

On the morning of the 26th of December all hands were called to
weigh anchor, when we made sail and stood out to sea [from Sydney].
. . . After breakfast all hands were called to muster, when the commodore thanked us for our good behavior while lying in port. He then
told us that we must look forward to a dangerous cruise, and said a few
words as to what our country and he himself expected of us in aiding
him in the endeavor to promote health and comfort, and as to the
necessity of economy in our rations and clothing.

When we were piped down, we took advantage of the fine weather
by sending up our stump to'-gallant-mast, bending new sails, and
building little hurricane houses of rough boards over the companion-
ways for the exclusion of the cold air. Drying stoves were slung between decks to make it more comfortable, and several barometers were
put up in various places with orders given to keep the temperature at
60°. By the 1st of January all the decks had been cleared of all loose
and useless articles, and everything snugly stowed away. Our battery
was made doubly secure, and everything put in good order for house-
keeping or rough and cold weather.

This was one of those days familiarly known on sea and land as
a "weather breeder." The sea was placid, but the sky lowering, and
had a wintry appearance to which we had been strangers for a long
time. We had been sailing rapidly in a due south course for several
days with a rising sea, and the weather had been misty.

January 5. At muster this morning three stowaways made their
appearance aft at the mainmast, and surrendered themselves. They
looked anything but convict-like, for they were dressed in the rig of
our crew, with blue trousers, blue flannel shirts, black silk neckerchiefs,

and black tarpaulin hats. The commodore was much surprised at their appearance, and informed us that we were mistaken if we expected that they would be harbored on board of his ship, and declared that if the ship was so fortunate as to weather the southern cruise, he should do his duty by sending them back to Sydney to be given over to the authorities. The stowaways were then entered on the ship's rolls for rations only, and stationed on the afterguard. . . .

January 22. Weather foggy. This morning we found bottom with eight hundred fathoms of line. The arming was covered with slate-colored mud. In the afternoon we took a second cast of the lead and found bottom at three hundred and twenty fathoms. The bottom same as before—slate-colored mud. The *Peacock,* while boxing off the ship from some ice under her bows, made a stern board which brought her in contact with an iceberg with such force as to crush her stern and larboard quarter boats, and carry away her bulwarks to the gang-ways. While getting out the ice anchor to heave the ship off, she gave a rebound which carried away her rudder and all the stanchions to the gangway. This second shock caused the ship to cant to starboard, when both jibs were given to her just in time to carry her clear of the iceberg. She had not moved more than a dozen lengths before a huge mass of ice fell from the iceberg in her wake. If this had happened twenty minutes before, it would have crushed the ship to atoms. As soon as we gained the open sea, Captain Hudson very wisely put the ship's head for Sydney, where she arrived in a shattered and sinking condition. For several days the weather had been foggy.

January 26. Hove to alongside of an iceberg, lowered a boat, and took in a supply of ice. Filled several of our tanks with it.

January 27. Weather fair. Wind from the sou'-sou'-west. All day working the ship out of an ice-floe. A long row of tabular icebergs were in sight from the south. Latitude 64° 1' south.

January 28. Weather fair. We were now surrounded by many tabular icebergs, from half a mile to three miles in length. We had run some forty miles through them, when we made high land ahead, eighteen or twenty miles to the other side of the ice barrier. We hove the lead and found bottom at thirty fathoms. Coarse black sand covered the arming.

At twelve o'clock the weather began to thicken, and the breeze to freshen, when we stood out of the bay.

At five o'clock all hands were called to close-reef topsails. The reef

161

points were frozen so stiff that we could not knot them. In getting spinning-lines around the sails several of the crew were so chilled and benumbed by the bitter cold that we had to sling them in bowlines, drag them from the yard, and lower them on deck.

At eight o'clock the ship was under her storm sails. It was bitterly cold, and every spray that touched the ship was converted into ice. At four bells all hands were called to work ship. We were in a high southern latitude, on an unknown coast, a terrific gale blowing from the south, accompanied by a blinding snow-storm, a narrow channel to navigate, and surrounded by icebergs. Such was our situation; and all that we could do was to be ready for any emergency, and to have all hands at their regular stations, while the good ship was being driven by the fury of the gale. Suddenly many voices cried out from the to'-gallant forecastle, "Icebergs on the weather bow!" then, "On the lee bow, and abeam!" Destruction seemed certain as we dashed on, expecting the almost inevitable crash. Return we could not, for we had just passed large bergs to leeward. The ship was kept on her course. Louder and more furious raged the gale. Now the lee guns were under water; the next instant the ship rose upright on an even keel.

At last we entered a narrow passage between two monster icebergs that were gradually closing together. Every officer and man was at his station with bated breath and blanched face; yet true to discipline there they stood like specters. We felt that we were death-doomed. One thought of the dear ones at home, a brief prayer to our God, then we nerved our hearts to meet our fate. But you know the song tells us that "there's a sweet little cherub that sits up aloft" to keep watch over poor Jack; and on this occasion of extreme danger, Providence was indeed kind. As our gallant ship sailed onward a glimmer of hope arose, and our hearts grew lighter and lighter as we heard the whistling of the gale grow louder and louder over our heads, while we gradually emerged from the passage. . . .

January 31. No moderation of the weather. At one o'clock a field of ice close under our lee. Wore ship instantly and just in time to avoid coming into contact with it. After lasting nearly thirty hours the gale abated, and then we made sail.

February 2. Found ourselves sixty miles to the westward of Piner's Bay.

February 3, 4, and 5. Foggy, chilly, and uncomfortable. Our sick list increasing rapidly.

February 6. The same thick weather. . . .

February 7. Weather much pleasanter. Sailed all day along a perpendicular, icy barrier, one hundred and fifty to two hundred feet high, with high land behind it. . . .

February 12. Sailed through a great deal of floe ice. Came up with a solid barrier which prevented our further progress. Land could be seen twenty or thirty miles distant. The air was very clear and the water smooth. We landed on an iceberg; and in a valley at the foot of a knoll, cutting through a thin skim of ice, we found a pond of delicious water. We were provided with leather bags for the purpose of watering the ship. We filled these with water, and, carrying them on board, filled several of our tanks. This iceberg was three miles in circumference. Imagine an iceberg three times larger than Boston Common, afloat, and drifting in the water. Such was the fact, however, and some icebergs are much larger. This one had at some time been aground, and had turned over, for we found on it heaps of stones, pebbles, gravel, and mud, where we landed. We saw several large boulders or rocks imbedded in it. What was exposed to view of one of them would probably weigh eight or ten tons. We obtained many specimens of the stones and pebbles. They were of basalt and red sandstone. These specimens from the Antarctic Continent were in great demand during the remainder of our cruise. We had a jolly time while on this iceberg, sliding, snowballing one another, and playing with the penguins and seals. As we had not got our "shore legs" on we received many a fall on the ice, which, we found, was very hard and flinty, and caused us to see a great many stars.

I never saw wild sea-animals so tame and innocent-looking as these seals. Three or four of us caught hold of an old sea-horse's tail, and he dragged us quite a distance. When we reached the edge of the berg we let go and he tumbled into the water. He soon came up again with two or three others, looked all about, and seemed much surprised at not finding us in the water with him. We captured several of these seals, called sea-lions, sea-elephants, or sea-tigers, and they form part of our collection at the Smithsonian Institute, at Washington, D. C. They are about ten feet long, and nearly as large around as a horse.

There were many fine fur seals in the Antarctic Ocean. It is, however, a singular fact that there are no walruses or auks seen in the Antarctic seas. On many of the icebergs were armies of penguins.

They are about twenty-four inches high. Some of them are dark gray, nearly black, with orange or light-gray breasts. On each side of their heads is a bunch of bright-yellow feathers. They stand erect and appear very dignified and soldier-like. They march in companies or regiments, following after the drum-major or king-penguin, who turns around at times to take a view of his old comrades. . . .

These birds, the penguins, keep excellent time with their file leader. It was very amusing to see them walk, they were so very awkward. If we annoyed them, they squawked furiously, flapped their wings, and showed fight. They would nip and bite so severely that even our thick clothing was poor protection from their attacks. On our return to the boat we captured several of them, the old king-penguin and a number of his followers, and, tying their legs, put them in the boat. When about half-way to the ship, they set up such a squalling and cackling that their comrades swimming about in the water would leap into our boat and sometimes completely over it, knocking our hats off, striking our heads and faces, and nipping us at every turn. They came in such numbers as to very nearly swamp our boat, and, to make the matter worse, the king and two or three others escaped, and then how they did lacerate us with their nippers! Just then, three big sea-lions came up alongside the boat and looked in. One of them boldly rested his head on the gunwale. I never saw such innocence pictured in a face as was in his. We expected that he would leap into the boat, or, by his weight on the gunwale, would swamp us, and thus give us all a chance to swim to the ship. Suddenly the old king-penguin, which we had again secured, made a desperate effort and regained his liberty, and, followed by two others, escaped from the boat. This seemed to pacify their comrades at large, and also the seals, for they all disappeared under water. . . .

February 17. To-day began with snow squalls. The snow, instead of being in flakes, was in grains, very hard and dry, and large as buckshot, though not at all like hail-stones. They were pure white. We were surrounded all day by a very large number of huge sperm whales, whose curiosity seemed to be greatly excited by our presence. They would come up close aboard, puffing and blowing like locomotives. They were covered with so many great barnacles that they looked like large rocks alongside the ship. When coming up to blow, the little whales, or calves, were as spry and active in their native element as kittens. It was not pleasant to have them so close aboard, and it was convincing proof that they knew not the enmity of man.

This night we had a splendid display of the *aurora australis*. It excelled everything of the kind we had ever witnessed, and appeared like some enchanted vision. Across the whole horizon, overhead, and all around were seen flashes of light showing all the prismatic colors. At the same time, or in quick succession, it flashed in all directions, and streamed up and down like the lightning's fitful glare. It would thicken at times like fog, and shut out from view the brilliant stars. Canopus and the Southern Cross were in the zenith at the time. While lying on our backs on the deck and looking up, we could command the entire magnificent view. . . .

February 21. Weather moderate with light westerly winds. At eight bells every appearance of bad weather. At two bells all hands called to muster, when the commodore thanked us for our exertions and good behavior during the trying scenes we had passed through, and congratulated us on the success that had attended us. He said that he should represent our conduct in the most favorable light to the government, and that he had no doubt that the government would grant us a suitable reward for our past services. He also informed us that he had determined to bear up and return north; so the ship's head was pointed towards New Zealand, three thousand miles distant. After giving three cheers for the Antarctic Continent, all hands were called to "splice the mainbrace. . . ."

. . . On the 22nd of July, while our first cutter, Lieutenant Alden and Midshipman Henry, and the *Leopard,* Lieutenant Underwood, were surveying the island of Malolo, they ran short of provisions. Lieutenant Underwood and Midshipman Henry, with several of the boat's crew, landed upon this island and attempted to purchase food from the natives. While engaged in trading, the hostage in the cutter under Lieutenant Alden jumped overboard and swam for the shore. Lieutenant Alden immediately leveled his rifle and shot at him, but he dodged the ball. The natives, seeing that the hostage had escaped, raised the war-cry, and then a bloody work commenced. Our officers and crew retreated to the water backwards, at the same time firing and warding off with their bowie-knife pistols the arrows and spears which were flying thick about their heads. Our little band fought bravely, and many of those savages were made to kiss the coral reefs. Midshipman Henry was knocked down by a blow from a club on the back of the head. He quickly arose, however, and seizing his assailant, plunged his bowie-knife deep into the savage's breast. The two then fell together, never to rise again.

Lieutenant Underwood, struck on the side of his head by a club in the hand of a gigantic savage, fell face downward into the water. This seemed to revive him, for he regained his footing and dealt the savage a terrible blow on his head with his bowie-knife pistol, which split his head nearly in two. He then turned towards the boats, when he was struck on the back of his head with a *ula,* or handy billy, which was thrown with tremendous force by a native a short distance off, and fell senseless into the water.

In the meantime Lieutenant Emmons in the *Greyhound* had joined Lieutenant Alden in the cutter, and then made for the shore to recover the bodies of their brother officers. They found them stripped of their clothing. Lieutenant Underwood was just alive, and as they lifted him he faintly breathed the words, "Tell—her—that—." These were his last. He had been married but a few weeks before we sailed from Norfolk. Beside him lay Joseph G. Clark, and not far from him Jerome Davis and Robert Furman. Close by the body of Henry were William Leicester and John Sac. They were all stunned. Clark's upper lip was partly torn away, and was hanging down to his chin. The natives were kept at a distance by the *Greyhound's* crew, while others were bearing the bodies of their shipmates to the cutter. We soon got under way and pulled for the ship. Arriving on board, every attention that affection could suggest was paid to the wounded. . . .

The next morning the *Flying Fish,* on board of which the bodies of the slain had been transferred, got under way and proceeded towards the island chosen for the place of burial.

The sun never rose more clearly, and nothing could have looked more beautiful and peaceful than did the little group of islands as we passed them in succession on our melancholy errand. Arriving at the last one, which was about ten miles from Malolo and uninhabited, we came to anchor. Two of the officers and three of the crew went on shore to select a place and dig a grave for both the victims. At one bell all hands were called to bury the dead. The two bodies were placed in the commodore's gig, side by side, wrapped in their country's flag, and rowed to the lonely little island, followed by other boats with the commodore, several of the officers, and twenty of the sailors (all dressed in white), who landed to pay this last tribute of respect to those who had gone through so many hardships and shared so many dangers with them.

The quiet of the scene, the solemnity of the occasion, and the smallness of the numbers were calculated to produce a deep impression. The bodies were borne to the grave, which was in the center of the little island, amid a small grove of ficus trees. It was a lovely spot that had been chosen. The grave was dug wide and deep, in the pure white coral sand. The funeral services were conducted so calmly, and yet with such feeling, that none who were present will ever forget that sad half-hour. After the bodies had been lowered, and the grave filled, three volleys were fired over it.

This pretty cluster of islands was named Underwood's Group, the little island, Henry's Island. We wandered about the beach a short time, then reshipped and returned to Malolo. Preparations were at once made to punish the actors in this foul deed. The rest of the day and during the night, the ship's small arms were prepared, and parties duly organized for the fight. Several boats, well manned and armed, were stationed around the island, so that none of the natives could escape. At nine o'clock we landed well armed, and provided with portfires and rockets (fiery spirits), which we had found so efficient on a former occasion. Orders were given to spare all women and children.

The first town we arrived at was entirely deserted. The natives had even taken all their household goods with them. We reduced it quickly to ashes, destroyed their yam and taro patches, and made the next town. When the natives first got sight of us, they sent up a shout of defiance. They exhibited no signs of fear, but rather defied us. While awaiting the arrival of Captain Ringgold's and Lieutenant Johnson's parties, we descended the hill, and advanced towards the ditch of the town. The natives boldly came to meet us, with a discharge of arrows, and exhibited the utmost confidence. They in truth believed their town to be impregnable, for it had hitherto withstood every attack made by the Fiji warriors. Its defenses showed no little engineering skill. A ditch twelve feet wide, and full of mud and water, surrounded the whole. Next came a strong palisade, built of cocoanut trunks, placed four or five feet apart, among which was here and there a living tree. This palisade also included a fence of wicker-work, about ten feet high, so strong and dense as to defy all attempts to penetrate or even see through it. Inside of this was a second ditch. In this ditch the natives sought shelter and defended themselves, only exposing their heads when they rose to shoot through the loop-holes left in the palisade. As soon as we neared the fortification, we spread out so as to outflank the skirmishers, and by a few rockets and a shower of balls showed them that they had different enemies from Fiji men to deal with. This compelled them to abandon all the outer works to destruction, and to retire within, where they all united in giving a loud shout of *"Lako-mai,"* "Come on," at the same time flourishing their war-clubs and spears.

Having arrived within about seventy feet, we fired on the fortification. Now was seen what many of those present had not before believed; the expertness with which these savages dodge a ball at the flash of a gun. Those who were the most incredulous before, were now satisfied that they could do this effectually. A stubborn resistance was kept up with musketry, arrows, and war-clubs, which lasted about twenty minutes. In this the women and children were as actively engaged as the men. They believed that it required a larger load to kill a large man than it did to kill a small man. The bows and arrows were for the most part used by the women.

The defense soon slackened, and many natives could be seen escaping from the rear with their dead and wounded on their backs. A rocket, of which several had already been tried without any visible effect, now struck one of the thatched roofs. Several natives sprang up to tear it off, but that moment was their last, as the roof immediately burst into flames. As soon as the flames were found to be spreading, a scene of confusion ensued that baffles description. The deafening shouts of *"Curlew, curlew, curlew,"* by the savages, with the cries and shrieks of the women and children, the roaring of the fire, the bursting of the bamboos, and an occasional volley from our rifles, will always be impressed on our memories. In about half an hour this whole town or stronghold of theirs was reduced to ashes. It was evident that large quantities of water, provisions, pigs, etc., had been stored up in the anticipation of a long siege. In the ditch we picked up a number of war-clubs, spears, bows and arrows, several old muskets, fish-nets, *tapa,* etc., and the cap of Lieutenant Underwood. Many of the dead were lying in the ditch.

Our party sustained but little injury. Only one man was struck by a ball, which did no other harm than to leave a scar on his right arm. Several were wounded by arrows, but only one, Samuel Stretch, dangerously. In crossing the island to another town, we found the

scenery extremely beautiful. In the valleys below us and on the declivi-
ties of the hills were to be seen yam and taro patches kept in the neat-
est order, with the small yam houses, or *lololo,* in the midst, surrounded
by groves of tall cocoanut trees and plantations of bananas. All looked
quiet and peaceful, in strong contrast to the exciting contest in which
we had been engaged, and the character of the ruthless and murderous
race who had been the occupants of the smiling valley.

Soon after descending the hill we came upon another stronghold.
We soon set fire to this town by throwing in rockets. It became too hot
for the savages, and as they attempted to escape in fives and tens, they
were riddled with bullets. Here we were re-inforced by Lieutenant
Murray's and Lieutenant Emerson's forces, who had destroyed several
towns. The natives made a stubborn resistance and even stood a
charge of bayonets. While these transactions were taking place on the
island, the water also became the scene of many conflicts. Every canoe
that attempted to escape from the island was overtaken by our boats,
destroyed, and its occupants became food for hungry sharks.

We destroyed all the towns, and by five o'clock all hands had returned on board ship. The boats on guard around the island were
relieved every four hours. The night passed as quietly as in a country
churchyard, save for the singing of some tropical bird, or the splashing
of the water, occasioned by some monster of the deep.

Early the next morning several natives were seen on the beach, waving pieces of white *tapa,* the emblem of peace with them. The commodore, with the interpreter in his gig, pulled for the shore. As they
neared the edge of the reef, which was bare now, it being low water,
all the men retired, leaving a young native woman standing with the
different articles of Lieutenant Underwood and Midshipman Henry
near her. She held a white cockerell in her arms, which she wanted
the commodore to accept. He declined to do so, but took the articles
of clothing. The commodore knew it to be the custom of the natives,
when defeated and at the mercy of their enemies, to beg pardon and
sue for mercy before the whole of the attacking party, in order that
all might be witnesses; and he also knew that they never acknowledged
themselves conquered unless this was done.

Many messages were delivered to the commodore by this young
woman from the chiefs, saying that they were sorry for clubbing and
killing our little chiefs. This, however, amounted to nothing. The commodore sent word to the chiefs and people that they must come and

beg pardon and sue for mercy before all our warriors, on a hill that he pointed out, on the south end of the island, saying that he should land there in a little while and receive them. In a few hours our whole force went ashore and took our station on the hill.

The day was perfectly serene, but the island, which a few days before had been one of the loveliest spots on earth, was now entirely desolate, showing the place of the massacre, ruined towns, and devastated plantations.

The eye wandered over the dreary waste, to the beautiful expanse of waters beyond and around, with the long lines of white, sparkling reefs, until it rested, far in the distance, on the small green island where we had performed the last rites to our murdered shipmates. A gentle breeze stirred the lofty palm trees and produced a moaning sound as in the forests of our own country. A feeling of depression, inseparable from the occasion, rested upon us and brought vividly to our thoughts the grief which these melancholy deaths would bring upon those who were far away. After watching several hours with much patience, we heard the sound of distant wailings, which gradually drew nearer. Presently the natives could be seen coming over the hills towards us, making a scene which will be long remembered. They at length reached the foot of the hill, when about forty of them advanced, crouching on their hands and knees, pausing occasionally to utter piteous moans and wails.

When within about thirty feet of us, they stopped, and an old chief, their leader, in the most piteous manner begged pardon, supplicating forgiveness and pledging that they would never do the like again to a *papalangi,* or white man. He said that they acknowledged themselves conquered, and that the island belonged to our big chief (the commodore), and that they were his slaves and would do whatever he desired. He said that their head chiefs and most of their wives had been killed. He offered several of the slain chief's daughters, as a present to the commodore.

During the whole time that the old chief was speaking the other natives remained bowed, with their faces to the ground.

A few words of advice were given them by the commodore, and they were then dismissed. They were not long in leaving; the chiefs' daughters with them. The young women were all very pretty.

Orders were now given to man the boats, and we reached the vessels at sundown. . . .[16]

CHAPTER III

Stand to the Guns

1861-1898

I N APRIL, 1861, the United States was plunged into Civil War. When the guns erupted, the Union was unfit for war at sea. Hurriedly, the Navy Department equipped merchant ships, ferryboats, and fishing smacks with cannon, and built gunboats and cruisers. Strategy dictated the blockade of 3,500 miles of Confederate coastline, the execution of amphibious landings with military support, the pursuit of enemy cruisers and privateers. The South preyed upon Union shipping and tried to break and run the blockade to assure a steady flow of supplies from Europe.

I

BLOCKADE DUTY

Month after month, year after year, in clear weather and foul, Yankee gunboats policed the enemy coastline, pouncing upon blockade runners, flushing out nests of Rebels. England stood ready to furnish the Confederacy with munitions and goods. Blockade runners stood poised at Nassau to dart through the cordon of Federal ships and unload cargoes essential for the South's prosecution of the war. Porous at first, almost watertight at the end, the Union blockade denied the Confederacy the tools of war. A letter of Commander John Rodgers, USN, the diary of Captain's Clerk Charles Post, the narrative of a sailor on the Sassacus, *and the letters of a seaman of the* Nansemond *give varying perspectives on blockade duty.*

> *USS Flag*
> *Port Royal Harbor*
> Dec 24th 1861

Dear Anne,

You are at home this evening—and merry Christmas is upon you —the enjoyment of giving and receiving presents—fixing poor little Willies stocking—my heart is with you though I am far enough away from any enjoyment—Marrying spoils a man for the service as far as indifference to getting home is concerned. Home home, rings the changes like bells. I feel sad just now, perhaps because you are so happy with your friends and my contrasted loneliness is wearisome— I am not so much given to the blues as to be accustomed to them. We are hoisting in coal just now—and tomorrow I presume we shall get to Tybee—where the situation is uncomfortable—not a very good harbor, and a continual preparedness for fight without any thing to do.

Yours,

J. R.[1]

(*From Post's diary*)

March 26th. Our duties have fairly begun. Here we are on the Wilmington blockade. Our station is on the southern channel of the northern entrance. At night the ship is required to be kept in the most perfect silence. No lights of any kind are shown. It reminds one of a great hunt, the way in which we lie, waiting for our *game*. Even the bells are reported to the officer of the deck, and not struck; the cable is ready to be slipped at a moment's notice. We are constantly under steam. At present there is a most romantic moon, which I have been getting rather spooney over, but it spoils sport. One of our ships took a prize the other night worth $500,000! "Next, please!" All my soiled clothes are stuffed in the air-port of my stateroom. They do not improve the ventilation.

March 27th. Tried fishing this morning. No luck. Had quite an excitement this afternoon. The flagship signalled strange vessel in sight. The stranger turned out to be the *Iroquois* back from Beaufort, where she has been coaling. I hope that she brings mail for us. My boarding cutlass was served out to me, to-day. So I feel quite war-like. We have just run in to our night position, quite close to the batteries. This is rather an agreeable relief from the deadly monotony of the day work. I am beginning to get quite interested in the game. It is very tantalizing to see daily the "Rebel" flag flying from the forts on shore. There are now two or three vessels in plain sight, lying under the batteries ready to run out. . . .

March 28th. This morning at breakfast the captain remarked, with a sort of twinkle in his eye, "We lost an anchor under the batteries last night, and I am going to get it, so you may have a lively morning. I left a boat over the place and we shall grapple for the cable." Just then the orderly made his appearance at the cabin door, and saluting said, "The officer of the deck desires me to report that the batteries have opened on us and that a shot has just passed over the quarterdeck." The captain laughed and said: "I thought that we should hear from them. Finish your breakfast Mr. Post, I shall not

beat to quarters. When you get through come up and see the fun."
Finish my breakfast! Well it seemed to be the correct thing to do, but
my last fish ball wandered about my mouth and failed to get pointed
for the trachea with perfect precision. I think he was somewhat troubled with similar difficulties. He went on deck and I almost immediately followed. They had got the cable and were engaged in hauling
it aboard with the anchor—a job which would take from 10 to 15
minutes—and there we were, a fair mark for "Johnny Reb" to practice at. Everyone was on a broad grin and appeared to enjoy the sport.
There was nothing to do, so I made up my mind that I might as well
have my after-breakfast pipe. We are allowed to smoke on the port
guard. This is a sort of platform outside of the rail of the ship, and
aft of the wheel-house, which one approaches by stooping down and
passing through a square port. We had our starboard side to the shore.
I lighted my pipe and stood with my elbows on the rail, looking inboard.

Several of my wardroom friends gathered on the port side of the
quarterdeck and commenced chaffing me, and explaining the dangers
from splinters, etc., of long-range shell-fire. Pretty soon there was a
puff of smoke from the battery, then a silence that seemed about an
hour, probably not much over 40 seconds, and some one said, "There
she comes," and sure enough there was a black speck in the air apparently coming right at our heads. No one ran, or showed any signs
of alarm, but my chaffing friends suddenly remembered little things
which they had forgotten to do in other parts of the vessel. I thought
that I too might as well see how the bow of the ship looked, but to
do this I had to stoop to crawl through the port. As I tried to do so
the shot fell in the water about 100 yards short. I at once put my pipe
back in my mouth and, as they slowly sauntered back, greeted them
with harmless banter. . . .

The batteries fired five or six more shots, none of which hit
us, and by that time we had our anchor catted and fished and
stood out of range. So now I have been under fire. There was
not a great deal of gore in this my first battle. I think that I can
honestly say, that, while a trifle worried, I was not badly scared.
Some of the old stagers tell me that that sort of thing is rather more
trying than when you have the excitement of hitting back. The Rebs
have some English *Whitworth* guns, and the old hands were very admiring of the way in which they were served. I caught a sea bass

to-day and we had it for dinner, and it was very good. There goes another shot. It is now bed time. There seems to be no row, on deck, so I suppose it is just ill nature on "Johnnie's" part. I think we got on their nerves this morning. I shall probably hear in my next mail how the N.A.B.S. [North Atlantic Blockading Squadron] made an attack, in force. How the *Florida* was disabled and limped out of range. Poor mother! . . .

April 1st. Pretty stupid work this blockading. In one of her letters, mother hopes that I will not become enamored with this life of adventure!! If I had been in search of the millenium I could not have come to a better place! We never see an enemy, from morning until night. I told her she could get a fair idea of our "adventures" if she would go on the roof of the house, on a hot summer day, and talk to half a dozen hotel hallboys, who are generally far more intelligent and agreeable than the average "acting officer." Then descend to the attic and drink some tepid water, full of iron-rust. Then go on the roof again and repeat this "adventurous process" at intervals, until she was tired out, and go to bed, with everything shut down tight, so as not to show a light. Adventure! Bah! The blockade is the wrong place for it.

At 3:30 a strange sail was reported. Gave chase. It turned out to be the brig *Perry* which vessel is stationed about 10 miles up the coast, at Masonborough Inlet.

April 2d. The captain thinks that there is a prospect of our getting away from this cursed blockade and going, perhaps, to the West India station. Anything to break this horrible monotony would be perfectly delightful. We are all tired out.

April 4th. Same dreary monotony.

April 5th. Muster of the crew this morning, it being Sunday. In the afternoon went up to the flagship to get news. Quite pleasant to be in motion, if only for a short time. This evening had a laugh at the look-out, who hailed, "Light Ho!" on the port quarter. Quite an excitement, until we found out that the fool had mistaken the moon for a light, as it rose out of the water like a ball of fire.

April 6th. A good deal of firing from the forts. No harm done and much powder wasted.

April 7th. Supply ship *Massachusetts* arrived to-day bringing fresh meat, ice and papers. No mail, as she came from Philadelphia. Ordered, by the flagship, to stand to sea after a sail reported in the northward. The sail was, of course, the brig *Perry. State of Georgia* arrived from Beaufort this evening. I suppose she brings letters. . . .

April 16th. This morning the watch on deck heard a steamer, slipped anchor, but could not find her. As soon as day broke we had the pleasure of seeing her under the shore batteries. We have received intelligence that 12 more are expected hourly. To-night we shall run very near shore and lay for them. . . .

April 17th. Like a fool, slept in my clothes, expecting some excitement before morning. In the afternoon a strange sail was reported to the northward. After standing out, for about 10 miles, overhauled her and sent a boat on board. She proved to be a schooner from Beaufort to Port Royal. This afternoon saw a big steamer in the southern entrance. Hope we shall catch her—not sanguine.

April 18th. *Mt. Vernon* returned bringing mail. . . .

April 21st. In the morning a new gunboat, the *Penobscot,* joined the squadron. Chased two vessels this morning. Of course, one was the brig *Perry!*

Captured a schooner last night. The *Mount Vernon* ran in within a quarter of a mile of the fort, and put a prize crew on board, in three fathoms of water. . . . This afternoon we had been lying by the *State of Georgia* and had hardly returned to our station when the *Daylight* began signalling; while we were answering her, we were in the middle, with signals at the peak main and fore, all at once. Rather confusing. I think though that we got them all straight. In the midst of it all came a gun from the *Perry.* A few more signals and then the whole fleet got under way—a sort of impromptu regatta. Soon all but the *Florida* turned back. We stood on for about 10 miles and are now lying within about a mile of the shore. The *Perry* has fired three more guns. Signals are seen in every direction. It looks as if there would be some sort of a scrap before morning.

April 23d. For once I was right. At about 3:30 a. m. I was called by Thomas, who said: "Wake up Mr. Post, for the love of Heaven! Shure, ain't the crew all at quarters and you not there. Haven't they fired off the little brass cannon right over your head and you sleeping shwately, all the time. Shure the captain's on deck, and there's a prize in sight." I sprang out of bed just as a rocket went off, as a signal to the rest of the fleet. When I arrived on deck, I found a pretty busy place. A vessel had come upon us as we lay at anchor. We had fired at her with the quarter-deck howitzer, right over my head. Thomas was right, I am a good sleeper. She had disappeared in the darkness, which was black as Erebus. You could not see six fathoms on either side. There was a drizzling rain, almost a fog. We slipped our anchor and ran in shore to cut her off, as close as possible, without taking ground. We now had nothing to do, but to lie to, look and listen and wait for morning. We were pretty sure that the chase could not be far off, for if she had been moving we should have heard her. We fired one or two guns as a warning to our fleet, and in hopes of clearing away the drift. Whether they had this effect or not I do not know, but as the dawn began to break, the scud rolled off to leeward in large masses. In the grey light, we saw flashes and heard guns to the southward, and discovered the *Daylight* engaging two shore batteries, between which lay the steamer which we were chasing, evidently aground. She had run in too far, in trying to get out of our way, during the darkness.

We at once stood in, using our 50 pound Dahlgren and 100 pound Parrott. The steamer evidently knew of the batteries and had run in for protection. The only trouble was that she had tried to get too close to her friends. The *State of Georgia* now made her appearance, using her long-range guns and signalling the *Daylight* and *Florida* to engage the enemy. It was a very pretty scrap for a few minutes. The *Daylight,* whose engine was disabled, headed to the southward using her starboard guns, their quick and sharp report, 32-pounders, sounding very funny amid the boom of the heavier metal on the larger vessels. A rapid but rather ineffectual fire on both sides was now maintained for about 20 minutes. The shore batteries fired a quantity of shells, but most of them exploded in the air, leaving little puffs of smoke to mark the spot. . . . We were just warming up to our work when the signal was hoisted for commanding officers to repair on board of the flagship. The captain came back to the ship at 8 a. m. The first thing which he said to me was, "Mr. Post, you had better get your breakfast; I have had a cup of coffee." All this time the ship was not really at quarters. Colors were now made, and the ship regularly called to quarters. I had a good breakfast, and got on deck at about 8:30, just in time to see the ball handsomely opened. The plan was for the *Georgia* and *Florida* to engage the batteries and for the *Penobscot,* a regular built gunboat, to run in and smash up the steamer. We advanced in echelon, the flagship leading, the *Florida* next, and the *Penobscot* following. Not having the proper fuses for the shells, for the 9-inch, we used two pivots. The *Georgia* delivered her broadsides handsomely and the little *Daylight* got in her 32's as she could. To our disgust the steamer also now slowly forged ahead. They had jettisoned most of her cargo, got her afloat, and soon were driving her full speed for the mouth of the river. The poor little *Penobscot* was entirely distanced and out of the race from the start. A running fight, in which the *Georgia* and *Florida* were the only participants, ensued, until we fairly got under the guns of Fort Fisher, when we reluctantly drew off. . . .

April 24th. Everything has gone back to our old routine. Helped the captain make out a report of our *action!!* to-day. . . .

April 26th. Sunday. Was made rather homesick to-day by the bay snipe, which had been whistling around us all day. One little fellow nearly came aboard.

April 27th. Sent a mail on board of the *Daylight,* who is going north for repairs. What luck some people do have! If one of the shells had only hit us the other day *we* should be going home to glory, cool drinks and our best girls. . . .

We had quite an affecting scene this afternoon. An old seaman holding the rating of carpenter's mate had been for some time unable to perform his duties, on account of age and increasing infirmities. He was a good man and had grown gray in the service. . . . The captain had applied for his transfer to a receiving ship, or a home, where the old man-of-war's man might find an asylum for the rest of his life.

When the boat came alongside, which was to take him to the *Daylight,* the captain called him upon the quarterdeck and told him that he was not sending him away because he was displeased with him, or because he had not tried to do his duty, but merely for his own good. He then took him kindly by the hand, wishing him good luck. Tears started in the eyes of the old tar. Turning around he touched his hat to the group of officers who were standing near, interested spectators of the scene, and then mounted the ladder which leads over the side. When he arrived at the top of the rail, he stood with one hand on the stanchion and the other raised to a salute, and in a tremulous voice with a good deal *of dignity* said, "I should have liked to have stayed with you, Captain Bankhead, if I had been able to do my duty." "You have done it, and now you have a right to rest." And so ended the career of an old supporter of the flag, who

179

had gone gray in the service. God bless the old sailor! I wish there were more just like him. . . .[2]

(*Sailor on the* Sassacus)

. . . Scarcely were twenty-four hours passed ere a sail was made and we gave chase. There was no black smoke to mark her as a blockade-runner, but all sails were to be overhauled without distinction. It proved to be merely a schooner heavily laden but having correct papers.

Another and another were chased with the same result, then a steam transport filled with our own soldiers, and the next day several craft of various description. But on the morning of the third day out, having arrived upon the appointed cruising ground, a thin curl of dark smoke was descried upon the horizon.

Down went the helm, around came the ship's prow. Four bells! and we were off for the anticipated prize. The wind blew freshly, dead ahead, and the white-capped waves tossed their spray over our bows, but so low were we in the water that it hindered us but little. An hour passed and yet another, and the wheel-houses and upper deck of the chase were above the horizon. . . . Speculations as to whether the chase were a prize or one of our own steamers had been all along rife, but her actions began to convince us. Evidently a swift steamer, the foam under her paddle-wheels, which could plainly be seen by a glass, as well as the increased volume of smoke from her fires, evidenced a desire to escape. . . .

It was estimated that now hardly three miles were between us, and at half past two o'clock in the afternoon a 100-pounder Parrott rifle was trained on her, and a shot fell just outside the foam of her wheels. Not a signal was shown, nor a sign of slackening speed returned, and in ten minutes the order was given, "Fire to hit." Another shot was fired, and anxiously we watched it, a little black speck in the air, as, splendidly in line, it struck apparently into her quarter. Colors were now flown from her peak, but the mist was too thick to enable us to read them, and still she kept her speed. . . . The gong sounded to quarters. Our whole battery was cleared for action, and every preparation made for the fight.

Was it the *Alabama* or *Florida?* What a chance for distinction to overtake and capture one of those noted pirates! The distance now rapidly diminished, and firing ceased; not a sound save the splashing wheels and rushing waters broke the stillness. Eagerness for the fight yet anxiety as to its result filled every heart. We were prepared for no disappointment aside from those of battle; and when we neared and could distinguish every part of the chase, and read the numbers still flying at her peak, and comparing their interpretation with the appearance of the ship, be convinced that it was indeed one of our own steamers, imagination can alone conceive the change in the mind of all from excitement to indignation.

It would be as impolitic as useless to add more; we turned about and steamed again for our station. Weeks afterward we heard from those who were on board that steamer that the reasons for her not having come to after the first fire were considerably at variance. One story was that we were taken for a new Anglo-Rebel ram that was expected; another, that the captain was in great haste.

Whatever may have been the reason it resulted in drawing the S—— from her station, so that on her return, at about dawn of day, another but thicker and blacker smoke was in sight, in toward the shore, about off Stump Inlet. Not only this, but a long, low hull, with raking masts and smoke-stack, lay below the smoke full in sight. Swiftly, like a hawk on its prey, the S—— sped toward her. Scarcely six miles away, clearly visible as she was to us, almost, indeed, within range of our guns, yet she tried to escape. Too close, however, inshore, under which her pilot had attempted to crawl along in the dusk past the innermost blockaders, she struck, and even then the utmost efforts were quickly made to save her. A kedge was led out from her quarter, bales on bales of goods were thrown overboard with almost incredible rapidity, but they had miscalculated our speed and draught. Ere more than the first effort could be made we were within range, and a shot whistled over their heads. Helter-skelter ran every one for the boats, and leaving every thing as it stood, with the engines still moving, they fled precipitately. A narrow creek led inland, and with all dispatch they pulled up into it and disappeared. . . . The surf dashed against her sides and at times completely washed her decks. Clouds of smoke and steam poured from her, mingling with the spray. It seemed certain that the rebels must have set her on fire, great as was their haste. Quick were the willing hands that lowered our boats almost before the anchor touched the bottom, but it was a perilous task to attempt through such a line of surf to pull boats never built or intended for the work. . . . Bravely the boats passed the first breakers, and soon tossing against the prize, one and another scrambled from them up the ship's side. . . .

The ship was not on fire, though it was evidently no fault of her former crew; for matches, signal-light, and all sorts of inflammable materials hastily piled together, but more hastily abandoned, declared their intention.

Yet, after all, fire would have given little trouble, for almost every part of the ship from keel to pilot-house was of iron. She was in most filthy condition. Paint had long since given place to white-wash, and whitewash to the effects of wind and rain. Heavy cases of goods from firms in New York, and of shoes marked as from Lynn, Massachusetts, were lying about the deck, or lifted half upon the rail in the attempt so hurriedly made to lighten ship. In the hold bales of dry goods were still swinging from the whips; while in the cabin all sorts of articles of toilet or apparel, hastily emptied trunks and valises, bottles and glasses, were strewn about the floor. Her log-book showed her to be the *Wild Dayrell,* of whose speed and successful trips to the Confederacy the public had often heard. . . .

All danger from fire or steam disposed of, attention was turned to continuing the laudable exertions of her former occupants. The tide seemed unfortunately to be falling; for though the surf was still as heavy, yet bare hillocks of sand began to appear in dangerous proximity to the S—— herself. To get ashore would have been almost to insure destruction; for every one knew that in twenty-four hours the rebels would have soldiers or a battery down upon the beach; and while they might at first prove little more than an annoyance, proper exertions for getting again afloat would be seriously interfered with. Prudently, the S—— retired a little further from the shoals, and again anchored to await the return tide. Meantime a strong hawser was made ready and men set to the task of lightening the prize, beginning with the coal which almost filled her bunkers. Most unfortunately, as is well known, a strong penchant exists in a Jack Tar for whisky, and, as is also generally known, he usually manages to get it by hook or crook if ever placed in its vicinity; the utmost vigilance, moreover, is hardly ever able to avert such an issue. There was no exception in this case. The most trusty men were sent below to stave in every barrel, jug, and jar of intoxicating liquor, and guards were stationed over them; but the men seemed to get drunk from the fumes, and as the guards were also soon drunk, it is fair to suppose they were drunk from sympathy.

The coal came up slowly. . . . In fact, the strong smell of whisky soon began to direct unmistakable suspicion toward the vicinity, and, in a word, so many men were getting under the influence of liquor that the officers were obliged to get them into the boats and abandon work.

With the rise of the tide another boat put off from the S———, with a hawser. It was safely carried through the breakers and made fast to the bow of the prize. . . .

When all was ready on the ships, and the tide nearly at its height, both engines were started, the hawser tautened, the prize yielded slowly, very slowly—stopped again, then stuck fast, one long, strong pull and snap! the cable parted in the hawse-hole. . . .

About midnight the hawser was again tautened, and though only the stars furnished their feeble light, the S——— was tasked her utmost to haul that ship from the strand. Again the hawser broke and the effort was given up. Lights now appeared on the shore, and back among the trees several could be seen moving hither and thither. Morning would probably bring the rebels upon us, and it was almost regretted that the steamer had not been at once destroyed. Morning brought no change, however, save that the *Wild Dayrell* was two hundred feet further on the beach. As the weather was clear and beautiful, a third trial was resolved upon.

Boats and crews were made ready as before, when another actor appeared in the drama. A sail was made out approaching from the direction of the Wilmington fleet. It proved to be the F——— man-of-war. She came up, and anchored.

Assistance was volunteered, and almost at the same moment four boats loaded with men and officers put off from her for the prize. . . . Without any ceremony, or so much as "by your leave," all orders were broken down, and like freebooters the new-comers began lightening ship in a very different manner from the first design. Had the commander of the stranger not made his appearance on the scene at this moment blood would have followed. . . .

He, being senior to the captain of the S———, gave orders to desist from work, as it was now apparent upon sounding about her that she never would float again. Orders were also added to save whatever provisions were needed by the crews of either vessel. . . .

All went along smoothly for nearly half an hour, till suddenly the sharp crack of rifles, and the whiz of a score of bullets overhead, hurried every body in preparation for the destruction. The blue lights and matches were this time more effectually piled together, and every part of the ship insured for complete and simultaneous combustion.

Then came the gauntlet of a quarter of a mile along the beach, from which the firing was constant. The wind was blowing directly on shore, and as nothing but muskets had yet been fired at us the sound seemed not to have reached the S——. The bullets whistled overhead, into the boat's sides, among the oars, and through hats and coats, but not a man had yet fallen. Sturdily the men lay to the oars till the boat fairly flew. It seemed utterly impossible to reach the ship without the loss of many men, and in spite of the peril of the situation we could not but feel a sort of contempt for such poor marksmen. But now they have seen from the ship the little curls of smoke out of the bushes, and an admonition to the rebels to retire is hurled from the hurricane deck—one, two, three howitzer shells burst over or in the infested shelter; and now not a marksman can be seen along the shore. The curling tongues of flame that now shot out from the decks of the *Wild Dayrell* showed that the torch had been faithfully applied; clouds of lurid smoke poured from the holds, and enveloped the whole of her light masts, sails, and rigging.

To insure complete ruin of her engines, and to preclude the remote possibility of her ever serving again either her owners or the rebels, both the S—— and F—— took position, and shot after shot was fired through the iron hull. Bursting shells soon tore immense holes in bows and stern, or threw masses of shattered deck and cargo high into the air.

In three hours the anticipated prize lay upon the beach a complete wreck.

Ere the night came again we were off for our outer station; but hours after dark the red light from the still smouldering fire marked to us the spot we had left. . . .[3]

(*Seaman on the* Nansemond)

Dear Cousin I now take my pen in hand to rite you a few lines to let you no that I am well and in good helth and I hope these few lines will find you the same. . . . you must excuse me for not riting sooner

When I [went] from your house I went to Boston and shiped in the navy . . . and went down to wilininton on the blockade and was trasferd to the nansemond. . . . she was a new york tug boat once she is the fastest one on the blockade   I supose you have seen acounts of her in the papers   we have destroid two blockade runers and captured one the margret & jessey   of corse, you herd about it so you see we have some prise money coming to us. . . .

I shiped coal passer   it is hard work but I gues that I can stand it. . . . I had my picter taken the other day and I guess that I will send it to you   it ant a very good one but you will look over that   I had a chew of tobaco in my mouth as usual   I think that I will nock of riting soon as I an giting tired. . . .

Dear Brother

I now take my pen in hand to rite a few lines to let you no that I am well and in good helth. . . . I supose that you no whare I am that I am in the navy   I like a bluddy fool went and shipped I could not let well enough alone so I went and shipped. . . . i wish that I was with you working in the woods I think it would be much better than going to sea. . . . we have all got trials and tribulations to bear for this is a hard world you no   at eney rate you and I have had it bout as hard as they everage but I hope that we shal come out all rite   yet I am an altred boy from what I was once   I have ben through meny a danger since I saw you and expect to go through meny more but it is no use to bid the devel good morning till you meat him. . . . I expect you think I dun rong when I left the army but I dont   I think I served them just rite   I was in two battles and came near dying twice and they would not discharge me and then I could not be contented but must ship in the navy. . . .

Cousin—I now take my pen in hand to rite you a few lines to let you no that I am still in the land of the living . . . we have had very bad wether through march but the wether is geting better now   I have had two fights latly one with the quarter gunner and I had one with Engineers yoman this morning and I didnot get whiped eather time the first one I just puntch till he was glad to go give it up   the other one his friends took his part or I would have nocked sevel bels out of him I tell you—I am rate on the mussel   theys git mistaken when [they] think of whiping me   not that I am braging i never interfear

185

with enney one except they comense it most all of the fellows are ashore to day I would not for there is nobody but nigars ashore here beaufort is a great old place new york cant hold a candel to this place I tell you the houses are twice as thick as they are in new york I came neer giting lost there one time wall to tell you the troth there is about seven acers of land between everys house. . . .

Cousin—

. . . we did not go to the blockade as soon as we expected to for we had to go up bogue sounds becaus they expeted that the rebs was coming to take this place we stayed up there a spell and then went on the blockade we stayed ther a spell without enney thing ocuring worth menshioning till the other night we had a little confab with the rebble ram we was lying on the bar as usual when the hawkwar a gun boat saw us and mistook us for a blockade runner which is often the case and let drive at us and just cleared our pilot house and bursted rate along side and then we signilised to her and found that it was one of our boats it was rather dark and we could not see a great wayes. in about two hours after that we saw a vessel pretty clost to us we didnot no [whether it was one] of our boats or not or whether it was a blockade runner or not we could not tell we sigenlised to her and she woud not ancer us pretty soon she showed a red lite and made towards us we saw then what she was we knew it was usles to stand and fight her so we fired a couple shots at her and then turned tale and was soon out of site of her in the dark. . . . I wish that I was with you I long to be my own master again to go where I like and to do as I like I dont like to be a slave nor I never will be a gain this is worse than slavery a blody site. . . .[4]

II

DEAR WILL

The Monitor *and* Virginia *(ex-*Merrimac*) engaged in the most spectacular naval duel of the war. The Confederate iron-clad* Virginia *thundered into Hampton Roads on 8 March 1862, annihilated two* *wooden ships of the Union Navy and, on the following day, clashed with the* Monitor, *newly arrived. The product of inventor John Ericsson, the iron-plated craft* Monitor *fought the Rebel for hours. Little damage was inflicted on either ship, but a bad leak forced the* Virginia *to retire. Union seaman J. P. Morse, who helped work the shore batteries, was more intent upon recording the event than upon grammar or spelling.*

Fort Munrow, March 13th, 1862

Dear Will,

I am going to give you a little of what we had here last Saturday and Sunday. Saturday afternoon a bout one o'clock the Merymack hove in site coming down the river and began to blaze away at the Congress and Comrland. The Merymack came up and pord a brod side in to the Congress and part on to the Comerland and ran into hur sarbour bows and pord a brod side through and through hur receiving deth in every direction. We were laying so near at the time that they took a horser to us from the Cumberland when they found that they were sinking, but they let us go again and we went in under shore and we went up to the camp and helped to work the guns on the batrey, but the shells were flying in every direction. But about the Merymack: she looks like a large house sunk down to the roof. You can not see anyone on board of hur. She is a devil's machine in the hands of his imps. The Congress ran on shore and struck hur colors and hoisted the white flag as she was on fire. She burnt all nite. It was the greatest fire works that I ever beheld. Her guns were going off at allmost as regular as tho they were fired by hur guners. At a bout twelve o'clock hur magazine blew up. It was the gratest site I ever beheld.

The Minasota got aground so that she could do nothing on Saturday, but on Sunday she did blaze a way well. The furst thing that we saw Sunday morning when we turned out was the Erison batrey [*Monitor*] and about eight o'clock they began. It was sport to see them go rite up to each other and pore brodsides in to each other, but I shall have to wate till I git home to tell you the rest as it is giting late and I have bin at work all day takeing in bales.

from yours

J. P. MORSE

You can let Charles see this and I gess it will take you both to read it.[5]

III

IT'S MADNESS TO REMAIN

The advance of the Union army led the Confederates to evacuate Portsmouth and Norfolk in May, 1862. Commodore Josiah Tatnall, convinced that it would be impossible to move the Virginia *up the James River on account of her draft, ordered her destroyed.*

The last week of December found the Monitor *lying under the guns of Fort Monroe, Virginia. Acting Assistant Surgeon Grenville Weeks was on board when she put out of Hampton Roads for duty with the South Atlantic Blockading Squadron off Charleston. This was the* Monitor's *last voyage.*

. . . On the afternoon of December 29, 1862, she put on steam, and, in tow of the *Rhode Island,* passed the fort, and out to sea under sealed orders.

General joy was expressed at this relief from long inaction. The sick came upon deck, and in the clear sky, fresh air, and sense of motion, seemed to gain new life.

The *Rhode Island,* like all side-wheel steamers, left in her wake a rolling, foaming track of waves, which the *Monitor,* as she passed over it, seemed to smooth out like an immense flat-iron. In the course of the afternoon, we saw the *Passaic* in tow of the *State of Georgia,* like a white speck, far in advance of us.

As we gradually passed out to sea, the wind freshed somewhat; but the sun went down in glorious clouds of purple and crimson, and the night was fair and calm above us, though in the interior of our little vessel the air had already begun to lose its freshness. We suffered more or less from its closeness through the night, and woke in the morning to find it heavy with impurity from the breaths of some sixty persons, comprising the officers and crew. Sunrise found us on deck, enjoying pure air, and watching the East. . . .

During the night we had passed Cape Henry, and now, at dawn, found ourselves on the ocean—the land only a blue line in the distance. A few more hours, and that had vanished. No sails were visible, and the *Passaic,* which we had noticed the evening before, was now out of sight. The morning and afternoon passed quietly; we spent most of our time on deck, on account of the confined air below, and being on a level with the sea, with the spray dashing over us occasionally, amused ourselves with noting its shifting hues and forms, from the deep green of the first long roll to the foam-crest and prismatic tints of the falling wave.

As the afternoon advanced, the freshening wind, the thickening clouds, and the increasing roll of the sea gave those most accustomed to ordinary ship-life some new experiences. The little vessel plunged through the rising waves, instead of riding them, and, as they increased in violence, lay, as it were, under their crests, which washed over her continually, so that, even when we considered ourselves safe, the appearance was that of a vessel sinking.

"I'd rather go to sea in a diving-bell!" said one, as the waves dashed over the pilot-house, and the little craft seemed buried in water.

"Give me an oyster-scow!" cried another—"anything!—only let it be wood, and something that will float over, instead of under the water!"

Still she plunged on, and about six-thirty p.m. we made Cape Hatteras; in half an hour we had rounded the point, and many on board expressed regret that the *Monitor* should not have been before the *Passaic* in doing so. Our spy-glasses were in constant use; we saw several vessels in the distance, and about seven p.m. discovered the *Passaic* four or five miles *astern* to the north of us, in tow of the steamer *State of Georgia*.

A general hurrah went up—"Hurrah for the first iron-clad that ever rounded Cape Hatteras! Hurrah for the little boat that is first in everything!" The distance between ourselves and the *Passaic* widened, and we gradually lost sight of her.

At half-past seven a heavy shower fell, lasting about twenty minutes. At this time the gale increased; black, heavy clouds covered the sky, through which the moon glimmered fitfully, allowing us to see in the distance a long line of white, plunging foam, rushing towards us —sure indication, to a sailor's eye, of a stormy time.

A gloom overhung everything; the banks of cloud seemed to settle around us; the moan of the ocean grew louder and more fearful. Still our little boat pushed doggedly on: victorious through all, we thought that here, too, she would conquer, though the beating waves sent shudders through her whole frame. Bearing still the marks of one of the fiercest battles of the war, we had grown to think her invulnerable to any assault of man or element, and as she breasted these huge waves, plunging through one only to meet another more mighty, we thought—"She is staunch! and will weather it!"

An hour passed; the air below, which had all day been increasing in closeness, was now almost stifling, but our men lost no courage. Some sang as they worked, and the cadence of the voices, mingling with the roar of waters, sounded like a defiance to Ocean.

Some stationed themselves on top of the turret, and a general enthusiasm filled all breasts, as huge waves, twenty feet high, rose up on all sides, hung suspended for a moment like jaws open to devour, and then, breaking, gnashed over in foam from side to side. Those of us new to the sea, and not appreciating our peril, hurrahed for the largest wave; but the captain and one or two others, old sailors, knowing its power, grew momentarily more and more anxious. . . .

The sea, like the old-world giant, gathered force from each attack. Thick and fast came the blows on the iron mail of the *Monitor,* and still the brave little vessel held her own, until, at half-past eight, the engineer, Waters, faithful to the end, reported a leak. The pumps were instantly set in motion, and we watched their progress with an intense interest. She had seemed to us like an old-time knight in armor, battling against fearful odds, but still holding his ground. We who watched, when the blow came which made the strong man reel and the life-blood spout, felt our hearts faint within us; then again ground was gained, and the fight went on, the water lowering somewhat under the laboring pumps.

From nine to ten it kept pace with them. From ten to eleven the sea increased in violence, the waves now dashing entirely over the turret, blinding the eyes and causing quick catchings of the breath, as they swept against us. At ten the engineer had reported the leak as gaining on us; at half-past ten, with several pumps in constant motion, one of which threw out three thousand gallons a minute, the water was rising rapidly, and nearing the fires. When these were reached, the vessel's doom was sealed; for with their extinction the pumps must cease, and all hope of keeping the *Monitor* above water more than an hour or two expire. . . .

A consultation was held, and, not without a conflict of feeling, it was decided that signals of distress should be made. . . .

Rockets were thrown up, and answered by the *Rhode Island,*

whose brave men prepared at once to lower boats, though, in that wild sea, it was almost madness.

The *Monitor* had been attached to the *Rhode Island* by two hawsers, one of which parted at about seven p.m. The other remained firm, but now it was necessary it should be cut. How was that possible, when every wave washed clean over her deck? What man could reach it alive? "Who'll cut the hawser?" shouted Captain Bankhead. Acting-Master Stodder volunteered, and was followed by another. Holding by one hand to the ropes at her side, they cut through, by many blows of the hatchet, the immense rope which united the vessels. Stodder returned in safety, but his brave companion was washed over and went down.

The men were quiet and controlled, but all felt anxiety. Master's-Mate Peter Williams suggested bailing, in the faint hope that in this way the vessel might be kept longer above water. A bailing party was organized by John Stocking, boatswain, who, brave man, at last went down. Paymaster Keeler led the way, in company with Stocking, Williams, and one or two others; and though the water was now waist-deep, and they knew the vessel was liable to go down at almost any moment, they worked on nobly, throwing out a constant stream of water from the turret.

Meanwhile the boat launched from the *Rhode Island* had started, manned by a crew of picked men. . . .

For hours they had watched the raging sea. Their captain and they knew the danger; every man who entered that boat did it at peril of his life; and yet all were ready. . . .

We watched her with straining eyes, for few thought she could live to reach us. She neared; we were sure of her, thank God!

In this interval the cut hawser had become entangled in the paddle-wheel of the *Rhode Island,* and she drifted down upon us: We, not knowing this fact, supposed her coming to our assistance; but a moment undeceived us. The launch sent for our relief was now between us and her—too near for safety. The steamer bore swiftly down, stern first, upon our starboard quarter.

"Keep off! keep off!" we cried, and then first saw she was helpless. Even as we looked, the devoted boat was caught between the steamer and the iron-clad—a sharp sound of crushing wood was heard—thwarts, oars, and splinters flew in air—the boat's crew leaped to the *Monitor's* deck. Death stared us in the face; our iron prow must go through the *Rhode Island's* side, and then an end to all. One awful moment we held our breath—then the hawser was cleared—the steamer moved off, as it were, step by step, first one, then another, till a ship's-length lay between us, and then we breathed freely. . . . The boat . . . lay, beating against our iron sides, but still, though bruised and broken, a life-boat to us.

There was no hasty scramble for life when it was found she floated; all held back. The men kept steadily on at their work of bailing—only those leaving, and in the order named, whom the captain bade save themselves. They descended from the turret to the deck with mingled fear and hope, for the waves tore from side to side, and the coolest head and bravest heart could not guaranty safety. Some were washed over as they left the turret, and, with a vain clutch at the iron deck, a wild throwing-up of the arms, went down, their death-cry ringing in the ears of their companions.

The boat sometimes held her place by the *Monitor's* side, then was dashed hopelessly out of reach, rising and falling on the waves. A sailor would spring from the deck to reach her, be seen for a moment in mid-air, and then, as she rose, fall into her. So she gradually filled up; but some poor souls who sought to reach her failed even as they touched her receding sides, and went down.

We had on board a little messenger-boy, the special charge of one of the sailors, and the pet of all; he must inevitably have been lost, but for the care of his adopted father, who, holding him firmly in his arms, escaped as by miracle, in placing him safely in the boat.

The last but one to make the desperate venture was the surgeon; he leaped from the deck, and at the very instant saw the boat being swept away by the merciless sea. Making one final effort, he threw his body forward as he fell, striking across the boat's side so violently, it was thought some of his ribs must be broken. "Haul the Doctor in!" shouted Lieutenant Greene, perhaps remembering how, a little time back, he himself, almost gone down in the unknown sea, had been "hauled in" by a quinine rope flung him by the Doctor. Stout sailor-arms pulled him in, one more sprang to a place in her, and the boat, now full, pushed off—in a sinking condition, but still bearing hope with her, for she was wood.

Over the waves we toiled slowly, pulling for life. The men stuffed their peajackets into the holes in her side, and bailed incessantly. We neared the *Rhode Island;* but now a new peril appeared. Right down upon our centre came the whale-boat sent to rescue others from the iron-clad. We barely floated; if she struck us with her bows full on us, we must go to the bottom. One sprang, and, as she neared, with outstretched arms, met and turned her course. She passed against us, and his hand, caught between the two, was crushed, and the arm, wrenched from its socket, fell a helpless weight at his side. . . . We were saved, and an arm was a small price to pay for life.

We reached the *Rhode Island;* ropes were flung over her side, and caught with a death-grip. Some lost their hold, were washed away, and again dragged in by the boat's crew. What chance had one whose right arm hung a dead weight, when strong men with their two hands went down before him? He caught at a rope, found it impossible to save himself alone, and then for the first time said— "I am injured; can any one aid me?" Ensign Taylor, at the risk of his own life, brought the rope around his shoulder in such a way it could not slip, and he was drawn up in safety.

In the mean time the whale-boat, nearly our destruction, had reached the side of the *Monitor,* and now the captain said—"It's madness to remain here longer; let each man save himself." For a moment he descended to the cabin for a coat, and his faithful servant followed to secure a jewel-box, containing the accumulated treasure of years. . . . In the heavy air the lamps burned dimly, and the water, waist-deep, splashed sullenly against the wardroom's sides. One lingering look, and he left the *Monitor's* cabin forever.

Time was precious; he hastened to the deck, where in the midst of a terrible sea, Lieutenant Greene nobly held his post. He seized the rope from the whale-boat, wound it about an iron stanchion, and then around his wrist, for days afterward swollen and useless from the strain. His black body-servant stood near him.

"Can you swim, William?" he asked. "No," replied the man. "Then keep by me, and I'll save you."

One by one, watching their time between the waves, the men filled in, the captain helping the poor black to a place, and at last, after all efforts for others and none for themselves, Captain Bankhead and Lieutenant Greene took their places in the boat. Two or three still remained, clinging to the turret; the captain had begged them to come down, but paralyzed with fear, they sat immovable, and the gallant Brown, promising to return for them, pushed off, and soon had his boat-load safe upon the *Rhode Island's* deck.

Here the heartiest and most tender reception met us. Our drenched clothing was replaced by warm and dry garments, and all on board vied with each other in acts of kindness. The only one who had received any injury, Surgeon Weeks, was carefully attended to, the dislocated arm set, and the crushed fingers amputated by the gentlest and most considerate of surgeons, Dr. Weber of the *Rhode Island.*

For an hour or more we watched from the deck of the *Rhode Island* the lonely light upon the *Monitor's* turret; a hundred times we thought it gone forever—a hundred times it reappeared, till at last, about two o'clock Wednesday morning, it sank, and we saw it no more. . . .[6]

IV

THE NOIS WAS TEROBLE

As the blockade around the Confederacy grew tauter, the Federal Navy, co-operating with Army units, assaulted coastal forts, towns, and cities. With the single exception of Richmond, the fall of no city was so important to the Union cause as New Orleans. Forts Jackson and St. Philip supplemented by a log and chain barrier stretched across the Mississippi River, and a flotilla of gunboats, two of them ironclads, guarded the southern approaches to the Crescent City. On 24 April 1862, Flag Officer David G. Farragut, intent upon the capture of New Orleans, moved his ocean-going, wooden squadron upriver toward the forts. The Yankee mortar vessels kept up a thunderous bombardment. On Farragut's flagship, the Hartford, *seaman Bartholomew Diggins was in the midst of the action.*

. . . On the night of the 23rd of April it was rumored, we were to attack the following morning, the rumor was made a certainty at 12 o'clock that night when the few men that had turned in were quitly notified to Stow there hammock, and the cooks ordered to have coffee ready at 1 A. M. We were all anxious that it come off. As we knew we had to go through with it, and the sooner it was over the better. While waiting further orders, the men gathered in little knots about the ship talking quitly of our chances, and fixing their little affairs in case the worst should happen.

One thing had a depressing effect on the men, their favorate officer Captain H. H. Bell had left the ship to take command of a divission of the fleet; except Lieut Thornton, the execetive officer, the men knew little of the officers as fighters. Farragut had no intercourse with the men. he seemd more like a passenger, spending most of his time seated on the propeler block on the poop deck, where he received and conversed with the other officers of the fleet.

the Captain of the ship Wainwright was as little known as the other officers at this time, he seldom having anything to say and spending most his time with Farragut on the poop deck or in his cabin.

during this evening and night the mortars were at their best, keeping a continual stream of shell in the air. it was a grand Sight but fearfull in effect. the shells could be plainly seen as they left the mortars each following the other through heavens like large stars, in a half circle-like path, and dealing death and distruction at the end of their mission.

A little before 1 A. M. the men were served with hot coffee and hard tack many thought that grog ought to be served, but the flag Officer was opposed to it. after that those that had any remaining preperation for the battle commenced to make them. The carpenters gang commenced preparing their plugs and patches to stop Shot holes, the carpenters mate had a canvas overhauls with leaden shoes suspended from long lines, that he might be suspended at any place over the ships side where a hole would occur. the guners mate was busey looking after the lock strings of the guns, filling the divission tubs with water for use in case of fire, and supplying buckets of sand which were placed in the rear of the guns to be scatered on the bloody deck to keep the men from sliping.

the Doctors and nurches were placing swinging cots at the main hatch for lowering the killed and wounded to a newly constructed Hospital in the main hold, those and many other preperations were going on through the ship, while we were waiting for the signal from the gunboat Itasca—which had been sent up to the forts to find if the opening made in the obstructions a few nights previous by Capt Bell and our firemen, still remained clear. if all was clear she was to display a light at her masthead, and all eys were now anxiously watching for that light. We saw the forts open fire on the Itasca, and could see that gallant little vessel, regardless of their fire hold her coarse up the river. the enemy now started fires along the river shore which was good evidence that they expected us. They now sent one of their largest fire rafts down. the last effort they will ever make to burn us below the forts, it like its numerous predecesor pass us without injurey.

At 2 AM the Itasca showed the wished for signal that all was clear. in a moment after our ship give the signal to the fleet to get under way and take their places in line. at the same time all hands were called onboard of us to up anchor. there was little nessesity for ordering, the men were all ready at the capstan bars. nothing will better elustrate the feeling of the men, than that the anchor was secured at the cathead in seven minutes from the time the order was given.

the whole fleet was soon under way and taking their places in line. all this was down quitly without bustle or nois. all seem anxious to conceal our intentions from the enemy. as soon as the ships began moving ahead the men went quitly to their places at the guns, a solam stillness prevailed, all that could be heard between the thundering of our mortars, was the revolutions of our own engine. it was a relief from the stillness to see the lively moovements of our vessels as they quitely took their assigned places in the line of battle, and at the same time all heading for the forts.

our progress up the river was very slow owing to the very strong curent, but good order prevailed. as soon as the head of the line was discovered by the enemy they opened fire on us, our men were all at the guns ready for action but our broadside guns could not bear on them. this is the most depressing experience of our various life. waiting to be engaged and under a heavy fire from the enemy, one has nothing to do to occupy the mind. the mind runs on the great uncertainty about to take place untill it is a relief when the battle opens.

the mortars now redoubled their fire, averaging a shell a minute from each mortar vessel. as we neared the forts the possition of the half cercle of boms in the air . . . it seemed they would soon be falling on our decks. the little gun boat Cayuga reached a breast of the forts about 3.30 a m. She being a little in advance of the rest of the fleet, received their full fire and noblely held her course up the

River. She was soon followed by the Varuna and Oneida. this much could be seen from our ship as we were only fireing our bow guns. our place in line was about the center of the fleet, the vessels a head together with the smoke from the forts aded to an already dark night, cut of from our view much of what was going on a head. as we rounded the point, and ranged up between the forts there was little to be seen but a great deal to be heard. The Boms from the mortar fleet now apeared to be comming down Strait upon us, and realy fell but a few feet distint. the action was now genral the fleet and forts were at their best, we had little to guide us but the flashing guns of the forts and Batterys, and those could not allways be seen, the smoke was so thick.

Our broad side guns were now in full action and ever man had all he could attend to. . . . the nois and roar at this time was teroble, and cannot be described, but to help the emagination, there was over three hundred guns and morrtars of the largest calabre in full blast, double this, by the explosion of shells fired by them then add to this the hissing and crashing through the air . . . confine this in a half mile square, it may give some idea of the nois and uproar that was taking place.

We now discovered on our port bow and coming strait for us, a large fire raft, it looked like the whole river surface was on fire ahead, the flames rising ten or fifteen feet untill they lost their firy tioungues in the thick smoke. as it come nearer we discovered what apeared to be the Ironclad Manasses alongside of it and towing it upon us. our helm was put quickly to port to avoid it. this run us hard a ground with our bowsprit over fort St. Phillippi, luckly the enemy thought we were going to land men, and ran from their guns, intirely deserting a powerfull water Battery. if this Battery had been bravely fought at this time it would have easly ended the career of the Hartford. but we did not escape the fire raft, and the guns of fort Jackson. as soon as we grounded the fire raft struct us under the port fore rigging, and swung her lenth alongside. the Manassas then cast off from her, and left us as they thought to distruction, turned and went up the river, to soon meet the fate he prepared for us.

Up to this time being over an hour at our terible work, the men stood bravely to their guns. as portions of the guns crews were killed and wounded, others would quickly fill their places. All the appliances of naval warfare was in full opperation. the swinging cot at the main hatch was in active service lowering the killed and wounded to the temporary hospital in the main hold. Sand was scatered on the bloody deck. the great tubs of water located in each Division was in great demand, the work and smoke creating thirst. the carpenters mate in his over alls swining over the side asisted by his men, Stopping shot holes. the mens faces darkened and smeared from the smoke and blood. the murderous smell of burned powder together with the smell of fresh blood. the screaming nois of shot and shell in the air, the lightning crash of those that struck us, all together made up a scene and created a feeling that can never be forgoten, and never known but by experience.

the hot weather since our arival in the river had softened the pitch in the ships seams causing it to run in long drops down the ships side. the tar in the rigging was of the same inflamible character. So that we were an easy prey to the flames of the fire raft. in a minute after it struck our side, the pitch from our seams was on fire. the fire spread rapidly up the fore and main rigging on the port side, this was the side we were fighting, the flames and heat drove the men from the guns, as powder could no longer be handled. On deck, the men found them selfs without occupation. this threw the men and most of the officers into the greatest confusion, for a few moments it looked like every one for himself. . . . the men were moving about the deck excitedly without object, & was standing near the main hatch wondering what next. when a masters mate came along and grabing up one of the main hatch gratings he started towards the forecastle with it. the ship seemed lost, and thinking the mate knew more about those things, than me, I grabed up a grating and followed him intending when the ship got too hot to jump over board. I had made but a few steps forward through the confused and excited men, when through all the nois and din I heard a voice. I turned and could just distingesh through the thick smoke the tall form of captain Wainwright. he was moving slowly forward through the excited people calling through a speaking troumpet. Take your places at fire quarters. then taping one, and calling another by name allways repeating, fire quarters, his calm fearless maner, and dignified bearing, had quick effect on the men, calmed the tumolt and restoring confidence, allmost making one ashamed of his fears. Farragut was walking at his side, and Lieut Comd Thornton was industresly placing the men, and directing their work. The captains order was quickly taking up by the men and passed through the ship, so that in a few moments every man was at his station and doing his best to combat the flames. at the first sight of captain Wainwright I droped my grating and started for the fire room hose. at this time also a shell exploded in the cabin, seting it on fire, which made considerable headway before it was discovered, the smoke and flames bursting through the windows, being the first notice of it.

Misfortunes seemed to crowed the old ship and it looked that only a miracle could save her. we were hard aground. the engines backing with all their power, and could not relieve her, in flames from water to masthead from the fire raft, the cabin ablaze from an exploded shell, and the ship the center of a terible storm of shot and shell, the crew in a death strugle with the flames, heat and smoke. the latter at time so thick that we were compelled to grope our way while conecting the hose. at the engine room Hatch I heard this conversation occur. Captain Wainwright hailed the engine room and inquired where is the chief engineer. Some one answered, "I dont know sir."

the Capt.   Who is in charge of the engines.

answer.   Mr. Purdy Sir

capt.   tell Mr. Purdy I want to see him

capt.   Mr Purdy are you doing all you can with the engines. You know we are in a bad way, if she dont back off.

Mr. Purdy.   the throttle is wide opened on the engines sir

capt.   is there any way you can increase her power

Mr. Purdy.   by reducing her water which would endanger the boilers

capt.   well try anything to get her a float. . . .

Mr. Purdy then went down in the fire room that he might better execute the captains orders reducing the water, and superentinding the management of the fires himself. in a few minutes the ship commenced jumping, the viberation was so great, from the revolutions of the engines that one could scarcely hold his feet. She come off, and cleared the fire raft at the same time, calling forth a spontaneous cheer from every man aboard. this cheering was an outburst of relief experienced by all, as we backed out in deep water. for notwithstanding the great exersions of all on board, we could make little headway against the fire while the fireraft remained alongside. the men fought the fire with renewed vigor and soon had it extinguished and were again at their places at the guns.

We all felt that the safety of the ship and crew was wholly due to captain Wainwright. his powerfull voice claimed the attention of the men. his tall form and commanding presence, and his cool, fearless manner, inspired all who saw or heard him, with his own courage, and made men feel that with such a leader there was nothing to fear from this time till his death he was the idol of his crew.

As we headed up stream we came close upon the Brooklyn, just passing Fort Jackson. the flashing guns from her sides brought a hearty cheer from the Hartford. we soon after emerged from the smoke and carnage between the forts to find ouselfs in the center of the enemys fleet. the McCrea passed close aboard of us and give us a broadside. she so nearly resembled our gunboats, that we were undecided wheather to fire and give her the benifit of the doubt. this same cause deceived others of our fleet, and the McCrea escaped the general destruction of the enemys fleet.

It was warm work still, but seemed only fun compared with what we had just been through. This incident, I believe passed intirely without record or farther notice. Yet it was one of the most daring and Recless acts of Bravery that I knew of throughout the war. it was a choice between giving up the Ship, or, blowing up the Ship, and Capt Wainwright chose the later. few of the ships company knew what was going on. the captain still stod near the engine room hatch, while Mr. Purdy remained in the fire room. Some of the firemen told me afterwards that they expected every moment to be their last, and the danger was increasing every moment untill She come off. nor was Mr Purdy less brave than his captain. he left the throtle opened on the engine and remained in the fireroom, forcing the fires on almost emty Boilers. if anything had happened to the boilers the people takeing part in this effort to get the ship afloat, not one of them would live to tell the tale.

We continued to fire just the same at anything and everything that did not fly our Flag. our attention was perticularly claimed by a large river steamer crowded with soldiers. she was approaching us apparently with the intention to board us. Captain Wainwright hailed her and demanded her surender. we delayed our fire for an answer and when it came, "No Never," a full broadside was our reply. it sent her drifting towards the shore in flames.

As we turned the bend on the Fort St. Phillippi side, we ran close upon the monster Iron clad Louisiana. She was lying under the

Farragut's Squadron passing the Confederate forts below New Orleans.

Lt. Cushing's torpedo boat sinking the Confederate
ironclad ram, *Albemarle*.

shadow of the Bank. we could not have noticed her, but for the heavy broadsides she gave us, we returned her broadsides and kept the fire on her untill we past up out of Range, with no more effect however than to dent her Iron Sides.

The gunboat Cayuga held the lead untill she reached the center of enemys fleet above the forts, when she was attacked on all side. the Varuna was next to arive and then the Oneida those three gun boats bore the brunt of the fight with the enemys fleet. the Varuna being the fastest got some distance a head of the others when she was enegaged by from the enemys gunboats. after a gallant strugle she was sunk, not untill she had sunk two of her adversarys. the balance of our fleet then come on the scene and made short work of the confederate gunboats distroying all that come within reach of our guns.

When the enemy fleet found themselfs worsted at all points the few that remained tryed to escape back to the forts, or up to the City. a few of them succeeded. The Ram Manasses was making harmless attemts to strike our vessels as they came up. she struck the Brooklyn, then crossed our bow. the Mississippi was in our rear. the Admiral signaled to her to engage the ram and run her down. the old Mississippi headed straight for her, intending to ram her, the Manasses escaped the butt, but received a full broadside at close range. The Mississippi began to turn to follow her pouring in broadsides all the time, when the Manasses finding no other escape ran along side of the bank, when her crew set her on fire and left her. She soon after swung from the bank and drifted down the river in flames.

We know had an opportunity to look about us, the banks on either side of the river was lined with the burning and sinking vessels of the enemy. the engines of some were still going and the large side wheels revolving with lightning rapidity, as if the vessels were making a wild effort to follow their crews through the woods.

as the thick smoke cleared away it revealed a beautiful morning, the bright sun just showing over the tops of the green trees that bordered the river. our fleet with few exceptions still in line of battle with flags flying from every mast head and peak steaming towards New Orleans with no ressestence and master of all the surroundings. We soon came upon our Gunboat Varuna where she had been sunk in a death strugle with the enemys fleet. her top gallant, forecastle was all that remained out of water, where the most of her crew and officers were hudled waiting to be taken off which was being done. We soon after arived at the Qurintine grounds, where the fleet anchored to have breakfast, and repair damages and care for the killed and wounded. . . .

we found a Confederate Regiment composed chiefly of germans. they displayed numerous white flags. After receiving their arms and equiptments they were paroled. they said they had been forced into the service and were as aglad of our success as we were, the balance of the day was consumed caring for the wounded and buring the dead, two of our guns was disabled, an enemy shot entered the mussell of one of them, breaking the mussel off half way to the breach.

at noon the fleet again started in the direction of New Orleans, the enemy in every way tryed to check our progress, sending down upon us great numbers of fire rafts, and burning ships, four and five full rigged ships, lashed together some of them loaded with cotton, would be swept down upon us by the rapid curent, in flames, at times blocking the river and making it difucult for our vessels to keep clear of them. at other times the whole surface of the river would be covered with bales of coton, Spars and debris from vessels which had burnt and sunk. as darkness aproached the sky in the direction of New Orleans was illuminated by the numerous fire ships sent down upon us which continued during the night. . . .

the following morning we up anchor. the fleet continued up to the city. the enemy now redoubled their efforts to obstruct our way. the officers and men remained at their stations, ready for any emergency. as we neared the city the destruction of property become greater, everything ahead indicated exitement and confusion, large volumes of smoke, occasional explosions at different points in the direction of the city. the face of the river seemed on fire. there was a continual procession of burning vessels passing down with the current. . . .

About 12 m 26 April we rounded the point that brought the city in sight. a large unfinished iron clad pierced for 16 guns passed us in flames. here was a sight not soon to be forgoten. warfs, vessels, and buildings on both banks of the River along the whole front of the city was all in flames. the city was hiden behind the thick smoke. another large Ironclad on the Stocks on the Algiers Side together with the Ship Yard was in flames. the fire fiend certainly had a feast. we continued our course up to the front of the city through almost a path of fire, the men standing at their places at fire quarters ready for any emergency. the hevens now added to the scene a terible storm of thunder and lightning, and rain fell in torrents.

The Hartford anchored abreast of the center of the city, the Pensacola and Mississippi ahead of us and the Brooklyn and Richmond astern, the smaller gunboats filling the space between the larger ships, and all forming a line that brought the whole city completely under the guns of the fleet. . . .[7]

V

AN ACT OF COURAGE

Frequently Confederates ashore harassed blockaders by sudden attacks. In the sounds of North Carolina during the spring of 1864, the Confederate ironclad ram Albemarle *sank the* Southfield *and battled the whole federal flotilla stationed there before steaming off. Several months later Lieutenant William B. Cushing, USN, set out in a specially constructed launch equipped with a spar torpedo in the bow to demolish the* Albemarle. *Cushing in his own words tells the story.*

. . . Fifty miles up the sound I found the Federal fleet anchored off the mouth of the river and awaiting the ram's appearance. Here I, for the first time, disclosed to my officers and men our object and told them that they were at liberty to go or not as they pleased. These, seven in number, all volunteered. One of them was Mr. Howorth, of the *Monticello,* who had been with me repeatedly in expeditions of peril. . . . Six were added to my original force. Amongst these was Assistant Paymaster Frank Swan, who came to me as we were about to start and urged that he might go, as he had never been in a fight. Disregarding my remark that it was a bad time for initiation he still made the request and joined us. He found an eventful night of it, being wounded and spending his next four months in Libby Prison and Salisbury.

The Roanoke River is a stream averaging one hundred and fifty yards in width and quite deep. Eight miles from the mouth was the town of Plymouth, where the ram was moored. Several thousand soldiers occupied town and forts and held both banks of the stream.

A mile below the ram was the wreck of the *Southfield* with hurricane deck above water and on this a guard was stationed to give notice of anything suspicious or fire rockets in case of attack. Thus it seemed impossible to surprise them or to attack with hope of success. Impossibilities are for the timid: we determined to overcome all obstacles. On the night of the twenty-seventh of October we entered the river, taking in tow a small cutter with a few men, the duty of which was to dash aboard the *Southfield* at the first hail and prevent any rocket from being ignited.

Fortune was with our little boat and we actually passed within thirty feet of the pickets without discovery, and neared the wharf where the rebels lay all unconscious. I now thought that it might be better to board and "take her alive," having in the two boats twenty men well armed with revolvers, cutlasses and hand grenades. To be sure there were thousands near by and ten times our number on the ship, but a surprise is everything and I thought that if her fasts were cut at the instant of boarding we might overcome those on board, take her into the stream and use her iron sides to protect us after, from the forts.

Knowing the town I concluded to land at the lower wharf, creep around and suddenly dash aboard from the bank, but just as I was sheering in close to the wharf a hail came sharp and quick from the iron-clad, in an instant repeated. I at once directed the cutter to cast off and go down to capture the guard left in our rear, and ordering all steam, went at the dark mountain of iron in front of us. A heavy fire was at once opened upon us, not only from the ship, but from men stationed on the shore, but this did not disable us and we neared them rapidly. A large fire now blazed up on the bank and by its light I discovered the unfortunate fact that there was a circle of logs around the *Albemarle,* boomed well out from her side, with the very intention of preventing the action of torpedoes.

To examine them more closely I ran alongside until amidship, received their fire and sheered off, for the purpose of turning, a hundred yards away and going at the booms squarely. This was my only chance of success and even if my boat were forced over the obstruction it could never get out again. But I was there to accomplish an important object and to die if needs be was but a duty. As I turned the whole back of my coat was torn out by buck shot and the sole of my shoe was carried away. The fire was very severe. In a lull of the firing the captain hailed us, again demanding what boat it was. All my men gave some comical answer and mine was a dose of canister which I sent amongst them from the howitzer, buzzing and singing against the iron ribs and into the mass of men standing fire-lit upon the shore.

In another instant we had struck the logs and were over, with headway nearly gone, slowly forging up under the enemy's quarter port. Ten feet from us the muzzle of a rifle gun looked into our faces and every word of command on board was distinctly heard.

Four more bullets now ploughed through my clothing in quick succession as I stood in the bow, the heel jigger in right hand and exploding line in left.

We were near enough then and I ordered the boom lowered until the forward motion of the launch carried the torpedo under the ram's overhang. A strong pull of the detaching line, a moment's waiting for the torpedo to rise under the hull, and I hauled in the left hand just cut by a bullet. The explosion took place at the same instant that one hundred pounds of grape at ten-feet range crashed in our midst and the dense mass of water thrown out by the torpedo came down with choking weight upon us. Twice refusing to surrender, I commanded the men to save themselves and throwing off sword, revolver, shoes, and coat, struck out from my disabled and sinking boat into the river. It was cold, long after the frosts, and the water chilled the blood while the whole surface of the stream was ploughed up by grape and musketry and my nearest friend was twelve miles away, but anything was better than to fall into rebel hands.

Death was better than surrender. I swam for the opposite shore, but as I neared it a man near me gave a great gurgling yell and went down.

The rebels were out in boats picking up my men and one of these attracted by the sound pulled in my direction. I heard my own name mentioned. I now struck out down the stream and was soon far enough away to again attempt landing. This time as I struggled to reach the bank I heard a groan in the river behind me, and, although very much exhausted, concluded to turn and give all the aid in my power to the officer or seaman who had bravely shared the danger with me and in whose peril I might in turn partake.

Swimming in the night with eye at the level of the water, one can have no idea of distance, and labors, as I did, under the discouraging thought that no headway is made. But if I were to drown that night I had at least an opportunity of dying while struggling to aid another. Nearing the swimmer he proved to be Acting Master's Mate Woodman, who said he could swim no longer.

Knocking his cap from his head I used my right arm to sustain him and ordered him to strike out.

For ten minutes at least I think he managed to keep afloat, when his presence of mind and physical force being completely gone, he gave a yell and sank like a stone, fortunately not seizing upon me as he went down. Again alone upon the water, I directed my course toward the town side of the river, not making much headway as my strokes were now very feeble.

My clothes were soaked and heavy and little chop seas splashed with a choking persistence into my mouth every time I gasped for breath. Still there was a determination *not* to sink, a will *not* to give up, and I kept up a sort of mechanical motion long after my bodily force was in fact expended.

At last, and not a moment too soon, I touched the soft mud and in the excitement of the first shock I half raised my body and made one step forward, then fell and remained half in the mud and half in the water until the daylight, unable even to crawl on hands and knees, with brain in a whirl and nearly frozen but with one thing strong in me, the fixed determination to escape. . . . As day dawned I found myself in a point of swamp that enters the suburbs of Plymouth and not forty yards from one of the forts. The sun came out bright and warm, giving me back a great portion of the strength of which I had been deprived before.

Its light showed me the town, swarming with soldiers and sailors, who moved about in an excited manner as if angry at some sudden shock. It was a source of satisfaction to me to know that I had pulled the wire that set all these figures moving in a manner quite as interesting as the best of the theatricals, but as I had no desire to be discovered by any of the dogs that were so plentiful around me, I did not long remain a spectator.

My first object was to get into a dry fringe of rushes that edge the swamp but to do this required me to pass over thirty or forty feet of open ground right under the eye of the sentinel who walked the parapet. Watching, until he turned for a moment, I made a dash to cross the space, but was only halfway over when he turned and forced me to drop down right between two paths and almost entirely unshielded.

Perhaps I was unobserved because of the mud that covered me and made me blend in with the earth. At all events the soldier continued his tramp for some time while I, flat on my back, waited another chance for action.

Soon a party of four men came down the path at my right, two of them being officers, and passed me so close as to almost tread upon my arm. . . . This proved to me the necessity of regaining the swamp, which I did by sinking my heels and elbows into the earth and forcing my body inch by inch toward it. For five hours then with bare feet, head and hands, I made my way, until I came at last to a clear place where I might rest upon solid ground. The cypress swamp was a network of thorns and briers that cut into the flesh at every step like knives and frequently when the soft mire would not bear my weight I was forced to throw my body upon it at length and haul along by my arms. Hands and feet were raw when I reached the clearing and yet my difficulties were but commenced. A working party of soldiers was in the opening engaged in sinking some schooners in the river to obstruct the channel. I passed twenty yards in their rear through a corn furrow and gained some woods below. Here I encountered a negro and after serving out to him twenty dollars in greenbacks and some texts of Scripture . . . I had confidence enough in his fidelity to send him into town for news of the ram. When he returned and there was no longer doubt that she had gone down, I went on again with a light heart and again plunged into a swamp so thick that I only had the sun for a guide and could not see ten feet in advance.

About 2 in the afternoon I came out from the dense mass of weeds upon the bank of one of the deep, narrow streams that abound there and right opposite to the only road in that vicinity.

It seemed Providential that I should come just there for thirty yards above or below and I never would have seen it and might have struggled on until worn out and starved and found a never-to-be-discovered grave. As it was, my fortune had led me to where a picket party of seven soldiers were posted, having a little flat bottomed, square-ended skiff, toggled to the root of a cypress tree that squirmed like a snake into the inky water. Watching them until they went back a few yards to eat, I crept into the stream and swam over, keeping the big tree between myself and them and making for the skiff.

Gaining the bank I quietly cast loose the boat and floated behind it some thirty yards, around the first bend, where I got in and paddled away as only a man could where liberty was at stake. Hour after hour I paddled, never ceasing for a moment, first on one side then on the other, while sunshine passed into twilight and that was swallowed up in thick darkness only relieved by the few faint star rays that penetrated the heavy swamp curtain on either side.

At last I reached the mouth of the Roanoke and found the open sound before me.

My frail boat would not have lived a moment in the ordinary sea there, but it chanced to be very calm, leaving only a slight swell which was, however, sufficient to influence my boat so that I was forced to paddle all upon one side to keep her on the intended course. After steering by a star for where I thought the fleet might be for, perhaps, two hours I at length discovered one of the vessels and after a long time got within hail.

My "Ship ahoy!" was given with the last of my strength, and I fell powerless with a splash into the water in the bottom of my boat and awaited results. I had paddled every minute for twelve successive hours and for four my body had been "asleep" with the exception of my two arms and brain.

The picket vessel *Valley City,* for it was she, upon hearing the hail at once slipped her cable and got under way at the same time lowering boats and taking precaution against torpedoes. It was some time before they would pick me up, being convinced that I was a rebel conductor of an infernal machine, and that Lieutenant Cushing had died the night before.

At last I was on board, had imbibed a little brandy and water, and was on my way to the flag ship commanded by Commander Macomb.

As soon as it became known that I had returned, rockets were thrown up and all hands called to cheer ship and when I announced my success, all the commanding officers were summoned on board to deliberate upon a plan of attack. In the morning I was again well in every way with the exception of hands and feet and had the pleasure of exchanging shots with the batteries that I had inspected the day previous. . . .[8]

When peace came, Americans turned from the sea to build a western empire. The Navy, in the face of public indifference, carried on while her ships rotted and personnel shrank. It continued to protect and promote national interests and to explore and chart remote regions. Finally in 1883 Congress appropriated funds to construct four steel cruisers. A corner had been turned and, by the eve of the Spanish-American War, the United States had a respectable force of modern vessels, including battleships.

VI

AND THEN THERE WAS ONE

While engaged in surveying Pacific waters in 1870, the Saginaw *grounded on a reef off Ocean Island, west of Midway. Lieutenant Commander Montgomery Sicard's official report describes the events which led to the breakup of the steamer under his command. He and his crew were marooned.*

Ocean Island, November 15, 1870.
Sir: I have to report the loss of the United States steamer *Saginaw,* under my command, on Ocean Island Reef, at about 3 o'clock on the morning of October 29.

The vessel left Midway Island late in the afternoon of October 28, bound for San Francisco with the contractors' party, (who had been working on the cut in the bar at that place.) Before shaping a course for San Francisco, my intention was to run over to Ocean Island, and see if there were any shipwrecked persons on it. . . .

Thinking to make Ocean Island Reef at daylight, I ordered myself called at 2 a. m., and also that the vessel should not make over four knots per hour, and that the officer of the deck should keep his watch on the forward part of the hurricane-deck, and keep the lookout vigilant. When I went on deck, about 2.15, I went on the hurricane-deck, took a look around with the glass; had some conversation with the officer of the deck regarding the lookout, handed him the glasses, and then sat down on the quarter-deck. . . .

About 2.20, the officer of the deck having reported that the ship had run by the deck-log thirty-five miles since 5 p. m., (28th) I ordered the mainsail taken in, and the engines stopped, (this I thought would reduce her speed to about one and a half knots per hour). . . . .

At 3 a.m. the officer of the deck reported that the vessel was going two and a half knots, which I did not consider too much, as she had still by the deck-reckoning eleven knots and four fathoms, and by patent log six knots and seven fathoms, to run to the reef. Almost immediately he hastened to me again, and reported breakers in sight; I hurried to the hurricane-deck, and saw at once that they were very close to the ship, so I ordered the topsails clewed up at once, and the engines backed. The men on the watch appeared paralyzed, and so slow that I had all hands called, and it was only by the greatest exertions of myself and the officer of the deck that the topsails were gotten in finally.

The engines were all the time backing slowly, but the pressure of steam was not enough to drive her astern with the topsails set, and just as they were clewed up she struck the reef. She bilged within ten minutes, and flooded the holds at once; and the forward body broke nearly off within an hour of the time of striking. The heavy swell on the reef did not give us any time, and the vessel went to pieces so fast that I could barely save some provisions, and all the boats but one, when the forward body was entirely under water, (except part of the spar-deck,) and broken up so as to be very unsafe for the men to go upon.

I worked all the 29th of October saving the necessaries of life; and the next morning I found the after-body of the vessel had been thrown more upon the reef, and then I succeeded in saving a few more articles. The paymaster's money-safe and part of his books were obtained, but no other articles of importance, the guns and all heavy articles sinking in deep water outside the reef and under a heavy sea. The logbook was saved. I feel most thankful to be able to say that all the ship's company and contractor's men were saved. The yeoman's books and stores, (being in the eyes of the ship,) were all lost, and most of the men lost and ruined their clothing. . . .

A very little of the engine and part of one boiler, with one paddle-wheel, and part of the shaft, protrude still above water; but it is utterly impossible to approach them, on account of the immense surf that breaks there constantly.

I have decided to send a boat (properly decked and equipped) to Honolulu, with news of our state; she will carry this letter; I have directed the officer in command, Lieutenant J. G. Talbot, (who volunteered with a crew of four men,) to charter a vessel to come up here and take the ship's company either to San Francisco or Honolulu, as seems to him most economical for the United States, (in case there is no United States vessel of war at Honolulu). . . .

Montgomery Sicard,[9]
Lieutenant Commander, Commanding
Rear Admiral John A. Winslow, U.S.N.
Commanding Pacific Fleet.

The Saginaw's *twenty-two foot gig with five men set out for Honolulu, 1,700 miles away, to enlist help. Coxswain William Halford, USN, endured that harrowing odyssey to Honolulu.*

. . . The only boat saved from the *Saginaw* wreck fit for any use was a small whaleboat 22 feet long used as a gig. This boat was taken out of the water and prepared for the relief trip. She was raised seven (7) or eight (8) inches amidship tapering off to four (4) inches at the stem and stern, and decking her over. Hatches were then cut in the deck so that we could sit down and row in case of calm weather. She was schooner rigged. We made new sails on the island using the cutter spars so as to give her more sail.

Everything was ready, provisions on board, and the day was appointed for sailing—Wednesday, November 16th, 1870. It was bad weather and it looked as if we would have more of it, so the Captain would not allow us to start until it had moderated.

Two days later, Friday, November 18th, 1870, it was fair so it was decided for us to start. All hands were mustered on the beach, the Captain had prayers, all hands joined in, services over, good-byes said, and after all shaking hands, we waded out to the boat, water breast high, and climbed on board, picked up our anchor, made sail, and were off on our trip. All hands were grouped together on the beach cheering us as long as we were within hearing.

We stood across the lagoon toward the opening in the reef and passed out into the open sea. We were now started on our 1,700-mile journey.

The boat was hauled up on the wind on the starboard tack and stood to the northward and eastward. We stood on this tack for three days making fair progress, the weather continuing moderate. When we got about 30° N. it began to change to colder and the wind variable. At last it hauled around to the N.W. and blew pretty strong, but this was in our favor to make our Easting, until it got too strong; then we had to heave to with a drag out to keep her head on to the sea, which we had to do two or three times. It moderated somewhat and just as we were taking the drag in and trying it again, the line parted so we lost it and part of the cable.

It was during this blow that our troubles commenced in earnest. Our provisions were calculated to last 25 or 30 days on one-quarter rations, but over one-half of the provisions were composed of rice and beans and in fact anything that was saved from the wreck had all been soaked with salt water, dried in the sun, then cooked and put in tins. When we commenced to use them they were fermented, causing cramps and dysentery. To have continued using them would have killed us all, so we held a consultation and decided to throw them overboard and put ourselves on shorter rations. We had a small quantity of dessicated potatoes, so we took three spoonfuls a day for a few days, then reduced it to two a day.

Muir and Andrews never got over the dysentery caused by eating the first spoiled food. Mr. Talbot got a little better but was very, very weak. Francis got over it, but was never strong again, as for myself it did not seem to affect me as it did the others.

We took the potatoes, soaked them in fresh water (the boat was ballasted with fresh water) to soften them and make them swell, and ate them. We had no way of heating them. When we left the island we had a lantern and a small heating apparatus, but the fifth day out we lost it. We had flint and steel, but no dry timber, it was wet the same as everything else in the boat on account of the leaking condition of the deck and upper works. We had about five (5) gallons of sperm oil for the light, but it was useless after the light was lost, so I proposed to use it on our potatoes. They tried it but they were so weakened that they could not retain it on their stomachs, so I had the oil to myself and that is what helped me so much. We had a small quantity of what had been hard bread before the wreck (ship's bread in those days was not put up in air-tight tins but just in gunny sacks). A few were saved, we had a little of it, but that was also lost.

After being out about twenty-five (25) days our provisions gave out altogether. We had made fair progress, but nothing was in sight. We had made our Easting as we thought and had stood to the Southward, hoping to pick up the Hawaiian Islands one and a half degrees farther west than we thought. About three days after our provisions gave out, we had the first real fine warm day since the wreck.

The boat had just steerage way, I was sitting on the tiller, the other four lying on deck in the sun sleeping, when a large bird (the Booby) landed on the deck and looked at me. I was afraid to rouse the others for fear of frightening the bird. I crawled along the deck and grabbed him. He didn't attempt to move. Wringing its neck, as I did not want to lose any of the blood, I just stripped off the feathers, divided in five parts and served it up as it was. I can assure you that nothing was wasted. That was the first food we had for three days, except a drop of water, and it was the last for two days more.

I was sitting at the tiller, the other four below the deck, when just as the day began to break I felt something strike me. I dropped my hand quick and got a small flying fish about four (4) or five (5) inches long. Shortly afterward quite a school came swimming along and quite a number landed on the deck. I secured six more, so we had a breakfast that morning. It seemed that someone was looking out for us. The day was breaking fast and I was looking around to see if there was anything in sight when I saw a dark lump astern, but waited a few minutes to make sure that it was land before waking the others. As it got a little clearer, I saw what it proved later to be, Tahoora or Kaula [Kawaihau] Rock, the Southwesternmost point of the land of the group. We had passed it during the night, so that meant we were 60 to 70 miles out. I woke them up and showed them the land. Served out the fish, of course we had to eat them raw, but we thought them very sweet. The sight of the land and the breakfast cheered us all up. Muir, Andrews, and Mr. Talbot were very weak from hunger and cold. Francis was stronger, but I could see he was failing fast this last week. I had lost considerable weight.

On account of the leaky condition of the boat it was all that Muir and Andrews could do to keep the boat clear of water. The upper works were already leaky. The bottom was tight when we started, but one day, just after getting the westerly winds, when we were running before a strong wind under a reefed square sail with a heavy following sea, we ran upon a large log, water-logged just awash, it was touch and go and she almost went over, but the following sea carried her over all right, but it strained the boat so that she was very leaky after-wards. I looked astern and saw a log 50 or 60 feet in length and about 4 feet in diameter that we had run over. It is a wonder she didn't capsize, but it wasn't to be. Funny things happen at times.

One night we came near losing a man overboard. I had just re-lieved Francis at the tiller, the other three were below. He went forward on the lee side and somehow got overboard. I didn't see him but heard him as he passed astern. The night was dark but the wind moderate. The boat was going only two or three knots. We had a strong fish line trailing astern all the passage, but never got a bite until he grabbed it, so I had him on board again before the others got out.

Well, after making the land and finding our position 60 or 70 miles to the S.W. of where we thought it was, the boat put around on the starboard tack and stood up to northward, hoping that the wind would haul more to N. and break us off, then we might fetch into land on the other tack on the Island of Niihau, which was in sight, but a long way to windward. We stood on all day and the next night, but instead of breaking off as we got to the northward, she began to come up. The wind kept hauling around until it got around to S.W. and came on to blow a regular Kona, with wind, rain, thunder and lightning, but the wind was in our favor, so we made direct for the Island of Kauai and got up off Black Head Sunday evening, Dec. 19, '70. The night was dirty and very dark. Mr. Talbot was sitting on deck. The other three below. I asked Mr. Talbot what he intended to do, run into Hanalei or remain out until morning. He seemed very low spirited and solemn like. I told him that it was very dark and the entrance narrow. I thought it best to shorten sail and head her out from the land until daylight. We had stood it so long we could stand it one more night. He said all right, so I shortened her down and headed her out from the land.

We then got to talking again. I tried to cheer him up, told him our troubles were over and what a good time we would have the next day when we got on shore, but it was of no use. He said "Halford, although we are very near the land, I don't think I will ever reach it alive." I tried to laugh him out of it, for I felt very different about it. I knew that I would pull through all right no matter what happened. I got him to lie down and told him that I would stay up all night, and let the others rest, for it seemed that I had more than my natural strength. The last two or three days, I could see poor Francis failing, and if he gave up it would be hard on me. Mr. Talbot stayed below for an hour or two, then got up. Francis and Andrews got up with him, Muir remained below. He insisted on me lying down, which I did, but much against my will. I went off in a doze, and when I awoke the boat was running off before the wind. I asked where we were going. They didn't answer me but hauled up on the wind again. I went off in another doze. The motion of the boat woke me this time. She was off before the wind again, and close down to the outer line of breakers. I didn't have time to get out of the hatch. Mr. Talbot sung out, "Put your helm down; haul aft your main sheet and get out of this!"

I said it was too late for that. The only chance for us was to drive her through it, but Francis obeyed the order, she came out broadside on to the breakers, and over she went, throwing me out of the hatch.

Andrews and Francis were washed away. I came up close to the boat, my arm went through the bights of some rigging, the masts being carried away when she went over. As the sea carried me away, the bights of the rigging tightened around my wrist and formed a close hitch. I hauled myself in close to the boat, found Mr. Talbot holding on to something and clawing at the bilge. I said, "Get to the stern and climb up on the bottom, I will follow you." He didn't answer but tried to do as I said. He got about half way out of the water, when the next rollers came in and rolled the boat over and over. He was then washed away.

After the rollers had passed, I managed to get on the bottom, still keeping the line fast to my wrist. I immediately stripped myself of all clothing, even let my belt and money go, didn't stop to take them off, but tore them down and let them fall. Just then the rollers came in again and rolled her over, but this time right side up. By this time we were over the reef and inside the breakers. I got upon deck thinking that I was all alone. It was then that I got quite a shock, sitting thinking for a few minutes, when I heard a terrible groan. I couldn't see anything until a flash of lightning came and showed me a dark object crawling out of one of the hatches. It didn't look like a human being. Anyway, I thought myself alone, but I roused myself and grasped it. It was only poor Muir. He had been under deck all the time, inside the boat. It must have been like a diving bell, but the poor fellow was crazy. I made him fast with a piece of the gear that was washing around. There was a mile comparatively speaking, of smooth water to the beach, but I didn't know it at the time. Something told me to keep to windward, so I hauled in a piece of one of the masts that was carried away when the boat went over, and used it as a pole to keep her head up. It was very lucky I did, for if I had gone 25 to 30 feet farther to leeward I should have been dashed on the rocks, whereas it was a beautiful shelving sandy beach where I landed. I stayed by the boat until well into the shore in about 5 feet of water.

Then I took the tin box containing the letters and papers. I knew where to put my hands on it. I had lashed the box to the after thwart the afternoon before. I made the box fast across my shoulder, and it made a good life preserver. Then I left the boat, taking Muir with me, reached shore all right and lay down to rest and think. Just above the sandy beach Muir was still groaning and raving. I was very restless, and being naked and cold. By this time the boat was well in shore, full of water and aground. I went off to her but couldn't find any clothing, so went back to the shore. When the water was about awash of my knees, I felt a pain in my left knee, put my hand down and found a piece of wood sticking out of it. A splinter of the mast must have struck me when in the breakers, but strange I never felt it until now. I pulled it out, then my head seemed to go around and I remember falling.

When I came to, it must have been hours afterwards, for the sun was well up and shining down on me. My feet were in the water and my head just above. I tried to get up but my leg refused duty. Then I looked around and saw a piece of driftwood, crawled to it, used it as a crutch then looked about for Muir. Found the tin box, but Muir was gone. Called his name several times, but got no answer. Then I thought that he had come to and gone off and left me. I then slung the box over my shoulder, looked around, saw some sheep or goats grazing a distance off. I made for them. . . . I knew then that there were natives not far off. Got around a clump of bushes, came right on top of a lot of native children playing.

As soon as they saw me they went scampering off screaming as if the Old Nick had them. I must have been a sight to behold! A couple of months' beard, long hair, dirty, naked, and wasted almost to a skeleton! No wonder the children were afraid of me! The grown people gathered around me in a few minutes, men and women with very little more clothing than what I had on myself. But there were none to speak English. I made motions to them for what I wanted, so the men took to the water and fairly carried the boat up on the beach. The women and children went hunting around and found Muir, only 50 feet back from where I had left him in a little gully. He was dead and black in the face. I sat down again and must have fainted.

When I came to there was a man leaning over me, rubbing me and speaking in English. His wife was sitting on her horse a short distance off and holding his. He took off his pants and overshirt and put them on me. Then put me on his horse and took me to his house a distance off. He was half white. He asked me who I was and where I came from; I told him. When we got to his house, he gave me a fresh water bath, rubbed me down . . . also dressed my wounds. I . . . then wanted to be up and doing for my shipmates must be getting in bad shape on the island. He took me over to Hanalei Harbor, Mr. and Mrs. Bindt at the Plantation House took charge of me and treated me as if I had been one of their own kin. . . .

There was a small schooner in the harbor, the *Wainona*, Captain Dudoit. He said he would take me up to Honolulu, but had to go to Waimea for a load of rice first. That didn't suit me, so I explained things to him. He then consented to start right off. We had light winds, took us 3 days to go 90 miles. We arrived off Honolulu Saturday forenoon, Dec. 24, '70. Schooner was anchored off the mouth of the harbor, so went on shore in a small boat. Went direct to the U. S. Consul's office, where I met the U. S. Minister, resident, told my story, delivered my papers and my work was done.

Seven hours after my reporting, the 200-ton schooner *Kona* left with provisions, clothing, and, in fact, everything that they thought would be needed. Two days after, the government steamer *Kilauea* left and arrived at the island Jan. 4th, '71, late in the afternoon with a duplicate lot of stores to those of the schooner *Kona,* for fear of an accident or calm weather. Took all hands on board on the 5th and brought them to Honolulu, arriving there about the 15th. The mail steamer from San Francisco arrived in Honolulu the night of Dec. 24, '70, and left again for San Francisco the evening of the 26th. At the U. S. Minister's request, I went on her as a passenger and reported to Admiral J. A. Winslow. Having reported, I went to the Navy Yard, Mare Island, to recuperate. I had improved wonderfully in the two weeks between the time of the capsizing of the boat and my stay in San Francisco during the night of Jan. 17, '71.[10]

VII

BOYD AND GORTZ DIED DURING THE NIGHT

The steamer Jeannette, *Lieutenant George W. DeLong, USN, set out from San Francisco in 1879 to explore the unknown approaches to the North Pole through the Bering Strait. Caught in the Arctic ice, the* Jeannette *drifted westward far beyond Wrangell Island and was finally crushed and sunk on 12 June 1881. For three months the crew battered its way in boats towards the Siberian coast until separated by a gale. The second cutter was never heard from again. DeLong in the first cutter and Engineer Benjamin Melville in the whaleboat reached the delta of the Lena River at widely separated points. DeLong's party died with the exception of two who, ordered south for aid, got word to Melville through natives. Melville searched for his commander and, in March, 1882, discovered his body with those of the other men at their last camp. DeLong's journal describes the last tragic days in the barren Arctic.*

October 1st, Saturday.—One hundred and eleventh day, a new month. Called all hands as soon as the cook announced boiling water, and at 6.45 had our breakfast; one half pound of deer meat and tea. Sent Nindemann and Alexey to examine main river, other men to collect wood. The doctor resumed the cutting away of poor Ericksen's toes this morning. No doubt it will have to continue until half his feet are gone, unless death ensues, or we get to some settlement. Only one toe left now. Temperature 18°.

At 7.30 Nindemann and Alexey were seen to have crossed, and I immediately sent men to carry one load over.

Left the following record:—

Saturday, October 1, 1881.

Fourteen of the officers and men of the U.S. Arctic Steamer Jeannette reached this hut on Wednesday, September 28th, and having been forced to wait for the river to freeze over, are proceeding to cross to the west side this A. M. on their journey to reach some settlement on the Lena River. We have two days' provisions, but having been fortunate enough thus far to get game in our pressing needs, we have no fear for the future.

Our party are all well, except one man, Ericksen, whose toes have been amputated in consequence of frost-bite. Other records will be found in several huts on the east side of this river, along which we have come from the northward.

GEORGE W. DE LONG,
Lieutenant U.S. Navy, Commanding Expedition.

At 8.30 we made the final trip, and got our sick man over in safety. From there we proceeded until 11.20, dragging our man on the sled. Halted for dinner; one half pound meat and tea each. At one went ahead again until 5.05. . . .

At least two miles an hour. Distance made good ten to twelve miles.

And where are we? I think at the beginning of the Lena River at last. . . . We saw two old huts at a distance, and that was all, but they were out of our reach, and the day not half gone. Kept on ice all the way, and therefore I think we were over water, but the stream was so narrow and so crooked that it never could have been a navigable water. My chart is simply useless. I must go on plodding to the southward, trusting in God to guide me to a settlement, for I have long since realized that we are powerless to help ourselves.

A bright, calm, beautiful day. Bright sunshine to cheer us up, an icy road, and one day's rations yet. Boots frozen, of course, and balled up. No hut in sight, and we halt on a bluff to spend a cold and comfortless night. Supper one half pound meat and tea. Made a rousing fire, built a log bed, set a watch (two hours each) to keep the fire going, and at eight P. M. crawled into our blankets.

October 2d, Sunday.—I think we all slept fairly well until midnight; but from that time it was so cold and uncomfortable that sleep was out of the question. At 4.30 we were all out and in front of the fire, daylight just appearing. Ericksen kept talking in his sleep all night, and effectually kept those awake who were not already awakened by the cold.

Breakfast five A. M. One half pound meat and tea. Bright, cloudless morning. Light N. airs. At seven went ahead, following frozen water wherever we could find it, and at 9.20 I felt quite sure we have gone some distance on the main river. I think our gait was at least two

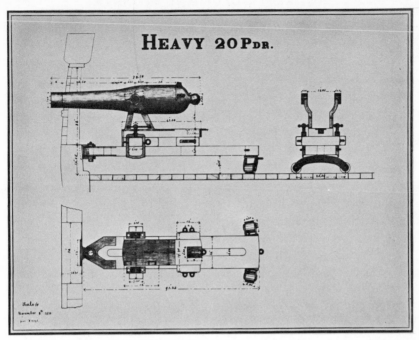

Heavy 20-pounder of the 1870's.

Sinking of the *Jeannette* in the Arctic—1881.

miles an hour, and our time under way two hours four minutes. I call our forenoon work at least six miles. . . .

Divine service before dinner. Dinner one half pound meat and tea. Started ahead at one P. M., and by 4.15 had completed two marching hours and made four miles. I was much bewildered by the frequent narrowing of the river to a small vein of ice, and the irregular rambling way in which it ran. Frequently it led us into a sand bank or deep snow, and our floundering around was both exhaustive of energy and consumptive of time. There is no use denying it, we are pretty weak. Our food is not enough to keep up our strength, and when we lose a night's sleep we feel it keenly. I had several bad falls on the ice this afternoon which shook me up pretty badly. A freshening N.E. wind had blown the efflorescence off the ice, and left smooth, clear spots as clear as glass. Frozen boots are but poor foot gear, and besides cramping the feet, are like boots of iron in walking. Slip, slide, and down you are on your back.

At 4.05 P. M. I saw more wood than we had sighted since our dinner camp, and but little ahead. I therefore called a halt and "camped," i.e., sat down, made a fire and got supper. Then we stood by for a second cold and wretched night. There was so much wind that we had to put our tent halves up for a screen, and sit shivering in our half blankets.

October 3d, Monday.—One hundred and thirteenth day. At midnight it was so fearfully cold and wretched that I served out tea to all hands, and on that we managed to struggle along until five A. M., when we ate our last deer meat and had more tea. Our remaining food now consists of four fourteenths pounds pemmican each, and a half starved dog. May God again incline unto our aid. How much farther we have to go before reaching a shelter or a settlement, He alone knows.

Brisk wind. Ericksen seems failing. He is weak and tremulous, and the moment he closes his eyes talks incessantly in Danish, German, and English. . . .

For some cause my watch stopped at 10.45 last night while one of the men on watch had it. I set it as near as I could come to the time by guessing, and we must run by that until I can do better. Sun rose yesterday morning at 6.40 by the watch when running all right. . . .

Our forenoon's walk I put at five miles. Some time and distance was lost by crossing the river upon seeing numerous fox-traps. A man's track was also seen in the snow, bound south, and we followed it until it crossed the river to the west bank again. Here we were obliged to go back in our tracks, for the river was open in places, and we could not follow the man's track direct. Another of the dozen shoals which infest the river swung us off to the eastward, too, and I hastened to get on the west bank again, reaching there at 11.50 for dinner. Our last four fourteenths pound pemmican.

At 1.40 got under way again and made a long fleet until 2.20. While at the other side of the river Alexey said he saw a hut, and during our dinner camp he again saw it. Under our circumstances my desire was to get to it as speedily as possible. As Alexey pointed out it was on the left bank of the river of which we were now on the right side looking south. But a sand bank gave us excellent walking for a mile, until we took to the river ice and got across it diagonally. Here, at 2.20, I called a rest, and Alexey mounted the bluff to take a look again. He now announced that he saw a second hut about one and a quarter miles back from the coast, the first hut being about the same distance south and on the edge of the bluff. The heavy dragging across country of a sick man on a sled made me incline to the hut on the shore, since, as the distance was about the same, we could get over the ice in one third of the time.

Nindemann, who climbed the bluff, while he saw that the object inland was a hut, was not so confident about the one on the shore. Alexey, however, was quite positive, and not seeing very well myself I unfortunately took his eyes as best and ordered an advance along the river to the southward. Away we went, Nindemann and Alexey leading, and had progressed about a mile when, splash! in I went through the ice up to my shoulders before my knapsack brought me up.

While I was crawling out, in went Gortz to his neck about fifty yards behind me, and behind him in went Mr. Collins to his waist. Here was a time. The moment we came out of the water we were one sheet of ice, and danger of frost-bite was imminent. Along we hobbled, however, until we came, at 3.45, abreast the point on which the hut was seen. Here Nindemann climbed the bluff, followed by the doctor. At first the cry was, "All right, come ahead," but no sooner were we all up than Nindemann shouted, "There is no hut here." To my dismay and alarm nothing but a large mound of earth was to be seen, which, from its regular shape and singular position would seem to have been built artificially for a beacon; so sure was Nindemann that it was a hut that he went all around it looking for a door, and then climbed on top to look for a hole in the roof. But of no avail. It was nothing but a mound of earth. Sick at heart I ordered a camp to be made in a hole in the bluff face, and soon before a roaring fire we were drying (and burning) our clothes, while the cold wind ate into our backs.

And now for supper! Nothing remained but the dog. I therefore ordered him killed and dressed by Iversen, and soon after a kind of stew was made of such parts as could not be carried, of which everybody except the doctor and myself eagerly partook. To us two it was a nauseating mess and—but why go on with such a disagreeable subject. I had the remainder weighed, and I am quite sure we had twenty-seven pounds. The animal was fat and—as he had been fed on pemmican—presumably clean, but—

Immediately upon halting I had sent off Alexey with his gun toward the hut inland, to determine whether that was a myth like our present one. He returned about dark, certain that it was a large hut, for he had been inside of it, and had found some deer meat, scraps, and bones. For a moment I was tempted to start everybody for it, but Alexey was by no means sure he could find it in the dark, and if we lost our way we should be worse off than before. We accordingly prepared to make the best of it where we were.

We three wet people were burning and steaming before the fire. Collins and Gortz had taken some alcohol, but I could not get it down. Cold, wet, with a raw N.W. wind impossible to avoid or screen, our future was a wretched, dreary night. Ericksen soon became delirious, and his talking was a horrible accompaniment to the wretchedness of our surroundings. Warm we could not get, and getting dry seemed out of the question. Nearly everybody seemed dazed and stupefied, and I feared that some of us would perish during the night. How cold it was I do not know, for my last thermometer was broken in my many falls on the ice, but I think it must have been below zero. A watch was set to keep the fire going and we huddled around it, and thus our third night without sleep was passed. If Alexey had not wrapped his sealskin around me and sat down alongside of me to keep me warm by the heat of his body, I think I should have frozen to death. As it was I steamed, and shivered, and shook. Ericksen's groans and rambling talk rang out on the night air, and such a dreary, wretched night I hope I shall never see again.

October 4th, Tuesday.—One hundred and fourteenth day. At the first approach of daylight we all began to move around, and the cook was set to work making tea. The doctor now made the unpleasant discovery that during the night Ericksen had got his gloves off and that now his hands were frozen. Men were at once set to work rubbing them, and by six A. M. we had so far restored circulation as to risk moving the man. Each one had hastily swallowed a cup of tea, and got his load in readiness. Ericksen was quite unconscious, and we lashed him on the sled. A S.W. gale was blowing, and the sensation of cold was intense; but at six A.M. we started, made a forced fleet of it, and at eight A.M. had got the man and ourselves, thank God, under the cover of a hut large enough to hold us. Here we at once made a fire, and for the first time since Saturday morning last got warm.

The doctor at once examined Ericksen and found him very low indeed. His pulse was very feeble, he was quite unconscious, and under the shock of the exposure of the past night he was sinking very fast. Fears were entertained that he might not last many hours, and I therefore called upon everyone to join with me in reading the prayers for a sick person before we sought any rest for ourselves. . . . Then setting a watch we all, except Alexey, laid down to sleep at ten A. M. Alexey went off to hunt, but returned at noon wet, having broken through the ice and fallen in the river.

At six P.M. all roused up, and I considered it necessary to think of some food for my party. Half a pound of dog was fried for each one and a cup of tea given, and that constituted our day's food. But we were so grateful that we were not exposed to the merciless S.W. gale that tore around us that we did not mind short rations.

October 5th, Wednesday.—One hundred and fifteenth day. The cook commenced at 7.30 to get tea, made from yesterday's tea leaves. Nothing can be served out to eat until evening. One half pound dog per day is our food until some relief is afforded us. Alexey went off hunting again at nine, and I set the men to work collecting light sticks enough to make a flooring for the house, for the frozen ground thawing under everybody has kept them damp and wet and robbed them of much sleep.

S.W. gale continues. Mortification has set in in Ericksen's leg and he is sinking. Amputation would be of no use, for he would probably die under the operation. He is partially conscious. At twelve Alexey came back, having seen nothing. He crossed the river this time, but unable longer to face the cold gale was obliged to return.

I am of the opinion that we are on Tit Ary Island, on its eastern side, and about twenty-five miles from Ku Mark Surka, which I take to be a settlement. This is a last hope. The hut in which we are is quite new, and clearly not the astronomical station marked on my chart. In fact this hut is not finished, having no door and no porch. It may be intended for a summer hut, though the numerous set fox-traps would lead me to suppose that it would occasionally be visited at other times. Upon this last chance and one other seem to rest all our hopes of escape, for I can see nothing more to be done. As soon as this gale abates I shall send Nindemann and one other man to make a forced march to Ku Mark Surka for relief. At six P.M. served out one half pound of dog meat and second-hand tea, and then went to sleep.

October 6th, Thursday.—One hundred and sixteenth day. Called all hands at 7.30. Had a cup of third-hand tea with one half ounce of alcohol in it. Everybody very weak. Gale moderating somewhat. Sent Alexey out to hunt. Shall start Nindemann and Noros at noon to make the forced march to Ku Mark Surka. At 8.45 A.M. our mess-mate Ericksen departed this life. Addressed a few words of cheer and comfort to the men. Alexey came back empty-handed. Too much drifting snow. What in God's name is going to become of us—fourteen pounds dog meat left, and twenty-five miles to a possible settlement? As to burying Ericksen, I cannot dig a grave, for the ground is frozen and we have nothing to dig with. There is nothing to do but to bury him in the river. Sewed him up in the flaps of the tent, and covered him with my flag. Got tea ready, and with one half ounce alcohol we will try to make out to bury him. But we are all so weak that I do not see how we are going to move.

At 12.40 P.M. read the burial service and carried our departed shipmate's body down to the river, where, a hole having been cut in the ice, he was buried; three volleys from our two Remingtons being fired over him as a funeral honor.

A board was prepared with this cut on it:

IN MEMORY
H. H. ERICKSEN,
Oct. 6, 1881.
U. S. S. *Jeannette.*

226

and this will be stuck in the river bank abreast his grave. His clothing was divided up among his messmates. Iversen has his Bible and a lock of his hair. Kaack has a lock of his hair.

Supper at five P. M.—one half pound dog meat and tea.

October 7th, Friday.—One hundred and seventeenth day. Breakfast, consisting of our last one half pound dog meat and tea. Our last grain of tea was put in the kettle this morning, and we are now about to undertake our journey of twenty-five miles with some old tea-leaves and two quarts alcohol. However, I trust in God, and I believe that He who has fed us thus far will not suffer us to die of want now.

Commenced preparations for departure at 7.10. . . . Under way at 8.30 and proceeded until 11.20, by which time we had made about three miles. Here we were all pretty well done up, and, moveover, seemed to be wandering in a labyrinth. A large lump of wood swept in by an eddy seemed to be a likely place to get hot water, and I halted the party. For dinner we had one ounce alcohol in a pot of tea. Then went ahead, and soon struck what seemed like the river again. Here four of us broke through the ice in trying to cross, and fearing frost-bite I had a fire built on the west bank to dry us. Sent Alexey off meanwhile to look for food, directing him not to go far nor to stay long; but at 3.30 he had not returned, nor was he in sight. Light S.W. breeze, hazy; mountains in sight to southward.

At 5.30 Alexey returned with one ptarmigan, of which we made soup, and with one half ounce alcohol had our supper. Then crawled under our blankets for a sleep. Light W. breeze; full moon; starlight. Not very cold. Alexey saw river a mile wide with no ice in it.

October 8th, Saturday.—One hundred and eighteenth day. Called all hands at 5.30. Breakfast, one ounce alcohol in a pint of hot water. Doctor's note: Alcohol proves of great advantage; keeps off craving for food, preventing gnawing at stomach, and has kept up the strength of the men. . . .

October 9th, Sunday.—One hundred and nineteenth day. All hands at 4.30 one ounce alcohol. Read divine service. Send Nindemann and Noros ahead for relief; they carry their blankets, one rifle, forty rounds ammunition, two ounces alcohol. Orders to keep west bank of river until they reach settlement. They started at seven; cheered them. Under way at eight. Crossed creek. Broke through ice. All wet up to knees. Stopped and built fires. Dried clothes. Under way again at 10.30. Lee breaking down. At one strike river bank. Halt for dinner—one ounce alcohol. Alexey shot three ptarmigans. Made soup. We are following Nindemann's track, though he is long since out of sight. Under way at 3.30. High bluff. Ice running rapidly to northward in river. Halt at 4.40 upon coming to wood. Find canoe. Lay our heads on it and go to sleep; one half ounce alcohol for supper.

October 10th, Monday.—One hundred and twentieth day. Last half ounce alcohol at 5.30; at 6.30 send Alexey off to look for ptarmigan. Eat deerskin scraps. Yesterday morning ate my deerskin footnips. Light S.S.E. airs. Not very cold. Under way at eight. In crossing creek three of us got wet. Built fire and dried out. Ahead again until eleven. Used up. Built fire. Made a drink out of the tealeaves from alcohol bottle. On again at noon. Fresh S.S.W. wind, drifting snow, very hard going. Lee begging to be left. Some little beach, and then long stretches of high bank. Ptarmigan tracks plentiful. Following Nindemann's tracks. At three halted, used up; crawled into a hole in the bank, collected wood and built fire. Alexey away in quest of game. Nothing for supper except a spoonful of glycerine. All hands weak and feeble, but cheerful. God help us.

October 11th, Tuesday.—One hundred and twenty-first day. S. W. gale with snow. Unable to move. No game. One spoonful glycerine and hot water for food. No more wood in our vicinity.

October 12th, Wednesday.—One hundred and twenty-second day. Breakfast; last spoonful glycerine and hot water. For dinner we tried a couple of handfuls of Arctic willow in a pot of water and drank the infusion. Everybody getting weaker and weaker. Hardly strength to get fire-wood. S. W. gale with snow.

October 13th, Thursday.—One hundred and twenty-third day. Willow tea. Strong S. W. wind. No news from Nindemann. We are in the hands of God, and unless He intervenes we are lost. We cannot move against the wind, and staying here means starvation. Afternoon went ahead for a mile, crossing either another river or a bend in the big one. After crossing, missed Lee. Went down in a hole in the bank and camped. Sent back for Lee. He had turned back, lain down, and was waiting to die. All united in saying Lord's Prayer and Creed after supper. Living gale of wind. Horrible night.

October 14th, Friday.—One hundred and twenty-fourth day. Breakfast, willow tea. Dinner, one half teaspoonful sweet oil and willow tea. Alexey shot one ptarmigan. Had soup. S. W. wind, moderating.

October 15th, Saturday.—One hundred and twenty-fifth day. Breakfast, willow tea and two old boots. Conclude to move on at sunrise. Alexey breaks down, also Lee. Come to empty grain raft. Halt and camp. Signs of smoke at twilight to southward.

October 16th, Sunday.—One hundred and twenty-sixth day. Alexey broken down. Divine service.

October 17th, Monday.—One hundred and twenty-seventh day. Alexey dying. Doctor baptized him. Read prayers for sick. Mr. Collins' birthday—forty years old. About sunset Alexey died. Exhaustion from starvation. Covered him with ensign and laid him in the crib.

October 18th, Tuesday.—One hundred and twenty-eighth day. Calm and mild, snow falling. Buried Alexey in the afternoon. Laid him on the ice of the river, and covered him over with slabs of ice.

October 19th, Wednesday.—One hundred and twenty-ninth day. Cutting up tent to make foot gear. Doctor went ahead to find new camp. Shifted by dark.

October 20th, Thursday.—One hundred and thirtieth day. Bright and sunny, but very cold. Lee and Kaack done up.

October 21st, Friday.—One hundred and thirty-first day. Kaack was found dead about midnight between the doctor and myself. Lee died about noon. Read prayers for sick when we found he was going.

October 22d, Saturday.—One hundred and thirty-second day. Too weak to carry the bodies of Lee and Kaack out on the ice. The doctor, Collins, and I carried them around the corner out of sight. Then my eye closed up.

October 23rd, Sunday.—One hundred and thirty-third day. Everybody pretty weak. Slept or rested all day, and then managed to get enough wood in before dark. Read part of divine service. Suffering in our feet. No foot gear.

October 24th, Monday.—One hundred and thirty-fourth day. A hard night. . . .

October 27th, Thursday.—One hundred and thirty-seventh day. Iversen broken down.

October 28th, Friday.—One hundred and thirty-eighth day. Iversen died during early morning.

October 29th, Saturday.—One hundred and thirty-ninth day. Dressler died during night.

October 30th, Sunday.—One hundred and fortieth day. Boyd and Gortz died during the night. Mr. Collins dying.[11]

229

VIII

SEA POWER

Captain Alfred Thayer Mahan, USN, published voluminously. He noted how in centuries past the fortunes of Great Britain rose under a government which understood and employed naval might correctly, while those of France fell through misuse. To assure American security, Mahan stressed the necessity of an Isthmian canal and the acquisition of naval bases in the Caribbean and the Pacific. While Mahan's ideas were influential in the United States, he received greater attention abroad. Impressed with these essays on sea power, the German Kaiser placed copies on board every imperial ship, while in England and Japan, Mahan's theories achieved popularity. The following is an extract from The Influence of Sea Power upon History, 1660-1783 *published in 1890.*[12]

The first and most obvious light in which the sea presents itself from the political and social point of view is that of a great highway; or better, perhaps, of a wide common over which men may pass in all directions, but on which some well-worn paths show that controlling reasons have led them to choose certain lines of travel rather than others. These lines of travel are called trade routes; and the reasons which have determined them are to be sought in the history of the world.

Notwithstanding all the familiar and unfamiliar dangers of the sea, both travel and traffic by water have always been easier and cheaper than by land. The commercial greatness of Holland was due not only to her shipping at sea, but also to the numerous tranquil water-ways which gave such cheap and easy access to her own interior and to that of Germany. This advantage of carriage by water over that by land was yet more marked in a period when roads were few and very bad, wars frequent and society unsettled, as was the case two hundred years ago. Sea traffic then went in peril of robbers, but was nevertheless safer and quicker than that by land. A Dutch writer of that time, estimating the chances of his country in a war with England, notices among other things that the water-ways of England failed to penetrate the country sufficiently; therefore, the roads being bad, goods from one part of the kingdom to the other must go by sea, and be exposed to capture by the way.

As regards purely internal trade, this danger had generally disappeared at the present day. In most civilized countries, now, the destruction or disappearance of the coasting trade would only be an inconvenience, although water transit is still the cheaper. Nevertheless, as late as the wars of the French Republic and the First Empire, those who are familiar with the history of the period . . . know how constant is the mention of convoys stealing from point to point along the French coast, although the sea swarmed with English cruisers and there were good inland roads.

Under modern conditions, however, home trade is but a part of the business of a country bordering on the sea. Foreign necessaries or luxuries must be brought to its ports, either in its own or in foreign ships, which will return, bearing in exchange the products of the country, whether they be the fruits of the earth or the works of men's hands; and it is the wish of every nation that this shipping business should be done by its own vessels. The ships that thus sail to and fro must have secure ports to which to return, and must, as far as possible, be followed by the protection of their country throughout the voyage.

This protection in time of war must be extended by armed shipping. The necessity of a navy, in the restricted sense of the word, springs, therefore, from the existence of a peaceful shipping, and disappears with it, except in the case of a nation which has aggressive tendencies, and keeps up a navy merely as a branch of the military establishment. As the United States has at present no aggressive purposes, and as its merchant service has disappeared, the dwindling of the armed fleet and general lack of interest in it are strictly logical consequences. When for any reason sea trade is again found to pay, a large enough shipping interest will reappear to compel the revival of the war fleet. It is possible that when a canal route through the Central-American Isthmus is seen to be a near certainty, the aggressive impulse may be strong enough to lead to the same result. This is doubtful, however, because a peaceful, gain-loving nation is not farsighted, and far-sightedness is needed for adequate military preparation, especially in these days.

As a nation, with its unarmed and armed shipping, launches forth from its own shores, the need is soon felt of points upon which the ships can rely for peaceful trading, for refuge and supplies. In the present day friendly, though foreign, ports are to be found all over the world; and their shelter is enough while peace prevails. It was not always so, nor does peace always endure, though the United States have been favored by so long a continuance of it. In earlier times the merchant seaman, seeking for trade in new and unexplored regions, made his gains at risk of life and liberty from suspicious or hostile nations, and was under great delays in collecting a full and profitable freight. He therefore intuitively sought at the far end of his trade route one or more stations . . . where he could fix himself or his agents in reasonable security, where his ships could lie in safety, and where the merchantable products of the land could be continually collecting, awaiting the arrival of the home fleet, which should carry them to the mother-country. As there was immense gain, as well as much risk, in these early voyages, such establishments naturally multiplied and grew until they became colonies; whose ultimate development and success depended upon the genius and policy of the nation from which they sprang, and form a very great part of the history, and particularly of the sea history, of the world. . . .

The needs of commerce, however, were not all provided for when safety had been secured at the far end of the road. The voyages were long and dangerous, the seas often beset with enemies. In the most active days of colonizing there prevailed on the sea a lawlessness the very memory of which is now almost lost, and the days of settled peace between maritime nations were few and far between. Thus arose the demand for stations along the road, like the Cape of Good Hope, St. Helena, and Mauritius, not primarily for trade, but for defence and war; the demand for the possession of posts like Gibraltar, Malta, Louisburg, at the entrance of the Gulf of St. Lawrence—posts whose value was chiefly strategic, though not necessarily wholly so. Colonies and colonial posts were sometimes commercial, sometimes military in their character; and it was exceptional that the same position was equally important in both points of view, as New York was.

In these three things—production, with the necessity of exchanging products; shipping, whereby the exchange is carried on; and colonies, which facilitate and enlarge the operations of shipping and tend to protect it by multiplying points of safety—is to be found the key to much of the history, as well as of the policy, of nations bordering upon the sea. The policy has varied both with the spirit of the age and with the character and clear-sightedness of the rulers; but the history of the seaboard nations has been less determined by the shrewdness and foresight of governments than by conditions of position, extent, configuration, number and character of their people—by what are called, in a word, natural conditions. It must however be admitted, and will be seen, that the wise or unwise action of individual men has at certain periods had a great modifying influence upon the growth of sea power in the broad sense, which includes not only the military strength afloat, that rules the sea or any part of it by force or arms, but also the peaceful commerce and shipping from which alone a military fleet naturally and healthfully springs, and on which it securely rests.

The principal conditions affecting the sea power of nations may be enumerated as follows: I. Geographical Position. II. Physical Conformation, including, as connected therewith, natural productions and climate. III. Extent of Territory. IV. Number of Population. V. Character of the People. VI. Character of the Government, including therein the national institutions.

I GEOGRAPHICAL POSITION—It may be pointed out, in the first place, that if a nation be so situated that it is neither forced to defend itself by land nor induced to seek extension of its territory by way of the land, it has, by the very unity of its aim directed upon the sea, an advantage as compared with a people one of whose boundaries is continental. This has been a great advantage to England over both France and Holland as a sea power. The strength of the latter was early exhausted by the necessity of keeping up a large army and carrying on expensive wars to preserve her independence; while the policy of France was constantly diverted, sometimes wisely and sometimes most foolishly, from the sea to projects of continental extension. These military efforts expended wealth; whereas a wiser and consistent use of her geographical position would have added to it.

The geographical position may be such as of itself to promote a concentration, or to necessitate a dispersion, of the naval forces. Here again the British Islands have an advantage over France. The position of the latter, touching the Mediterranean as well as the ocean, while it has its advantages, is on the whole a source of military weakness at sea. The eastern and western French fleets have only been able to unite after passing through the Straits of Gibraltar, in attempting which they have often risked and sometimes suffered loss. The position of the United States upon the two oceans would be either a source of great weakness or a cause of enormous expense, had it a large sea commerce on both coasts.

England, by her immense colonial empire, has sacrificed much of this advantage of concentration of force around her own shores; but the sacrifice was wisely made, for the gain was greater than the loss, as the event proved. With the growth of her colonial system her war fleets also grew, but her merchant shipping and wealth grew yet faster. . . .

The geographical position of a country may not only favor the concentration of its forces, but give the further strategic advantage of a central position and a good base for hostile operations against its probable enemies. This again is the case with England; on the one hand she faces Holland and the northern powers, on the other France and the Atlantic. . . .

The advantage of geographical nearness to an enemy, or to the object of attack, is nowhere more apparent than in that form of warfare which has lately received the name of commerce-destroying, which the French call *guerre de course*. This operation of war, being directed against peaceful merchant vessels which are usually defenceless, calls for ships of small military force. Such ships, having little power to defend themselves, need a refuge or point of support near at hand; which will be found either in certain parts of the sea controlled by the fighting ships of their country, or in friendly harbors. The latter give the strongest support, because they are always in the same place, and the approaches to them are more familiar to the commerce-destroyer than to his enemy. The nearness of France to England has thus greatly facilitated her *guerre de course*. . . .

If, in addition to facility for offence, Nature has so placed a country that it has easy access to the high sea itself, while at the same time it controls one of the great thoroughfares of the world's traffic, it is evident that the strategic value of its position is very high. Such again is, and to a greater degree was, the position of England. . . .

But for the loss of Gibraltar, the position of Spain would have been closely analogous to that of England. . . .

At the present day, looking only at the geographical position of Italy, and not at the other conditions affecting her sea power, it would seem that with her extensive seacoast and good ports she is very well placed for exerting a decisive influence on the trade route to the Levant and by the Isthmus of Suez. This is true in a degree, and would be much more so did Italy now hold all the islands naturally Italian; but with Malta in the hands of England, and Corsica in those of France, the advantages of her geographical position are largely neutralized. . . .

Circumstances have caused the Mediterranean Sea to play a greater part in the history of the world, both in a commercial and a military point of view, than any other sheet of water of the same size. . . . A study of the strategic conditions of the Mediterranean . . . will be an excellent prelude to a similar study of the Caribbean. . . .

The second remark bears upon the geographical position of the United States relatively to a Central-American canal. If one be made, and fulfil the hopes of its builders, the Caribbean will be changed from a terminus, and place of local traffic . . . into one of the great highways of the world. Along this path a great commerce will travel, bringing the interests of the other great nations, the European nations, close along our shores, as they have never been before. With this it will not be so easy as heretofore to stand aloof from international complications. The position of the United States with reference to this route will resemble that of England to the Channel, and of the Mediterranean countries to the Suez route. . . .

In case of a contest for supremacy in the Caribbean, it seems evident from the depth of the South Pass of the Mississippi, the nearness of New Orleans, and the advantages of the Mississippi Valley for water transit, that the main effort of the country must pour down that valley, and its permanent base of operations be found there. . . . Furthermore, as her distance from the Isthmus, though relatively less, is still considerable, the United States will have to obtain in the Caribbean stations fit for contingent, or secondary, bases of operations; which by their natural advantages, susceptibility of defence, and nearness to the central strategic issue, will enable her fleets to remain as near the scene as any opponent. . . .

II PHYSICAL CONFORMATION—The peculiar features of the Gulf coast, just alluded to, come properly under the head of Physical Conformation of a country, which is placed second for discussion among the conditions which affect the development of sea power. . . .

Numerous and deep harbors are a source of strength and wealth, and doubly so if they are the outlets of navigable streams, which facilitate the concentration in them of a country's internal trade; but by their very accessibility they become a source of weakness in war, if not properly defended. The Dutch in 1667 found little difficulty in ascending the Thames and burning a large fraction of the English navy within sight of London; whereas a few years later the combined fleets of England and France, when attempting a landing in Holland, were foiled by the difficulties of the coast as much as by the valor of the Dutch fleet. . . .

Before and during the great Napoleonic wars, France had no port for ships-of-the-line east of Brest. How great the advantage to England, which in the same stretch has two great arsenals, at Plymouth and at Portsmouth, besides other harbors of refuge and supply. . . .

Besides the contour of the coast, involving easy access to the sea, there are other physical conditions which lead people to the sea or turn them from it. . . . When Richelieu had put an end to civil war, Frenchmen did not take to the sea with the eagerness and success of the English and Dutch. A principal reason for this has been plausibly found in the physical conditions which have made France a pleasant land, with a delightful climate, producing within itself more than its people needed. England, on the other hand, received from Nature but little, and, until her manufactures were developed, had little to export. Their many wants, combined with their restless activity and other conditions that favored maritime enterprise, led her people abroad; and they there found lands more pleasant and richer than their own. Their needs and genius made them merchants and colonists, then manufacturers and producers; and between products and colonies shipping is the inevitable link. So their sea power grew.

But if England was drawn to the sea, Holland was driven to it; without the sea England languished, but Holland died. . . . The poverty of the soil and the exposed nature of the coast drove the Dutch first to fishing. Then the discovery of the process of curing the fish gave them material for export as well as home consumption, and so laid the corner-stone of their wealth. Thus they had become traders at the time that the Italian republics, under the pressure of Turkish power and the discovery of the passage round the Cape of Good Hope, were beginning to decline, and they fell heirs to the great Italian trade of the Levant. Further favored by their geographical position, intermediate between the Baltic, France, and the Mediterranean, and at the mouth of the German rivers, they quickly absorbed nearly all the carrying-trade of Europe. . . . Other causes concurred, but their whole prosperity stood on the sea power to which their poverty gave birth. Their food, their clothing, the raw material for their manufactures, the very timber and hemp with which they built and rigged their ships (and they built nearly as many as all Europe besides), were imported; and when a disastrous war with England in 1653 and 1654 had lasted eighteen months, and their shipping business was stopped, it is said "the sources of revenue which had always maintained the riches of the State, such as fisheries and commerce, were almost dry. Workshops were closed, work was suspended. The Zuyder Zee became a forest of masts; the country was full of beggars; grass grew in the streets, and in Amsterdam fifteen hundred houses were untenanted."

. . . The case of Holland then has strong points of resemblance to that of Great Britain now; and they are true prophets . . . who warn her that the continuance of her prosperity at home depends primarily upon maintaining her power abroad. Men may be discontented at the lack of political privilege; they will be yet more uneasy if they come to lack bread. It is of more interest to Americans to note that the result to France, regarded as a power of the sea, caused by the extent, delightfulness, and richness of the land, has been reproduced in the United States. In the beginning, their forefathers held a narrow strip of land upon the sea, fertile in parts though little developed, abounding in harbors and near rich fishing-grounds. These physical conditions combined with an inborn love of the sea, the pulse of that English blood which still beat in their veins, to keep alive all those tendencies and pursuits upon which a healthy sea power depends. Almost every one of the original colonies was on the sea or on one of its great tributaries. All export and import tended toward one coast. Interest in the sea and an intelligent appreciation of the part it played in the public welfare were easily and widely spread; and a motive more influential than care for the public interest was also active, for the abundance of ship-building materials and a relative fewness of other investments made shipping a profitable private interest. How changed the present condition is, all know. . . . When the day comes that shipping again pays, when the three sea frontiers find that they are not only militarily weak, but poorer for lack of national shipping, their united efforts may avail to lay again the foundations of our sea power. Till then, those who follow the limitations which lack of sea power placed upon the career of France may mourn that their own country is being led, by a like redundancy of home wealth, into the same neglect of that great instrument. . . .

Except Alaska, the United States has no outlying possession—no foot of ground inaccessible by land. Its contour is such as to present few points specially weak from their saliency, and all important parts of the frontiers can be readily attained—cheaply by water, rapidly by rail. The weakest frontier, the Pacific, is far removed from the most dangerous of possible enemies. The internal resources are boundless as compared with present needs; we can live off ourselves indefinitely in "our little corner," to use the expression of a French officer to the author. Yet should that little corner be invaded by a new commercial route through the Isthmus, the United States in her turn may have the rude awakening of those who have abandoned their share in the common birthright of all people, the sea.

III EXTENT OF TERRITORY—The last of the conditions affecting the development of a nation as a sea power, and touching the country itself as distinguished from the people who dwell there, is Extent of Territory. This may be dismissed with comparatively few words.

As regards the development of sea power, it is not the total number of square miles which a country contains, but the length of its coastline and the character of its harbors that are to be considered. As to these it is to be said that, the geographical and physical conditions being the same, extent of sea-coast is a source of strength or weakness according as the population is large or small. A country is in this like a fortress; the garrison must be proportioned to the *enceinte*. A recent familiar instance is found in the American War of Secession. Had the South had a people as numerous as it was warlike, and a navy commensurate to its other resources as a sea power, the great extent of its sea-coast and its numerous inlets would have been elements of great strength. The people of the United States and the Government of that day justly prided themselves on the effectiveness of the blockade of the whole Southern coast. It was a great feat, a very great feat; but it would have been an impossible feat had the Southerners been more numerous, and a nation of seamen. What was there shown was not, as has been said, how such a blockade can be maintained, but that such a blockade is possible in the face of a population not only unused to the sea, but also scanty in numbers. Those who recall how the blockade was maintained, and the class of ships that blockaded during great part of the war, know that the plan, correct under the circumstances, could not have been carried out in the face of a real navy. Scattered unsupported along the coast, the United States ships kept their places, singly or in small detachments, in face of an extensive network of inland water communications which favored secret concentration of the enemy.

Behind the first line of water communications were long estuaries, and here and there strong fortresses, upon either of which the enemy's ships could always fall back to elude pursuit or to receive protection. Had there been a Southern navy to profit by such advantages, or by the scattered condition of the United States ships, the latter could not have been distributed as they were; and being forced to concentrate for mutual support, many small but useful approaches would have been left open to commerce. But as the Southern coast, from its extent and many inlets, might have been a source of strength, so, from those very characteristics, it became a fruitful source of injury.

The great story of the opening of the Mississippi is but the most striking illustration of an action that was going on incessantly all over the South. At every breach of the sea frontier, war-ships were entering. The streams that had carried the wealth and supported the trade of the seceding States turned against them, and admitted their enemies to their hearts. Dismay, insecurity, paralysis, prevailed in regions that might, under happier auspices, have kept a nation alive through the most exhausting war. Never did sea power play a greater or a more decisive part than in the contest which determined that the course of the world's history would be modified by the existence of one great nation, instead of several rival States, in the North American continent. But while just pride is felt in the well-earned glory of those days, and the greatness of the results due to naval preponderance is admitted, Americans who understand the facts should never fail to remind the overconfidence of their countrymen that the South not only had no navy, not only was not a seafaring people, but that also its population was not proportioned to the extent of the sea-coast which it had to defend.

IV NUMBER OF POPULATION—After the consideration of the natural conditions of a country should follow an examination of the characteristics of its population as affecting the development of sea power; and first among these will be taken, because of its relations to the extent of the territory, which has just been discussed, the number of the people who live in it. It has been said that in respect of dimensions it is not merely the number of square miles, but the extent and character of the sea-coast that is to be considered with reference to sea power; and so, in point of population, it is not only the grand total, but the number following the sea, or at least readily available for employment on ship-board and for the creation of naval material, that must be counted.

For example, formerly and up to the end of the great wars following the French Revolution, the population of France was much greater than that of England; but in respect of sea power in general, peaceful commerce as well as military efficiency, France was much inferior to England. In the matter of military efficiency this fact is the more remarkable because at times, in point of military preparation at the outbreak of war, France had the advantage; but she was not able to keep it. Thus in 1778, when war broke out, France, through her maritime inscription, was able to man at once fifty ships-of-the-line. England, on the contrary, by reason of the dispersal over the globe of that very shipping on which her naval strength so securely rested, had much trouble in manning forty at home; but in 1782 she had one hundred and twenty in commission or ready for commission, while France had never been able to exceed seventy-one.

Again, as late as 1840, when the two nations were on the verge of war in the Levant, a most accomplished French officer of the day, while extolling the high state of efficiency of the French fleet and the eminent qualities of its admiral, and expressing confidence in the results of an encounter with an equal enemy, goes on to say: "Behind the squadron of twenty-one ships-of-the-line which we could then assemble, there was no reserve; not another ship could have been commissioned within six months." And this was due not only to lack of ships and of proper equipments, though both were wanting. "Our maritime inscription," he continues, "was so exhausted by what we had done [in manning twenty-one ships], that the permanent levy established in all quarters did not supply reliefs for the men, who were already more than three years on cruise."

A contrast such as this shows a difference in what is called staying power, or reserve force, which is even greater than appears on the surface; for a great shipping afloat necessarily employs, besides the crews, a large number of people engaged in the various handicrafts which facilitate the making and repairing of naval material, or following other callings more or less closely connected with the water and with craft of all kinds. Such kindred callings give an undoubted aptitude for the sea from the outset. . . .

It may be urged that such reserve strength has now nearly lost the importance it once had, because modern ships and weapons take so long to make, and because modern States aim at developing the whole power of their armed force, on the outbreak of war, with such rapidity as to strike a disabling blow before the enemy can organize an equal effort. To use a familiar phrase, there will not be time for the whole resistance of the national fabric to come into play; the blow will fall on the organized military fleet, and if that yield, the solidity of the rest of the structure will avail nothing. To a certain extent this is true; but then it has always been true, though to a less extent formerly than now. . . .

England is at the present time the greatest maritime nation in the world; in steam and iron she has kept the superiority she had in the days of sail and wood. France and England are the two powers that have the largest military navies; and it is so far an open question which of the two is the more powerful, that they may be regarded as practically of equal strength in material for a sea war. In the case of a collision can there be assumed such a difference of *personnel,* or of preparation, as to make it probable that a decisive inequality will result from one battle or one campaign? If not, the reserve strength will begin to tell; organized reserve first, then reserve of seafaring population, reserve of mechanical skill, reserve of wealth. . . .

The whole question of the value of a reserve, developed or undeveloped, amounts now to this: Have modern conditions of warfare made it probable that, of two nearly equal adversaries, one will be so prostrated in a single campaign that a decisive result will be reached in that time? Sea warfare has given no answer. . . .

V NATIONAL CHARACTER—The effect of national character and aptitudes upon the development of sea power will next be considered.

If sea power be really based upon a peaceful and extensive commerce, aptitude for commercial pursuits must be a distinguishing feature of the nations that have at one time or another been great upon the sea. History almost without exception affirms that this is true. Save the Romans, there is no marked instance to the contrary.

All men seek gain and, more or less, love money; but the way in which gain is sought will have a marked effect upon the commercial fortunes and the history of the people inhabiting a country.

If history may be believed, the way in which the Spaniards and their kindred nation, the Portuguese, sought wealth, not only brought a blot upon the national character, but was also fatal to the growth of a healthy commerce; and so to the industries upon which commerce lives, and ultimately to that national wealth which was sought by mistaken paths. The desire for gain rose in them to fierce avarice; so they sought in the new-found worlds which gave such an impetus to the commercial and maritime development of the countries of Europe, not new fields of industry, not even the healthy excitement of exploration and adventure, but gold and silver. They had many great qualities; they were bold, enterprising, temperate, patient of suffering, enthusiastic, and gifted with intense national feeling. When to these qualities are added the advantages of Spain's position and well-situated ports, the fact that she was first to occupy large and rich portions of the new worlds and long remained without a competitor, and that for a hundred years after the discovery of America she was the leading State in Europe, she might have been expected to take the foremost place among the sea powers.

Exactly the contrary was the result, as all know. Since the battle of Lepanto in 1571 . . . no sea victory of any consequence shines on the pages of Spanish history; and the decay of her commerce sufficiently accounts for the painful and sometimes ludicrous inaptness shown on the decks of her ships of war. Doubtless such a result is not to be attributed to one cause only . . . the government of Spain was in many ways such as to cramp and blight a free and healthy development of private enterprise; but the character of a great people breaks through and shapes the character of its government, and it can hardly be doubted that had the bent of the people been toward trade, the action of government would have been drawn into the same current. The great field of the colonies, also, was remote from the centre of that despotism which blighted the growth of old Spain. As it was, thousands of Spaniards, of the working as well as the upper classes, left Spain; and the occupations in which they engaged abroad sent home little but specie, or merchandise of small bulk, requiring but small tonnage. The mother-country herself produced little but wool, fruit, and iron; her manufactures were naught; her industries suffered; her population steadily decreased. Both she and her colonies depended upon the Dutch for so many of the necessaries of life, that the products of their scanty industries could not suffice to pay for them. . . .

242

The English and Dutch were no less desirous of gain than the southern nations. Each in turn has been called "a nation of shop-keepers"; but the jeer, in so far as it is just, is to the credit of their wisdom and uprightness. They were no less bold, no less enterprising, no less patient. Indeed, they were more patient, in that they sought riches not by the sword but by labor, which is the reproach meant to be implied by the epithet; for thus they took the longest, instead of what seemed the shortest, road to wealth. . . .

The tendency to trade, involving of necessity the production of something to trade with, is the national characteristic most important to the development of sea power. Granting it and a good seaboard, it is not likely that the dangers of the sea, or any aversion to it, will deter a people from seeking wealth by the paths of ocean commerce. Where wealth is sought by other means, it may be found; but it will not necessarily lead to sea power. Take France. . . . The French navy has known periods of great glory, and in its lowest estate has never dishonored the military reputation so dear to the nation. Yet as a maritime State, securely resting upon a broad basis of sea commerce, France, as compared with other historical sea-peoples, has never held more than a respectable position. The chief reason for this, so far as national character goes, is the way in which wealth is sought. . . .

The noble classes of Europe inherited from the Middle Ages a supercilious contempt for peaceful trade, which has exercised a modifying influence upon its growth, according to the national character of different countries. The pride of the Spaniards fell easily in with this spirit of contempt, and co-operated with that disastrous unwillingness to work and wait for wealth which turned them away from commerce. In France, the vanity which is conceded even by Frenchmen to be a national trait led in the same direction. . . .

In Holland there was a nobility; but the State was republican in name, allowed large scope to personal freedom and enterprise, and the centres of power were in the great cities. The foundation of the national greatness was money—or rather wealth. Wealth, as a source of civic distinction, carried with it also power in the State; and with power there went social position and consideration. In England the same result obtained. The nobility were proud; but in a representative government the power of wealth could be neither put down nor overshadowed. . . .

243

In yet another way does the national genius affect the growth of sea power in its broadest sense; and that is in so far as it possesses the capacity for planting healthy colonies. Of colonization, as of all other growths, it is true that it is most healthy when it is most natural. . . .

The fact of England's unique and wonderful success as a great colonizing nation is too evident to be dwelt upon; and the reason for it appears to lie chiefly in two traits of the national character. The English colonist naturally and readily settles down in his new country, identifies his interest with it, and though keeping an affectionate remembrance of the home from which he came, has no restless eagerness to return. In the second place, the Englishman at once and instinctively seeks to develop the resources of the new country in the broadest sense. In the former particular he differs from the French, who were ever longingly looking back to the delights of their pleasant land; in the latter, from the Spaniards, whose range of interest and ambition was too narrow for the full evolution of the possibilities of a new country.

The character and the necessities of the Dutch led them naturally to plant colonies; and by the year 1650 they had in the East Indies, in Africa, and in America a large number, only to name which would be tedious. They were then far ahead of England in this matter. But though the origin of these colonies, purely commercial in its character, was natural, there seems to have been lacking to them a principle of growth. "In planting them they never sought an extension of empire, but merely an acquisition of trade and commerce. They attempted conquest only when forced by the pressure of circumstances. Generally they were content to trade under the protection of the sovereign of the country." This placid satisfaction with gain alone, unaccompanied by political ambition, tended, like the despotism of France and Spain, to keep the colonies mere commercial dependencies upon the mother-country, and so killed the natural principle of growth.

Before quitting this head of the inquiry, it is well to ask how far the national character of Americans is fitted to develop a great sea power, should other circumstances become favorable.

It seems scarcely necessary, however, to do more than appeal to a not very distant past to prove that, if legislative hindrances be removed, and more remunerative fields of enterprise filled up, the sea power will not long delay its appearance. The instinct for commerce, bold enterprise in the pursuit of gain, and a keen scent for the trails that lead to it, all exist; and if there be in the future any fields calling for colonization, it cannot be doubted that Americans will carry to them all their inherited aptitude for self-government and independent growth.

VI CHARACTER OF THE GOVERNMENT—In discussing the effects upon the development of a nation's sea power exerted by its government and institutions, it will be necessary to avoid a tendency to over-philosophizing, to confine attention to obvious and immediate causes and their plain results, without prying too far beneath the surface for remote and ultimate influences. . . .

It would seem probable that a government in full accord with the natural bias of its people would most successfully advance its growth in every respect; and, in the matter of sea power, the most brilliant successes have followed where there has been intelligent direction by a government fully imbued with the spirit of the people and conscious of its true general bent. Such a government is most certainly secured when the will of the people, or of their best natural exponents, has some large share in making it; but such free governments have sometimes fallen short, while on the other hand despotic power, wielded with judgment and consistency, has created at times a great sea commerce and a brilliant navy with greater directness than can be reached by the slower processes of a free people. The difficulty in the latter case is to insure perseverance after the death of a particular despot. . . .

As the practical object of this inquiry is to draw from the lessons of history inferences applicable to one's own country and service, it is proper now to ask how far the conditions of the United States involve serious danger, and call for action on the part of the government, in order to build again her sea power. It will not be too much to say that the action of the government since the Civil War, and up to this day, has been effectively directed solely to what has been called the first link in the chain which makes sea power. Internal development, great production, with the accompanying aim and boast of self-sufficingness, such has been the object, such to some extent the result. In this the government has faithfully reflected the bent of the controlling elements of the country, though it is not always easy to feel that such controlling elements are truly representative, even in a free country. However that may be, there is no doubt that, besides having no colonies, the intermediate link of a peaceful shipping, and the interests involved

245

in it, are now likewise lacking. In short, the United States has only one link of the three.

The circumstances of naval war have changed so much within the last hundred years, that it may be doubted whether such disastrous effects on the one hand, or such brilliant prosperity on the other, as were seen in the wars between England and France, could now recur. In her secure and haughty sway of the seas England imposed a yoke on neutrals which will never again be borne; and the principle that the "flag covers the goods" is forever secured. The commerce of a belligerent can therefore now be safely carried on in neutral ships, except when contraband of war or to blockaded ports; and as regards the latter, it is also certain that there will be no more paper blockades.

Putting aside therefore the question of defending her seaports from capture or contribution, as to which there is practical unanimity in theory and entire indifference in practice, what need has the United States of sea power? Her commerce is even now carried on by others; why should her people desire that which, if possessed, must be defended at great cost? So far as this question is economical, it is outside the scope of this work; but conditions which may entail suffering and loss on the country by war are directly pertinent to it. Granting therefore that the foreign trade of the United States, going and coming, is on board ships which an enemy cannot touch except when bound to a blockaded port, what will constitute an efficient blockade? The present definition is, that it is such as to constitute a manifest danger to a vessel seeking to enter or leave the port. This is evidently very elastic. Many can remember that during the Civil War, after a night attack on the United States fleet off Charleston, the Confederates next morning sent out a steamer with some foreign consuls on board, who so far satisfied themselves that no blockading vessel was in sight that they issued a declaration to that effect. On the strength of this declaration some Southern authorities claimed that the blockade was technically broken, and could not be technically re-established without a new notification. Is it necessary, to constitute a real danger to blockade-runners, that the blockading fleet should be in sight? Half a dozen fast steamers, cruising twenty miles off-shore between the New Jersey and Long Island coast, would be a very real danger to ships seeking to go in or out by the principal entrance to New York; and similar positions might effectively blockade Boston, the Delaware, and the Chesapeake. The main body of the blockading fleet, prepared not only to capture merchant-ships but to resist military attempts to break the blockade, need not be within sight, nor in a position known to the shore. The bulk of Nelson's fleet was fifty miles from Cadiz two days before Trafalgar, with a small detachment watching close to the harbor. The allied fleet began to get under way at 7 A.M., and Nelson, even under the conditions of those days, knew it by 9.30. The English fleet at that distance was a very real danger to its enemy.

It seems possible, in these days of submarine telegraphs, that the blockading forces in-shore and off-shore, and from one port to another, might be in telegraphic communication with one another along the whole coast of the United States, readily giving mutual support; and if, by some fortunate military combination, one detachment were attacked in force, it could warn the others and retreat upon them. Granting that such a blockade off one port were broken on one day, by fairly driving away the ships maintaining it, the notification of its being re-established could be cabled all over the world the next. To avoid such blockades there must be a military force afloat that will at all times so endanger a blockading fleet that it can by no means keep its place. Then neutral ships, except those laden with contraband of war, can come and go freely, and maintain the commercial relations of the country with the world outside.

It may be urged that, with the extensive sea-coast of the United States, a blockade of the whole line cannot be effectively kept up. No one will more readily concede this than officers who remember how the blockade of the Southern coast alone was maintained. But in the present condition of the navy, and, it may be added, with any additions not exceeding those so far proposed by the government, the attempt to blockade Boston, New York, the Delaware, the Chesapeake, and the Mississippi, in other words, the great centres of export and import, would not entail upon one of the large maritime nations efforts greater than have been made before. England has at the same time blockaded Brest, the Biscay coast, Toulon, and Cadiz, when there were powerful squadrons lying within the harbors.

It is true that commerce in neutral ships can then enter other ports of the United States than those named; but what a dislocation of the carrying traffic of the country, what failure of supplies at times, what inadequate means of transport by rail or water, of dockage, of lighterage, of warehousing, will be involved in such an enforced change of the ports of entry! Will there be no money loss, no suffering, consequent upon this? And when with much pain and expense these evils have been partially remedied, the enemy may be led to stop the new inlets as he did the old. The people of the United States will certainly not starve, but they may suffer grievously. As for supplies which are contraband of war, is there not reason to fear that the United States is not now able to go alone if an emergency should arise?

The question is eminently one in which the influence of the government should make itself felt, to build up for the nation a navy which, if not capable of reaching distant countries, shall at least be able to keep clear the chief approaches to its own. The eyes of the country have for a quarter of a century been turned from the sea; the results of such a policy and of its opposite will be shown in the instance of France and of England. Without asserting a narrow parallelism between the case of the United States and either of these, it may safely be said that it is essential to the welfare of the whole country that the conditions of trade and commerce should remain, as far as possible, unaffected by an external war. In order to do this, the enemy must be kept not only out of our ports, but far away from our coasts.

Can this navy be had without restoring the merchant shipping? It is doubtful. History has proved that such a purely military sea power can be built up by a despot, as was done by Louis XIV; but though so fair seeming, experience showed that his navy was like a growth which having no root soon withers away. But in a representative government any military expenditure must have a strongly represented interest behind it, convinced of its necessity. Such an interest in sea power does not exist, cannot exist here without action by the government. How such a merchant shipping should be built up, whether by subsidies or by free trade, by constant administration of tonics or by free movement in the open air, is not a military but an economical question. Even had the United States a great national shipping, it may be doubted whether a sufficient navy would follow; the distance which separates her from other great powers, in one way a protection, is also a snare. The motive, if any there be, which will give the United States a navy, is probably now quickening in the Central American Isthmus. Let us hope it will not come to the birth too late. . . .[13]

CHAPTER IV

Commence Firing

1898-1918

B Y THE last decade of the nineteenth century, the United States had become a great industrial nation and, having linked East and West by railroad, Americans looked beyond the continental limits to the fertile islands of the Pacific and Caribbean. Proud and confident, spurred by politicians, newspaper editors, and missionaries, they sought to take the blessings of democracy to the world's underdeveloped countries. With public opinion at high pitch, revolution erupted in the Spanish dependency of Cuba. The cruelty of Spanish rule, together with American business involvement in Cuba, led Americans to demand intervention.

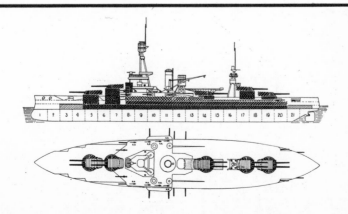

I

REMEMBER THE *MAINE*, TO HELL WITH SPAIN

Tragically and unexpectedly, in Havana Harbor on the evening of 15 February 1898, the battleship Maine *blew up. Spanish responsibility was never proved, but the slogan "Remember the* Maine, *to Hell with Spain" ignited the war. Commanding the* Maine *on that fateful night was Captain Charles D. Sigsbee, USN.*

. . . I was in my quarters, sitting on the after-side of the table in the admiral's cabin. . . .

I had completed a report called for by Mr. Theodore Roosevelt, Assistant Secretary of the Navy, on the advisability of continuing to place torpedo-tubes on board cruisers and battle-ships. I then wrote a letter home. . . .

At taps ("turn in and keep quiet"), ten minutes after nine o'clock, I laid down my pen to listen to the notes of the bugle, which were singularly beautiful in the oppressive stillness of the night. The marine bugler, Newton, who was rather given to fanciful effects, was evidently doing his best. During his pauses the echoes floated back to the ship with singular distinctness, repeating the strains of the bugle fully and exactly. . . .

I was inclosing my letter in its envelope when the explosion came. . . . It was a bursting, rending, and crashing roar of immense volume, largely metallic in character. It was followed by a succession of heavy, ominous, metallic sounds, probably caused by the overturning of the central superstructure and by falling debris. There was a trembling and lurching motion of the vessel, a list to port, and a movement of subsidence. The electric lights went out. Then there was intense blackness and smoke.

The situation could not be mistaken: The *Maine* was blown up and sinking. For a moment the instinct of self-preservation took charge of me, but this was immediately dominated by the habit of command. I went up the inclined deck into the starboard cabin. . . . My first intention was to escape through an air-port, but this was abandoned in favor of the more dignified way of making an exit through the passageway leading forward through the superstructure. I groped my way through the cabin into the passage, and along the passage to the outer door. The passage turned to the right, or starboard, near the forward part of the superstructure.

At the turning, some one ran into me violently. I asked who it was. It was Private William Anthony, the orderly at the cabin door. He said something apologetic, and reported that the ship had been blown up and was sinking. He was directed to go out on the quarter-deck, and I followed him. . . .

I stood for a moment on the starboard side of the main-deck, forward of the after-superstructure, looking toward the immense dark mass that loomed up amidships, but could see nothing distinctly. There I remained for a few seconds in an effort to grasp the situation, and then asked Anthony for the exact time. He replied: "The explosion took place at nine-forty, sir."

It was soon necessary to retire from the main-deck, for the after-part of the ship was sinking rapidly. I then went up on the poop-deck. By this time Lieutenant-Commander Wainwright and others were near me. Everybody was impressed by the solemnity of the disaster, but there was no excitement apparent; perfect discipline prevailed. . . .

The flames increased in the central superstructure, and Lieutenant-Commander Wainwright . . . went forward on the poop-awning, making a gallant inspection in the region of the fire, but was soon obliged to report that nothing could be done. The fire-mains and all other facilities were destroyed, and were not available for the service.

We then began to realize more clearly the full extent of the damage. One of the smoke-stacks was lying in the water on the starboard side. . . . As my eyes became more accustomed to the darkness, I could see, dimly, white forms on the water, and hear faint cries for help. Realizing that the white forms were our own men, boats were lowered at once and sent to the assistance of the injured and drowning men. . . . Only three of our fifteen boats were available—the barge, the captain's gig, and the whale-boat. The barge was badly injured.

Two of these were manned by officers and men jointly. How long they were gone from the ship I cannot recall, but probably fifteen minutes. Those of us who were left on board remained quietly on the poop-deck.

Nothing further could be done; the ship was settling rapidly. There was one wounded man on the poop; he had been hauled from under a ventilator on the main-deck by Lieutenants Hood and Blandin just as the water was rising over him. Other boats, too, were rescuing the wounded and drowning men. Chief among them were the boats from the *Alfonso XII*, and from the steamer *City of Washington*. The visiting boats had arrived promptly, and were unsparing of effort in saving the wounded. The Spanish officers and crews did all that humanity and gallantry could compass. During the absence of our boats the fire in the wreck of the central superstructure became fiercer. The spare ammunition that had been stowed in the pilot-house or thrown up from the magazines below was exploding. It continued to explode at intervals until nearly two o'clock in the morning. . . .

Presently Lieutenant-Commander Wainwright came to me and reported that our boats had returned alongside the ship at the stern, and that all the wounded that could be found had been gathered in and sent to the Spanish cruiser and the *City of Washington* and elsewhere. The after-part of the poop-deck of the *Maine*, the highest intact point above water, was then level with the gig's gunwale, while that boat was in the water alongside. We had done everything that could be done, so far as could be seen.

It was a hard blow to be obliged to leave the *Maine;* none of us desired to leave while any part of her poop remained above water. We waited until satisfied that she was resting on the bottom of the harbor. Lieutenant-Commander Wainwright then whispered to me that he thought the forward ten-inch magazine had been thrown up into the burning material amidships and might explode at any time, with further disastrous effects. He was then directed to get everybody into the boats, which was done. It was an easy operation, one had only to step directly from the deck into the boat. . . .[1]

In April, 1898, the United States declared war on Spain. The events of the conflict seemed to prove Mahan's dictum that sea power is cardinal, especially if employed against a disorganized foe. American

strategy was to strike Spain's island outposts: Cuba, Puerto Rico, the
Philippines.

II

MANILA BAY

Commodore George Dewey's squadron attacked the Spanish fleet
anchored in Manila Bay on 1 May 1898. Gunner Joel C. Evans,
in charge of the Boston's *forward ammunition supply, recounts the*
battle.

. . . It was a little after half-past five o'clock when the roar of a
gun on our deck above let me know that we had taken a hand in the
game. It was an eight-inch monster, and before its echo below had
died away the call for ammunition came. I think that was the proud-
est moment of my twenty-four years in the navy. I had sent many a
shell above to hit or miss a sand-bank or some old hulk for target practice, but we knew now that every one "meant business." On the bridge
Captain Wildes would shout what was wanted, and the word came to
us from those assisting above in hoisting. Each projectile was slung
ready for use, the powder in copper cylinders and the fixed ammunition for the rapid-firing guns in boxes. The men worked coolly, with
nothing troubling them but the heat and curiosity. Their eagerness to
know what was going on was overwhelming, and impelled them to
rush to the ports to discover the cause of extraordinary activity on
deck or of lulls in the firing. I had little opportunity for this, as I had
to be particularly careful that no error was made in the ammunition,
and that not a second was lost. What between orders for full and reduced charges, steel and shell, I was kept busy all the time. . . .

My own feelings were so lost in anxiety to do well with the ammunition that for the first hour and a half I thought little of what
was being done above.

After this I became exhausted from the heat, loss of sleep, and
lack of proper food; and when we were ordered to cease supplying
ammunition I went on deck and lay down on the desk in the chart-

U.S. Battleship *Maine* blowing up in Havana Harbor.

Battle of Manila Bay.

house. Below, the thermometer was at 116°, and the fresh air was a great relief. From this vantage-point I could see the destruction we had wrought, and was informed of all that had happened.

The most exciting incident of the battle, perhaps never exceeded in its audacity and its fearful results for the attacking party, was the attempt of two torpedo-boats to destroy the *Olympia*. They waited as she approached, and then came at her full speed. The *Olympia* poured a storm of big shells about them, but they presented such a small target at the distance of several miles that they were not hit, and each moment of their nearer approach was filled with suspense and dread for all on our ships. Insignificant as they were, they might send the flag-ship to the bottom of the bay, and every shot directed at them carried a prayer for its success. When within eight hundred yards the *Olympia* used her secondary battery, and almost drowned the torpedo-boats in a rain of projectiles. The one which led suddenly paused, and then, coming on a few feet, blew up and sank with her crew. The other fled for the beach, and was found there the next day, a mere sieve, battered and blood-stained.

The engagement was a general one by this time, and forts and ships fired at one another with the fury of desperation on one side and perfect confidence on the other. The *Boston* was ordered to look after the *Reina Christina* and the *Castilla,* and we went as close to them as we might with any degree of prudence, steaming in an ellipse and firing the port battery. Then we ported our helm and gave them the starboard guns.

The *Boston* did not escape unscathed. We were struck a number of times. The shot that had disturbed us below nearly ended Captain Wildes's life. He was on the bridge, with sun helmet, palm-leaf fan, and cigar, when the shot hit the foremast three feet over his head, passed from starboard to port, cutting a shroud in the fore-rigging, and burst ten feet from the side, the recoil sending the base-plug back on deck. The captain watched the shell's progress intently, and then resumed his smoking. Of all the officers on the bridge he was the only one who did not try to dodge the missile. He simply said, "We were lucky, gentlemen! . . ."

We made five trips past the forts and fleet, peppering the *Reina Christina* whenever able. Just two hours after the beginning of the battle we hauled out, and, withdrawing a few miles, the order was given for breakfast. Then it was that I went on deck. I could not eat, but was fortunate enough to get a cup of Paymaster Martin's coffee. The men had cold comfort, as the galley fires had been ordered extinguished at 4 A.M. They were wearied and hungry, and ate the bread and meat with good appetites. . . . Meanwhile we had our eyes glued on the ships we had been maiming, and were gratified to see the *Reina Christina* burst into flames, followed by the *Castilla*. . . .

My men were talking excitedly about the fight, and naturally their versions were different. Some were sure that the *Boston* had done all the damage inflicted on the Spanish, and others that we had been badly hurt. The *Baltimore* led back, the *Olympia* seeking to save her ammunition, which was almost spent. The *Boston* was the third ship in the return. The *Baltimore* faced the Cavite forts at close range, and for twenty minutes fired without cessation. A mine field burst a thousand yards from her, but without damage. The *Baltimore* then steamed ahead two hundred yards, the *Olympia* taking her place for the same length of time. The *Boston* was favored at the end of forty minutes, when we attacked the sea face of the forts where the *Olympia* had been. We got so near inshore that our stern was in the mud, and we were as steady as a rock. I think there were only three guns then firing from the fort, and our first eight-inch shell dismounted all three. We then fired at all Spanish property within range, and, knowing that it was the end of the battle, took pride in accurate firing and measured ranges.

In the second fight I sent up ammunition until 11:30, about three-quarters of an hour. All my men were naked except for shoes and drawers, and I wore only a cotton shirt in addition. Three in the after powder division fainted from the heat, but none of my force was overcome. The heat was really fearful. The powder smoke settled down, choking us and half blinding some, and only the love of the work kept us going. The Chinese stood the heat better than we did.

The *Boston* stayed by the batteries until they were silent. All this time the two Spanish vessels were ablaze. The *Don Antonio de Ulloa* had the attention of most of us, and finally went down with her colors flying. By an accident to her engine-room telegraph, the *Boston* was cut out of the job of going inside and destroying all the vessels, and the *Petrel* did the work. Then the cheering became general, and as ship after ship passed in their manoeuvers the men shouted themselves hoarse with joy. The signal was set that none had been killed on any vessel of ours. It is not easy to convey a proper idea of the enthusiasm and delight at the news that our men were all safe, after the hell we had been through for hours. We could hardly believe it. . . .[2]

III

THE FLEET CAME OUT AND
WENT TO DAVY JONESES LOCKER

Thousands of miles away, Rear Admiral Cervera's fleet, sailing from Spain, eluded American patrols and slipped into Santiago Harbor on the eastern end of Cuba. Rear Admiral William T. Sampson blockaded the port.

The destruction of Cervera's fleet was vital. A military expedition, hastily organized, landed in Cuba and successfully penetrated the main line of land defenses for Santiago. Cervera had two choices— surrender or escape. On 3 July 1898 the Spanish ventured out to break through the blockade. American ships chased Cervera's force along the Cuban coast, pumping in shells without receiving effective return fire. One by one the Spanish ships were beached and destroyed. The battle is seen through the eyes of Seaman Cross on the Battleship Oregon.

. . . *July 4.* The fish has come out to see us. On the 3rd the Spanish fleet came out of the Harbor to fight and get a way if posable. (I would have put this down on the 3rd But I dident have time and was too tired that night so I put it off for today.) Well the Fleet came out and went to Davy Joneses locker. it was Just 9.25 A.M., first call sounded on our ship for Quarters and we all had our best dudds on; we wer going to listen to the Articles of War this morning and to have chirch right affter, But we never did. all of a suden the Ordly on watch made a dive for the Cabin head first, and told the old man the Fleet was coming out of the Harbor. the old man jumpt up a standing. as soon as some of the men seen the ships there, they went to there Quarters with out any further delay. I was standing on the Quarter Deck waiting for the last call to go. I heard the news and looking around the affter Terets seen the first one. I thought she looked

(Right) Jim Hickey, No. 2 Gun Forr'ard Turret, USS *Olympia*. (Below) Gunners on board a cruiser grabbing a breath of fresh air.

Biger than a Mountain. But then I thought affterwards we could cut her down to her natchral size. . . .

By 9.27 the Oregon fired the first shot of the Battle of July 3rd 1898 at the first ship that come out of the Harbor. I dont remember the ships as they come out, But we went in to meet them and passed them som good shots as they cep coming. about 7 or 9 minuts after they got started good, one of our 6 inch guns blew up one of the Torpedo Boats, struck her squar amidships, she sunk like a rock with all on board, and right hear is where I had to stop for a moment to admire one of there Guners. I do think he was one of the bravest men I ever had the pleasure to look upon. That man must have known he was going to a shure Deth, he stud on Deck and cep firing at us all the time, and the last time I seen him he was Just going up in the air.

As the ships came out of the harbor they sircled to the right, or Westward, and Capt. Clark knew they were trying to escape. they did not think the old Oregon was such a runer as she was a fighter, so we Just tailed on with them and giving them shot-for shot. In about 20 minuts the first ship went on the Beach, plumb knocked out, and 15 minuts later the secon one went on the Beach, a short ways from the first. Then came the tug of war for we had to run to catch the Vizcaya and the Colon, but we catched them both. the Vizcaya was about 4000 yards ahead and the Colon was about 3 miles ahead, and the poor men in the fireroom was working like horses, and to cheer them up we passed the word down the ventlators how things was going on, and they passed the word back if we would cut them down they would get us to where we could do it. So we got in rainge of the Vizcaya and we sent her ashore with the secondary Battry and 6 inch guns, and then we settled down for a good chase for the Colon. I thought she was going to run a way from us. But she had to make a curv and we headed for a point that she had to come out at. We all think there is no man in the Navy like Capt Clark, he is a Brave man, he stud on the Forward 13 inch turet through the thickest of this fight and directed his ship to the final results. . . .[3]

With the defeat of Spain, the United States discovered herself a world power, administering extraterritorial possessions, exercising protectorates. Maturity brought responsibilities.

IV

THE TRAIN TO PEKING

In response to urgent calls from the American legation at Peking, the protected cruiser Newark *arrived at the mouth of the Pei-ho River, near the port of Tientsin, and dispatched battle-ready marines by rail to Peking in May, 1900. Aroused over the encroachments of the European powers, the Chinese had formed a society, the Boxers, pledged to exterminate all "foreign devils." Early in June landing parties of American seamen were ordered to join the forces of other nations, then assembled at Tientsin, for the relief of the Peking legations. Attached to this expedition was Midshipman Joseph K. Taussig of the* Newark.

. . . It is probable that never again will history repeat the story of eight nations combining their naval forces in land operations against a common enemy. These nations were the American, Austrian, British, French, German, Italian, Japanese and Russian. This combined force became known as "The Seymour Relief Expedition," taking its name from Vice Admiral Sir Edward Seymour of the British Navy, who, by virtue of his seniority, became the commander of the expedition; and from the fact that its mission was the relief of the besieged legations at Pekin.

Our American leader was the late Rear Admiral Bowman H. McCalla, who was then a captain, commanding the *Newark*. . . . With the British contingent were . . . Admirals Jellicoe and Beattie. Both were young men, the former being captain of the battleship *Centurion* and chief-of-staff to Admiral Seymour; the latter a lieutenant on one of the ships. With the Germans was Captain von Usedom—an officer of unusually high attainments. There were other officers, too numerous to mention here, who afterwards became famous in their respective services. . . .

AT TAKU. A more desolate anchorage than that off Taku cannot be imagined. From the deck of the ship not a vestige of land is in sight. The wide expanse of muddy greenish yellow water is depressing. The Taku bar, formed by the continuous silt from the Pei-ho River,

261

is the barrier which forces vessels to anchor so far off shore. When we arrived late in the afternoon of May 27, the French cruiser *D'Entre-casteaux,* the French gunboat *Surprise* and three Chinese cruisers were the only vessels present. The French admiral was ashore. He returned the following day and his two ships immediately stood out to sea. The French admiral apparently felt no cause for alarm. However, events on shore were moving rapidly, although the information was meager and slow in reaching us. This was before the days of radio, and our ship was anchored twelve miles off shore. . . .

At five o'clock in the morning of May 29, I was rudely awakened by the captain's orderly, who said: "The Captain says get ready to go ashore immediately; uniform, heavy marching order. Be prepared to remain four or five days." On deck everything was hustle and bustle. The first contingent of sailors, about sixty in number, with Ensign Daniel W. Wurtsbaugh in charge, were packing haversacks and knap-sacks. Canteens were being filled; one day's ration served out for each man's haversack; 180 rounds of rifle ammunition in each belt. The three-inch field piece, with ammunition, stores, and water, was being placed in the sailing launch. Extra water and stores were lowered into the steam launch. At seven-thirty we shoved off from the ship, the steam launch taking the sailing launch and cutter in tow.

Little did we appreciate the coming difficulties. Tide and wind were both against us. When about three miles from the ship the steam launch ran aground on the bar. We lightened her by transferring some men into the already crowded sailing launch and cutter. In this way we ploughed through the soft mud for a short time. Then the steamer stuck fast. The sailing launch and cutter cast off—the former making sail. The cutter, of which I was in charge, had over fifty men in her. . . . At one o'clock, five and a half hours after leaving the ship, we landed at Taku, a tired, hungry lot. Our rations of canned corn beef and hardtack were devoured with relish.

Here we found the marines who had left the ship about four o'clock that morning. There were about fifty in the company com-posed of the guard of the *Newark* and that of the *Oregon,* which latter had been embarked on the *Newark* just before leaving Nagasaki. Cap-tain John T. Meyers was in command. . . .

On to Tientsin. The Europeans at Taku advised an immediate start for Tientsin, it being rumored that on the following day no armed foreigners would be permitted to pass the forts. An unsuccessful attempt was made to get passage for our little force on the railroad. The only remaining means of conveyance was the Pei-ho River. A tug and a large covered lighter were chartered, and into this lighter we were packed. Immediately on starting all hands were required to go inside under cover so as not to be visible when passing the forts. Our discomfort was great. Not only was it very hot, but the lighter had been used for carrying mud, and had not been cleaned. It was a great relief when finally we were allowed on deck and had the opportunity to view our surroundings. . . .

It was not until 11:00 P.M. that we arrived at Tientsin and disembarked. Here we found the entire foreign colony, headed by a brass band, awaiting us. They were much worried over the possibility of Boxer atrocities. Excitement was running high. We, being the first foreign contingent to appear, were made welcome with enthusiasm and wide open arms. As our battalion formed on the dock some one in a distinctly foreign (to us) voice shouted: "Three cheers for Uncle Sam!" They were given with a will, all nationalities vociferously participating. . . .

Insofar as the outward appearances of the foreign section of Tientsin were concerned there was no cause for alarm. The place was exceedingly clean and well policed. Business was progressing in the liveliest manner. . . .

However, in spite of these serene outward appearances, there must have been a decided feeling of unrest among those who were in a position really to understand the situation. Captain McCalla and the American consul, Mr. Ragsdale, wished to send the company of marines to Pekin immediately. But the Chinese authorities would not permit the armed force to travel on the railroad. During the next few days after our arrival, foreign naval detachments from the ships of Great Britain, France, Russia, Germany, Japan, Italy, and Austria arrived. Something must have suddenly occurred in Pekin to bring these ships to Taku, where, only a few days previously, the U.S.S. *Newark* was the only foreign man-of-war in the roads.

On May 31, the pressure brought by the powers became too great for the authorities further to refuse the use of the railroad. Accordingly a special train was made up, and into this a combined force of about four hundred sailors and marines was packed. . . . This was the little force that protected our legation in the long siege of the following months. Much has been written of their gallant activities. . . .

263

In the meantime, those of us who were left in Tientsin moved our quarters from Temperance Hall to the compound of the American Board Mission. This, like other compounds in Tientsin, was enclosed by a high brick wall. . . . We had one three-inch field piece with seventy-two rounds of shrapnel, and one Colt automatic gun mounted on a tripod.

There was much difference of opinion in Tientsin as to whether there really was to be trouble, or whether the whole unsettled situation would soon blow over. Every day rumors indicated that the Boxers were becoming more and more active, and that they were gradually approaching the city with a view to repeating the massacre of 1870. However, large forces of Chinese Imperial troops were encamped nearby, and at Yang Tsun, eighteen miles distant. It was certain that Tientsin was safe so long as the Chinese government remained friendly, and these troops remained loyal. But there were some missionaries who were outspoken in their belief that the foreigners had more to fear from these regular Chinese troops than from the Boxers.

For a while all was quiet in Tientsin and we settled down to routine life. . . .

More detachments of sailors and marines from the continously augmented foreign men-of-war at Taku continued to arrive at Tientsin.

On or about June 6 the railroad line between Pekin and Tientsin was cut. This, of course, was serious. Then definite news was received that the Boxers were burning railroad stations and foreign missions; that some missionaries had been murdered and native Christians were hurrying towards Tientsin for protection. These occurrences resulted in the *Newark* sending ashore a second company of fifty bluejackets under the command of Ensign C. E. Gilpin.

Our vigilance increased, especially at night. The part of Tientsin occupied by the foreigners was divided into sections, each guarded by a different nation. Many streets were barricaded. Our men slept out in the open, the field piece at hand ready for immediate action. Sentries were stationed at points on the large plain guarding all approaches from that direction, and on the Taku road, the main thoroughfare between the native and foreign cities. Attempts to run a train through to Pekin met with failure. Telegrams indicated that the situation was becoming more and more serious. Additional legation guards were asked for. There was no way of getting them to Pekin except by marching the intervening eighty miles.

On the evening of June 8 the telegraph line had been cut, completely isloating Pekin from the rest of the world. A meeting of foreign consuls and naval commanders assembled that evening to estimate the situation and determine on a course of action. . . . The generally accepted version is that the meeting was getting nowhere when Captain McCalla lost patience and arose. He is imputed to have made a statement to this effect: "I don't care what the rest of you do, but my legation is in danger and I am going immediately to start for its relief." Be that as it may, I was aroused at midnight by Ensign Wurtsbaugh and instructed by him to call all hands at four o'clock, pack effects, have breakfast, and be ready to march to the railroad station at six o'clock.

When we arrived at the station, expecting to find plenty of rolling stock available, much to our surprise we found the main track and sidings occupied by several trains containing the battalions of Her Britannic Majesty's Ships *Centurion, Endymion,* and *Aurora.* We learned they had left their ships at midnight, made the long boat trip to Taku (they evidently crossed the bar at high tide), made up the trains, and arrived ahead of us. . . .

Not only did the British have control of all the rolling stock, but Vice Admiral Seymour had placed Captain E. H. Bayley of the *Aurora* in charge of the station and all the equipment. Well do I remember Captain McCalla's irritation at this state of affairs. . . .

Things were finally straightened out and the American detachment, consisting of 112 officers and men, were given space in the first train. . . .

It was not until afternoon that the trains finally got underway and started us on a sixteen day campaign between Tientsin and Pekin. . . .

Embarked in the trains which started from Tientsin for Pekin on June 9, 1900, for the purpose of relieving our besieged legations were the naval battalions of eight different nations. It was not until several days later that our maximum strength of approximately 2,100 was reached. Of this number the British, Russians and Germans formed the much larger part. . . .

Pulling out from the railroad station early in the afternoon, the trains proceeded in a normal manner for twenty-five miles. The country was flat, dotted with the innumerable grave mounds of centuries. The ground was dry and sun baked, the crops insignificant and parched. The plain was studded with villages and cities as far as the

265

eye could reach. . . . This part of the country certainly made a sorry appearance due largely to the extended drought for which the foreigners were being held responsible by the Boxers.

At Yang Tsun, the first important city, which is eighteen miles from Tientsin, we passed a large number of troops encamped on the banks of the Pei-ho River. They were a part of the Chinese Imperial Army under General Neigh. . . .

Seven miles beyond Yang Tsun occured the first forced stop. Here we found a few rails and ties torn up, probably the work of a marauding band of Boxers. These were replaced in short order and we proceeded. From then on, during the next five miles, we encountered frequent recurrences of the few missing rails and ties. . . .

This railroad was under British supervision, so the trains were on the left track. This was fortunate, as, for some unknown reason, most of the damage had been done to the other track, which we did not stop to repair. With the American battalion was a lithe six-foot coal passer who had previously worked as a section hand on a railroad. He was the only one in the whole force who knew how to drive a spike. For the first few days he was worth his weight in gold. After that there was so much spike driving to be done, Chinese coolies were hired for this purpose.

It was decided to encamp by this trestle for the night. A double line of sentries with pickets were posted around the trains. Detachments turned to and gathered the partly burned railroad ties for fire wood. While engaged in this work we came across the trunks of three dismembered bodies, the heads, legs, and arms being scattered about. This gruesome sight, evidently the work of Boxers, had a salutory effect on the vigilance of our sentries. . . .

The next morning at five o'clock the Americans and British commenced to repair the trestle. This being completed the trains moved on. But now our progress was very slow. The farther from General Neigh's army at Yang Tsun, the bolder had the Boxers become. And their destructiveness increased with their boldness. By three o'clock we were near Lofa Station which is thirty-five miles from Tientsin. Here we had our first experience with the Boxers. An alarm was given by some one shouting, "Man the Cars!" Immediately there was confusion. Some contingents got in the cars, and some under the cars. Captain McCalla ordered us to form skirmish line alongside the train. We then advanced and saw ahead about a dozen Chinamen whom we

266

recognized as Boxers by their red caps, belts, and anklets, and by their red and white flags. Each one carried a huge knife or long spear. They slowly and steadily advanced making many salaams and gestures—a most picturesque group. We had heard these poor superstitious creatures thought they were bullet proof and that their peculiar movements turned the missiles aside giving them nothing to fear. When fire was opened they had no time to appreciate the fallacy of their belief. In a few moments they were riddled with bullets, all, of course, being killed.

Our skirmish line then advanced through a nearby village but saw no more Boxers. The village had been temporarily abandoned.

Shortly before dark we arrived at Lofa. This was a watering place for the engines. But the waterworks were demolished, the station destroyed, and both tracks and switches badly torn up. So this, our second night's camping site, still left forty-five miles between us and the legations at Pekin. . . .

The water supply was beginning to be a serious problem. All the water used came from wells, and that for drinking purposes had to be boiled. It first had to be tested to insure freedom from poison. The Chinese coolies impressed into service about this time for repairing the railroad never hesitated to drink the water. This, of course, was the best possible test. No wells were found to have been tampered with in any way. It was evident that the Chinese, who invariably deserted their villages on our approach, intended to return as soon as we passed on. While many of the wells were artesian, their flow was very meager owing to the long dry spell then prevailing. At Lofa it became necessary to water the engine. The pumping apparatus having been demolished, a thirty-yard bucket line was formed. For six hours, long into the night, our very weary men labored to fill the 4,500 gallon tender. . . .

As it now became apparent that our advance to Pekin would take much longer than originally anticipated, steps were taken to insure the necessary food and stores reaching us. A supply train, to be in charge of Paymaster Jewett and guarded by a few marines, was scheduled to leave our position daily in the evening for Tientsin and to return the following morning. This train for several days passed back and forth through General Neigh's army at Yang Tsun. It brought us plenty of canned goods and mineral water . . . [and] car loads of rails, ties, spikes, and fish plates, from the train yards at Tientsin. And, what was best of all, it brought about 100 Chinese coolies to work on repairing the railroad. . . .

The next town of importance was Lang Fang, five miles beyond Lofa, and just half way between Tientsin and Pekin. The intervening tracks were in fairly good condition, but on reaching Lang Fang we found both tracks torn up for at least a mile, a very serious situation that would require a number of day's work. Up to this time, the British and Americans, with the aid of the Chinese coolies, had done all the repair work on the tracks. It was extremely hard work, consisting of digging out the rocky road bed, carrying the ties sometimes for more than a hundred yards, lifting the heavy rails and setting them in place, and driving spikes. It was novel work for sailormen; but the rapidity of construction was marvelous. . . .

While at Lang Fang the Boxers made their first real serious attack on our trains. A large body of them—several hundred in number— suddenly appeared out of a nearby village and orchard. Armed with spears and knives, and with banners waving, they approached the trains at a full run. Before them flew five Italian sailors, who, contrary to the orders, had gone foraging beyond the picket line. Down the track came the Italians running for their lives. But they were not speedy enough, and all were cut down by their pursuers. . . .

The rapidly advancing Chinese were close aboard when fire was finally opened. Soon the rifles started to pop and the Boxers to drop. On they came, however, until hand to hand encounters began taking place. Captain McCalla took his orderly's rifle and shot several Boxers as they bore down on him with waving knives. One British officer stuck his sword in a Boxer's mouth. For a while the situation seemed desperate. Now, the rapid rat-tat-tat of a machine gun added its welcome noise to the din. Hundreds of bullets were swept across the front of the Chinese mob. They began to waver. Then as suddenly as they had at first appeared, they turned and fled. It is remarkable that our only casualties were the five Italians caught in the orchard. The Boxers left 102 dead on the field. . . .

We made a collection of knives, spears, and banners. On one of the banners was printed in Chinese ideographs, "Death to all Foreigners: by order of the Government." Things were taking a more serious aspect. . . .

It became apparent if we continued to repair the railroad all the way to Pekin and keep our line of communication open to the rear, the time of arrival at Pekin would be indefinitely postponed and we might get there too late. It was accordingly agreed to repair the road only so far as Anting, fifteen miles from Lang Fang. From there we would abandon the railroad in the evening and make a forced night march of about twenty-five miles to Pekin. But several days were still consumed in making repairs to the road beyond Lang Fang. The construction train was sent ahead. Preceding it went a reconnoitering party of British marines. . . .

From this time on it became the policy to burn every village that harbored Boxers. They made wonderful blazes. Foraging parties were organized to kidnap mules, horses, carts and other impedimenta for our expected forced march. . . .

About three miles from Anting was a village where more than the usual amount of damage had been done to the tracks. The British marines found quantities of railroad material stored in the narrow village streets. They surprised a large party of Boxers in the inn and killed them all. The town was burned. Then the unexpected happened. Captain McCalla received orders from Admiral Seymour to bring the construction train back to Lang Fang. A new and most serious situation had arisen. The track near Yang Tsun had been torn up for miles. The Chinese army which had been encamped there presumably protecting the railroad had disappeared, we knew not where. Our communications were cut in the rear leaving our little force of 2,100 sailormen in the heart of China with nothing to rely on for ultimate extraction excepting a very limited amount of ammunition and supplies and an unlimited amount of resource and courage.

The construction train put back as near Yang Tsun as the torn-up tracks would permit. Here, on the morning of June 17, one week after leaving Tientsin, we found ourselves repairing the railroad only twenty miles from that place. And instead of working towards Pekin, we were going the other way. For two days we labored, the main body in the other trains remaining at Lang Fang. We had had no word from Pekin or Tientsin for some time. We knew nothing of what was going on between Tientsin and the sea. . . .

The afternoon of June 18, while the construction train was still working in the neighborhood of Yang Tsun, all the other trains carrying the entire force returned. . . . That morning while at Lang Fang they had been attacked by a large body of Boxers supported by Imperial Chinese troops. There was a fierce battle in which it was esti-

269

mated the Chinese lost 500 killed, while the allies lost several killed and about forty wounded. It was the first time that gun fire had been employed against us. Captain von Usedom, of the German Navy, the senior officer at Lang Fang, knew that regular Chinese troops had taken part in the engagement as several of their standards were captured. Seeing that it would be futile to attempt to make Pekin under these circumstances, and even to hold Lang Fang, he had ordered the retreat to Yang Tsun, burned all the rolling stock in his rear and thereby placed twenty-five miles between the advancing Chinese Army and our little force. It was a desparate situation.

At a meeting of the senior officers it was decided to . . . try to get back to Tientsin. Yang Tsun is eighteen miles from Tientsin by the railroad and about thirty miles by river. We had no land impedimenta. The Germans had seized three large junks suitable for conveying the wounded and such few stores as remained. We Americans obtained several smaller boats into which were placed knapsacks, haversacks, and blankets.

The morning of June 19 saw us ready for the start back to Tientsin, the river route being chosen. Our legations at Pekin were left to their own salvation. . . .

The reason for the sudden turning of the Chinese armies against us was not known at the time. Nor did we find out until after our return to Tientsin. What happened was this:

The naval commanders off Taku had no information from the legations at Pekin nor from our little relief expedition for several days. All effort to communicate with us failed. They held a meeting and, unfortunately, made a decision based on false premises. They *assumed* that the Chinese armies were against us. Therefore the only thing to do was to consider that a state of war existed, to bombard the Taku forts, land a large force, and proceed to the relief of Pekin. All the naval commanders agreed to this procedure excepting the American, Rear Admiral Louis Kempff. He held that such drastic action was unwarranted, and refused to allow the United States ships to take part in the bombardment. Later events proved that Admiral Kempff was absolutely right in the stand he took.

It was this bombardment of the Taku forts by the allied navies that turned the Chinese armies against us. . . .

The morning of June 19 found all detachments busy preparing to move. It was a grave undertaking. All realized that this was a retreat.

Our expedition was a failure; our legations were in dire straits; and we, ourselves, were in a predicament from which we would be lucky to escape.

Nothing was to be carried except absolute necessities. One horse was given to Vice Admiral Seymour; Captain McCalla rode a small white mule. The other mules were used as pack animals to carry water, stores, and ammunition for the three-inch field piece. Each American bluejacket carried 180 rounds of rifle ammunition in his belt, and seventy rounds in his haversack. The haversacks were then jammed with canned goods and hardtack. The only artillery in the whole force were the American three-inch field gun and two British muzzle-loading nine-pounders. . . .

At noon we started. It having been decided to follow the left bank of the Pei-ho, we crossed on the bridge and ferried the field piece in a junk. As each nationality crossed we advanced sufficiently to make room for them in our rear. It was not until four o'clock that the whole force was ready and the real movement towards Tientsin began. Progress was slow, the bugle frequently sounding a halt. . . .

Night found us only a few miles from our abandoned trains, the positions of which were marked by flame and smoke. They had been set on fire to prevent falling into the enemy's hands. The sentries being posted we turned in for a few hours' sleep, the only disturbance being the routine watch standing and the frequent heehawing of the five mules.

At six in the morning the column was again under way. Fairly good progress was made until ten o'clock. The advance guard was then resting, waiting for the main body to close up. The point reported a body of men advancing towards us. Captain McCalla directed me to take a few men and reconnoiter. Passing through a recently deserted village on our left, it was seen that the approaching group was composed of about 200 Boxers. The field piece was rushed to the fore, and skirmish line formed behind a mud wall. At first only banners could be seen owing to a rise in the road. The Boxers, when within about 800 yards, opened fire with what we estimated at approximately thirty rifles, the bullets flying high over our heads. As we did not return the fire, on they came. When within 500 yards our field piece spoke. At the first shot the Boxers halted. Two more shots and they turned and fled into a village a short distance in their rear. We advanced on the double across the open space and through the village. Not a Boxer was to be seen. They had a most uncanny way of disappearing. . . .

This section of the country was particularly well adapted for defense. The numerous villages, the flat fields interlaced with mud walls, and the thousands of grave mounds, made it possible for the Chinese to harass us without exposing themselves. From this time on they would retire from village to village and open fire from concealed positions. In many instances their rifles would be thrust through the mud walls of houses. We would halt and form skirmish line. Then one or two volleys would be fired followed by the order to charge. On the double we would rush forward only to find the village deserted, the Chinese having taken position in the next town, a few hundred yards away. . . . On several occasions it was necessary for Admiral Seymour to order flanking parties across the river before it was deemed wise to charge. Late in the afternoon we were brought to a halt at a village where the enemy rifle fire, judging by the noise, had been greatly augmented.

The American skirmish line was strengthened by the addition of first the British, and then the French and Japanese. Our field gun and the British nine-pounders were placed in action. Still the ragged volleys from the village continued. The Germans took up a position in the rear of the skirmish line and fired over our heads. This was not at all comfortable. Before their fire was stopped one of their bullets struck one of the marines of our point in the back. As he was carried to the rear he shouted: "Hey, fellows, here goes a dead marine killed by a damned Dutchman. . . ."

The Japanese captain was the first to divine what was going on in the Chinese village. He simply shouted: "Fire crackers!" The order was given to fix bayonets, followed by the charge. The mixed line of American, British, French and Japanese rushed forward on the double, all yelling at the tops of our voices. We passed through the village, and, as usual, not the vestige of a Chinaman was to be seen. . . .

That night we witnessed a spectacle never to be forgotten. It was decided to bivouac between two villages and the river. To make our position secure, both towns were set on fire. All through the night the conflagration raged, throwing a lurid light over the weary sailors sleeping by their stacked arms. No enemy could approach without detection at a long distance. For the time being, a sense of security prevailed.

At daylight we found before us about a mile of open plains with the city of Pietsang beyond. This we traversed unmolested, but on nearing the city fire was opened from a point in the river bed where there was a sharp turn to the right. To the usual musketry fire, which now showed appreciable increase in volume, was added that from field pieces throwing shrapnel. There was no longer any doubt that regular Chinese troops were opposing us.

The city of Pietsang occupies both banks of the Pei-ho. It was evident, in view of what had just taken place, that a force would have to be despatched across the river. The Russians, Germans and Japanese were ferried to the right bank; a heavy shrapnel fire was opened on the Russians as they landed forcing them to take shelter behind some joss houses. When they were joined by the Germans and Japanese the advance started on both sides of the river simultaneously.

We on our side, the American, British, and French, proceeded close to the river bank, keeping under cover of houses whenever possible and firing on the Chinese whenever seen, which was seldom. Bullets and shell were flying thick, but most of them seemed to pass overhead.

We slowly advanced through the entire city, the Chinese retreating before us and finally making a determined stand in a strong position about 500 yards beyond the edge of the city. Here we were held in check for some time. The French sailors were now mixed in with our skirmish line. Well do I remember how difficult it was to get them to cease firing when the order was given. After dislodging the Chinese from their strong position we advanced by quick rushes from mud wall to mud wall. . . .

There was a sudden cessation of the opposition, and, for a short time we advanced without molestation. It was the calm before the storm. We were following the river levee on top of which was a road. It now made a sharp turn to the right. Here the Chinese made their most determined stand up to this time. From a large village, which was uncovered to the front by the turn in the levee, they opened up on us.

Then suddenly a troop of cavalry, about 300 strong, appeared on our left flank. They opened fire with carbines. The range was too great, and we could see the puffs of dust made by the bullets hitting the ground. The three-inch field piece had been hauled on the levee for use against the Chinese in the village ahead; but, owing to the heavy enemy fire, had to be withdrawn under cover of the embankment. Its fire was then directed at the cavalry. A few well aimed shots were sufficient to disperse that threat.

It now became necessary to cross the levee in order to gain protection from the Chinese in the village ahead. The men who had been dragging the field piece were exhausted. Captain McCalla directed that my section exchange places with them. While the change was taking place the movement across the levee began. The men who had been relieved from the field piece were already passing over and I followed close behind. On gaining the top of the levee I saw our men lying down supposedly under cover of the bank, firing into the village ahead.

Bullets were flying thick, but we had become so used to them they passed on almost unnoticed. Great then was my surprise when I felt a tremendous blow on my right hip which knocked me flat. I was the only one on the top of the levee at the time. In my desire to get under cover as soon as possible, and not being able to get up, I slid down the levee bank on the side towards the river. There I remained, for how long I have never known, but until picked up some time later by a British lieutenant and a couple of bluejackets.

It seems that on crossing the river to obtain shelter from the village ahead, we exposed ourselves to the fire from the Chinese in a village on the opposite bank. We did not know that the Russians, Germans, and Japanese on the other side of the river had not advanced as fast as we had. Accordingly for a time we were in the serious predicament of having the enemy on three sides of us. The result was more casualties than had heretofore been experienced, and a renewed sense of our desperate situation.

After driving the enemy from their position a halt was called for much needed rest and food, and to take stock. A number of wounded men and a few dead had been collected in one spot. The dead were buried; and the wounded taken to the river and placed on the junks. My billet was on top of a lot of boxes containing canned goods. We Americans had no doctor with our detachment. . . . To the British doctors, who had more of their own to attend than they really had time for, fell the lot of looking out for us. . . . About four hours later Surgeon MacNamara of the *Endymion* set my leg, wrapped a bandage around it (there were no splints available) gave me an injection of morphine, and moved on to the next patient.

That day, June 21, there was no further advance, and as usual there was no disturbance during the night. However, the Chinese began their attacks again as soon as the movement started in the morning. All that day the little column, with its increasing number of casualties, struggled forward in the same manner as on the previous day.

The three-inch field piece was consigned to the river, all its ammunition having been exhausted. It had proved a most valuable weapon, and its loss was serious. The care of the wounded was getting to be more and more of a difficult problem. The junk ahead of the one I was in ran aground in a very precarious position. Several of the wounded were again struck by bullets. A British midshipman and several bluejackets extricated the junk from its dangerous position, only later to have it struck by a shell and sunk. The wounded were transferred to the other two junks thereby filling them almost to the limit of their capacities.

Camp was broken at 2:00 A.M., it being hoped that a night movement would prove more rapid. But it was not to be so, as the harassment soon commenced. It looked like another long day of continual fighting with now rapidly depleting ranks, ammunition, and food.

At about 9:00 A.M., the fire from the Chinese suddenly ceased and for a short time the column proceeded unopposed. This we knew augured something unusual. The column was approaching a number of substantial looking buildings surrounded by a high wall and a moat. Two Chinamen hailed from the top of the wall asking who we were and what we were doing. The answer, through an interpreter, was, "Peaceful foreigners going to Tientsin." Instantly a heavy fire was opened from the compound.

This place, of course, could not be left in our rear. It *had* to be taken.

A large flanking party of British Royal Marines under command of Major Johnstone was sent far to the rear where it crossed the river, and made a wide detour. While the main body was keeping the Chinese busy, this flanking force after what to us seemed an interminable period, suddenly appeared in the rear of the compound giving the Chinese a startling surprise. It must be that they thought these marines composed an entirely new force, and a much larger one than it really was, for without more ado the Chinese abandoned their wonderfully strong position and fled. . . .

We found ourselves in possession of the Hsiku arsenal. Here was enough artillery for an army. . . . That this place was so easily taken seemed a miracle. It was our salvation. All detachments were set to work fortifying. Within a short time it was felt that we could withstand the attacks of many thousands of Chinese as long as the food held out.

All the wounded officers, excepting Captain Jellicoe who had been shot through the lungs and had to remain in a sitting posture, were placed in a large room which contained numerous siege guns and boxes of ammunition stacked to the ceiling. I was between a Russian lieutenant and a German lieutenant, while near my feet was a British midshipman. . . .

The next day the Chinese besiegers kept up a continuous bombardment of shrapnel, but made no assault. This might have been due to the dust storm that was raging. Outside it was blinding, while inside the buildings the dirt found its way through the windows which had no glass, and the shutters of which had to be left open to give light. It did absolutely no good to wash. We wounded, with our begrimed clothes and faces, were terrible looking sights. But as there were large quantities of medical stores in the arsenal we were all made more comfortable; in my own case by a splint which suited my particular fracture.

The second night rockets were again fired and this time it was reported that answering signals were seen from Tientsin. So we hoped for a speedy relief.

The following day, June 25, a cloud of dust was seen approaching. It did not come from the direction of Tientsin. Rumors immediately ran rife.

First one would come in and tell us it was a relief column approaching; and then some one else would say, "no, it is Chinese cavalry." For an hour or more we were left in suspense and doubt. Finally there was no mistaking that the approaching dust cloud was caused by our relief forces. . . .[4]

The United States' steady naval expansion in the first decades of the twentieth century was accompanied by technological experiments —the submarine and airplane.

The Holland submarine.

Barry, (USTB)—1905.

V

THE *OCTOPUS*

In 1895 inventor John P. Holland contracted with the Navy to build the submarine Plunger *but, upon completion, the government rejected her. In 1900, however, the Navy accepted the* Holland, *which received Hull Number 1—the first of a list of submarine hull numbers that approached 300 prior to World War II. Between 1900–1914 the Navy accepted twenty-five submarines. Considered boats, not ships, and skippered by no one above the rank of lieutenant, junior grade, these early experiments carried only a handful of men and were not designed for long cruises. Holland himself in 1900 discusses the future of the submarine, and Frank Cable, an electrical engineer employed as superintendent of construction for the Electric Boat Company, describes his strange cruise in 1907.*

When the first submarine torpedo-boat goes into action, she will bring us face to face with the most puzzling problem ever met in warfare. She will present the unique spectacle, when used in attack, of a weapon against which there is no defense. You can pit sword against sword, rifle against rifle, cannon against cannon, iron-clad against iron-clad. You can send torpedo-boat destroyers against torpedo-boats, and destroyers against destroyers. But you can send nothing against the submarine boat, not even itself. You cannot fight submarines with submarines. The fanciful descriptions of the submarine battle of the future have one fatal defect. You cannot see under water. You cannot fight under water. You cannot defend yourself against an attack under water, except by running away. If you cannot run away, you are doomed. Wharves, shipping at anchor, the buildings in seaport towns cannot run away. Therefore, the sending of a submarine against them means their inevitable destruction.

To-morrow, if we had a fleet of submarines big enough, they could protect New York harbor completely against an attack by the combined surface fleets of the world. But our shipping and our city would still be at the mercy of our enemies, if they had even one submarine, manned by a fearless crew of experts. You could not mine against her, for she would countermine. You could not close the harbor against her, even with a net-work of torpedoes and chains stretched across the Narrows, reaching from the surface to the bottom of the channel. From a safe distance she would simply send a torpedo against the network that would blow it to pieces, giving all the passage-way she wanted to go in and out. You could not chase her with a fleet of your own submarines, because you could more easily find a needle in a haystack than a sixty-five foot cylinder in a place like New York Bay. And if, by accident, you did find her, she would be out of sight in a flash. Then, too, the pursuing boats could never tell under water whether it was one of their own number or of the enemy. This difficulty might be met by sending only one submarine in pursuit; but, in that case, the prospect of finding the quarry would be about as promising as dredging with a butterfly-net for a half-dollar that had been thrown into the bay.

No; as nearly as the human mind can discern now, the submarine is indeed a "sea-devil," against which no means that we possess at present can prevail. She can pass by anything above or beneath the waves, destroy wharves and shipping and warships at anchor, throw shells into the city and then make her way out again to sea. She can lie for days at the bottom of the harbor, leaving only when she has used up all her stored power except what is required to carry her back to the open, where she can come to the surface a speck on the water. She would never have to expose herself for more than a second at a time during all her work of destruction in the harbor. This would be when she rose to discharge her gun to shell the city. The recoil of the gun would send her down again and out of sight. The chance of hitting her would be one in a million, even if the harbor was a floating battery, which it would not be very long while the submarine was at work. Her torpedoes she could discharge without coming to the surface at all.

It may be that the tacticians can solve the problem. To me it is the most profound puzzle. To me there seems but one solution, and that is too Utopian for serious consideration. Nations with sea ports will have to refrain from making war. It is probably safe to trust the ingenuity of man to provide the means for preventing such a contingency. . . .

For twenty-one years I have been experimenting with submarine craft. I have travelled in submerged boats under all sorts of conditions and with all sorts of crews. All my work has been experimental, the most dangerous stage of any mode of travel. Yet I have never had an accident. On one occasion, an engineer who thought he knew more about my boat then I did gave me a few uncomfortable minutes. Before putting out for a trial dive, he cut off the automatic attachment that supplied us with air. Before I had realized what the trouble was, our supply of air was permitted to get so low that my nose began to bleed. But when the engine was stopped, the reserve buoyancy sent the boat to the surface like a cask, and we had only to open our hatch to get relief. Certainly, that is a fair showing for nearly a quarter of a century of work. . . .[5]

[Cable] There is little romance in a dip of twenty-four hours under old ocean. When it was generally known at the Fore River Yards, at Quincy, Massachusetts, that the United States government demanded, among other tests, that I should take my crew of thirteen into the hold of the Octopus and remain that length of time beneath the waves, the order did not create any great excitement. This probably, was due in large measure to our confidence in the boat itself. Most of us knew the thorough manner in which it had been constructed. . . .

The Octopus was built by the Fore River Ship Building and Engine Company of Quincy, Massachusetts. She is one hundred and five feet long, has a fourteen-foot beam, and draws twelve feet of water in a light condition. She is of two hundred and seventy tons displacement, has five hundred horsepower on the surface, and is equipped with twin screws driven by gasolene-engines. She has a splendid electric storage-battery system for use in submerged work. Submerged she is driven by two fifty-two horse-power electric motors.

When driven by her gasolene-engines the Octopus can make eleven nautical miles an hour, on the surface. Driven submerged by her motors she can make ten nautical miles. Her official time is 10.004 knots.

The previous record submergence test was seventeen hours. This was made by the ill-fated French boat Lutin.

When the hatch was fastened down and we sank quietly to the bottom of Narragansett Bay at four o'clock on the afternoon of May 15th, I had with me [fourteen] petty officers and crew, precisely the same number as were on board the French submarine. . . .

Every member of this crew hailed from Quincy, with the exception of West, who was a Salem lad. The crew had been trained under my own personal supervision, and acted as a unit. Without flattering them I can truthfully say that they were as brave and cool a set of men as ever gathered together under any flag. Momm, the mate, is a man of great experience and resource. Nindeman has sailed all over the world. He is one of the few survivors of the ill-fated *Jeannette* expedition. The men were fully alive to what may happen to a vessel in the course of a twenty-four hours' submergence beneath the waves. But they were quite cheerful about it. Nobody indulged in gloomy forebodings. There was no looking up and taking a last glimpse of the sky, nor any theatrical attitudinizing of the kind. They all faced their contemplated twenty-four hours' imprisonment as they would have carried out any orders. It was done cheerfully, and without any idea that the eyes of the world—at least the eyes of the great navies of the world—were upon them.

When the hatch was closed, and the necessary preparations were completed, I glanced at the crew, and I must say that I experienced a thrill of pride as my eye rested for a moment on the well-knit and hardy forms and the fearless, resolute faces of my companions.

"Boys," I said, "we are now going to be locked up together for quite a spell, and we must try to make it as little tedious as possible. Let's give three cheers for the boat and her builders."

One of the tests we had to make was to run the motors for four hours after starting up. This was done by putting her nose against the dock so that, although running the motors, we really did not alter our position materially. Two tenders, the *Hist* and the *Starling,* were in attendance for fear some vessel, ignorant of the fact that we lay beneath them, might, after we had sunk to the bottom, drop a heavy anchor on us and thus crush in the shell of our little craft.

We had dinner at six o'clock. The boat had been entirely cut off from the outside air and we were wholly dependent upon our compressed or "canned" supply. The great motors gave out a strange, humming sound. The crew conversed at first in low, constrained tones, but became more lively as the meal progressed. Everybody sat down to dinner except two men on watch. The meal was prepared by Marcus West, who acted as chef during the test. He used an electric stove, and care was taken to cook nothing which would give out noxious fumes. Our menu was as follows:

Consommé
Roast chicken
Cold roast beef
Cold ham
Chicken salad—Lobster salad
Vegetables
Boiled potatoes
French green peas
String beans
Dessert
Pie—Cake—Crullers
Tea—Coffee

There were no cigars, no lights, except that given out by the electric bulbs, being allowed in the boat. This abstention from tobacco was the only hardship undergone by the crew during their stay on board the vessel.

By seven o'clock the meal was over, the dishes were cleared away, the cloth was removed, and the men had disposed themselves about the boat, lounging, chatting, reading, and a game of freeze-out was started at the table.

At eight o'clock, after running the motors for four hours, as I have described, the men were ordered to stations, the boat trimmed by admitting water to the ballast tanks, and we commenced to descend. There was slightly perceptible jar, the *Octopus* quivered just a little from stem to stern, then she heeled over a trifle to port, righted, and rested lightly, on an almost even keel, in the mud and ooze at the bottom of Narragansett Bay. The men returned to their game, and now that the great wheels of the motors had ceased to revolve, except for the low buzz of voices, or an occasional ripple of laughter from the card-players, profound silence prevailed.

The first thing I did after submerging was to set a watch of two men, which was changed every two hours. The duties of these men were to look after all the interior of the boat, so that if any leak occurred they could take care of it. The *Octopus* had a bell immersed in a tank of water, which could be struck by means of air pressure. On the *Starling*, her steam-yacht tender, was another bell. This equipment by means of which we communicated with each other consists of a bell and a set of telephone receivers. It is the same device which is in use on light-ships and on many seagoing craft. We exchanged signals every hour, so as to let those on the *Starling* know that everything was all right. . . .

At ten o'clock I ordered all hands, except the two on watch, to turn in. The rubber mattresses were blown up with compressed air, all lights but one solitary shaded electric bulb were "doused," and soon my crew were sleeping as peacefully and soundly as they would have done in their quarters at the Fore River Yards. I, also, stretched myself upon my mattress, but the sleep which came so readily to the others did not at first answer to my call. For the next two hours, and in fact until long after midnight, several thoughts crowded upon me to which my mind had hitherto been a stranger.

As I half dozed on my rubber mattress, there suddenly appeared to me in great black letters a head-line I had read in the "Boston Globe" months before: "Submarine in Fatal Plunge Drowns Fourteen." Instantly all the terrible details of the sinking of the *Lutin* flashed across my mind. I seemed to see the ill-fated craft one hundred and thirty-seven feet below the surface in the harbor of Bizerta, Tunis, the overturned accumulators, the stifling fumes, the struggle for breath in the suddenly darkened hull.

I roused myself from this gloomy reverie, knowing full well the careful construction of our craft, and that I had with me a crew of men expert in every detail. No fear of a like disaster to the *Octopus* disturbed my dreams. . . .

At about six a.m. I got up and, waking the mate, we made together a thorough inspection of the hull. Notwithstanding we went over every inch of the interior surface, we could discover no signs of leakage. There was not even any moisture on the inner shell of steel.

At about seven o'clock I ordered the hands turned out. I was impressed by the freshness of the air. Up to this time we had had no occasion to draw upon our compressed supply. Some surprise was expressed that the air was not more vitiated. The exposure of litmus showed but slight discoloration from the presence of carbonic acid.

The air-flasks have a pressure of two thousand pounds to the square inch. These flasks are tested to double the working air pressure placed upon them.

Of course it didn't seem exactly like getting up in the morning. There was nothing but the ship's chronometer to assure us that it was seven a. m. After a look through the periscope I piped all hands to breakfast. . . .

At eight o'clock we struck the usual signal to the *Starling,* and in addition to the stereotyped answer, received a brief resumé of the morning's news. . . .

About nine o'clock one of the boys came up and informed me that "C. Bergh had an organ." I did not at first exactly comprehend how an instrument of that magnitude had been smuggled into the interior of the *Octopus* through her narrow hatchway; but I was ultimately given to understand that Mr. Bergh's instrument was a mouth-organ. The sailor modesty of Mr. Bergh would not permit his essaying anything more classic than "Waiting at the Church" and "Home Sweet Home," but he was loudly applauded. I doubt if Caruso ever had a more appreciative audience. Good music or bad, it broke the tedious spell which seemed to settle on the crew after breakfast was over. If ever I have to spend another twenty-four hours cut off from the world in a submarine, I shall certainly see that a pipe-organ is part of the equipment.

And this brings me to the reflection that, even in time of war, the monotony of life below the waves, shut out from the world, excluded from a view of the fleeting clouds and from the sound of the waters, except as some faint murmur reaches the ear through the double steel shell of the submerged craft, must always constitute one of the chief obstacles to prolonged existence in a submarine. It is the feeling of being cut off from the world, and not the fear of suddenly intruding waters and death by drowning, that is uppermost in the mind of the imprisoned. The mere fact that one cannot breathe the air of heaven creates a maddening longing to be once more on the surface. The knowledge that you are confined within the steel walls of your submarine prison makes you long for freedom.

. . . Jules Verne drew an enticing picture of life below seas in his splendid romance of the *Nautilus;* but I am unable, from my own experience, to say much for its attractiveness. Perhaps some embittered recluse like Captain Nemo might find it enjoyable; but we must remember that the Frenchman's submarine was a very different affair from the fighting-machine in which we were imprisoned. The involuntary passengers of the *Nautilus* were conducted to a splendid dining-apartment glittering with china, porcelain, and glass, and were fed with strange, delicious dishes prepared from the flora and fauna of the sea. . . .

In one respect, however, we felt that we were as well off as Captain Nemo and his crew. Jules Verne tells us that in the *Nautilus* men's hearts never failed them. And so it was with those bottled up in the *Octopus,* knowing well the skill and care that had been put into her construction.

When the time of our imprisonment had expired the *Octopus* responded instantly to the action of her powerful pumps, and as the water ballast was forced from her tanks she gradually, and on an even keel, rose up through the water, freeing herself without a shock from the ooze in which she had been embedded and riding securely upon the surface.

When the hatch was opened and the members of the trial board descended into the hold, they found the atmosphere perfect. So little of our compressed-air supply had been used—only one forty-fifth— that at that rate of consumption, providing we had been sufficiently stocked with water and provisions, we could have remained for forty-five days beneath the waves.[6]

VI

I WORE ONLY A BICYCLE TIRE

A momentous event in naval aviation history was Eugene Ely's successful landing and take off from the armored cruiser Pennsylvania *anchored at San Francisco in 1911. The reports of Captain C. F. Pond, commanding the* Pennsylvania, *and Ely preserve the drama of this historic flight, which demonstrated the feasibility of the carrier.*

A special platform had previously been erected on board at the Navy Yard, Mare Island, Cal. This platform, somewhat modified from the one used by Mr. Ely in his flight from the U.S.S. Birmingham at Hampton Roads, Va., was 119 feet 4 inches in length, 31 feet 6 inches width in the clear, extending from the stern to the bridge-deck over the quarter-deck and after 8-inch turret, the forward end being 5 feet higher than the after end, and with a fantail of same width and 14 feet 3 inches in length sloping at an angle of about 30 degrees, over the stern. At the sides were fitted guard rails of 2-inch by 12-inch planking, and guide rails of 2-inch by 4-inch scantling, 12 feet apart, extended throughout its length. These guide rails, evidently intended to aid the aviator in determining his direction upon landing were of little or no use in that connection, but served a useful purpose in holding the lines connecting the sand bags at a proper height from the platform. . . .

Every possible precaution was taken to insure the safety of the aviator. As fitted at the navy yard, the platform bore at its forward end a canvas screen extending from the platform to the temporary searchlight platform on the mainmast underneath the lower top, intended to catch the aviator and his machine should all other means fail, and, 10 feet from its forward end, a 2-inch by 12-inch plank extending across the face of the platform. These, and especially the plank, were very crude devices, and had they come into use would probably only have caused serious if not fatal injury to the aviator and his machine. Abaft the solid plank stop and spaced about 6 feet apart were fitted two canvas screens about 20 inches in height. These, together with the slight slope of the platform, were the only means provided in the original construction to check or stop the flight of the machine. It was very evident that something more was needed and after several consultations with Messrs. Curtiss and Ely, during which several schemes were considered and rejected, it was finally decided to adopt a system of sand bags such as had been successfully used to check automobiles at racing meets.

Accordingly 22 pairs of bags were placed on the platform, each bag containing 50 pounds of sand, accurately weighed to insure uniformity of action, so as not to slue the machine, each pair being connected with a 21-thread line hauled taut across the face of the platform over the guide rails. These bags, spaced about 3 feet apart, covered about 75 feet of the length of the platform. As it turned out they were ample for the purpose and worked perfectly and none of the other devices were called into play. On either side of the platform, awnings were spread, extending to the life-boat davits, to catch the aviator should he be thrown over the edge of the platform. Life preservers were supplied and expert swimmers stationed, while boats lay off on either side for use in case of necessity.

The flying machine, a Curtiss biplane, had been fitted with a central skid, its lower face about 5 inches above the plane of the wheels on which the biplane stood when at rest, to which were attached three pairs of flat steel hooks intended to catch the lines connecting the sand bags. These hooks, though simple in design, were extremely ingenious. . . . It is only necessary to add that they functioned perfectly. The machine was further fitted with two metal air tanks, one on either side and with a hydroplane forward for use in case, through accident, the landing was made in the water. There were no other special fittings, and the machine landed on its rubber-tired wheels, as upon ordinary occasions. Ely himself wore a life preserver about his shoulders improvised from the inner tube of a bicycle tire.

The ship was riding to the flood tide with the wind, a light breeze of about 10 to 15 miles about three points on the starboard quarter, the most disadvantageous point, both accelerating the speed of the aeroplane and sweeping it off its course. The U.S.S. *Maryland* lay about 1000 yards, two points abaft our starboard beam, and the U.S.S. *West Virginia* about 500 yards on our port bow.

The flight from the aviation field at Tanforan, 10 miles distant in an air line, was made at a speed of about 60 miles an hour, as determined by the time of flight, and at an elevation of about 1500 feet. When about a half mile distant the aeroplane made a graceful dip, passing directly over the *Maryland* at an elevation of about 400 feet, then circling and continuing its descent passed over the bows of the *West Virginia* at an elevation of about 100 feet, and completing the turn at about 500 yards on our starboard quarter headed directly for the ship. When about 75 yards astern it straightened up and came on board at a speed of about 40 miles an hour, landing plumb on the center line, missing the first lines attached to the sand bags—but catching the next lines, and stopping within 30 feet with 50 feet to spare, nothing damaged in the least, not a bolt or brace started, and Ely the coolest man on board.

Hardly two minutes had elapsed from the time the aeroplane was first sighted, and no one had imagined he would make the landing on the first turn. The sand bags worked perfectly, stopping the machine, weighing, with the aviator, about 1000 pounds, with a speed of 40 miles an hour, within 30 feet, and, as Ely stated, with no perceptible jar. Six pairs of bags did the work, being hauled in over the guide rails close to the machine, the other five pairs being only slightly disturbed. The bags were caught, four on the first set of hooks, three on the second, and four on the third set. As the aeroplane came on board, the upward draft from the wind striking the starboard quarter of the ship lifted it bodily and gave it a slight list to port. . . . When the size and weight of the machine, its speed of approach, the elevation from which it descended, and the effect of the wind are considered, the marvelous skill, accuracy of judgment and quickness of brain of the aviator may be imagined. The slightest error of judgment meant serious, if not fatal, injury to both the aviator and his machine. Three feet more of elevation would have forced him to plunge directly into the canvas screen, and three to ten feet less elevation would have caused him to strike the fantail with consequences which can only be surmised.

The flight from the ship, an hour later, was comparatively tame. The aeroplane took the air easily, dipping to within about 10 feet from the surface of the water and then rising to an elevation of about 2000 feet over the city. Within a very few minutes Ely was back on the aviation field, landing within 10 feet of the starting line.

As a result of this experiment and of my observations on the aviation field, I desire to place myself on record as positively assured of the importance of the aeroplane in future naval warfare, certainly for scouting purposes. For offensive operations, such as bomb throwing, there has as yet, to my knowledge, been no demonstration of value, nor do I think there is likely to be. The extreme accuracy of control, as demonstrated by Ely, while perhaps not always to be expected to the same degree, was certainly not accidental and can be repeated and probably very generally approximated to.

There only remains the development of the power and endurance of the machine itself, which, as with all mechanical things, is bound to come. There will be no necessity for a special platform. The flight away may be made either from a monorail or from a stay, and either from forward or aft, but preferably forward, while the return landing may be made on the water alongside, and the aviator and his machine afterwards brought on board. In fact, Curtiss has already demonstrated at San Diego the feasibility of not only landing upon the water, but under certain conditions the practicability of also flying from the surface of the water. . . .

[Ely] There was never a doubt in my mind that I would effect a successful landing on the deck of the *Pennsylvania*. I knew what a Curtiss biplane would do, and I felt certain that if the weather condi-

Eugene Ely's plane before landing on the U.S. cruiser *Pennsylvania*.

tions were good there would be no slip. The atmospheric conditions at the field appeared to be good, but, as I discovered after I got up in the air a few hundred feet, there was a good stiff breeze blowing. The quality of the air was good. It was heavy and moist and of even pressure. The temperature was cold enough to make me uncomfortable, but I cannot say that the coldness was severe enough to incapacitate me or to interfere with the free use of all the members of my body.

As I came out over the bay above Hunters Point, I was about 1200 feet up. It was cloudy, smoky and hazy. I could not see the ships at first and did not locate them until I was within about two miles of them.

I was spinning along at about 60 miles an hour with the wind directly behind me, and when I sighted the *Pennsylvania* I saw that the stern was pointed into the wind, and when about a mile away I veered off to pass over what I supposed was the flagship *California*. As I neared her I dropped down from 1000 to about 400 feet in salute to the admiral. This ship, however, proved to be the *Maryland,* as the *California* was not in the bay, and I swung around the *West Virginia* coming down to about 100 feet above the water, and pointed my machine for the *Pennsylvania*. I then made a sharp turn about 100 yards astern of that ship, gradually dropping down.

But there was an appreciable wind blowing diagonally across the deck of the cruiser, and I had to calculate the force of this wind and the effect it would have on my approach to the landing.

I found that it was not possible to strike squarely toward the center of the landing, so I pointed the aeroplane straight toward the landing, but on a line with the windward side of the ship. I had to take the chance that I had correctly estimated just how many feet the wind would blow me out of my course.

Just as I came over the overhang at the stern, I felt a sudden lift to the machine, as I shut down the motor, caused by the breaking of the wind around the stern. This lift carried me a trifle further than I intended going before coming in actual contact with the platform.

If anything I was brought to a stop a little too short and it probably would have been better to have had a little less weight in the sand bags.

The pneumatic life preserver that I had used during the flight from the *Birmingham* in Hampton Roads had proved cumbersome, inter-

GREAT
ENCOURAGEMENT
FOR
SEAMEN.

ALL GENTLEMEN SEAMEN and able-bodied LANDSMEN who have a Mind to diftinguifh themfelves in the GLORIOUS CAUSE of their COUNTRY, and make their Fortunes, an Opportunity now offers on board the Ship RANGER, of Twenty Guns, (for FRANCE) now laying in PORTSMOUTH, in the State of NEW-HAMPSHIRE, commanded by JOHN PAUL JONES Efq; let them repair to the Ship's Rendezvous in PORTSMOUTH, or at the Sign of Commodore MANLEY, in SALEM, where they will be kindly entertained, and receive the greateft Encouragement.---The Ship RANGER, in the Opinion of every Perfon who has feen her is looked upon to be one of the beft Cruizers in AMERICA.----She will be always able to Fight her Guns under a moft excellent Cover ; and no Veffel yet built was ever calculated for failing fafter, and making good Weather.

Any GENTLEMEN VOLUNTEERS who have a Mind to take an agreable Voyage in this pleafant Seafon of the Year, may, by entering on board the above Ship RANGER, meet with every Civility they can poffibly expect, and for a further Encouragement depend on the firft Opportunity being embraced to reward each one agreable to his Merit.

All reasonable Travelling Expences will be allowed, and the Advance-Money be paid on their Appearance on Board.

IN CONGRESS, MARCH 29, 1777.

RESOLVED,

THAT the MARINE COMMITTEE be authorifed to advance to every able Seaman, that enters into the CONTINENTAL SERVICE, any Sum not exceeding FORTY DOLLARS, and to every ordinary Seaman or Landfman, any Sum not exceeding TWENTY DOLLARS, to be deducted from their future Prize-Money.

By Order of CONGRESS,

JOHN-HANCOCK, PRESIDENT.

DANVERS: Printed by E. RUSSELL, at the Houfe late the Bell-Tavern.

fering with the free use of my arms and legs, so on this occasion, I wore only a bicycle tire and found it was much better, as it did not hamper my movements at all. . . .[7]

In 1914 war enveloped Europe. The United States remained neutral until Germany's unrestricted submarine warfare provoked Congress to declare war on 6 April 1917. Upon arriving in England, Rear Admiral William S. Sims, USN, quickly grasped the severity— not fully revealed to the public—of the German submarine campaign. Allied shipping losses had risen to 540,000 tons in February and threatened to reach an unprecedented height of 900,000 tons. Continued sinkings on such a scale spelled disaster. Final victory hinged on the Allies' ability to cope with enemy submarines.

VII

TORPEDOED AND SINKING FAST

On the date of Admiral Sims' first appeal to Washington, the Navy Department ordered Destroyer Division Eight under Commander Joseph K. Taussig, USN, to prepare for sea. Weathering a stormy passage, this first American squadron approached the Irish coast on 4 May. Each four-stacker, repaired and briefed at Queenstown, got under way to patrol an area of 900 square miles. Lieutenant Commander Ralph C. Parker's letters to his wife; Commander Taussig's narrative; the official report of Lieutenant William Gresham, an armed guard officer on the merchant ship Aztec; *describe the battle for the Atlantic.*

April 13, 1917

There is absolutely no news. We are standing by for what may betide, with not the faintest idea of what it may be. Of course, we are drilling all the time, and perfecting our readiness for action in every way, but there is a total absence of that excitement and sense of something impending that one usually associates with the beginning of

WHAT THE NAVY IS DOING

Photograph by W. A. Nightingale, U. S. N.   Press of Navy Recruiting Bureau, New York

HEROES OF THE DEEP ⚓

n this war the ARMED GUARD, all enlisted men, are making the Epic of the Navy. For two hours and a half the armed guard of the S. S.
the Hun, compelling the U-boat to submerge damaged. Enemy fired two hundred rounds of shrapnel, one shot exploded in the armed guard's mess room,
ng it completely, others hitting the ship with minor damage.
truck by shrapnel, but giving as they took, our men won out and kept their heads. Here is the youthful fibre of the Navy, kids almost alongside of their
but now veterans and according to their commander, "behaving cooly throughout the engagement, doing their duty."

ENLIST IN THE NAVY

The dramatic contrast between the recruiting posters of the Revolutionary War
and World War I, is shown on page 291 and above.

war. Indeed, I think that the only real anxiety is lest we may not get into the big game at all. I do not think any of us are bloodthirsty or desirous of either glory or advancement, but we have the wish to justify our existence. With me it takes this form—by being in the service I have sacrificed my chance to make good as husband, father, citizen, son, in fact, in every human relationship, in order to be, as I trust, one of the Nation's high-grade fighting instruments. Now, if fate never uses me for the purpose to which I have been fashioned, then much time, labor, and material have been wasted, and I had better have been made into a good clerk, farmer, or business man.

I do so want to be put to the test and not found wanting. Of course, I know that the higher courage is to do your duty from day to day no matter in how small a line, but all of us conceal a sneaking desire to attempt the higher hurdles and sail over grandly.

You need not be proud of me, for there is no intrinsic virtue in being in the Navy when war is declared; but I hope fate will give me the chance to make you proud. I have been having lots of fun in command myself, and good experience. I have taken her out on patrol up to Norfolk twice, where the channel is as thin and crooked as a corkscrew, then into dry dock. Later, escorted a submarine down, then docked the ship alongside of a collier, and have established, to my own satisfaction at least, that I know how to handle a ship. All this may not convey much, but you remember how you felt when you first handled your father's car. Well, the car weighs about two tons and the W——— a thousand, and she goes nearly as fast. You have to bring your own mass up against another dock or oilship as gently as dropping an egg in an egg-cup, and you can imagine what the battleship skipper is up against, with 30,000 tons to handle. Only he generally has tugs to help him, whereas we do it all by ourselves.

The war is far harder on you than on me. The drill, the work of preparing for grim reality, all of it is what I am trained for. The very thought of getting into the game gives me a sense of calmness and contentment I have never before known. I suppose it is because subconsciously I feel that I am justifying my existence now more than ever before. And that feeling brings anybody peace.

May 19, 1917
General Post Office, London
On the trip over, we were steaming behind the R———, when

all at once she steered out and backed, amid much running around on board. At first we thought she saw a submarine and stood by our guns. Then we saw she had a man overboard. We immediately dropped our lifeboat, and I went in charge for the fun of it. Beat the R_____'s boat to him. He had no life-preserver, but the wool-lined jacket he wore kept him high out of water, and he was floating around as comfortably as you please, barring the fact that his fall had knocked him unconscious. So we not only took him back to his ship, but picked up the R_____'s boat-hook, which the clumsy lubbers had dropped—and kept it as a reward for our trouble.

We are being somewhat overhauled, refitted, etc., in the British dock-yard here. Navy yards are much the same the world over, I guess. I will say, however, that they have dealt with us quickly and efficiently, with the minimum of red tape and correspondence. We have become in fact an integral part of the British Navy. Admiral Sims is in general supervision of us, but we are directly in command of the British Admiral commanding the station. Of the U-boat situation, I may say little. There is nothing about which so much is imagined, rumored and reported, and so little known for certain. Five times, when coming through the danger zone, we manned all guns, thinking we saw something. Once in my watch I put the helm hard over to dodge a torpedo—which proved to be a porpoise! And I'll do the same thing again, too. We are in this war up to the neck, there is no doubt about that—and thank Heaven for it!

Kiss our son for me and make up your mind that you would rather have his father over here on the job than sitting in a swivel-chair at home doing nothing.

May 26.

I never seem to get time to write a real letter. All hands, including your husband, are so dead tired when off watch that there is nothing to do but flop down on your bunk—or on the deck sometimes—and sleep. The captain and I take watch on the bridge day and night, and outside of this I do my own navigating and other duties, so time does not go a-begging with me. However, we are still unsunk, for which we should be properly grateful.

I have seen a little of Ireland and like New York State better than ever. It is difficult to realize how matter-of-fact the war has become with every one over here. You meet some mild-mannered gentleman and talk about the weather, and then find later that he is a survivor from some desperate episode that makes your blood tingle. I would that we were over on the North Sea side, where Providence might lay us alongside a German destroyer some gray dawn. This submarine-chasing business is much like the proverbial skinning of a skunk—useful, but not especially pleasant or glorious.

June 8.

Once more I get the chance to write. We are in port for three days, and that three days looks as big as a month's leave would have a month ago. Everything in life is comparative, I guess. When we live a comfortable, civilized, highly complex life, our longings and desires are many and far-reaching. Now and here such things as sleep, warmth, and fresh food become almost the limit of one's imagination. Just like the sailor of the old Navy, whose idea of perfect contentment was "Two watches below and beans for dinner."

You get awfully blasé on this duty—things which should excite you don't at all. For instance, out of the air come messages like the following: "Am being chased and delayed by submarine," "Torpedoed and sinking fast." And you merely look at the chart and decide whether to go to the rescue full speed, or let some boat nearer to the scene look after it. Or, if the alarm is given on your own ship, you grab mechanically for life-jacket, binoculars, pistol, and wool coat, and jump to your station, not knowing whether it is really a periscope or a stick floating along out of water.[8]

[*Taussig*] . . . It should be remembered that during these days of the patrol the submarines did not have much to fear from the destroyers unless they were come upon unawares. This was a difficult thing to accomplish as the submarine had the great advantage of seeing the destroyer before being seen. The submarine commander then had the choice of staying under until the destroyer passed out of sight, or he could with impunity show himself provided the distance was great. In fact the submarines occasionally did allow themselves to be sighted, but always disappeared before the destroyer got close enough to do harm. Their tactics in this matter changed after the convoy system was adopted and after there were sufficient depth charges to develop the barrage. The great value of the destroyer on patrol, was its ability to keep the submarines down at times when it was necessary for them to be on the surface, in order to make successful attacks on merchant vessels. . . .

The first submarine sighted on the *Wadsworth,* that we know was a submarine, was mistaken for a drifter. These fishing boats were frequently encountered in certain areas, especially along the inside patrols. They carried a small sail aft to keep themselves headed into the wind while fishing with drift nets out. On several occasions on hazy days we had passed one or more of these vessels, at times mistaking the sail for the conning tower of a submarine. And when a submarine was actually sighted we thought at first its conning tower was the sail of a drifter. As usual the guns were manned, but when the command to open fire was finally given the submarine disappeared at the same time, and no shots were fired. Of course all hands were much disappointed. We spent several hours in the vicinity looking for its wake in the hope of getting a chance to drop our two depth charges—but no such luck came to us.

On our next patrol following this incident the *Wadsworth* was ordered by radio to meet the British Hospital ship *Karapara* which was returning from Gallipoli with sick and wounded, and bound for Bristol. It was necessary at this time to escort hospital ships as the submarines had recently torpedoed two of them. The two nights we were with the *Karapara* were beautiful moonlight ones, permitting the high white sides of the big ship to be seen for miles. It was uncomfortable duty. With a sigh of relief we parted company a few miles from Bristol at four o'clock in the morning and started back for our patrol station. It seemed to me that I had just lain down on my bunk in the chart-house when the officer of the deck called through the speaking tube: "Submarine on the surface!" The engine room telegraphs rang for full speed ahead as I rushed to the bridge.

It was just daylight, the atmosphere was unusually clear, and there on the horizon about six miles away was the submarine. Of course she had seen us, so I was determined that this submarine should not get down without being fired at. The forecastle gun commenced firing at 11,000 yards. No sooner had the first splashes appeared near the supposed submarine when to our consternation she commenced to make smoke, flash a searchlight, and make other signals. Our submarine was the British patrol boat *P-14.* None of the eight shots fired at this great range had hit her, but they came close enough for her to know that she was being made a target of.

297

P-14 and *Wadsworth* steamed toward each other and, when close enough to pass the time of day, both vessels stopped. The following conversation then took place:

P-14: "I say, I wish you would take a good look at us."

Wadsworth: "We are very sorry we fired at you, but we mistook you for a German submarine on the surface."

P-14: "I say, I am sorry I stopped you on your way."

Wadsworth: "Oh that's all right; goodbye!"

P-14: "Goodbye, old top!"

The *P-14* was one of the first patrol boats built to be used as submarine decoys. They were designed to look like submarines from a distance. Later on the *P* boats were constructed to resemble small merchant ships.

In reporting this incident to Admiral Bayly his comment was: "Such things will happen in war. I am glad *P-14* was not hit. . . ."

. . . Contacts with submarines were not the only exciting and interesting episodes in connection with the patrol duty. For instance there were the mystery ships with which we worked in conjunction. . . . During our first stay at Queenstown we had been let into the secret of these ships, or Q-boats as they were generally called. We were shown two of them fitting out. One was a sailing ship and one a merchant tramp steamer. So we knew of their existence and had been instructed concerning what action to take in case of an "S. O. S." coming from them. The general rule was that so long as they used their merchant ship distinguishing call we were to keep clear no matter how persistently they called for help; but as soon as they resorted to their special man-of-war call it meant that help was immediately wanted. While the *Wadsworth* on several occasions picked up the "S.O.S." from these ships, assistance was never required by any that was near enough for us to aid.

One day early in the game, while proceeding quietly along on our patrol station, we sighted a merchant vessel, which was immediately approached in accordance with the custom. This was an unusually trim looking vessel as far as lines were concerned, but otherwise could create no suspicion. As we closed she hoisted the Uruguayan flag and we made out in large letters on her side, *Maldonado-Montevideo*. Running close aboard we hailed, asking where from, where going, and what cargo. To which came the reply from the grey haired skipper: "From Montevideo bound for Liverpool loaded with wool."

World War I destroyer hunting submarines in the Atlantic.

Deciding she was not big enough to escort, the *Wadsworth* resumed her patrol. On our next arrival at Queenstown I was surprised to meet the master of the *Maldonado*. That ship was a *Q* boat (one of the converted sloops), and was returning to Queenstown when we spoke to her. Of course before she arrived there, probably during the night after our meeting, she had painted out all references to Uruguay. The captain, a retired naval officer, then in the reserve, was very much pleased and amused at the way he had fooled us.

Survivors, like submarines, were rarely seen by some destroyers, and frequently encountered by others. . . .[9]

[*Gresham*] From the day that we left New York the weather was very rough, gales blowing almost continuously. We had gun drills twice a day and target practice several times, using as targets barrels which we threw overboard. As we came into the danger zone the tension increased to a point where few of us took any large amount of time for sleep.

As we neared the French coast on April 1, I had not had my clothes off for days. Every bluejacket in my crew had slept in his clothes and had his peajacket, pistol, and lifebelt where he could get at them quickly. That night about 9.30 I was standing on the waste deck, starboard side. There was a heavy sea running, the wind was blowing a moderate gale. The moon was up, but the sky was overcast with dark rain clouds, with frequent squalls. We were running with no lights at all. Every port was covered. The chief engineer came by behind me.

As he passed he said: "Mr. Gresham, this is a pretty ticklish night, isn't it?" I answered: "I consider this the most dangerous night we have had, and if we get by to-night I feel we will be pretty safe."

I had barely gotten these words out of my mouth when there was a flash like a sheet of lightning, with a mass of water thrown up in the air. The flash was followed by a report below and a terrific jolt. The ship was lifted upward and to starboard, and then immediately settled down with a starboard list. She began to go down by the head so fast that between the forecastle and the bridge her well deck was awash in a couple of minutes. The explosion had put the electric plant and the wireless out of commission, making it impossible to send out an S O S. The ship was in utter darkness, and there was a hail squall.

In less time than you can tell it, the crew were all out of their quarters and up on deck. I ordered my men to man the guns. But as the foreward part of the ship was awash, No. 1 crew could not get to their posts. But at No. 2 gun, in the stern, its crew was standing by in a moment. In the meantime I went up the ladder to the top of the charthouse and began with my binoculars to search for a submarine. It was raining hard, and I could see nothing. After searching about three minutes I came down and gave the order to my men to put the Colt automatic gun in No. 1 boat and stand by to abandon ship.

I went into my cabin to get some confidential papers. When I tried to unlock the door of the locker it would not open. I smashed the panel, took out the papers and went back to the top of the charthouse to make a further search for a submarine, but without result. Then I went below on the waste deck, starboard side, and made another search from there, but I could see nothing.

By this time the ship's crew had lowered all three of the boats, and the men were already in them, all except the third mate and myself. The boat on the weather side had been smashed on being lowered but I did not know this at the time. The third engineer had stuck by his post in the engine room till the very last. His name was Herbert Collins and he had his nerve right with him. He stopped the engines and shut off the oil pump, which at once put the fires out and kept the ship from catching fire. The boatswain of the ship could also be mentioned. Up in the forecastle, which was already filling fast, he saw the men were all out of their quarters before he left. It should also be said of poor Epolucci that he was busy till the last helping the crew of the ship who were having trouble with their boat. It cost him his life, for he went with them and their boat must have gone down.

Meanwhile, the third mate and I were still on the ship. I could now feel she was sinking fast. I could hear the water coming into the fire room and sizzling on the hot boilers. It splashed up through the fire room hatches. By this time No. 3 boat had shoved off and No. 1 boat was waiting. The third mate kept calling me to leave the ship. I went to the rail and asked if all of my men were in the boat. I was told they were. The third mate and I then slid down the boat falls. In the boat I discovered that Epolucci was missing, but they told me he had gone in No. 3 boat, so I gave the word to shove off. This was not easy, for the sea was running high, but at last we managed to get clear. We stood away and for a while we could just make

301

out the black shape of the vessel against the sky, and could see the men in No. 3 boat, which was not far distant. Then another squall blew up, with a heavy rain, and everything was blotted out. When the rain stopped the *Aztec* was no longer in sight, nor could we see anything of the other boat.

My boat was small and had all it could carry. There were 11 of my gunners, the captain of the *Aztec,* the first mate, the third mate, the third engineer, the boatswain, the wireless operator, and one mess-man—19 of us in all. We were packed so tight we could use only one pair of oars. There was not elbow room for more, and as the seas were still running high, we had all we could do to keep from capsizing. Twice I think we nearly did. In an effort to steady the boat we got out a sea anchor of canvas and threw it over the bow. But it didn't work. Then I shifted it to the stern and ordered my men to pull against it. This helped us keep the boat's head to the seas, but even so our chances looked slim, so I ordered, first, the Colt automatic thrown overboard, and after that several hundred pounds of ammunition, provisions, and water, distress signals, etc., that had, of course, been placed in the boat early in the voyage to be ready for such an emergency.

We were drenched to the skin, the wind was so cold it cut into us, and there were frequent squalls of hail and rain. The captain was still suffering from the violent nausea caused by the gases he had inhaled at the time of the explosion. The messman was in his under-clothes, and the third engineer wore only the thin overalls which he had worn in the hot engine room. One of my men gave him his pea-jacket, and we huddled the half-naked messman close under our bodies to give him all the warmth we could.

For about three hours we fought out there in the darkness and cold, but we were making no headway at all. We shipped a lot of water and it took constant bailing to keep us afloat. This bailing, moreover, was difficult because we were jammed in so close together. Three times the seas broke over our heads, soaking us good and plenty, and twice nearly swamping our boat. I believe that all that saved us was the morale and training of my bluejackets. Every man of the lot was as steady as a rock, and in all those hours not one of them so much as let out a whimper or failed to put all he had in him into the execution of every command.

After hours that seemed long to us, I saw a little white light in the distance. It changed to red and then to green. The men were tremendously excited and wanted to let out a yell. But for a while I kept them quiet. We were not in shape for a submarine then. But there was a lighthouse nine or ten miles away with a bright flashing light, and when the strange boat came between us and the light I saw it was not a submarine. We fired our pistols and burned one of our red Coston lights. But then we had to wait awhile, for that French patrol boat when it saw our light was just about as skittish as I had been at first myself. It went on by. After making a big circle, however, it came back to within hailing distance and verified our helpless condition. Our red light was out, but the captain of our ship had with him a flashlight, and kept it turned upon our boat to show the Frenchman what we were.

They hove us a line, which we caught with an oar, and then the only question left was how we were to get aboard. The sea had by that time increased to a point where it seemed a certainty that we would be smashed to a pulp if we tried to bring our small boat alongside. So I explained it to the men.

"Boys," I said, "we have made a good fight and the only thing for us to do now is to keep it up a little longer—possibly until daylight— on the chance of the storm letting up a bit."

In about half an hour it did seem to let up a little. The French boat swung around and made a lee for us, and when we came in close alongside we left our boat like bullfrogs jumping off a log. Practically every man at once made a spring up for the Frenchman's side. I was last to go, and in my jump the boat dropped from under me. I hung on to the gunwale, however, and a French sailor caught me by the coat.

The boat which picked us up was a converted trawler doing patrol duty. It was in command of a French naval officer, with a crew of 21. They were a fine lot of men. Their boat was a clumsy little old tub, but they had named it the *Jeanne d'Arc,* and they could not have been prouder if it had been an ocean liner. There was only one of them who could speak a little English, and we couldn't speak any French at all, but we got along in fine shape from the start.

They could not have been kinder. They heated up some red wine below in an old battered tin kettle, and opened a can of beef. But the French officer and I were the only ones who could eat anything. The rest of our crew were still too sick from shock and exposure. Those little Frenchmen opened their lockers, and got out all the spare clothes they had. They insisted on fitting all of us out, although I could see they had little to spare. In fact, more than one generous Frenchman that night gave away his best and only suit of clothes.

Meanwhile the French officer had brought out a chart, and I showed him the spot where our ship was blown up. Most of the talking was done by signs, but the Frenchmen seem to be good at that, and they soon got all they needed to know. In a very few minutes we were back on the scene of the explosion hunting for our other boat. Another French patrol soon joined us, but though we searched until 9 in the morning we could find no trace of boat No. 3, and it has never been heard of since. It must have been capsized in the storm.

We reached Brest in due time. The French on the dock were greatly excited when they learned who we were. I went to Paris and in a few days my men followed me there. Nothing was too good for them. They were entertained at tea parties and suppers and taken about in automobiles. I left Paris and went to Boulogne and crossed the Channel to Folkestone. We did not wait in London, for I had orders to come home by the *Manchuria*, which was due to sail the next day at noon. Our voyage was uneventful, but we were all glad enough to catch sight of the American coast.[10]

(Parker's letters to his wife continued.)

August 3

Once in a while some of us gets a torpedo fired at him, and only luck or quick seamanship saves him from destruction. Some day the torpedo will hit, and then the Navy Department will "regret to report." But the laws of probability and chance cannot lie, and as the total U-boat score against our destroyers so far is zero, you can figure for yourself that they will have to improve somewhat before the Kaiser can hand out many iron crosses at our expense.

We had a new experience the other day when we picked up two boatloads of survivors from the _____, torpedoed without warning. I will say they were pretty glad to see us when we bore down on them. As we neared, they began to paddle frantically, as though fearful we should be snatched away from them at the last moment. The crew were mostly Arabs and Lascars, and the first mate, a typical comic-magazine Irishman, delivered himself of the following: "Sure, toward the last, some o'thim haythen gits down on their knees and starts callin on Allah; but I sez, sez I, 'Git up afore I swat ye wid the axe-handle, ye benighted haythen; sure if this boat gits saved't will be the Holy Virgin does it or none at all, at all! Git up,' sez I."

The officers were taken care of in the ward-room—rough unlettered old sailormen, who possessed a certain fineness of character which I believed the deep sea tends to breed in those who follow it long enough. I have known some old Tartars greatly hated by those under them, but to whom a woman or child would take naturally.

What you say about my possibly being taken prisoner both amuses and touches me. The former because it seems so highly unlikely a contingency. Submarines do not take prisoners if they can help it, and least of all from a man-of-war. But I have often thought of just what I should do in such a case, and I have decided that it would be far better to die than to submit to certain things. In which case, I should use my utmost ingenuity to take along one or two adversaries with me.

August 27.

I am still in command of the ship and love it, but there is a difference being second in command and being It. It makes you introspective to realize that a hundred lives and a $700,000 ship are absolutely dependent upon you, without anybody but the Almighty to ask for advice if you get into difficulty.

It is not so much the submarines, which are largely a matter of luck, but the navigating. Say I am heading back for port after several days out, the weather is thick as pea-soup, and I have not seen land or had an observation for days. I know where I am—at least I think I do—but what if I have miscalculated, or am carried off my course by the strong and treacherous tides on this coast, and am heading right into the breakers somewhere, or perchance a mine-field! Then the fog lifts a little, and I see the cliffs or mountains that I recognize, and bring her in with a slam-bang, much bravado, and a sigh of relief. Don't you remember the days when you thought son was dying if he cried—or if he didn't? Well, that's it!

Don't get the idea that I have no recreations. We walk and play golf, go to the movies on occasion, and there is always a jolly gang of mixed services to play with.

September 20.

I am still in command and loving every minute of it. With any other captain than ours it would be a comedown to resume my place as a subordinate. But in his case I think that all mourn a little when he is away.

Oh, it's great stuff, this being in command and handling the ship alone. Particularly I enjoy swooping down on some giant freighter, like a hawk on a turkey, running close alongside, where a wrong touch to helm or engine may spell destruction, and then demanding through a megaphone why she does or does not do so and so. I have learned more navigation and ship-handling since being over here than in all my previous sea-going experience. In the old ante-bellum days one hesitated to get too close to another ship, even with the required navigation lights on. Now without so much light as a glowworm could give, we run around, never quite certain when the darkness ahead may turn into a ship close enough to throw a brick at.

However, I am back in the ranks again now, as the captain has resumed command.[11]

(Taussig's narrative continued.)

. . . The night work was very trying, especially on the inside stations where there were more patrol vessels, and more ships passing through certain confined areas, than were found farther out. For the patrol craft the risk of collision was much more imminent than that from a submarine. This was not so for the merchant vessels as their speeds were generally less and, on account of their size, they could usually be seen at much greater distances, thereby giving them more opportunity to maneuver to avoid collision. There were not many of the first thirty-five destroyers that, at some time before the war ended, did not have a more or less serious collision. At night when an object is first seen, the difficulty in distinguishing what it is and how far away it is, is great. Especially is this so on very dark nights, no moon, overcast, but clear atmosphere. This fact was vividly brought to my notice by an incident which occurred considerable time after we had been operating without lights, and when we were accustomed to picking up ships at night. It was on a night like that just referred to, atmosphere very dark but clear. As was customary I was sleeping in all my clothes, on the bunk in the chart-house, when aroused by the call through the speaking tube: "Submarine on the surface!" followed by the rush of feet as the forecastle gun crew took their stations. We had always thought that our one best chance for getting a submarine was to fall in with one suddenly at night, and resort to ramming. Here evidently was the chance. Ensign Norman P. Earle was officer of the deck. He pointed out to me the small black spot saying excitedly:

"Captain, it's a submarine, I can see it's higher in the middle than on the ends—shall we open fire?" The gun's crew had picked up the spot and were waiting the word. The ship was now rushing along at close to 25 knots.

"How long has it been since you sighted this?" I asked.

"It must be nearly a minute now—I'm sure it's a sub," was the reply.

"Better not open fire yet," I said. "If it's a sub it should either be submerged by this time or we should be on top of it right now."

Fire was not opened. The dark spot got bigger and bigger. Soon through my night glasses, I could make out the high sides, two smoke-stacks, and four masts of a large steamer. We went close enough for me to recognize our old friend the White Star liner *Adriatic,* a vessel something over 600 feet long! Such were the difficulties (and disappointments) of night work in the patrol areas.

But with all the uncertainty of the thing, together with the occasional excitement and interesting episodes, there was a great deal of monotony about the patrol. There were many days when our bright lookouts saw nothing that could give us a thrill. There were many days of discomfort when, owing to rough seas, the excessive rolling of the ship made eating off tables impossible, and sleeping in bunks difficult. The howling of the wind through the rigging had the tendency to get on one's nerves after several continuous days of it. Most of us slept in our clothes, not removing them during the tour of duty. One captain was taking a bath when a submarine was sighted and the general alarm gongs rang. It is rumored that he stopped bathing. One day while visiting with that delightful officer, Commander Shershton, of H. M. S. *Snowdrop,* he made mention of getting a call at night and going on the bridge in his pajamas.

"Do you mean to tell me," I said, "that you take off your clothes at night?"

"Certainly," he replied. "When a call comes I throw on a dressing gown, and up I go."

"How long have you been doing this duty?" I asked.

"Nearly three years," was the answer.

"Well," I said, "when I have been doing this patrol duty for three years, I am going to put on my pajamas too."

I had then been at it for just three months.

The patrol duty was quite different from convoy duty. When the change was made we no longer steamed around for days at a time by ourselves. Thereafter, we always—or nearly always—had company. . . .

While the operations of United States destroyers resulted in a decrease in sinkings, there were still far too many of these latter to warrant an optimistic viewpoint as to the final outcome. There had been, for a long time, a struggle for the upper hand between those in favor of the adoption of the convoy and those opposed to it. . . . Finally the convoy advocates succeeded in persuading the Admiralty to try a few experimental ones. These proved successful, and from that time on the transition gradually took place, the destroyers being withdrawn from patrol duty as their services as escort vessels were required.

It took some little time to get the convoy system properly organized. For a while the destroyers would travel light one way. That is, we would take a convoy to sea, and come back to port without one; or would go to sea without a convoy and bring one back. This of course was an uneconomical employment of the destroyers; so as soon as the number of convoys increased sufficiently, and the organization and administration of their operations straightened out, the outbound convoys were so timed in departure that the destroyer escorts would proceed with them to the limit of the submarine danger zone, and then join company with an inbound convoy. By this method all the destroyers worked both ways. . . .

These early convoys made a great difference in the work and responsibilities of the senior destroyer captains, who by virtue of their seniority became the escort commanders. While on patrol we had only our own ships to look out for unless we happened to be in company with a single merchant ship. But when the convoy started we immediately became division or squadron commanders with the tactical duties involved, and the responsibility not only of the escort vessels but, to some extent, of the convoyed vessels as well.

There was also some administrative work and paper work involved which had not been on our shoulders previously. For example when we received the operation order from headquarters the escort commander would, usually, on the morning of sailing, have a conference at Admiralty House with the masters of the vessels that composed the convoy. Here the plan of procedure was explained, instructions given as to methods to be followed under different circumstances, admonition to keep closed up, lights out at night, etc. These merchant captains had never before traveled in formation. They were now to be initiated under peculiarly trying conditions where they must not only keep position accurately, but by day they must zigzag, and by night they must keep their lights out. Many of them did not like the idea at all, some few bucked it, but the greater number came around in good shape and did their best to make the convoy system the success which it eventually proved to be. Before sailing each time, the escort commander had to issue an operation order to his force, and on return to port he was required to submit a report on the operations. Neither of these had been required while the patrol was in effect. . . .

Let us follow through the mode of procedure in one such instance.

The escort commander would receive an operation order from the commander-in-chief. This gave the information concerning the convoy, its makeup, etc., the composition of the escort, and the time of departure. It was accompanied by the copies of all orders issued to the individual ships composing the convoy. These orders were:

(a) Sailing orders.

(b) A sketch showing the position of all vessels in convoy.

(c) A sketch of the zigzag plan to be followed.

The sailing orders were complete as to detail in regard to: (1) time of getting under way; (2) order in which ships should pass out through the boom; (3) directions for passing through the swept channel; (4) the courses to be steered with positions to be passed through by the convoy so long as it remained together; (5) what to do in case escort leaves before dispersing position is reached; (6) the speed of the convoy; (7) the zigzag to be used, and for how long.

In addition the escort commander was given an envelope marked "secret," which contained the information, orders, and instructions concerning the inbound convoy which was to be met after the parting of company with the outbound one. These instructions were often quite bulky as they usually contained orders for the ocean escort commander and the commodore of the convoy.

When a convoy left the United States, Halifax, Dakar, or wherever its starting point was, the destination of the different ships was not always known; or if they had been given a destination, this was changed after departure without their knowledge. This information had to be conveyed to the commander of the convoy so that the vessels could be rearranged in formation to facilitate the separation of the convoy into groups bound for English West-coast ports, Channel ports, or French ports.

There was also furnished the escort commander information of all convoys at sea or which would be at sea during the time he would be out. This was so as to avoid crossing one another at night. When two convoys met or crossed on a dark night it created an ugly situation which no one cared to encounter.

Having received the orders from the commander-in-chief, the escort commander would arrange for the aforementioned meeting with all the merchant captains at Admiralty House. There would then be a conference of the captains of the escort vessels on board that of the senior escort commander, after which the latter would issue an operation order to his force. . . .

At the appointed time the destroyers would get underway and stand out to sea. This was usually about two hours in advance of the convoy. The escort would then spread out and make a "sweep" for a distance of ten miles off the lightship. This was to search for submarines and, if there should be any present, to keep them under while the merchant ships were leaving harbor, passing through the swept channel, and forming up afterwards. This latter was usually a slow process owing to the inexperience of the personnel in tactical maneuvers. The escort vessels would return from their scouting in time to join the convoy on its arrival off the lightship. Here would commence a shepherding process where the merchant ships were the sheep and the destroyers the collies. It was something of an effort to round the convoy into shape, but when once done, and we were finally on our way, we settled down to routine zigzagging with only now and then a break in the formation caused by some ship not keeping position.

In these early merchant convoys the ships in formation were placed at intervals of 1,600 yards and at distances of 400 yards. This gave a comparatively wide front and shallow depth. The destroyers or other escort vessels were stationed ahead and on the flanks, with one astern to keep the ships closed up and to be in position to attack any submarine that might pass through the formation. The speed of these convoys was, of course, determined by that of the slowest ship, which frequently was not over eight knots. Then about one knot in advance was lost through the zigzag, and usually another knot was lost owing to the prevailing westerly sea which knocked down the speed of all ships.

For forty-eight hours or more the convoy would proceed to the westward. Then when reaching the dispersing point, or if the dispersing point had not been reached by dark of the day on which due, the signal would be made for the convoy to separate, and each vessel would be left to its own resources for the remaining trip across the Atlantic. The destroyers would assemble, and the escort commander would set a course and designate a speed to take the force to a daylight position well in advance of the rendezvous for the incoming convoy. A radio would be sent to the ocean escort requesting his time of arrival at the rendezvous. These merchant convoys were usually several hours late and often much more, which necessitated the escort vessels proceeding farther to the westward than originally contemplated.

At daylight, having obtained a position well in advance of the on-coming convoy, scouting line would be formed, the distance between ships depending on the known accuracy of our own position, and the visibility conditions. Westward the scouting line would proceed, and usually at the expected time, or a little later, one of the scouting vessels would sight smoke or masts or the hull of a ship, again depending on atmospheric conditions. This destroyer would flash out the code word for "contact." All others knowing his position in line would immediately alter course so as to assemble on the convoy. No further signals were necessary, each destroyer knowing his place and taking it, immediately beginning to patrol at a distance of from 800 to 1,200 yards from the nearest merchant ship. The escort commander would then communicate with the commodore of the convoy, giving him such orders as were directed by the Admiralty. These orders were either signalled by semaphore, shouted through a megaphone, or, if the sea was sufficiently smooth, sent aboard by a heaving line from the merchant ship to the destroyer.

Another two days would be taken up in the eastward passage. Then re-arrangement of the vessels of the convoy would take place in order to facilitate the separation of vessels bound for destinations in accordance with the Admiralty instructions. A radio would be received from the escort commander of the Plymouth destroyers asking for our position relative to their designated rendezvous, which was the position where the convoy would separate into two parts, or perhaps three.

Then the British destroyers would make contact and assemble, the convoy would be divided, the British escort going with the ships bound for the English Channel and French ports, the American escort proceeding with those bound for Irish and West English ports. This procedure varied at times according to the destinations of the ships and the escort vessels available.

If there were only a few of the convoy proceeding up the Saint George Channel and the Irish Sea, some of the Queenstown destroyers would immediately return to base, thereby being ready that much sooner for the next assignment.

If there was no submarine activity in the Irish Sea and Bristol Channel we would drop our convoy off the Smalls lighthouse which is at the western end of the southern Welsh peninsula. Here the final instructions would be given each master as to the route to be followed until arrival at Liverpool. If there was submarine activity in the Irish Sea the destroyers would have to continue as far as the Skerries. When it came near the time for the destroyers to part company with the convoy they were all on *qui vive* for the radio order, "Return to port." Immediately on its receipt, hard over would go the rudder, black smoke would come from the stacks, and speed increased to 20 knots for the run back to Queenstown. We may have been out six, seven, or even eight days, during which time we had been more or less on a nervous strain, there had been considerable discomfort for at least a part of the time, and the fresh provisions had not lasted through. The three days' rests before us at Queenstown looked very tempting, and we could not get there too soon. . . .

Our chief difficulty with the convoys at first was the keeping of the ships together in a reasonably well defined formation. There was always a tendency to straggle on the part of some. This was not entirely the fault of the deck officers, but often due to the fireroom and engine room forces. They were not used to steaming at an absolutely uniform number of revolutions minute after minute, and day after day. Some of the vessels of the convoy were making close to their maximum cruising speed, so when fires were cleaned the steam pressure dropped, and of course the speed was reduced, with the resultant falling behind of the ship concerned. The destroyers, at times, were kept busy rounding up the stragglers. In order to get a better viewpoint and to be in position to prod the laggards I always stationed my own ship, the *Wads-*

worth, to cover the rear of these slow convoys. As we patrolled back and forth across the rear of the formation it was a simple matter to hail or signal any ship that was falling behind. . . .

During the early convoys the ships were widely scattered at daylight. The reasons for this were timidity on the part of those officers who were afraid of collision, and partly because the ships carried dimmed side and stern lights. At dark the ships would begin to open out and continue to do so, so long as the lights on the next ship could be seen. And these lights invariably showed farther than was intended. Gradually *all* lights were dispensed with, and it was found that the ships would then keep closed sufficiently to see the hulls of those next aboard. . . .

Communications were a particularly difficult problem at first. Some of the ships carried only one radio operator, and no signalmen who understood the semaphore system. It was usually necessary in such cases to deliver a message by word of mouth through a megaphone. And this was not always easy when the wind was howling and a big sea was running. Often would the reply come back, "I don't hear you," when in reality was meant, "I do not *understand* you." At times there would be French, Italian, or Scandinavian ships sprinkled through the convoy. These often were a problem because sometimes they did not understand the English language. But we found out that while on most of these ships they did not understand *plain* English, they did have a working knowledge of good old English seagoing swear words. Commander Fremont told of his troubles in getting an Italian tramp merchant ship to understand a message. He tried international flag hoist, semaphore, radio, and megaphone; but all to no avail. Finally he ran close aboard and shouted through the megaphone: "You blank blank, blankety blank, when I hoist flag X you head south blank blank quick, savvy?" and without a moment's hesitation came the answer:

"All right, Sir!"

The signaling gradually improved with the placing of trained signalmen on every ship in the convoy, and, although the radio communication never reached a really satisfactory state, still it worked in emergencies. . . .

It was my good fortune not to have a ship of any merchant convoy of which I commanded the escort, torpedoed. At times submarines were sighted, but they were kept down without getting in a

313

position for attack. In these early days of the convoy there were strict orders that no escort vessel should leave the formation to hunt submarines. Of course if a submarine was sighted, the nearer destroyers would go after it and keep it under until the convoy was well out of range. But the destroyer would then cease the hunt and rejoin the convoy. Later, when depth charge barrages were in order, this was changed so that if a submarine was located, the destroyer would continue the hunt until all possible chance of getting the sub was gone.

One dark night while the *Wadsworth* was patrolling across the rear of a slow convoy, the officer of the deck, Ensign N. P. Earle, shouted through the speaking tube: "Dropped a depth charge, sir!" Immediately afterwards as I was jumping up the ladder to the bridge the explosion took place, followed shortly by the explosion of the second charge which had also been let go. The officer of the deck had seen what he felt sure was the luminous wake of a submarine running submerged. It passed from our quarter to ahead as if the submarine were going to attack the convoy from the rear. Both depth charges being gone, we circled looking for results. In a few minutes the radio operator through the speaking tube reported:

"*Trippe* reports striking a submerged object which listed her fifteen degrees." This of course was the submarine whose wake we had seen. Either our charges dropped close enough to shake him up or he was going ahead with his attempted attack when he unexpectedly bumped the *Trippe*. At any rate there was no attack on the convoy. A half hour later the radio operator reported hearing a German submarine fairly close aboard calling excitedly on the radio as if wanting help. Of course we could not decode the message, but were satisfied that this fellow had been sufficiently damaged to be making appeals for help to his nearest confrere.

The detonations of depth charges near the ships of a convoy always gave them the impression that they were struck by something, and, until they were used to it, would so report to the escort vessels. Once in a while a ship would *think* herself torpedoed; and there were instances of their actually stopping and beginning to abandon ship by lowering boats, when the sole cause of their discomfiture was the explosion of a depth charge probably a half mile or more away.

While there was considerable monotony in convoy duty, there were many things to keep one interested or uncomfortable. For example, there would be a machinery breakdown, necessitating the taking of the vessel in tow; or a ship would have its cargo shift leaving us to wonder whether she would turn turtle. If a ship was torpedoed there was the problem of picking up the survivors, or if the ship remained afloat, the problem of getting her into port. And of course we had a reasonable number of false alarms. I remember one case in particular where the escort destroyers were on a scouting line standing towards our expected inbound convoy. The atmosphere was unusually clear. Suddenly the masthead lookout reported:

"Conning tower of a submarine dead ahead."

We could not see it from the bridge, and shortly afterwards a rain squall in that direction shut out the horizon from view. The lookout was positive he had seen the submarine, so I sent radio to the ocean escort:

"Submarine sighted between the convoy and escort."

Shortly after this the rain squall passed by, and there, showing over the horizon, were the topmasts of the convoy which had for its ocean escort the auxiliary cruiser *Moldavia*. This was a large merchant ship with two smokestacks, and it dawned on me at once that what the lookout had mistaken for the conning tower of a submarine were the two smokestacks, almost in line, over the horizon. So I sent radio to the *Moldavia:* "False alarm, lookout mistook smokestacks for conning tower."

The Commodore was evidently not pleased with the scare we had given him, and when we ran close aboard to deliver orders he shouted in a sarcastic tone:

"I congratulate you on your fine lookout."

Which remark I ignored by answering:

"I have the following orders for you from the Admiralty," and went ahead and gave him the orders. . . .[12]

VIII

WE COUNTED THE HOLES IN OUR PLANES

A naval aviation unit was the first American military organization, except for Army medical detachments, to land in France. Naval avia-

tion forces expanded rapidly, until in November, 1918, they num-
bered 1,300 officers, 15,000 men, 500 planes, 50 kite balloons, 3
dirigibles. The Yale University Aviation Unit of twenty-nine members
was the nucleus of the Naval Reserve Flying Corps, whose recruits
were college boys and civilian pilots. At Killingholme on the English
east coast, in France at Dunkirk and eleven other bases, and in Italy
naval aviators guarded shipping lanes, flew patrols, and escorted
bombing missions over enemy lines. Lieutenant (j.g.) David S. Ingalls
records day-to-day events and Lieutenant Kenneth MacLeish's letter
to a friend typifies the idealism of the Yale Unit.

. . . Now in regard to the actual work. There were several sorts of patrols. First, the sea patrol which consisted in flying low, always in sight of the fleet, to guard against seaplanes during the coastal destroyer patrols up to Ostend and Zeebrugge, or during a shoot. As there were seldom any enemy seaplanes to be seen, and as one always looked forward to a cold bath if the motor failed, this was a stupid job, never preferred to line patrols.

Of these, in good weather, there were usually two a day—at the time when the Huns were out en masse—between ten and twelve in the mornings and five and six in the evenings. At these times always at least two flights went, one above the other for protection. Two large groups made the most confusing affair imaginable; machines of friend and foe seemed to be everywhere. Twice I remember seeing two Huns collide, with the most gratifying result. In bad weather there were small patrols, perhaps under the clouds along the lines, or up the coast to look for some daring seaplane merchant, for the Hun seaplanes were fond of bad weather.

Between the regular patrols any one who wished could go out by himself, or more often persuade a couple of pals to accompany him, on a search for lone two-seaters spotting or photographing near the lines. Besides these patrols there was considerable escort work to be done, accompanying day bombers to Bruges or some other objective. But this was monotonous, for the Huns would not often attack such numbers, thirty or thirty-five machines.

Every so often bombing raids on Hun aerodromes or on the Mole at Zeebrugge were carried out. These were very interesting and can probably be best illustrated by the description of one in particular. One of the most successful was against the Varsennaire Aerodrome, about twenty miles behind the lines, southeast of Ostend and used for day scout and night bombers. For the bombing, Camel squadrons were picked, with a Dolphin squadron above as protection. One squadron of Camels were to carry phosphorus bombs, which set fire to anything near on exploding, and the rest were to carry the customary twenty-five pound shrapnel bombs. Certain parts of the aerodrome were assigned to each squadron as its target, and certain hangars or huts assigned to each man.

After several false starts, the show finally began about half an hour before sunrise on what turned out to be a perfect day, for the Allies. There was considerable confusion in getting off in the dark, as a Camel is a difficult machine to fly even in the day-time, but finally every one was climbing toward 10,000 feet at which altitude we were all to meet at a certain time over Dunkirk. As one went up, the dawn grew brighter and at 10,000 feet it was possible to make out the other machines. The leaders of the different flights were firing signal lights to help their men get together, just as the sun became visible over the horizon, and eventually all fell into line in their places. Then the leader flew along the coast until midway between Ostend and Zeebrugge, where he turned toward the land, diving across the shore line.

The Huns were evidently asleep, and no Archie was put up until all the machines were down to about 200 feet, roaring over the country towards the objective, plainly visible. Now the squadrons split up to fly over their parts of the field, and descending to about 150 feet, dropped their bombs. The shrapnel bombs cause a ghastly looking explosion and the phosphorus give out clouds of smoke, so the field upon looking back seemed like Dante's Inferno.

Lined up in front of one row of hangars was a squadron of Fokkers with their engines warming up, from which, as we approached, men had run to shelter. Turning back toward these, we all dove, setting many machines on fire, and riddling all of them with bullets. For several minutes all the machines were diving, zooming, turning, and shooting from every side resulting in a grand mêlée and many near-collisions. Finally the leader fired a Véry light, the signal to return. Then the countryside appeared to be covered with Camels streaking for the lines at about 100 feet up. And now revenge was wreaked upon the Archie, for whoever saw the bursts from battery anywhere near him turned, dove and shot, driving the crews hurriedly to shelter and silencing every battery near their path. Soon the flock reached the lines where the remaining ammunition was expended at the Hun trenches, when all flew back to their respective aerodromes. . . . Fortunately no one was hurt and the reports together with the photos taken soon after proved the great success of the raid.

These large raids did not occur frequently, as a large amount of their success depends upon the element of surprise, but during a "push" the work was similar. For then the squadrons went over the trenches into Hunland, but at different times, so that there was always a squadron over the enemy's lines of communication looking for something to bomb. The target was not often determined beforehand, except when a large congestion of troops was reported, but the squadron flew about until something worth while was observed. . . .

On my fourth day at 213, I went on two patrols, on which we saw no Huns . . . soon after returning from the second, about 4 P.M., I had my Camel filled with gas and oil and set out alone to see what was doing. When I had climbed to about 18,000 feet, which is a fairly safe altitude, I flew over the lines between Nieuport and Ypres for about fifteen minutes. It was growing dark and I saw no Huns, only a few British flights at different times. Finally just before dark I decided to go down low and see if I could find a Hun two-seater spotting for batteries. I descended slowly till I reached about 12,000 feet. I had been looking below most of the time, and nothing had appeared anywhere. I was suddenly surprised by seeing three monoplanes flying parallel to me 500 feet higher and to the rear. They must have seen me, for they turned and dived. I was disgusted with myself for being caught and started for the lines, diving a little.

In thirty seconds, they got within range and began to shoot. All I could do was sit, watch them, turn from side to side, climb, and dive slightly, trying to dodge. . . . They kept coming and tracers flew on all sides. They would dive, shoot, zoom up, and repeat. Finally they got close, and as one turned off and started to zoom up, I turned at him, fired a few shots, and quickly started home again. He immediately dove and beat it. When I straightened out, I could see only one and heard lots of shooting. I supposed the other was below shooting up at me. It was a rotten feeling. I couldn't see where the deuce he was and the shooting kept up.

I turned, dove, kept on, and soon he appeared again above me. For a minute more they both stayed about fifty yards directly behind me, shooting. For no reason both turned and dove toward the ground. I turned and fired, diving, glad to shoot and not be shot at. But they outdove my machine. I didn't seem to hurt them. I pulled up and started for the lines about two miles off. That last two minutes was the worst part. I kept expecting to hear some one shooting at me, as I didn't know how many more might have come up during our chase. I sat turning round and round, looking above and below, surprised that no one started to shoot. When I got back and saw the half dozen holes in the machine I realized that I had been a perfect fool. It was a good lesson, because when flying over Hunland I always felt so safe. Nothing happens, and you see no one, and it doesn't seem that there could possibly be any danger anywhere in the peaceful heavens.

September 20. Successful trip. I was a flight commander at 213 and all three flights were sent out as protection at 218, a day bombing squadron. We set out when they telephoned that they had started, and climbed so that we all met over LaPaune. On such trips, one flight of Camels went on each side, slightly above and to the rear of the day bombers, while the third flight flew about 4000 feet above to guard against Huns who might dive. We went along the coast two or three miles out to sea and turned in between Ostend and Zeebrugge. Just after we crossed the coast and were being Archied, I was flying with my four members of the flight on the right side of the bombers. I saw four Fokkers coming straight at us from the right side, some distance off. We flew along for some time and then as they continued to approach I turned and headed for them, my flight following. We approached head on and I shot straight at their leader, turning and zooming just as we almost met. I could see the four Huns and two other Camels all lined up, while my two last men had turned off and were some distance above. I headed at one of the Huns and fired. He immediately dived; I didn't follow, having a dread of being caught low down over German land.

When I looked around now I saw only three Fokkers at a distance, some of the bombers way off, and one Camel above. . . . I turned after the bombers to keep near and protect them. The Fokkers flew about, but didn't come near. Soon the bombers started to return. One had a poor motor and was below and behind the rest. I saw two Fokkers start for him, so I did, too. One of them was directly behind shooting at the bomber. The other somehow had got a little ahead and was doing nothing. I approached at right angles and, deciding that the first-named Hun was the most dangerous, fired at him. He went down with smoke coming out of his machine. I turned and started for the other Hun. He could not have seen me, for I had a perfect shot at him. I don't know how I could have missed, for I almost ran into him. He turned over on his back and went into a spin. I watched him go until he got near the ground, when I heard some one shooting and saw three Fokkers coming up at me, shooting. . . . I dove and fired at the nearest.

They split up and dove off in different directions. I immediately turned and started after the bomber, who was hurrying toward the coast. But as I started out, the Huns pulled up and fired from beneath and behind. All the British machines had now crossed the coast. I kept after them, while these three beggars kept shooting from an impossible distance, until I crossed the coast. The first Hun I had shot was officially confirmed as being destroyed in flames. But some one reported having seen the other pull up after spinning and flatten out apparently O.K. Two of my flight, hit in the gas tanks the first thing, had barely managed to get home.

On September 24th, a chap named Hobson and I went out about 5.30 P.M. to look for a two-seater photographing. This was the closest shave I had. We flew along the lines, got disgusted and started for home. It was getting dark. As we left the lines I saw Archie over LaPaune and there picked up a machine heading toward Ostend on our side of the lines. I fired my gun to attract Hobson's attention and set out in pursuit, for Archie on our side of the lines meant a Hun. Hobson woke up and started, too, but at some distance behind. I got within range. The Hun was an old Rumpler, the slowest I ever saw, and he just kept on. I dove under him and came up from below. But he was so slow that I overshot. . . . I dove again. He would turn one way to give his observer a shot. I would try to keep under him, making a bigger circle, so his observer could not shoot. A few seconds, and I tried to come up below him again. His machine was too slow and I almost overshot, but succeeded in firing a few rounds from just beneath.

Nothing happened. I dropped and continued working for a good position, fed up at not being able to get one. On a turn he very nearly got me. Before I could make the outside circle, his observer fired ten shots, the tracers all going by between the struts on my left side. We were ten yards off at the time and I could see the two Huns perfectly in their black helmets. It was fascinating to be so close. All the time we were getting further over the lines, and I was getting madder. I gave up the careful, cautious tactics, got straight behind him, and kept firing for 100 rounds.

At last a big puff of smoke came up like an explosion and I felt fine. I turned and dove down to the ground to chase myself home. When over the lines and not high enough to be safe from Archie, the stunt is to race just over the ground at about 200 feet. I had not seen Hobson anywhere. I got near the ground south of Ostend and tore along watching, hoping that no Huns would dive from above. The only danger in this low flying is from the machine guns. . . . I knew fairly well where they were thickest, and went along for five minutes without a shot. Then suddenly I heard a rat-tat, my motor stopped, gas poured out of the tank below the seat, and clouds of white vapor rose from it.

The machine was thrown into a sort of dive and when I pulled on the stick, I found that the elevating controls did not respond. I switched on the gravity tank. The motor picked up just over some trees and, as the Camel is very tail-heavy with motor on, the nose came up and I missed the trees by inches. I found that the wires to go down with were O.K., the rudder worked, but the ailerons answered weakly. But the motor kept hitting on about six of the nine cylinders and I went along all right. Evidently I had run into a bad place, for I was shot at till I crossed the lines. Usually one turns, zooms, etc., when in this predicament, but I expected the rest of the controls to go any second. . . . I sat still and by using the rudder kept going as fast as possible in little turns toward home. It was a relief to get out of shot across the lines. Then I had to land. I didn't dare go up high, but flew down low experimenting with the machine and seeing just what I could do. When I reached the aerodrome I came in slowly over the trees on the side and, using the motor, managed to land.

The machine was shot up. One burst of bullets had perforated the tank under my seat. All but one strand in the wires that cause one to go up were severed, as well as a number of strands in those to go down. One aileron had been hit at a hinge, and there were a few holes in the wings. Hobson had returned. He had been back of and above me, fired, and had seen the Hun burst into flames and crash. We felt fine, and I got a new machine next day.

September 18. Yesterday while flying along the coast, I noticed the enemy kite balloon which, in good weather, is always up near Ostend for observation purposes. It looked like easy meat. When we returned to the aerodrome I suggested to the flight that we go get the beggar. Although only one fellow in the squadron had ever tried for a kite balloon, they all fell for it immediately. This morning three of our flight asked the C.O.'s permission and filled our guns with incendiary tracer bullets. Another flight having offered to escort us, six machines started out about 10 A.M.

A thick layer of clouds covered the sky at 8000 feet, so we flew down the coast just under them. Opposite Ostend we turned in and, nosing over slightly to get up more speed, approached the kite balloon in a big curve. Not until we had almost reached the coast did the Archie open up. As we were only 7000 feet up, it was some Archie. One shell broke just under my right wing, through the fusilage in front on my knees, a piece of the cowl striking me on the knee and giving me a start.

The Archie on this coast is about the best the Huns have. . . . During the three minutes we were diving toward the kite balloon, the Huns were pulling it down. We got to it at about 4000 feet, all diving at different angles. We all fired. Nothing happened. I turned and dove again, shooting at the big, fat target. Looking back I saw a blaze flare up in the bag, then it crumpled in a great mass of flames, and dropped directly on the three balloon sheds which promptly caught fire. It was a lovely sight. *"Beaucoup bon,"* thinks I, hearing no machine guns and seeing no Huns anywhere in the sky. A minute or so of peace and quiet and then I saw a machine racing along abreast of me, about a mile off and at the same altitude. This gave me a start, as I thought it meant a scrap, but presently I recognized it as Smith's machine, so I joined him and we jogged along for home. On the way I happened to notice a lot of German barracks, wooden buildings among trees. Our incendiary ammunition was just the stuff to pull off a surprise party. I fired at them and was delighted to see them smoke up. I must have hit some straw to touch'em off in such elegant fashion. We were machine-gunned from the ground, but nothing to worry about. Ducking it, we reached the pleasant atmosphere of home.

We counted the holes in our planes and reported that the excursion had been successful. Our observers and photographers discovered that the burning balloon had lit up the three enormous sheds in which extra balloons were stored and burned them to the ground. The General commanding our forces was bucked up and called up our C.O. to say how pleased he was.

September 28th, the Allied push started, and our squadron was compelled to do low bombing and shooting up behind the enemy lines. On the first trip we started early in the morning of a rainy day with a strong wind. The entire squadron, with bombs attached, went up at once, in three flights. We climbed to 4000 feet and, as we got near the lines, we dove gently so as to arrive at about 300 feet up on the other side. Due to the confusion and hurry of the German troops, our machine gun work was excellent. On the main road to the front, near Thourout, we saw a complete artillery train. Our leader dived and we followed, loosing our bombs. The execution was terrible and the whole column was demoralized. We stayed around, diving at the remains and shooting horses, men, etc. . . .

On another raid the C.O. was chasing a poor bloke who was legging it on a bicycle for dear life. Pretty soon this German blighter hopped off the road and ducked behind a stone wall. When the C.O. banked around to see where his quarry had gone, the fellow up and heaved a brick at him. It smashed a tremendous hole in a wing of the plane. Imagine a man stoning an aeroplane!

During these two months I flew 108 hours, 45 minutes; 63 flights over the lines; 13 combats; 2 low bombing raids on aerodromes; 1 low bombing raid on the Mole; 10 low bombing raids behind the lines during the Allied push.

(MacLeish's letter)

Paris, March 19, 1918

Dear Henry:

I just received your letter telling me of Stuffy Spencer's death and telling me to be careful. I'll be careful, Henry, but you all at home simply *must* realize this! We all feel it so strongly and it's such a consolation that it seems a pity you can't share it. We are all men with more or less red blood, and, thank God, we have ideals which are really worth while. You couldn't consider us men unless we believed in those ideals firmly enough to fight for them. They are *all,* in our lives that are really worth while in these trying times. To enumerate them would simply be to repeat what men, much more able than we, have said many times before. But I doubt whether you appreciate the real foundation from which they spring. It is simply this—a true and sacred love for all you friends and relatives at home . . . the majority of men over here, whether conscious of it or not, are "selfless" or nearly so. They can't be anything else. So, then, we *will* defend those ideals—if necessary with our lives—for unless we did, we could never have any self-respect. If you can understand this much, you must be able to understand what follows: We must all give up this life sooner or later, but it is not granted to all to give it up so nobly, as to us. To me the finest miracle in life is to be able, in the last few moments on this earth, to revolutionize one's entire existence, to forget a life of failure and weakness, and to die a hero.

The Gates of Honor are open to us, those lucky ones of us who are over here. We need not fear that we are not prepared to die, for no matter what we *have* been, in the last glorious moments we can die, not as the ordinary man, but fighting for the ideals we hold so sacred. Is there a nobler death? So you see, Henry, old pal, we're *lucky*, every one of us. Don't think for a moment that we have any regret—even the joys of life are secondary to the true happiness one experiences in dying for the ideals he knows are right. Don't think we have any fears. What is there to fear in such a glorious death? And don't grieve, Henry. There's nothing to be sorry about. . . .

If "Stuffy" had died before the war, I should have grieved, but we are at war—circumstances are topsy-turvy—I'm *not* sorry. I'm proud as I can be that "Stuffy" was once a dear friend of mine. I'm proud to have known him. You can't be proud of a man and sorry for him at the same time; therefore be *proud* of him. . . .

I'm going to the front to-morrow. I don't think anything will happen to me. If it should be my lot to make the supreme sacrifice, you'll know that I did it gladly, and that I bought life's most marvelous reward, Honor, at a dirt cheap price, and that I was happy, ever so happy, that it was granted to me, unworthy as I am, to give up my life for my friends, who, fundamentally, are my ideals.

So there you are, Henry, and there's not any end to my preaching. I'm not looking for trouble, and, therefore, probably won't find any. "Wally" Winter was shot down by Huns recently. He dove his machine and when he tried to pull out of the dive it was so shot to pieces that it collapsed. Those who saw the fight said the scrap "Wally" put up was the most magnificent and inspiring thing they had ever seen in their lives.[13]

CHAPTER V
This Is Not a Drill
1918-1945

DURING the peace that followed the Armistice of 11 November 1918, the Western World reacted against war and made determined efforts toward an international reduction of armaments. Such cut-backs in the 1920's thrust naval operations into the background, but advances in aviation caught the public imagination.

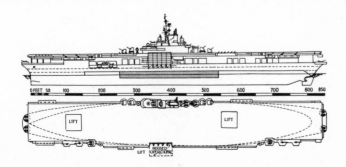

I

THE TRANSATLANTIC FLIGHT

Cramped by limited appropriations and the tendency to under-estimate its importance, naval aviation pioneered the first transatlantic flight in history. While sixty destroyers and other surface craft patroled the course, three Navy Curtiss (NC) flying boats took off from Long Island, New York, in May, 1919 for Newfoundland and, via the Azores, for Lisbon, Portugal and Plymouth, England. In command of that historic flight was Commander John H. Towers, who tells his own story.

. . . Much of the preliminary work had already been started through the routine channels, all under the utmost secrecy, and it was desired to keep the whole plan secret until it was almost time to under-take the flight. Unfortunately, however, through an error my orders were given out for publication when issued, in accordance with the usual peacetime custom of the Navy, and the cat was fairly out of the bag. Instructions were given that no information of any positive na-ture was to be given out, and to me was passed the job of keeping the correspondents satisfied and happy, but not telling them anything. It was a most interesting work, and very educating.

The so-called TA section got busy at once and things began to hum. I will not go into detail as to the work which the preparation involved, but will point out some of the features, just to show the ramifications. The invitations to the Allied countries had to be handled separately through the State Department, also permits obtained through the same channels for air and surface craft to use the ports of the various countries which they were expected to touch. Detailed inspections had to be made of the various ports to determine the relative merits. Personnel had to be selected not only for the crew of the seaplanes, but for the handling crews on the base ships. Complete lists of material for the seaplanes and for all the base ships had to be drawn up and assembled. Some of this material was not even in existence, and had to be designed, developed and tested. Special charts had to be engraved. Many special tables had to be worked out.

The NC-1 as completed was only a starting-point from which to work out the seaplanes for the transatlantic flight, and a most careful schedule of experiments and tests had to be laid down. Last, and biggest of all, the whole problem of base and patrol ships had to be worked out. Base ships had to be selected which could meet requirements, and fitted with gasoline tanks, special equipment, etc., required. The destroyers had to have a special radio installation, and a lot of equipment, such as star shells, meteorological apparatus, etc. The number of destroyers was astonishing. Our final plan called for a destroyer every fifty miles, and there was approximately four thousand miles to be covered. As there could be no chances taken of delaying the flight by not having destroyers in position, in very few cases could it be figured on to use the same destroyer twice.

The approved plan recommended a start from Newfoundland during the week of the full moon of May fourteenth, which meant that the seaplanes must get away from Rockaway at least a week sooner, in order to have time to get things tuned up at Newfoundland, and to have a few days to wait for favorable weather. . . .

In the meantime the work at Rockaway had been going ahead in spite of many difficulties. Two fires within a week had seriously crippled the station. A big storm caught the NC-1 at her mooring, and in spite of all efforts to save her she dragged her moorings and went ashore, one wing being wrecked and the hull damaged. This limited our project to three seaplanes, and as experiments were necessary up to the latest possible moment, it was decided to use the NC-2 for that purpose, and then shift one wing of the NC-2 to the NC-1. A change in the current along the shore kept sweeping the sand over the marine railway used for getting the NC boats out of the water and the constant services of a small dredge were required to keep this track clear.

On April twenty-first the bulk of the work in Washington had been completed, and I moved, with the transatlantic section, to Rockaway, where most of the activity was concentrated. A definite date of

World War I United States Naval Air Station, Brest, France.
Hydroplane starting out on patrol.

NC-4 on Taugus River, Lisbon, Portugal.

starting, or rather, a definite date before which we would not start had to be given to the destroyers, and on April twenty-fourth, at a conference of all the commanding officers of the vessels which would participate, I gave this date as May fifth. During the last days of April the vessels began to slip out of New York to take up their stations. It just happened that when the division of superdreadnaughts which were to act as meteorological ships passed through Ambrose Channel we were out in two of the big seaplanes, making some tests, so we swooped down close to the ships. They gave us a wonderful cheer, wished us good luck by wireless, then headed out for the mid-Atlantic to take up their posts.

Work was going ahead day and night. Newspaper men were permitted to see the preparations, and realized that the date of departure was not far off, but none of them seemed to grasp the obvious date, viz.: at the period of the coming full moon. The NC-3 was finished and ready, the NC-4 was having the final touches put on, and the NC-1 was being rapidly modified. The new hangar was not quite complete, and so it was necessary to keep all three seaplanes in one hangar. This was a constant source of worry, as it meant that if a fire got started in that hangar we were ruined.

On Saturday, May third, in accordance with orders from Washington, the NC-1, NC-3, and NC-4 were placed in commission. This was the first time aircraft had been commissioned in the Navy, and given a real individuality, like a ship. On this same date I made the assignment of crews, taking the NC-3 as flagship, assigning the NC-4 to Lieutenant-Commander Read and the NC-1 to Lieutenant-Commander Bellinger.

Weather conditions indicated a possible start on Tuesday, May sixth, so on Sunday evening, in accordance with a promise I had made to the correspondents, I announced May sixth as the possible date of starting for Halifax. At two-fifteen Monday morning I was awakened by excited calls to me from the hall outside my door in the barracks, and my first thought was—"Fire!" I looked out toward the big NC hangar, about a quarter of a mile away, and there I saw a dull-red glow, obviously caused by a big fire inside. The crew had been filling the NC-1 with gasoline, and a spark from the electric pump jumped, and in a second that whole section was aflame. The twenty men on duty dashed for fire-extinguishers, and with hundreds of gallons of chemicals succeeded in protecting the vital parts of the

NC-1, but before it could be got under control the fire had destroyed one whole wing of the NC-1 and a big part of the tail of the NC-4.

Things looked hopeless, as first examination indicated that at least a week would be required to repair those two seaplanes. Then we happened to think of the set of good wings taken off the NC-1 after the storm, and realized that they were for the same side as the burned wings, and everything brightened up. Telephone calls were sent in to the naval inspectors and to the Curtiss Engineering Company at Garden City, and before daylight truckloads of mechanics began to roll in. Our men had stripped off most of the burned parts. By midnight Monday night both the NC-1 and the NC-4 were repaired and ready to fly!

At daylight Tuesday morning, May sixth, all three seaplanes were on the beach and all hands were standing by, ready for the start. Mr. Weather had changed his mind, however, and it not only did not look favorable at Rockaway, but was reported as bad all up the line of destroyers. At ten o'clock I finally announced that there would be no start that day, and went in to call up Mr. Bowie of the Weather Bureau, to find out what he thought of the prospects in the immediate future. He did not consider that there would be any change until the end of the week, as conditions were most unsettled, and he fully realized that we wanted good conditions for the first hop, so we might have good rehearsals for the more difficult legs ahead.

Wednesday was bad, and Thursday did not hold much hope, according to the weather charts on Wednesday evening, but late Wednesday night conditions began to improve and word was passed to stand by for a start on Thursday.

Everything was ready shortly after daylight, but I wanted to get the final report from Mr. Bowie before shoving off. It came at 9:45 A.M. and said: "Conditions favorable." There were a few quick "good-bys," the inevitable photographs caught as we were slipping into helmets, goggles, etc., and, at 10 A.M. we were off. As we cleared the end of Rockaway Point, we swung around and headed for Montauk, the NC-1 and the NC-4 taking up position on each side of the NC-3. In the NC-3 were Commander H. C. Richardson and Lieutenant D. H. McCulloch, pilots; Lieutenant-Commander R. A. Lavender, radio officer; Lieutenant Braxton Rhodes and Machinist L. R. Moore, engineers; and forward, with me, Lieutenant-Commander R. E. Byrd, who was to go as far as Newfoundland as assistant navigator.

Byrd had been in charge of all the navigational preparations, and I desired to have him along so that we could thoroughly test out the instruments on the first two hops and make any modifications which we might deem desirable.

As we passed the air station at Montauk we could see the entire personnel out on the dirigible field, and we exchanged radio greetings. Lavender also telephoned forward several messages which he had received, including one from Hon. Franklin D. Roosevelt, Acting Secretary of the Navy, wishing us the best of luck. We passed over Block Island, up over Vineyard Haven Sound and across Monomoy Point just south of Chatham. The visibility was excellent and the whole southeastern part of Massachusetts was in plain view. The air was smooth and warm and everybody aboard was wearing a big smile.

As we passed Chatham we changed course to the northward, heading up the line of destroyers for Seal Island, off the southwest point of Nova Scotia. At this time we were flying at thirty-five hundred feet altitude. This was a little high for determining our drift, but the air was so smooth I did not want to come down until we sighted the first destroyer, and found out how far out we were in our calculations. I found out we were several miles to the eastward, so telephoned to the pilots to come down to about two thousand feet, and we had no further trouble. Just about this time Lavender telephoned that a message had been received from the NC-4, saying that they were having engine trouble, were running on three engines, and might have to land. She began to drop astern and descend, and we thought she was landing close to destroyer number one, as that vessel was still in sight, so we proceeded on course and NC-1 followed.

Byrd spent the afternoon vibrating between the forward and after cockpits, trying smoke bombs, sextants, etc. My cockpit was not very large, and with all the charts, chart desk, sextants, drift indicator, binoculars, chronometers, etc., stacked in there, very little room was left. As I wore a telephone all the time, wires were trailing all about me, and Byrd and I were continually getting all mixed up like a couple of puppies on leashes. Occasionally one of the pilots would come forward for a cup of coffee and a sandwich, or to take a look at the chart to find out how we were progressing. All these little festivities were rudely broken up about the middle of the afternoon, when a squall hit us.

We headed down through it and telephoned to Lavender to roll in his trailing antenna, before the weight on the end hit the water and the whole thing was jerked off. From time to time until we landed at Halifax the air was very rough. We sighted Seal Island, and a little later made out the coast of Nova Scotia, and off that coast we struck very rough air. We lost sight of the NC-1 in the haze, but finally made out the entrance to Halifax Harbor ahead and landed near our buoys at 7 P.M. Rockaway time, which was eight-thirty Halifax time, the flight of five hundred and forty-two miles having taken just nine hours.

Ten minutes later the NC-1 came roaring in. We secured to our moorings, gave orders to overhaul crews as to refueling, and went on board the *Baltimore,* where Captain Cluverius received us, and after we got off our flying clothes and cleaned up, we sat down to a nice hot dinner. There were many correspondents on board as well as interested visitors, including the American consul, and while we were dining, we gave them a running summary of the flight.

No news had been received of the NC-4, other than that she was down and destroyers were searching, so I filed a telegraphic report to the Navy Department, announced that, weather permitting, NC-1 and NC-3 would leave at 8 A.M. next day for Trepassey, Newfoundland; read a multitude of telegrams which had been received for me, and then turned in. Lieutenant-Commander McAddie, probably better known as Professor McAddie, of Blue Hill Observatory, was on the *Baltimore* to give us advice as to weather, and he assured me that we would have good weather the following day.

I was called several times during the night to receive important telegrams, the most pleasing of which was one which came shortly before daylight saying that the NC-4 was on the water off Chatham, Massachusetts, and was heading for the air station near that place.

We were all up before daylight, and everything was apparently ready for the start, the engineers having worked with the repair crews most of the night, but a daylight inspection disclosed something which had been overlooked, viz.: that there were several cracked propellers. The *Baltimore* had spare ones on board, but they did not have enough hub plates. We were in a dilemma, when Byrd, who had been in command of our air station at Halifax during hostilities, remembered that he had turned some of these hubs over to the Canadians. He dashed over to the dockyard in a speed boat, and came back with the hubs. By the time both seaplanes were finally ready it was too late to start.

McAddie promised us good weather for the next day, so we made the best of it, and planned to get off the following morning.

The NC-3 had trouble with one engine-starting motor, so, as the NC-1 was cruising around on the water, all ready to go, I gave Bellinger the signal and he got off and headed out. Shortly afterward we followed, but noticed trouble when thirty-eight miles out, and landed on the water. Examination disclosed another cracked propeller. It might have held for many hours, but if it didn't there was a good chance of a piece as it flew off going into the forward part of the hull and decapitating somebody, so I decided to return to Halifax. Lavender sent a radio message asking that a new propeller be prepared for us, and we flew back, got it, put it on, caught a quick lunch while the work was being done, and got away at 12:40 P.M. McAddie said the good weather would hold out for at least eight hours, but that the wind would be strong as we got farther north. It was! We proceeded up the coast of Nova Scotia, which is most forbidding looking, with very few signs of habitation, and, upon passing Cape Canso, headed out for the island of St. Pierre.

Just about this time we ran into strong winds and rough air. We went up to get out of the disturbed air, but found the wind blowing about forty-five miles an hour and almost dead against us, so we came down about one thousand feet and pushed through it. No difficulties were experienced in the navigation, and St. Pierre was sighted when we were about fifty miles from it. Upon reaching this island we made a sharp change of course and ran down-wind for the southwest point of the Avalon peninsula. I signaled to go up, so that we would get the stronger winds of the high altitudes, and we climbed to five thousand feet.

It was bitterly cold, about zero, I should say, but with the help of the wind, we were making one hundred and twelve miles an hour, so we stuck it out. Down below were hundreds of icebergs, which from our height reminded me of sheep in pasture. I happened to look back at one time and saw Moore climbing around up among the engines, exposed to the full force of our rush through the air. It nearly froze me to look at him.

Cape Pine was sighted, and with our speed we reached it quickly, but we were at five thousand feet, and had to land in a very small harbor, which none of us had ever seen before. Furthermore it was surrounded by high hills and the wind was working itself up into a gale. After coming down through about the roughest air I have ever experienced, we finally landed and taxied full speed to our moorings. There we found the NC-1 which had arrived about an hour and a half before. Everything was secured for riding out the heavy wind, and arrangements were made for bringing both planes up to the *Aroostook* for refueling as soon as the weather moderated, which it did early next morning.

Getting on the *Aroostook* seemed almost like getting home. She was our so-called mother-ship, scheduled to follow us to Plymouth, and on her were our clothes, extra toilet articles, and all the things one travels with. Each person had been limited to five pounds of personal baggage on the seaplanes, and five pounds is not much. Richardson and I, being the two seniors, had been assigned the pilot-house for sleeping quarters, and this had been fitted up with two real brass beds. Since the pilot-house was built largely of glass, we had the privacy of the proverbial goldfish, but we didn't mind that in the least. The rest of the officers and men were given quarters about the ship. Richardson, Bellinger and I messed with the commanding officer, Captain Harvey Tomb, and altogether had a very comfortable time of it. . . .

Word was received from Read on May thirteenth that he was all ready to leave Chatham, and expected to get away the following morning. I suggested his making one hop of it from Chatham to Trepassey, but he got such a late start he did not find this practicable, so he put into Halifax, and came up to Trepassey on May fifteenth. We had been waiting for weather, and May fifteenth looked very promising, from the reports received from the route and from the four battle-ships, stationed two on each side four hundred miles apart and dividing the distance from Newfoundland to the Azores into equidistant parts.

I hated the thought of starting without Read, but, on the other hand, the weather people advised a start, and couldn't promise that good weather would hold along the course, so I determined to make a try on the afternoon of May fifteenth. The seaplanes were loaded to nearly twenty-nine thousand pounds total, which would give a good margin of safety on gasoline to reach Ponta Delgada, but, on the other hand, made it very doubtful if we could get off the water in crosswind. We could not. After spending two hours in NC-3 and everybody on board getting soaked through with spray, I decided it would be almost suicidal to go into the air in that condition, and called it off. Just at this time, nearly dusk, we saw NC-4 standing in, and I think everybody was glad we hadn't succeeded.

All three seaplanes went to their moorings and work was started at once to get a new engine into the NC-4 in place of the old one put in at Chatham and to reduce the load in all three to twenty-eight thousand three hundred pounds. The crew of the NC-3 was much heavier than either of the other crews, and we could not safely cut down this weight by taking out gasoline, so I decided to try it with a little over twenty-eight thousand three hundred, and put off Lieutenant Rhodes, one of the engineers, if we couldn't get off successfully.

Daylight on the sixteenth found us studying the weather. Mr. Greeg of the Weather Bureau and Lieutenant Barratt, Navy Aerographer, received and plotted reports, sent up sounding balloons and gazed off into space, but remained noncommittal. About noon they began to cheer up and I quietly gave orders to be ready to leave at three o'clock. Barratt and Greeg finally said they believed conditions would be satisfactory, wind southwest to west, and partly cloudy during the early part of the run. A rush dispatch was received from the Weather Bureau just about the same time, predicting favorable conditions.

Sandwiches and coffee were put aboard, engines warmed up, and all three planes slipped their moorings. NC-3 was to get off first, followed by NC-4 then NC-1. We waited until NC-1 and NC-3 reported all ready, then taxied over close to shore, put on full power and headed across the narrow harbor. We just failed to get off before reaching the other side, so came back and tried again, and again just failed. I signaled to the motorboat to come alongside, and transferred Rhodes and the battery radio set, as previously decided upon. NC-4 during this time tried out, got off, circled and landed again. We then made our third trial, and got off at 7:30 P.M. followed by NC-4 and NC-1, and all stood out to sea.

It was cold, rough and rather hazy, and we were flying with a bigger load than had ever been carried by any sea-plane, so the first few minutes were anxious ones. With great difficulty I managed to distinguish the NC-1 and the NC-4 astern of us, so struck off down the line of destroyers.

Those who think that having destroyers fifty miles apart made navigation as easy as "walking down Broadway" should have been with us that evening. It was not until darkness came on, and they began to fire star shells at five-minute intervals from the anti-aircraft guns that I could even think of anything but finding the next destroyer. They could not be expected to be exactly on position, and if we didn't find them exactly where we expected to, there was always the question, are they wrong or are we?

As it got dark it also got overcast, and thus made flying very difficult for the NC-3 pilots, as our lighting system developed defects, and the lights on the pilots' instrument-boards were out. The moon finally came up, but the clouds nearly obscured it. My pilots telephoned that they would like to go above the clouds, so that they could have the moon and stars for reference. I signaled to go up. NC-1 and NC-4 were on the other side of us, and about two miles astern. We climbed through the clouds, and at forty-five hundred feet found smoother air and a beautiful clear heaven. . . .

These hours above the clouds over the mid-Atlantic at night I shall always regard as the most impressive of my life. The engines were running beautifully, all forty-eight cylinders spitting short purplish flames, with a roar which from below must have sounded like an express-train. . . .

I foolishly added one more thrill through my stubbornness. The destroyers had been instructed to fire all star shells to the northwest, with guns elevated to an angle of seventy-five degrees, it being our plan to pass to the southward of all destroyers, and thus avoid danger of being hit. I had set a course which was taking us by the destroyers, just south of them, like clockwork, when finally as we approached one, it was evident that we would pass just to the northward of it. I thought it was out of position, and I didn't want to change course. Besides, I could see it, and thought they could see us through the then thin clouds, so I kept right on. Having timed their firing, I knew they were due to fire just about where we were in line. We were at forty-five hundred feet, so the shell was due to explode five hundred feet below us. Either the destroyer didn't see us or they didn't believe in deviating one iota from their instructions, for right on the second I saw the flash from the gun. The shell exploded just under us. I looked back and both Richardson and McCulloch looked as though they would like to take the navigating out of my hands.

The rest of the night was uneventful. As dawn began to break we looked for a hole in the clouds in order to go down where we could see the destroyers. We could not get down in time to see number fourteen, but finally found a hole and got through shortly before we were due to see number fifteen. We found the weather slightly hazy and threatening, and very shortly encountered heavy rain squalls. I believed number fifteen was to northward, and was looking that way for her, when one of the pilots called my attention to the dim outlines of a vessel to the southward. We were already past it, but eased over in that direction to get a better look. The rain shut off our vision, so I assumed it was number fifteen and changed course accordingly, to bring me back on the line. We then encountered fog, which together with the rain squalls lasted the rest of the flight, and brought us to grief.

Number sixteen was not seen, nor was number seventeen, so I reached the conclusion that I had mistaken some other vessel for number fifteen and that we were probably to the southward of the course, and changed course to run parallel, hoping that we would run out of the fog and see some station vessel. I knew from radio news that both the NC-1 and NC-4 were having similar difficulties, but it was now a case of each navigator trying to solve his own problems. We tried the radio compass, but with no result. We also tried different altitudes, but as soon as we escaped the fog we struck clouds. The fog was at times so thick that even the wings seemed blurred to one in the bow. The rain came in bursts, and its effect on the pilots as it drove in their faces was finally to bring on drowsiness. The medical officer at Rockaway had both forewarned and forearmed me for such an emergency, so I opened up the medical kit and got out a double dose of strychnin, which I gave to Richardson, who was in worse shape than McCulloch. About an hour later I repeated the dose. It brought him around all right.

When I figured we were due to be approaching Flores Islands, the strain became severe, for we could not see more than one hundred yards, and I doubt if we could have avoided the mountains if they had loomed up ahead. Finally at eleven o'clock I got just a glimpse of the sun. I grabbed my sextant and got a quick reading of the altitude. We were tossing about so that the bubble used for the artificial horizon was very unsteady, but I quickly worked out the sight and drew in the line of position. This line passed through Pico, so I changed course to head up the line, not knowing just where on it I might be, in fact, not being at all sure of my position.

It got very thick again, and Moore came forward to tell me that he had a bare two hours of fuel left. I went aft to the pilots, apprised them of the situation, and asked their opinion as to the advisability of landing, so that we could stop the engines, take a radio compass bearing on the *Columbia* at Horta, and, having found our position, proceed to the nearest port. We looked over at the surface of the sea, and though we could see it but dimly, decided that a landing and getaway could be made safely, so engines were throttled and we started down. When we got too close to put on power and get up again, all realized that the sea was too rough. We hit the top of a wave, jumped to the top of the next, and then landed on the slope of the third with such force that I expected the hull to collapse. We were down!

Before landing we had sent out a radio signal, announcing our intention and giving what I believed to be our approximate position. We had also been sending out approximate positions every half hour, so I thought the destroyers would find us in a few hours. An examination of the seaplane showed the hull badly crushed above the water line, some of the main longitudinals broken, a rather bad leak under the pilots' cockpit, and the forward center engine-beds bowed.

As we had not been getting replies to our radio signals for some hours, Lavender set out to make a thorough inspection of this system, and found the ground wire broken just under the after propeller. I then realized that our signals had not been going out and that no one knew where we were. Signals intercepted that afternoon stated that last message had been received from NC-3 when passing destroyer number sixteen, so evidently our outfit had failed us shortly after that time. We immediately fixed the radio so that messages could be sent by running one engine, and spent an hour calling. The NC-4 had reached Horta, the NC-1 was down in fog and in bad shape, and the NC-3 was missing, and radio signals were flying about so fast that our poor little messages were smothered. We could hear instructions being given to search between sixteen and seventeen for NC-3, and as we were four hundred miles farther east we began to feel alarmed, especially when a little later we heard a storm warning go out from Horta.

All preparations were made for riding out the storm. We decided our sea anchor was too big for the weather which was coming and rigged up two canvas buckets instead. Stock was taken of food, and I discovered that our few remaining sandwiches had, along with almost everything else in the hull, been dashed in the bilge when we struck the water and were water-soaked. The emergency rations were intact, and we had five small cakes of milk chocolate. There was plenty of water in the radiators, and, although it was full of rust and had some oil in it, thirsty men could and did drink it. Wires were examined and tightened up, colors were hoisted upside down as a distress signal and the Véry pistol was oiled up and loaded, ready for use at night.

As evening came on the wind increased. We continued to send out radio calls until the sea got so rough we could not run the engine without great danger of wrecking the seaplane. At dusk, watches were set as lookouts. The hull was pumped out and those who felt like it curled up there and tried to sleep. We were wet and cold and were pitching and rolling, so, tired though we were from the all-night and half-day flight, very little sleep was had. I was up practically all night, trying to get sights on the stars or moon to determine our position, and plotting our drift before the wind. It was too cloudy for any good sights, however.

About four o'clock Sunday morning, May eighteenth, the real storm broke. The wind suddenly increased to gale force, and brought with it a driving rain. All hands were turned out, for it was now a fight for life. The pump was manned, pilots put at controls to keep us headed into wind and a close watch kept on the sea anchor and wing pontoons. After getting control of the water in the hull, we took the hose off the pump and Moore and I rigged it up to the oil tank, to put oil on the sea. It made a fairly good slick, but we were drifting so fast it was no use to us, so I decided to save the oil in case we had a chance to run the engines.

About 7 A.M. the good old NC-3 began to break up. First the left lower wing got a big sea which broke all the ribs, then the tail went under and broke the lower elevator. The wind at this time was blowing something over fifty miles and later got up over sixty. Seas were about thirty to thirty-five feet and very steep. The real calamity occurred at 9 A.M. when a heavy cross-sea carried away our left-wing pontoon.

I did not think we could last much longer, but we got out the harness which the engineer wore when climbing around among the engines and took turns strapping ourselves out on the opposite wing so that the additional weight would keep the broken wing out of the water. Pumping was kept up continuously, as the leaks were getting worse. There was no rest for anybody.

Just at noon the air cleared and I got a meridian altitude of the sun, which, applied to a poor time sight taken in the early forenoon, gave me a position forty-five miles southeast of Pico, the highest island in the Azores. Richardson spotted the dim outline of the mountain above the clouds. It was so near and yet so far, for the gale was taking us directly away from it and down into the broad South Atlantic. We did try to send a radio signal, however, and nearly wrecked ourselves before we could stop the engine. We put over the big sea anchor to check our drift, but it broke immediately, so we put the buckets back over. By the improvised scheme of having a bit of broken rib dropped over at the stern, and timing it till it passed the bow, knowing the length of the hull I could get a fair estimate of drift, which, of course, was stern first. So watching our course I kept a good record of our positions.

Night began to come on, and things looked very blue. We had heard instructions sent to use every available vessel in the search, but they were still searching out in the mid-Atlantic.

We had also heard how the crew of the NC-1 had been rescued by the Greek ship *Ionia,* after being over six hours adrift, and taken into Horta, while efforts were being made to save the remains of the NC-1. Destroyers were having a bad time of it in the gale, and the various captains told me afterward they had no idea we were still alive. We also heard the report of the NC-4 telling how through a rift in the fog they had sighted land, which proved to be the southwest corner of Flores; how they had flown on to Fayal, to again get lost, and finally landed about eight miles from Horta in the lee of the island of Fayal, where they got their bearings and finally made Horta.

Sunday night was something to try to forget. None of us expected to live through it, though I am glad to say we kept our opinions to ourselves. We were all dead tired, but there had to be three on watch all the time, and the other two intermittently engaged in pumping, so no sleep was possible. I kept awake by smoking and letting the spray dash over me occasionally. The heaviness cleared toward midnight and I got some good star and moon sights, which fixed our position definitely. By this time we had learned that by careful manipulation of the controls we could make the seaplane drift a little across the wind, and I tried to make a course to San Miguel on which Ponta Delgada is located. It was dangerous work, for if we got pointed too far the waves would undoubtedly wreck us, and if we didn't point off we would meet our end somewhere in the South Atlantic, if we lived that long.

Toward morning the water got so deep in the hull that I feared we were slowly sinking. Six hours of pumping got it down to where we felt safe again, but it nearly wrecked us physically. One man had to lie in the water down under the gasoline tanks to keep debris from stopping up the suction while the others pumped, then they would change so that the wet man could get warm.

At nine-thirty Monday morning I got a sun sight which showed that we were getting well to the eastward, and at ten-thirty Moore sighted land astern, at a distance which I estimated to be about forty-five miles. It was San Miguel. The effect on all hands was astonishing. We had been adrift two days in a storm and hadn't seen a thing but water. The sea was still high, with heavy winds blowing, and we didn't know if the old wreck would hold together, but now there was real hope. . . .

We continued to pump, but with a different spirit. With my binoculars I was able to identify points on San Miguel, and laid a course which would bring us close to the west end, where we could sail down along the coast before the wind. As we got closer in to shore we reversed our colors and hoisted our pennant. We were afraid to try to run an engine to send a signal, so the ships at Ponta Delgada had no idea of our proximity, until the United States Marine Battery stationed in the hills west of Ponta Delgada sighted us and reported to naval headquarters by radio. Lavender was listening in, and heard the message, and immediately the air was full of messages—"Look again; can't be NC-3," etc. The marines came back with word that the seaplane had threes plastered all over it. A destroyer came roaring out of the harbor, and when she got close I saw it was the *Harding*, Commander H. E. Cook, commanding. We sent a signal by blinker light for her to merely stand by, as we intended making port without aid if possible.

Just after this another wave took off my remaining wing pontoon and we very nearly capsized, but by this time we were off the entrance to the harbor, so we started the three serviceable engines, and with Moore on one wing, Richardson on the other, Lavender working signals, McCulloch at the controls, and myself in the bow we came slowly into Ponta Delgada, amid a perfect bedlam of whistles, sirens, twenty-one-gun salutes, waving of flags and wild dashing about of dozens of motor-boats.

Our final effort at a sea-anchor, consisting of a bundle of wreckage from the wings, trailing by the radio antenna wire, was still trailing out, and the confusion was increased by two of the motor-boats getting snarled up in this like a pair of kittens in a spool of thread. Finally we reached our buoy and were taken off by the Admiral's barge, and landed at Admiralty House, where we were greeted by Rear-Admiral R. H. Jackson, accompanied by Captain Ward Wortman of the destroyer force, and by the Governor of the Azores and the Mayor of Ponta Delgada.

We were so unsteady on our feet from a combination of weakness and sudden change to solid ground that we could not walk without assistance. The inhabitants gathered around Admiralty House and gave us a big ovation, then we got a chance to bathe and shave and finally got what we needed most—food. I sent off my report by cable to Washington and received the latest news from the NC-1 and NC-4; then turned in.

In my capacity as division commander and in execution of my orders I expected to proceed to Lisbon, with Read, in the NC-4 and so informed the Navy Department, but they decreed otherwise, and after Read reached Ponta Delgada, and Bellinger, with his crew, came in by destroyer, I received authority to proceed by destroyer with the personnel of the NC-1 and NC-3. So midnight of May twenty-first the *Stockton* slipped out with all of us on board, and at six o'clock in the afternoon of May twenty-third we arrived in Lisbon, and transferred to the U.S.S. *Rochester,* where I reported to Rear-Admiral Plunkett and we settled down to await the arrival of the NC-4, which was weather-bound in Ponta Delgada.

Those few days in Lisbon were most pleasant. We spent them in sightseeing and being generally entertained. Lisbon is a second Monte Carlo, so the evenings were far from dull. Finally, on May twenty-seventh we got word that the NC-4 had started. There was a great assemblage on the *Rochester* that afternoon to witness her arrival, which was accompanied by great enthusiasm from the hundreds of thousands of Lisbonites afloat and ashore. When Read and his crew got on board the *Rochester,* we of the NC Division were all decorated by the Portuguese Minister of Marine on behalf of the President of Portugal.

Early the next morning the *Rochester* put to sea for Plymouth, where we arrived on the afternoon of May twenty-ninth. Arrangements were made for the reception of the NC-4, and on the morning of May thirtieth a radio message was received that she had started. A small water leak caused her to land at Mondega River, and because of delay there she only went as far as Ferrol, Spain, that evening, then came on to Plymouth the next day, when again there was a big gathering on the *Rochester*. After being greeted by the representatives of the British government, the crew of the NC-4, accompanied by the remainder of the personnel of the NC Division and by Admiral Plunkett and his staff, proceeded by motor-boats to the Barbecon, where impressive ceremonies were held on the exact spot from which the Pilgrims had embarked for America. . . .

On Monday the crew of the NC-4 and I were decorated with the Cross of the Royal Air Force, and on Tuesday the whole party proceeded to Paris, where we had four more days of gaiety, then to Brest to take passage home on the U. S. naval transport *Zeppelin*. We arrived in New York on June twenty-seventh, after an absence of just fifty-one days, in which enough had happened to be spread over the average life of a man and furnish quite sufficient excitement and amusement.

The flight had become a matter of history. . . .[1]

II

PROGRESS IS CRUEL ONLY TO THE FEW

The Navy experimented with dirigibles but hopes for the huge airships ended in successive disasters—the Shenandoah *broke up during a thunderstorm in Ohio, 1925; the* Akron *went down off the New Jersey coast, 1933; the* Macon *ended her career off the West Coast, 1935. The tragic loss of the* Akron *is described by the widow of one of the officers on board and by one of the survivors, Lieutenant Commander Herbert V. Wiley.*

The baby had finished his nightly sham battle against tub, water, and his father, and after he had eaten lustily we had tucked him drowsily into bed. Jim had wandered out into his newly planted garden and thither I followed him. The fact that I stumbled a little with fatigue made the sight of his quiet figure and broad back all the dearer to me. He was on his knees, digging gently with one finger into the soil; and I slumped down on the sand beside him, resting my elbows on my knees.

"Not a sprout yet," he murmured. . . . "What do you reckon has happened to the darned things?"

"My dear," I said earnestly, "how would it do to leave them rather quietly in the soil—I mean the sand—for a few days so that they can make up their minds about this sprouting business. . . ."

"If they really would get down to business I'd leave them alone. There are gardens everywhere in Lakehurst and yet the baby is still waiting for that super-chow we've planned for him."

"Might it not speed up the process if there was suddenly a little less water in the lake and a little more of it just hereabouts?" I suggested affably. "After all, there is a drought, you remember."

For answer Jim rolled over on his back, caught one of the dog's long curly ears in his hands, and rubbed it as he grinned drowsily.

"I was on the point of suggesting the lake, but only in connection with a swim. Leave it to the aerologists to place moisture where nature intended. Anyhow, this being my first garden, I can't set a bad precedent. How about a shot or two of Badminton and then a cool swim? Dinner's under way, I take it."

I straightened my back, which ached a little, and wondered vaguely how I could manage to hold a racket in a hand afflicted with a burnt finger. But the proposition was too tempting, and in a moment Jim had brought out my sneakers and was stretching the net across the little patch of stubbly grass which we called a court.

The swift flight of the tiny feathered ball seemed to renew my energy and we were soon fiercely intent upon the game. Somewhere in the back of my mind I was wondering, as usual, how anyone could be as quiet as Jim was, and yet so gay. At that moment a soft purring noise forced its way into my consciousness. I stopped the swing of my racket so suddenly that I nearly pitched headlong in my effort to stand still and listen. Jim, too, had swung around with his back to me and was searching the sky.

"I know, I know!" I cried idiotically. "It's the same noise that we heard over Boston that night. Jim, can it possibly. . . ."

"There she is," he said softly, and started at a dog trot for the edge of the lake where the view of the sky was less obstructed than it was on the court. Climbing up on a log bench by the water, he sat on its back with his feet on the seat. His eyes were the only part of his relaxed body which gave me an inkling of his excitement.

While we had played our game the color of the lake had deepened into its evening purple, and at our backs the sunset was softening. Out of it came the airship; and the manner of its moving was beautiful. Few inanimate objects attain beauty in the pursuance of their courses, and yet, to me, at least, the flight of this ship was far lovelier than the swooping of a bird or the jumping of a horse. For it seemed to carry with it a calm dignity and a consciousness of destiny which ranked it among the wonders of time itself.

It was the *Akron* returning from her first western cruise; and this was our first sight of her. My hand was so cold and trembling that I drew it away from Jim's and clasped it over my other in my lap. Jim's eyes had become dreamy and speculative, yet alert.

I wondered if it were only the beauty of the ship which aroused my emotions so keenly or if it were because I vaguely realized that our lives would become so involved in her fate. . . .

Several weeks later Jim came home with the news that he was to make his first flight in the *Akron* at dawn the next day. The "zero hour" had been set for 4:30 A.M. and he carried with him a soft-spoken alarm clock. It did but little good, however, for my excitement made sleep almost impossible. At last Jim awoke and switched off the alarm before it had had time to fulfill its mission. When he saw that I apparently had one eye open he came over to say good-by. After he went down stairs I slid out of bed and followed him, blinking sheepishly as I walked into the lighted dressing-room. He glared at me with a terrible fierceness but in a few moments we were drinking hot coffee quite merrily. As we perched on the kitchen table a new sound came through the windows, a sound for which I seem to have waited through great spaces of time during my next months at Lakehurst. It was a whistle whose note resembled that of a fog horn and which, I learned, announced the intended approach or departure of the ship. It had a long throaty note which made me shudder a little and which seemed to be the very breath of the still, dark morning through which we groped our way to the car.

The tall walls of the hangar soon became visible ahead of us in the darkness. Inside and on top of it were many lights which gave the building an air of busy preoccupation. Jim drove around one side of it, pulled his bag from the rear seat of the car, and went off into the towering walls. I parked the car near the front of the hangar and waited. The revolving signal beacon on the roof kept up its slow, swirling movement, and I, a mere earth traveler, felt lost and insignificant in a world of new conquests and alien interests.

The waiting seemed endless and the sky began to brighten slowly. My impatience had increased to an almost unbearable pitch when at last I saw a sailor climb into a tiny engine-room which was built into the framework of the huge door of the hangar. In a moment the singing noise of electric motors began and inch by inch the doors slid back, letting a stream of light out into the darkness about me. Soon they were far enough apart to enable me to see the black iron mast to which the rounded nose of the *Akron* was coupled. When the doors were entirely opened (a process which took about ten minutes) I saw that the mast and the ship were being pulled along some tracks by an engine. As the ship came abreast of my car I climbed out and stood in absolute awe with head far back to watch the enormous, seemingly endless, silver shape move slowly past me. It was at that time that I had my first adequate idea of her size and fully appreciated her great length of nearly 800 feet. For, after she had passed me, the atmosphere seemed very bright and I noticed that the sun had come up behind her.

Swarming groups of sailors walked casually by her sides and held her guy ropes as she was drawn down the tracks, her nose and stern held rigidly by the mechanical handling gear. When she reached the "hauling-up" circle her rear fin was freed from the heavy beam which held it and a taxi wheel was substituted. Then she was swung down into the "mooring" circle with her nose into the wind and other adjustments were completed. Already she seemed so small that I was sure I had ridiculously overestimated her size.

At last the sailors released her yaw lines; and at the command, "Up Ship" she slipped her moorings and floated free of her mast, the wind pushing her back ever so little. Suddenly her engines began to purr, at first very gently and then louder and louder until their steady hum was a splendid rhythm of strength. Her tilted propellers took command of her, she ceased floating and almost leapt forward, seeming to feel no hesitancy nor uncertainty. The red, white, and blue coloring on her fins and the great star on her breast sparkled in the sunlight. Her beauty embodied such a sense of strength that I remembered I had heard her called a "roving mountain peak."

My elation went with her, however. As I climbed back into the car and rattled homeward I wondered jealously why I was fated to be tied to the earth. But as I left the car a swarm of rollicking puppies attacked me and we raced to the shore of the lake. After all, the earth was glorious, and the puppies knew it. We romped on the shore until I heard another kind of chirping inside the house and went in to see the always amazing phenomenon of round pink cheeks and merry eyes.

Late in the summer when the ship was due to dock at 4:30 A.M. two of us determined to go up to the landing field to watch her come in. The weather appeared to be rather foggy as we slipped out of the quiet house but it was still too dark to be sure. When my hand touched the steering wheel of the car I found it dripping with moisture; and as we paused at the sentry house on the Air Station I saw by the car lights that the mist was almost a rain.

"Ugh," I thought. "This doesn't promise a happy landing."

We parked the car and waited; but the density of the fog increased as the dawn began. Even the neon lights on the aerology building a short distance from us were invisible. The dreary note of the station whistle penetrated the foggy morning for ten seconds every minute.

Many times during several hours of waiting we distinctly heard the humming motors of the *Akron* above our heads. Once or twice we could even see the long black shadow of the ship silhouetted against the opaque fog, and we would become tense with baffled excitement. But in an instant it would disappear and with it the muffled sound of the engines, leaving us desolate in the thick pearl grey of the enveloping fog, wondering if we had been seeing a specter. The continual moaning of the fog horn accentuated the feeling.

Suddenly I turned and saw one of the most beautiful sights I have ever known. The fog had rolled back in just one place and through it the sunlight poured radiantly. Between these walls of grey the ship appeared, her upper half still veiled in long wisps of delicate grey while her lower portion was glistening and silvery. The fog horn ceased, the air seemed to clear abruptly, and the ship came steadily, even placidly, down to her mast. . . .

Some months later I had my first chance to watch airplanes hook on to the ship while both were in flight. It was at night and "the Admiral" was aboard. Jim had said good-by early in the evening just before the moan of the zero hour whistle had sounded. Several hours later I became conscious that the air outside the house was vibrating with the roar of planes and the softer purr of the ship. Snatching up a coat I ran out into the night and looked up. . . .

All around the *Akron* flew her planes, just discernible by the lights on their wing tips. I could see that they were in formation or soaring and diving through the air before they settled in the steady, persistent climb up to the trapeze. Just as the ship passed over the house one of the planes made contact with the ship, hung motionless for a moment, then swooped down and away in a perfect spiral as another plane shot forward to take its place under the ship.

I wondered whether some persons would resent the intrusion of these inventions of man upon the natural beauty of the starry night: whether they would prefer the intermittent twinkling of the stars to the rhythmic pulsations of the lights aboard the ship. To me it was a happy demonstration of the harmonious co-operation possible between natural elements which had seemed to remain the same since time began and the triumphant dreams of earth creatures. . . .

A plane flew up under the *Akron,* hovered for a few moments in the light around the trapeze, and then was drawn slowly into her black hull. The port closed, the ship faded into the night, and I went slowly back into the old house where I could only sit and stare into the fire.

Next morning while I was ardently trying to disprove the proverb that cooks are born and not made, I again heard the *Akron* overhead. My experimental mood fled with me as I ran out into the sunshine. There was the ship indeed; but what a different ship! No air of mystery surrounded her now. She was another creature, her hull ablaze with sunlight, while she slipped lazily along in the still air like a huge droning bee. All around her buzzed her coterie of mosquito-like planes. . . . One by one they crept up to the ship for a few moments, then disappeared inside her as she sailed out of sight, much as a motherly old hen clucks to her brood and settles snugly down over them to rest.

Often the weather around Lakehurst was wild. The old trees surrounding our house would double up and moan as the relentless winds twisted and tore at them. My dog would creep close to my bed and stare with wide eyes when I arose in the middle of the night to inspect the antiquated furnace. Then I would crawl back to bed after a furtive glance at the baby and would lie for long minutes to await the return of sleep, wishing that the wind did not shake even the bed in which I lay. As the lightning flashed I would cover my eyes with my balsam pillow and tell myself that although there was a storm here, the weather was probably serene or at least navigable not far away. I began dreamily to picture the weather as a pleasant field dotted with mushrooms which were the storm areas, and this crude idea consoled me. The *Akron* I knew to be three times stronger than the *Shenandoah*. She had already ridden out storms which would have wrecked the latter ship; and I was proud that she kept rigidly to her flight schedules. She was fulfilling her destiny. . . .

One afternoon in early April I was standing in the nursery door gloating over a lovely little table and chair which had been sent up from the South for the baby's birthday. Jim and I had opened the crate together that noon, out on the front "stoop" over which an old wisteria vine cascaded its lavender blossoms.

While I was looking into the nursery an arm rested across my shoulders and Jim's voice said musingly:

"It'll be great to see both of them sitting there. This summer we'll rig up a workshop and I'll learn to use the new tools you got me. We'll try our hand at a bow and some arrows for you first, and then —oh, lots of things for the nursery. Did I tell you there is a zero hour at six tonight?"

"Dinner at five, then," I said mechanically. "I've planned an amazing salad."

We had a very gay meal, for we were in our most ardent window-shopping mood, where possibilities are far more exciting than actualities. Our coffee we had while we sat on the living-room settee, Jim holding his saucer with his left hand while he made wobbly drawings of a toy bench with his right.

The arrival of a friend's car interrupted us and Jim went off to the station, saluting me with a smile as he ran down the steps. After he had gone I stood at the window for a long time watching the feathery glory of the pale green larch tree.

"It is far too early for the sun to have set," I thought vaguely.

I had planned to see the ship go out but was delayed for awhile in leaving the house. As I approached the landing field I noticed with surprise that a fog, about 100 feet above the ground, was creeping over the mooring circle. Broad beams of light were being played on the *Akron* as the last preparations were made for her flight.

Those lights went out, her own broke into their twinkling rhythm, and the command, "Up Ship" was given.

And then a strange thing happened. A moment before her sailing she appeared vital and strong. But as she ascended, the swirling mist seemed to take possession of her tentatively at first as if it were afraid of what it was doing, and then more imperatively. Her lights took on a ghostly hue and her gleaming shape became dim and elusive. For a few moments she was faintly visible to us. Then the mist renewed its purpose. And the ship had disappeared. . . .

[*Wiley*] . . . the ship began to descend rapidly from 1,600 feet, and I dropt the emergency ballast forward, and the fall was stopt at 800 feet. . . . We rose rapidly and leveled off easily at 1,600 feet. While we were falling the engines speeded to full speed; when we regained altitude they changed to standard speed. About three minutes later the air became exceedingly turbulent, and the ship was tossed about violently.

I knew we were near the center of the storm, because the air is most disturbed toward centers, and I called all hands to the landing-stations—that is, I gave the signal to have them available, and not in their bunks. The ship took a sharp lurch and the rudder-control wires of the upper rudder carried away. Then they broke. I unclutched the upper rudder and tried to steer with the lower rudder. I was on the right side of the control power and supervised the rudder, and the captain was on the left side supervising the elevator wheel—the wheel that sends you up and down.

The elevator man reported several times that the ship was falling, and I heard the report 800 feet. By this time the bow of the ship nosed to about 20 degrees, but even then we were falling quite rapidly. In the fog nothing could be seen. I asked the altitude, and the answer was 300 feet. I gave the order to stand by for a crash, and the signal was rung to the engine car. Then we hit the water. We had, as I remember, a list to starboard—my side of the car—

and water—I remember—rushing in my window carried me out of the other window—the window the captain was standing by.

I tried to swim as rapidly as I could to get from under the ship, and finally I came to the surface. I could see the ship drifting away from me when the lightning flashed. The bow was pointed up in the air and the whole structure was a general wreck. I saw two lights on what I thought was the stern, and looking to the side of them I saw the lights of a ship. I also thought I could see the glare of Barnegat lighthouse.

I swam toward the ship and after about ten minutes found a board about three feet square which I clung to the rest of the way. I saw several men in the water, but none very close that I thought I could help.

When I got about 400 yards from the ship (the tanker *Phoebus*), the wind changed and the waves began hitting me in the face instead of rising from behind me. The captain put his ship broadside the sea and it floated down toward us. I think he had heard the cries of some of the men in the water. I swam easily to the steamer, and they threw a life-ring to me and hauled me aboard.

(The officer's widow resumes her story.)

. . . A few days ago I went into the hangar again. Its fourteen stories' height yawned almost empty above me.

Over at one side the gallant old *Los Angeles* looked tired and desolated. How the *Akron* had glistened, had breathed vitality in every sweeping line!

In one corner I saw a small pile of junk: old and distorted duralumin frames and some moldy pieces of fabric.

"Is that something they're experimenting with?" I asked.

My escort said nothing for a minute and then, quietly, "That is all we've been able to salvage of the *Akron*."

I needed to take a deep breath and so I turned away. There in another corner groups of men were working among stacks of shining new duralumin pieces.

"And that?" I said hastily.

"That is for shipment to the west coast. It's for the new ship."

"Oh, I am glad," I murmured. "Progress is cruel only to the few. . . ."[2]

III

THE LAST SIGNAL FROM LIEUTENANT FITCH

In the air, under the sea, progress exacted its price. Lieutenant Commander Edward Ellsberg, deep-sea diver engaged in rescue work, and a submariner relate their experiences.

Swinging to port as she passed the white can buoy marking the end of the mile course off Provincetown the S-4 finished her submerged run. Spray driven by a stiff wind dashed over the periscopes, making observations on the range buoys difficult.

Inside the control room, crowded with men at their diving stations, Lieutenant-Commander Jones gave the order to emerge. The stern diving plane moved to "Hard rise. . . ."

CRASH!

A terrific blow slammed the S-4 drunkenly to port, knocked down the rising bow, and heeled the submarine sharply over. The shock tripped out the circuit breakers on the switchboard. In the darkness the blue-jackets found themselves thrown in a tangled heap to the port bilges. The vessel rocked irregularly as a destroyer rode over her deck.

The forward periscope suddenly rose out of its well as if plucked by a giant hand outside, and then as quickly dropped back, jamming itself in a maze of tangled hoisting wires.

Bow down, stern in air, the S-4 lay over to port and under the horrified gaze of the men on the *Paulding's* bridge disappeared from sight. . . .

The rescue ship *Falcon,* just arrived over the wreck, was swinging to a flimsy mooring in a gathering storm while Eadie explored below. Eadie came up, reported, "Hole in the battery room, starboard side; six men alive in torpedo room; no damage aft of battery room, but no sounds in after half of ship."

There was little time for any action. If the battery room only was flooded, the thirty-four men aft might be alive but unconscious. Blowing water out of the undamaged ballast tanks should bring the boat up. The officers on the *Falcon* elected to try it.

Diver Carr took down a hose which he coupled to the ballast tank blow line. The *Falcon* blew without result. The S-4 had more than the battery room flooded—certainly the control room, perhaps the whole stern.

Evidently the six men forward were all that were left. The storm was getting worse. The *Falcon* could not work much longer. Diver Michels went down to couple a hose to the compartment salvage line which led to all compartments including the torpedo room.

The weather was very bad. Michels, going down in darkness with the waves heaving the *Falcon* wildly, soon found himself badly tangled in the wreckage on the S-4's deck. Eadie, roused from his bunk, went down again, worked desperately for two hours in icy water to free Michels, then sent him up, unconscious and frozen.

Diving had to cease.

Through the oscillator, the *Falcon* talked with Lieutenant Fitch, who answered by rapping in Morse code with his wrench.

Fitch reported the salvage air line flooded, the air bad, his oxygen nearly gone.

The storm kept up.

Late the second day, wet, frozen, starved, thirsty, half stifled from foul air, Lieutenant Fitch inquired, "Is there any hope?"

We signaled back, "There is hope. Everything possible is being done," but we well knew that nothing was possible till the storm abated.

At midnight we received a message to transmit to Lieutenant Fitch: "Your wife and mother constantly praying for you." Our oscillator spelled the message out. No answer from the S-4. We kept sending the message. At 6:20 A.M. the third day came the last signal from Lieutenant Fitch—three raps—acknowledgment. That was the end.

The next day the storm abated. After some difficulty in dragging (the storm had carried away our marker buoys) we located the S-4 again.

Lieutenant Fitch had reported the air salvage line flooded shortly after Michels' ill-fated attempt to connect a hose to it. While the storm rolled on we racked our heads and studied the S-4 plans minutely to discover some way of getting air directly into the torpedo room. A message came from a submarine captain in far-off San Diego, "Try the S-C tube. . . ."

We decided to cut the rubber diaphragms off the copper tubes, where they extended through the T arms, on the inside terminal of the S-C device, clamp air hose to the tube ends, and attempt to ventilate and exhaust through the S-C tubes. We hoped that Lieutenant Fitch, expecting us to hit on this method, had rigged his listening gear and opened the check valve on the inside terminal of the S-C device while he had the strength to move about.

A grappling hook finally caught in the boat. Wilson and Eiben, sliding down the line, made their way forward and connected hoses to the S-C tubes. I turned on the air. An anxious moment watching the gauge; the pressure dropped, the air went through!

We blew fresh air in and vented foul air out on the chance in a million that someone might revive. But foul air, cold and dampness had done their work.

There was nothing left to do but raise the boat. Winter was upon us. Diving days would be scarce, and diving extra hazardous. But raise the boat we must.

What was the extent of the damage? Would the injured hull stand the strains of lifting without breaking in two? I donned a diving rig and dropped overboard from the *Falcon* to find out.

Down through icy water I slid, and shortly stood on the narrow bow of the S-4, alongside the S-C tube over the torpedo room. A few fish swam around me. I walked slowly aft, impeded by the water and the drag of my life line and air hose.

Over the battery room I reached the spot where the deck was torn away; dropping down a few feet I clambered over the cylindrical hull to the gun, where the deck was good again. The gun, muzzle down, was slewed to port. I climbed over it and reached the conning tower, when I recollected that I had as yet seen no hole piercing the hull itself. That was my job.

I turned about, climbed back over the gun and started forward over the exposed cylindrical hull when I had to stop. A fine mud, stirred up by my previous passage, filled the water and made it impossible for me to see the submarine. Balancing myself on the slippery cylinder, I tried to figure out my direction when a surge above jerked my lifeline, pulled me off my feet, and I found myself sliding down the side of the S-4.

As I went over, a projecting plate flashed in front of my helmet. My hand seized it. I hung there and found what I had dived to see.

I was hanging from a torn steel plate over the gash in the submarine's side and looking directly into the S-4's death wound. It was not a very large hole, quite small in fact, hardly large enough for a man to crawl through, but it was enough.

However I did not spend much time inspecting it. I felt a cold trickle down my right arm. Looking up at my hand, I saw that the jagged plate I was hanging from had cut open my glove and the air in my suit was leaving me. I must get that hand down. Seeing some plates sticking from the side I tried to push myself up with my legs, but these plates also felt ragged and likely to cut the suit further. Another glance at my hand showed I was losing too much air. I let go, fell clear of the S-4, and disappeared in the black mud alongside.

I was lying on my right side in soft ooze. It was utterly dark. I instinctively pushed with my right arm to straighten up. The arm cut through the mud without effect. I struggled to regain my feet and felt under me torn steel plates which had dropped from the submarine. I ceased struggling. If I cut my suit any worse buried in that muck, I might be in a bad way.

If I could not get up, my shipmates at the surface could pull me up. Over the telephone I asked them to heave on my lifeline. They did, but I felt no strain. My line was foul or something—if it were caught in the torn side of the submarine over me, a few heaves across those razorlike plates would cut my air hose in two. And that meant "finis." Hurriedly I yelled out to stop heaving. They stopped.

I lay still and thought. I must extricate myself . . . by floating myself out of the mud. Keeping my torn right glove low, I opened the air valve on my suit wider and started to inflate the suit. It worked; I felt my helmet rise, break through the mud into the dim light of the ocean floor. Quickly, I throttled the air to avoid breaking free and ballooning up to the surface with a sure case of the "bends."

Alternately I opened and closed the air valve, lifting myself by inches till I was out to my waist. Glancing up, I could see my air hose now rising vertically, clear of everything. Again making myself heavy, I asked for a pull and a moment later I was clear of the mud, dangling on my life line. The submarine was invisible.

My job was done. I had inspected the damage, and had been down nearly an hour. The tenders on the *Falcon* started me on the slow ascent to the surface.

The salvage job started. After three months, the S-4 was raised. . . .

The day the S-4 sank, the wife of one of the officers trapped inside her, speaking from anguish of her heart, exclaimed:

"He's gone. They never raise those boats till after everybody's dead!"

She was right. . . .[3]

[*Submariner*] . . . What happens in a submarine when it goes to the bottom and cannot rise?

. . . Well, you may recall the S-5, which went down off Delaware Breakwater a few years ago. I was one of the forty men who were bottled up in that boat for thirty-seven hours. What happened on the S-5 is typical of what happens on any submarine that can't make the surface.

We were off Delaware Breakwater due for a crash dive—a quick plunge planned for emergencies—and a submerged run. The small circular deck hatches, one for'ard leading down to the torpedo-room and one aft into the engine-room, were secured. The for'ard diving rudders, under the bow, were spread out like the flappers on a whale. Amidships in the control-room, thick with smoke from burning oil, a dozen sailors were on the job, twisting valves, throwing switches and turning wheels. The Diesel engines had been shut off, and the boat was moving under electric power.

The skipper had just dropped down through the hatch from the conning tower and we were settling nicely when all of a sudden it seemed as if the whole Atlantic Ocean had come rushing in on us. A sailor had left a valve open. No one got excited. As quickly as we could we got that valve closed—but not before sixty tons of salt water had poured in. By that time the nose of the boat was pointed down at an angle of about fifteen degrees. This sent the water rushing for'ard and in a few minutes the torpedo-room was entirely flooded. The added weight in the bow pulled her nose down rapidly until when we hit bottom, in thirty-five fathoms of water, our keel was nearly vertical.

Fortunately, nobody suffered much more than a slight jar when the S-5 shot down and stuck her nose in the mud.

But there was a lot of fast scrambling by the men who were in the torpedo-room when the water went roaring into it. Everyone kept cool, though, and in a jiffy we had the watertight door between the torpedo and the control rooms securely fastened.

After we hit bottom our first move was to shift the water ballast in the outer tanks so as to bring the craft back to something like an even keel. Then we tried to bring her to the surface, but she wouldn't budge, and there we were stuck fast with more than two hundred feet between us and air.

If any of the bunch down there had had a yellow streak, it would have shown then. But the whole lot of them were game. They talked and acted as though they were going through an everyday experience. The only bird who showed any nervousness was the chap who'd left the valve open. And he wasn't scared because he was afraid of death, but because he feared someone would call him a dumb-bell or that an officer would bawl him out.

After a while I noticed that little itchy feeling in my nose which men of the undersea service are more afraid of than anything else. It means that water has gotten into the batteries and is generating chlorine gas.

I looked at the skipper, and it wasn't hard to guess that he had felt the same sensation. My first thought was of the gas masks, but then I remembered that we had enough of them for no more than half the men we had on board. Within a few seconds the whole crew began coughing and sneezing, and every man realized what had happened. But there wasn't the slightest sign of panic. . . .

There was only one thing to do—batten the compartment doors where the batteries were stored and shut out the fumes. That meant that we'd have to desert the control-room with its signaling apparatus and duck into the two aft compartments with the engines and electrical equipment.

It's no cinch to crowd forty men into such close quarters and still maintain discipline, but we managed it. And the boys didn't lose their sense of the comic either. As we were crowding into every available bit of space, one of the sailors, a New Yorker, observed: "This ain't half as bad as a five o'clock jam in the subway. Plenty of room here, huh?" and he slid in between a dynamo and the shell of the boat.

Meanwhile the skipper blew out the aft ballast tanks, letting the sub bend upward again, so that we had to brace ourselves to keep from sliding together in a heap. When the boat, with her nose in the mud and her stern pointing up, steadied a bit, we found, by tapping around the propeller shaft, that a few feet of her stuck up above the water line.

I don't think any of us officers believed we could punch a hole through the steel wall with the machinists' tools we had, but we couldn't let the men know how hopeless and helpless we felt. So we started chopping away with the tools we had and under the most trying conditions. . . .

The men worked in relays, and after hammering away for twenty-four hours we got a hole in her big enough to stick an arm through. With the first whiffs of fresh air everyone's spirits rose. But nobody kidded himself into believing that we were much closer to rescue.

We attached the white undershirt of one of the men to a piece of tubing, shoved it up through the hole and prayed that some ship would see it and recognize it as a distress signal.

You can imagine how we felt as we looked out through that tiny hole and watched first one ship and then another sail past us. We knew, of course, that the part of our boat that was out of the water couldn't be seen from any distance—that it probably looked like a buoy from a distance of five hundred yards.

Then, after twenty-four of the most uncomfortable hours I ever want to spend under the sea, the lookout of an old Shipping Board coaster saw our signal. The captain, a fine old Swede, put out in a small boat to investigate. He had been off his course and, seeing our distress signal, first thought it was a buoy.

He didn't have any tools aboard his ship that would cut into the steel sides of our sub, so he went scouting along the coast for a rescue ship. Fortunately, he found one that had the necessary equipment for rescue work of this kind, and after chopping away for eight hours, they had a hole big enough to drag us through. We had been captives exactly thirty-seven hours. . . .[4]

Depression swept around the world during the 1930's and attempts at armament reduction ended in failure. Japan invaded Manchuria, Germany rattled its sabers, Italy undertook the conquest of Ethiopia. As international relations deteriorated, the Roosevelt Administration

stepped up naval construction. Hitler issued ultimatum after ulti-
matum until in 1939 war was declared in Europe.
   Suddenly, without warning on

IV

7 DECEMBER 1941

0800
Enemy air raid Pearl.   This is not a drill.

0816
To all ships and stations: Hostilities with Japan commenced with air raid on Pearl X.

0832
To all ships present Pearl: Japanese submarine in harbor.

0901
To Midway: Pearl Harbor bombed X No indication direction attack X Take off   Attempt to locate and sink Japanese force X.

0902
To Wake: Pearl bombed by Japanese X Be on alert.

0911
To all sector commanders Pearl.   Do not fire on our planes coming in.

0920
To Comtaskforce One: Battleships remain in port until further orders X Send all destroyers to sea X Destroy enemy submarines X Follow them by own cruisers to join Halsey X.

8 DECEMBER, 0450 [GCT]
To the Chief of Naval Operations: In spite of security measures,

Pearl Harbor—7 December 1941.

surprise attack by Japanese damaged all battleships except *Maryland*. Moderate damage to *Tennessee* and *Pennsylvania*. *Arizona* total wreck. *West Virginia, Oklahoma, California, Nevada* seriously damaged. *Utah* and *Oglala* turned over. *Honolulu, Helena, Raleigh* unfit for sea. *Vestal, Curtiss*, damaged. *Shaw, Cassin, Downes* complete loss. Airplane losses severe. Following remains: About 13 B-17, 9 B-18, 30 pursuit, 10 patrol planes, one patrol plane squadron at Midway. All available Army bombers requested to be sent Oahu. Following damage to enemy: Number of enemy aircraft destroyed. One enemy submarine sunk, probably two more. Now have 2 Carriers, 7 Heavy Cruisers, 3 Squadrons Destroyers and all available planes searching for enemy. Personnel behaving magnificently face of furious surprise attack. Personnel casualties heavy in *Oklahoma* and *Arizona*.

(Lieutenant Commander Samuel Glenn Fuqua, a survivor from the battleship Arizona, *testifies to the events of 7 December 1941.)*

I was in the [*Arizona's*] ward room having breakfast. There was a short signal on the air raid siren of about one second duration. I notified the anti-aircraft control officer, who was in the ward room at the same time, to man the anti-aircraft batteries. He told me that he thought they were just testing the loud speakers . . . as the loud speaker system had gone out previous to the attack.

I said, "No. That sounds like an air raid alarm to me." However, I still thought there was a possibility that someone had brushed against the handle of the alarm.

After the anti-aircraft control officer on duty had left the ward room, I proceeded to the telephone in the ward room and telephoned to the officer of the deck to pass the word, "Anti-aircraft batteries." When I was unable to get him on the phone I proceeded to the port side of the quarterdeck. As I came out the port side of the quarterdeck there was a plane flew up overhead at a height of 50 feet with machine guns firing. I glanced up and I saw it was a Japanese plane. Then I proceeded to No. 4 turret to the starboard side of the quarterdeck, on the double.

When I rounded the No. 4 turret I saw the officer of the deck up forward and reported to him to sound general quarters and pass the word . . . to set material condition ZED as final damage control condition for battle. . . .

. . . About this time I heard a plane overhead. I glanced up. I saw a bomb dropping which appeared to me was going to land on me or close by.

The next thing I remember I came to on deck in a position about six feet aft the starboard gangway. I got to my feet and looked around to see what it was that had knocked me down. Then I saw I was lying about six feet from a bomb hole in the deck. This bomb had hit the face plate of No. 4 turret, had glanced off that and gone through the deck and had exploded in the captain's pantry. . . .

Then I glanced up forward and saw the whole midship a mass of flames in that section of the ship. . . .

Then I ran forward to make preparation to fight the fire. There I met Major Shapler, United States Marine Corps, who had just come down from the after defense station.

He told me at this time that he observed a bomb go down the stack. As the fire hoses were laid out in the quarterdeck in an effort to fight the fire, there was no water in any hose.

At this time, which I judge to be about 0815, the ship had apparently broken in two as there was water lying on the deck just abaft of the break of the deck at frame 88.

I then attempted to keep the fire back by dipping water from the side in buckets and by the use of the CO_2 fire extinguisher. We were able to keep the fire from spreading aft until we could pick the wounded up off the deck and place them in boats to transfer them to Ford Island. . . .

I would judge about 8:15 or 8:20 I saw a tremendous mass of flames, the height of 300 feet, rise in the air forward, and shook the ship aft as if it would fall apart like a pack of cards.

It was then I realized that the forward magazine had exploded. I then directed that the after magazine be flooded. This was done, but the man who flooded the after magazine was not saved. . . .

At this time, about 8:20, all the guns on the boat had ceased firing.

Being that the ship was no longer in a fighting condition, I ordered the remaining people in the after turrets to abandon ship. The only possible thing that I could see that could be done at this time was to transfer the wounded and those burned, who were running out of the flames, to Ford Island.

With the assistance of a rescue boat from the USS *Solace,* approximately 100 men who were burned and wounded were transferred to Ford Island. After this operation was completed, at about 0845, I made a thorough search of the after part of the ship, which was accessible, for wounded and uninjured personnel.

About 0845 I directed that the forward lines of the USS *Vestal,* which vessel was tied up to the port side astern, be cut. This was done and I believe the *Vestal* cut their own after lines. . . .

I finally left the ship myself about 0915, and proceeded to the receiving barracks at Pearl Harbor to report in. I learned later from the battle report of the USS *Vestal* that the *Arizona* received one torpedo hit and possibly two; these torpedoes passing under the stern of the *Vestal* and apparently striking the *Arizona* up about frame 35 on the port side. However, this was not possible to verify as the entire forward part of the ship was destroyed. . . .

After the fire, which was put out after burning for a period of two days amidships, I went on board to search for the bodies. We found the admiral's body on the boat deck, or we found a body which I believe to be the admiral's body on the boat deck, just at the foot of the flag bridge ladder. The captain's body was never found. However, the captain's ring and some coat buttons were found on the flag bridge.

Ensign D. Hein, United States Navy, was on the bridge during the attack. In some manner he got off the bridge. I discovered him about two days after the attack in the United States Naval Hospital in Pearl Harbor. In his statement he stated that he saw the captain himself and a quartermaster on the bridge. He also stated that the quartermaster reported to the captain that there was a bomb hit either by or on No. 2 turret. The next thing he reported was that the ship was sinking like an earthquake had struck it, and the bridge was in flames. He was lying on the deck in front of the wheel, and he struggled to his feet and ran off the bridge down the flag bridge to the port side and fell onto the boat deck.

Those are his words: The boat deck was a mass of flames, and the men were dying all around. He said that he thought he would lie down and die with them. Then he thought that he would go down the port side of the quarter-deck and lie down there, which he did.

In picking up the wounded off the deck aft, he was one of the persons I apparently put in the boats. . . .

(Ensign Nathan Frederick Asher attests to the courageous counter-measures of the destroyer Blue.*)*

I was seated in the Wardroom with three other officers from the *Blue* when the gangway watch notified me that the *Utah* had been torpedoed by Japanese aircraft. I immediately dashed out of the Wardroom and ordered to sound the general alarm and to pass the word to man all battle stations.

I proceeded to the bridge and there I saw a number of Japanese airplanes diving at ships in Pearl Harbor. I called the engine room and told the engineer to light off No. 2 boiler. No. 1 boiler was already lit off for auxiliary purposes.

I told the control man to notify the control to open fire immediately on enemy planes. I did not wait for any signal to open fire because I had heard some machine-gun fire from other ships in the harbor.

We had no ammunition by the guns; all ammunition was in the magazine. We had approximately 960 rounds of .50 caliber machine-gun bullets belted at each machine. We opened fire with our machine guns at approximately five minutes after 8, and about seven minutes after 8 we opened up with our 5-inch guns, with our main battery, at the Japanese planes diving in the harbor.

The signal was hoisted in our sector to prepare to get under way, and we had already made our preparation, and upon the execution of that signal I ordered the chain unshackled and we cut loose our wire to free ourselves from the buoy in the quickest manner, and we proceeded out of the channel through the north channel out of Pearl Harbor.

While we were under way we maintained our fire at the Japanese planes diving at the ships and we saw four planes that I think we shot down—four planes in the attack.

Before we got under way No. 4 gun crew shot a plane which crashed near Pearl City. When the crew saw that the plane was down, they stopped shooting and proceeded to pat each other on the back. Then the chief gunner's mate went back there, thinking there was a casualty because he did not hear the firing. Then they went back to their battle stations and continued fire.

When we got abeam where the *Utah* had been torpedoed we noticed a lot of wood floating in the water. I presume that came from the topside of the *Utah* after she had gone down. We stopped our engines so we could drift through it without causing any damage to our hold plating.

When we were abeam of Westlock Channel we saw a series of bombs, which I first thought was the ammunition dump going up but which I now believe was just a series of six bombs dropped by planes which dove at us.

When we neared the entrance of the Channel we were attacked by approximately three or four planes, and we were hit by none.

When we were abeam Weaver Field, I went at 25 knots. There was a mine sweeper in front of me, and I did not see his paravane and I ran through his paravane and I believe I cut it in two.

Before we had gotten under way I received a signal over the voice radio to sortie eastward, and I believe that came from Batdiv 4. I set the course 120 through and proceeded to a regular assigned sector, patrol sector 3. When I got to the middle sector, I slowed down to 10 knots and started patrolling, using the echo range.

About 20 minutes after we slowed down I noticed that we had our first contact about 1300 yards. I developed the contact and dropped four depth charges. . . .

. . . I ran by the spot where I dropped the depth charges and turned around and picked up what I thought was the same contact and I didn't know whether it was the first contact or another because the second contact was in approximately the same position. I dropped two additional depth charges. I then turned around and observed a large oil slick on the water, and we observed bubbles coming to the surface along the length of approximately 200 feet.

At that time everybody on the bridge thought the submarine was coming to the surface; so I ordered action to the starboard and to man the batteries ready to open fire if she did surface, but nothing ever developed from that. So I believe that submarine was sunk.

Then we proceeded patrolling, and in about 30 minutes after that the *St. Louis* came steaming out, and we got our third contact, and that contact was in the vicinity of the *St. Louis*.

I hoisted the signal emergency unit. I believe it was 2:10. I do not recall the exact number. I headed at flank speed to the spot and dropped two additional depth charges. I circled around and observed an oil slick over that depth charge from that contact. I did not see any air bubbles rising to the surface as on the second attack.

Japanese plane falling in flames into the Pacific.

Then the *St. Louis* sent us a visual to screen. I took the screen and we proceeded at a course 180. We were joined by the *Monaghan* and the *Phillips,* and the *Blue* took the screen station to the port bow of the *St. Louis,* and the *St. Louis* sent us a signal.

They had received word that there were enemy ships off Barbers Point. The *St. Louis* sent us a signal to proceed to engage the enemy. We cleared the ship for action—we started to clear the ship before we got under way from Pearl Harbor. Then we got our torpedoes ready for torpedo attack. We had nine torpedoes ready for attack and we got our smoke devices ready to lay a screen. We headed for Barbers Point but did not see anything, and we later joined the rest of the force, which consisted of the *St. Louis* plus Desron 1, Desron 6, the *Detroit,* the *New Orleans,* and the *Phoenix.*

We joined that force, and the *Blue* was directed to take a station five miles off in place of the *Detroit;* so we joined the remainder of our division. While we were proceeding to join the rest of our division, the torpedo war head fell on deck and started to roll around. I was forced to slow down to five knots, and the chief torpedo man grappled with the war head and chucked it over the side on my orders because I did not think we had time to lash it securely.

Then we joined the rest of our force and later on formed the disposition for that night. . . .[5]

V

THE WAR AT SEA

There is no better introduction to World War II naval operations than Fleet Admiral Ernest J. King's summary.

. . . The major strategic decision of the war provided first for the defeat of Germany and then for the defeat of Japan. Both of these tasks have now been accomplished and we can view in clearer perspective the two major campaigns which led to victory. The contrast between them is at once apparent. The war in Europe was primarily a ground and air war with naval support, while the war in the Pacific was primarily a naval war with ground and air support.

In the European war, sea power was an essential factor because of the necessity of transmitting our entire military effort across the Atlantic and supporting it there. Without command of the sea, this could not have been done. Nevertheless, the surrender of the land, sea and air forces of the German Reich on 8 May 1945 was the direct result of the application of air power over land and the power of the Allied ground forces.

In the Pacific war, the power of our ground and strategic air forces, like sea power in the Atlantic, was an essential factor. By contrast with Germany, however, Japan's armies were intact and undefeated and her air forces only weakened when she surrendered, but her navy had been destroyed and her merchant fleet had been fatally crippled. Dependent upon imported food and raw materials and relying upon sea transport to supply her armies at home and overseas, Japan lost the war because she lost command of the sea, and in doing so lost—to us—the island bases from which her factories and cities could be destroyed by air. . . .

Thus our sea power separated the enemy from vital resources on the Asiatic mainland and in the islands which he had seized early in the war, and furnished us the bases essential to the operations of shore-based aircraft from which the atomic bombs finally were despatched, and on which troops and supplies were being massed for the invasion of Kyushu and Honshu. The defeat of Japan was directly due to our overwhelming power at sea.

The destruction of the Japanese Navy followed the Nelsonian doctrine that naval victory should be followed up until the enemy fleet is annihilated. Of 12 battleships, 11 were sunk; of 26 carriers, 20 were sunk; of 43 cruisers, 38 were destroyed; and so on throughout the various types of ships, which collectively constituted a fleet considerably larger than ours was before the war began. The few ships that remained afloat were for the most part so heavily damaged as to be of no military value.

In striking contrast is the record of our ships. Although 2 old battleships were lost at Pearl Harbor, 8 new battleships have since joined the fleet. Against 5 aircraft carriers and 6 escort carriers lost, we completed 27 carriers and 110 escort carriers. While we lost 10 cruisers, 48 new cruisers have been commissioned. We lost 52 submarines and built 203. The capacity of the United States to build warships, auxiliary ships and merchant ships, while supporting our forces and our allies all over the world, exceeded all former records and surpassed our most sanguine hopes. . . .

In the successful application of our sea power, a prime factor has been the flexibility and balanced character of our naval forces. In the Atlantic the German Navy was virtually limited to the use of submarines, without surface and naval air support. In the Pacific, Japanese sea power was hampered by army control, and Japanese naval officers lacked the freedom of initiative so necessary to gain and exercise command of the seas. On the other hand, while ours was a vast fleet, it was also a highly flexible and well balanced fleet, in which ships, planes, amphibious forces and service forces in due proportion were available for unified action whenever and wherever called upon. . . .

With the possible exception of amphibious warfare, which covers a field of considerably broader scope, the outstanding development of the war in the field of naval strategy and tactics has been the convincing proof and general acceptance of the fact that, in accord with the basic concept of the United States Navy, a concept established some 25 years ago, naval aviation is and must always be an integral and primary component of the fleet. . . . Because of it mobility and the striking power and long range of its weapons, the aircraft carrier has proved itself a major and vital element of naval strength, whose only weakness—its vulnerability—demands the support of all other types, and thereby places an additional premium on the flexibility and balance of our fleet. The balanced fleet is the effective fleet. . . .

The epic advance of our united forces across the vast Pacific, westward from Hawaii and northward from New Guinea, to the Philippines and to the shores of Japan, was spearheaded by naval aviation and closely supported by the power of our fleets. In these advances, some of the steps exceeded 2000 miles and the assaulting troops often had to be transported for much greater distances. The Navy moved them over water, landed them and supported them in great force at the beaches, kept them supplied and, particularly at Okinawa, furnished air cover during weeks of the critical fighting ashore.

The outstanding development of this war, in the field of joint undertakings, was the perfection of amphibious operations, the most difficult of all operations in modern warfare. Our success in all such operations, from Normandy to Okinawa, involved huge quantities of specialized equipment, exhaustive study and planning, and thorough training, as well as complete integration of all forces, under unified command. . . .

The end of the war came before we had dared to expect it. As late as August 1943 strategic studies drawn up by the British and United States planners contemplated the war against Japan continuing far into 1947. Even the latest plans were based upon the Japanese war lasting a year after the fall of Germany. Actually Japan's defeat came within three months after Germany's collapse. The nation can be thankful that the unrelenting acceleration of our power in the Pacific ended the war in 1945.

The price of victory has been high. Beginning with the dark days of December 1941 and continuing until September 1945, when ships of the Pacific Fleet steamed triumphant into Tokyo Bay, the Navy's losses were severe. The casualties of the United States Navy, Marine Corps and Coast Guard reached the totals of 56,206 dead, 80,259 wounded, and 8,967 missing. Many of these gallant men fell in battle; many were lost in strenuous and hazardous operations convoying our shipping or patrolling the seas and skies; others were killed in training for the duties that Fate would not permit them to carry out. All honor to these heroic men. To their families and to those who have suffered the physical and mental anguish of wounds, the Navy includes its sympathy in that of the country they served so well. . . .[6]

VI

SHE VANISHED BENEATH THE JAVA SEA

During the dark days of December the Allies reeled under Japan's initial onslaughts. By mid-February, 1942 Singapore had fallen. The Japanese threatened Java. Naval Aviator Walter G. Winslow on board the cruiser Houston *reports her heroic action in Sunda Straits against Herculean odds.*

On the night of February 28, 1942, the U.S.S. *Houston,* Admiral Tommy Hart's former Asiatic flagship, vanished without a trace somewhere off the Northwest coast of Java. The mystery of the *Houston* remained complete until the war ended and small groups of survivors were discovered in Jap prisoner of war camps, scattered from the island of Java through the Malay Peninsula, the jungles of Burma and Thailand, and northward to the Islands of Japan.

Of the 1,008 officers and men who manned her, approximately 350 escaped from the sinking ship, only to be captured in the jungles of Java, or as they floundered helplessly in the sea. Of the original survivors, only 266 lived through the ordeal of filth and brutal treatment meted out to them in Japanese prisoner of war camps.

To me the story of the U.S.S. *Houston,* especially the last three weeks of her valiant battle against tremendous odds, is one of the great Epics of the United States Navy. . . .

What happened to the *Houston* that night is a nightmare of many years standing, yet each incident of that wild battle lives in my mind as vividly as though it happened only minutes ago.

On that fateful evening of February 28, 1942, I stood on the quarter-deck contemplating the restful green of the Java Coast as it fell slowly behind us. Many times before I had found solace in its beauty, but this night it seemed only a mass of coconut and banana palms that had lost all meaning. I was too tired and too preoccupied with pondering the question that raced through the mind of every man aboard, "Would we get through Sunda Strait?"

There were many aboard who felt that, like a cat, the *Houston* had expended eight of its nine lives and that this one last request of fate would be too much. Jap cruiser planes had shadowed us all day and it was certain that our movements were no mystery to the enemy forces closing in on Java. Furthermore, it was most logical to conclude that Jap submarines were stationed throughout the length of Sunda Strait to intercept and destroy ships attempting escape into the Indian Ocean.

Actually there wasn't any breathing space for optimism, we were trapped, but there had been other days when the odds were stacked heavily in the Japs' favor and we had somehow managed to battle through. . . . I turned and headed for my stateroom. I had just been relieved as Officer-of-the-Deck and the prospect of a few hours rest was most appealing.

The wardroom and the interior of the ship, through which I walked, was dark, for the heavy metal battle ports were bolted shut and lights were not permitted within the darkened ship. Only the eerie blue beams of a few battle lights close to the deck served to guide my feet. I felt my way through the narrow companion way and snapped on my flashlight briefly to seek out the coaming of my stateroom door. As I stepped into the cubicle that was my room, I took a brief look around and switched off the light. . . .

I slipped out of my shoes and placed them at the base of the chair by my desk, along with my tin hat and life jacket, where I could reach them quickly in an emergency. Then I rolled into my bunk and let my exhausted body sink into its luxury. The bunk was truly a luxury, for the few men who were permitted to relax lay on the steel decks by their battle stations. I, being an aviator with only the battered shell of our last airplane left aboard, was permitted to take what rest I could get in my room.

Although there had been little sleep for any of us during the past four days, I found myself lying there in the sticky tropic heat of my room fretfully tossing and trying for sleep that would not come.

The constant hum of blowers thrusting air into the bowels of the ship, the *Houston's* gentle rolling as she moved through a quartering sea, and the occasional groaning of her steel plates combined to bring into my mind the mad merry-go-round of events that had plagued the ship during the past few weeks.

Twenty-four days had elapsed since that terrifying day in the Flores Sea, yet here it was haunting me again as it would for the rest of my life. My mind pictured the squadrons of Jap bombers as they attacked time and again from every conceivable direction. After the first run they remained at altitudes far beyond range of our anti-aircraft guns, for they had learned respect on that first run when one of their planes was blasted from the sky and several others were obviously hit and badly shaken. But that first salvo almost finished the *Houston*. . . . There had been no personnel casualties that time but our main anti-aircraft director had been wrenched from its track, rendering it useless, and we were taking water aboard from sprung plates in the hull.

That day the crew had only the steady barrage from the anti-aircraft guns and Captain Rooks' clever handling of the ship to thank for keeping them from the realms of Davy Jones. But there was one horrible period during that afternoon when the Nips almost got us for keeps. A five-hundred pound bomb, and a stray at that, hit us squarely amidships aft. Some utterly stupid Jap bombardier failed to release with the rest of his squadron and Captain Rooks could make no allowances for such as him. The salvo fell harmlessly off the port quarter but the stray crashed through two platforms of the main mast before it exploded on the deck just forward of number three turret. Hunks of shrapnel tore through the turret's thin armor as though it were paper, igniting powder bags in the hoists. In one blazing instant all hands in the turret and in the handling rooms below were dead. Where the bomb spent its force, a gaping hole was blown in the deck below which waited the after repair party. They were wiped out almost to a man. It was a hellish battle which ended with forty-eight of our shipmates killed and another fifty seriously burned or wounded. . . .

We put into Chilatjap the following day, that stinking fever ridden little port on the South Coast of Java. Here we sadly unloaded our wounded and prepared to bury our dead. It seemed that in the hum of the blowers I detected strains of the Death March—the same mournful tune that the band played as we carried our comrades through the heat of those sunburned, dusty streets of Chilatjap. I saw again the brown poker-faced natives dressed in sarongs, quietly watching us as we buried our dead in the little Dutch cemetery that looked out over the sea. I wondered what those slim brown men thought of all this.

The scene shifted. It was only four days ago that we steamed through the mine fields protecting the beautiful port of Soerabaja. Air raid sirens whined throughout the city and our lookouts reported bombers in the distant sky. Large warehouses along the docks were on fire and a burning merchantman lay on its side vomiting dense black smoke and orange flame. The enemy had come and left his calling card. We anchored in the stream not far from the smouldering docks where we watched Netherlands East Indian soldiers extinguish the fires.

Six times during the next two days we experienced air raids. Anchored there in the stream we were as helpless as ducks in a rain barrel. Why our gun crews didn't collapse is a tribute to their sheer guts and brawn. They stood by their guns unflinchingly in the hot sun, pouring shell after shell into the sky while the rest of us sought what shelter is available in the bullseye of a target.

Time and again bombs falling with the deep throated *swoosh* of a giant bull whip exploded around us, spewing water and shrapnel over our decks. Docks less than a hundred yards away were demolished and a Dutch hospital ship was hit, yet the *Houston,* nicknamed "the Galloping Ghost of the Java Coast" because the Japs had reported her sunk on so many similar occasions, still rode defiantly at anchor.

When the siren's bailful wailing sounded the "all clear," members of the *Houston's* band came from their battle stations to the quarterdeck where we squatted to hear them play swing tunes. God bless the American sailor, you can't beat him.

Like Scrooge, the ghosts of the past continued to move into my little room. I saw us in the late afternoon of February 26, standing out of Soerabaja for the last time. Admiral Doorman of the Netherlands Navy was in command of our small striking force. His flagship, the light cruiser *De Ruyter,* was in the lead, followed by another Netherlands light cruiser, the *Java.* Next in line came the British heavy cruiser *Exeter* of *Graf Spee* fame, followed by the crippled *Houston.* Last in the line of cruisers was the Australian light cruiser *Perth.* Ten allied destroyers made up the remainder of our force. . . .

Our force was small and hurriedly assembled. We had never worked together before, but now we had one common purpose. . . . We were to do our utmost to break up an enemy task force that was bearing down on Java, even though it meant the loss of every ship and man among us. In us lay the last hope of the Netherlands East Indies.

All night long we searched for the enemy convoy but they seemed to have vanished from previously reported positions. We were still at battle stations the next afternoon when at 1415 reports from air reconnaissance indicated that the enemy was south of Bowen Island, and heading south. The two forces were less than fifty miles apart. A hurried but deadly serious conference of officers followed in the wardroom. Commander Maher, our gunnery officer, explained that our mission was to sink or disperse the protecting enemy fleet units and then destroy the convoy. My heart pounded with excitement, for the battle later to be known as the Java Sea Battle was only a matter of minutes away. . . .

In the darkness of my room the Japs came again just as though I were standing on the bridge . . . a forest of masts rapidly developing into ships that climbed in increasing numbers over the horizon . . . those dead ahead, ten destroyers divided into two columns and each led by a four stack light cruiser. Behind them and off our starboard bow came four light cruisers followed by two heavies. The odds weigh heavily against us for we are outnumbered and outgunned.

The Japs open fire first. Sheets of copper colored flame lick out along their battle line and black smoke momentarily masks them from view. . . . I wonder why our guns don't open up, but as the Jap shells fall harmlessly a thousand yards short I realize that the range is yet too great. The battle from which there will be no retreat has begun.

At twenty-eight thousand yards the *Exeter* opens fire, followed by the *Houston*. The sound of our guns bellowing defiance is terrific, the gun blast tears my steel helmet from my head and sends it rolling on the deck.

The range closes rapidly and soon all cruisers are in on the fight. Salvos of shells splash in the water ever closer to us. Now one falls close to starboard followed by another close to port. This is an ominous indicator that the Japs have at last found the range. We stand tensely awaiting the next salvo, and it comes with a wild screaming of shells that fall all around us. It's a straddle, but not a hit is registered. Four more salvos in succession straddle the *Houston,* and the lack of a hit gives us confidence. The *Perth,* 900 yards astern of us, is straddled eight times in a row, yet she too steams on unscathed. Our luck is holding out.

Shells from our guns are observed, bursting close to the last Jap heavy cruiser. We have her range and suddenly one of our eight-inch bricks strikes home. There is an explosion aboard her. Black smoke and debris fly into the air and a fire breaks out forward of her bridge. We draw blood first as she turns out of the battle line, making dense smoke. Commander Maher, directing the fire of our guns from his station high in the foretop, reports our success to the Captain over the phone. A lusty cheer goes up from the crew as the word spreads over the ship.

Three enemy cruisers are concentrating their fire on *Exeter.* We shift targets to give her relief, but it is not long after this that *Exeter* shells find their mark and a light cruiser turns out of the Jap line, smoking and on fire. Despite the loss of two cruisers, the intensity of Jap fire does not seem to diminish. The *Houston* is hit twice. One shell rips through the bow just aft of the port anchor windlass, passes down through several decks and out the side just above the water line without exploding. The other shell, hitting aft, barely grazes the side and ruptures a small oil tank. It too fails to explode.

Up to this point the luck of our forces had held up well, but now there is a rapid turn of events as the *Exeter* is hit by a Jap shell which does not explode, but rips into her forward fireroom and severs a main steam line. This reduces her speed to seven knots. In an attempt to save the *Exeter*, whose loss of speed makes her an easy target, we all make smoke to cover her withdrawal. The Japs, aware that something has gone wrong, are quick to press home an advantage, and their destroyers, under heavy support fire from the cruisers, race in to deliver a torpedo attack.

The water seems alive with torpedoes. Lookouts report them approaching and Captain Rooks maneuvers the ship to present as small a target as possible. At this moment a Netherlands East Indies destroyer, the *Koertner*, trying to change stations, is hit amidships by a torpedo intended for the *Houston*. There is a violent explosion and a great fountain of water rises a hundred feet above her, obscuring all but small portions of her bow and stern. When the watery fountain settles back into the sea it becomes apparent that the little green and grey destroyer has broken in half and turned over. Only the bow and stern sections of her jack-knifed keel stick above the water. A few men scramble desperately to her barnacled bottom, and her twin screws in their last propulsive effort turn slowly over in the air. In less than two minutes she has disappeared beneath the sea. No one can stand by to give the few survivors a helping hand for her fate can be ours at any instant.

It is nearing sundown. The surface of the sea is covered with clouds of black smoke, which makes it difficult to spot the enemy. It is discovered that Jap cruisers are closing in upon us, and our destroyers are ordered to attack with torpedoes in order to divert them and give us time to reform. Although no hits are reported, the effect of the attack is gratifying for the Japs turn away. At this point the engagement is broken off. The daylight battle has ended with no decisive results; however, there is still the convoy, which we will attempt to surprise under the cover of night.

We check our losses. The *Koertner* and H.M.S. *Electra* have been sunk. The crippled *Exeter* has retired to Soerabaja, escorted by the American destroyers, who have expended their torpedoes and are running low on fuel. The *Houston, Perth, De Ruyter,* and *Java* are still in the fight, but showing the jarring effects of continuous gunfire. Only two destroyers remain with us, H.M.S. *Jupiter* and H.M.S. *Encounter*. . . .

During the semi-darkness of twilight we steam on a course away from the enemy in order to lead any of their units which might have us under observation into believing that we are in retreat. When darkness descends we turn and head back.

Shortly after this H.M.S. *Jupiter,* covering our port flank, explodes mysteriously and vanishes in a brief but brilliant burst of flame. We are dumbfounded, for the enemy is not to be seen yet we race on, puzzling over her fate and blindly seeking the transports.

An hour passes with nothing intervening to interrupt our search, and then high in the sky above us a flare bursts, shattering the darkness. Night has suddenly become day and we are illuminated like targets in a shooting gallery. We are helpless to defend ourselves, for we have no such thing as radar, and the plane merely circles outside our range of vision to drop another flare after the first one burns itself out, following it with another and still another.

We cannot know for sure, but certainly it is logical to assume that the enemy is closing in for the kill. Blinded by the flares, we wait through tense minutes for the blow to come.

On the ship men speak in hushed tones as though their very words will give our position away to the enemy. Only the rush of water as our bow knifes through the sea at thirty knots, and the continuous roaring of blowers from the vicinity of the quarter-deck, are audible. Death stands by, ready to strike. No one talks of it although all thoughts dwell upon it.

The fourth flare bursts, burns, and then slowly falls into the sea. We are enveloped in darkness again. No attack has come, and as time passes it becomes evident that the plane has gone away. How wonderful is the darkness, yet how terrifying to realize that the enemy is aware of our every move and merely biding his time like a cat playing with a mouse.

The moon has come up to assist in our search for the convoy. It has been almost an hour since the last flare, and nothing has happened to indicate that the enemy has us under observation. During this period Ensign Stivers has relieved me as officer of the deck. I climb up on the forward anti-aircraft director platform and sprawl out to catch a bit of rest before the inevitable shooting begins. I hardly close my eyes before there comes the sound of whistles and shouting men. I am back on my feet in a hurry and look over the side. The water is dotted with groups of men yelling in some strange tongue which I cannot understand. H.M.S. *Encounter* is ordered to remain behind to rescue them.

Now we are four, three light cruisers and one heavy. We plow on through the eerie darkness. Suddenly out of nowhere six flares appear in the water along our line of ships. They resemble those round smoke pots that burn alongside road constructions with a yellow flame. What exactly are they, and how did they get there? Are they some form of mine, or is their purpose to mark our path for the enemy? No one dares to guess. Either eventuality is bad enough.

As fast as we leave one group astern, another group bobs up alongside. We cannot account for them, and this oriental deviltry is as bewildering as it is confusing. None of us has ever seen a phenomenon before. We continue to move away from them, but other groups of floating flares appear.

The uncertainty of what is to follow is nerve wracking. We look back and there, marking our track on the oily surface of the sea, are zig-zag lines of flares which rock and burn like goulish jack-o-lanterns. We leave them on the far horizon and no more appear. We are again in welcome darkness.

At approximately 2230, lookouts report two large unidentified ships to port, range 12,000 yards. There are no 'friendly ships within hundreds of miles of us, therefore these are the enemy. The *Houston* opens up with two main battery salvos, the results of which are not determined, and the Japs reply with two of their own which throw water over the forecastle. With this exchange of fire the Japs disappear in the darkness and we make no effort to chase them, for we need all of our ammunition to sink transports.

There is no relaxing now. We are in the area where anything can happen. Hundreds of eyes peer into the night seeking the convoy, as we realize that the end of our mission is approaching.

During the night the order of ships in column has been shifted. The *De Ruyter* still maintained the lead, but behind her comes the *Houston,* followed by the *Java* and *Perth* in that order.

A half hour passes without incident, and then with the swiftness of a lightning bolt a tremendous explosion rocks the *Java* 900 yards astern of the *Houston.* Mounting flames envelop her amidships and

379

spread rapidly aft. She loses speed and drops out of the column to lie dead in the water, where sheets of uncontrolled flame consume her.

Torpedo wakes are observed in the water, although we can find no enemy to fight back. The *De Ruyter* changes course sharply to the right, and the *Houston* is just about to follow when an explosion similar to the one that doomed the *Java* is heard aboard the *De Ruyter*. Crackling flames shoot high above her bridge, quickly enveloping the entire ship.

Captain Rooks, in a masterpiece of seamanship and quick thinking, maneuvers the *Houston* to avoid torpedoes that slip past us ten feet on either side. Then joined by the *Perth,* we race away from the stricken ships and the insidious enemy that no one can see. How horrible it is to leave our allies, but we are powerless to assist them. Now that Admiral Doorman has gone down with his blazing flagship, the Captain of the *Perth* takes command, for he is senior to Captain Rooks, and we follow the *Perth* as she sets a course for Batavia.

What an infernal night, and how lucky we are to escape. It seems almost miraculous when the sun comes up on the next morning, February 28, for there have been many times during the past fifteen hours when I would have sworn we would never see it.

The *Houston* was a wreck. Concussions from the eight-inch guns had played merry hell with the ship's interior. Every desk on the ship had its drawers torn out and the contents spewn over the deck. In lockers, clothes were torn from their hangers and pitched in muddled heaps. Pictures, radios, books, and everything of a like nature were jolted from their normal places and dashed on the deck. . . .

The ship itself had suffered considerably. Plates already weakened by near hits in previous bombing attacks were now badly sprung and leaking. The glass windows on the bridge were shattered. Fire hose strung along the passageways were leaking and minor floods made it sloppy underfoot.

The *Houston* was wounded and practically out of ammunition, but there was still fight left in her, plenty of it.

These events accompanied by many others played upon my mind in the minutest detail, until at last my senses became numb and I relaxed in sleep.

It was nearly 2400 when, *Clang! Clang! Clang! Clang!,* the

nerve shattering "General Alarm" burst through my wonderful cocoon of sleep and brought me upright on both feet. . . .

Clang! Clang! Clang! Clang! The sound echoed along the steel bulkheads of the ship's deserted interior. I wondered what kind of deviltry we were mixed up in now, and somehow I felt depressed. I grabbed my tin hat as I left the room and was putting it on my head when a salvo from the main battery roared out overhead, knocking me against the bulkhead. We were desperately short of those eight-inch bricks and I knew that the boys weren't wasting them on mirages. . . .

As I climbed there was more firing from the main battery, and now the five-inch guns were taking up the argument. I realized that it was getting to be one hell of a battle and I started running. On the Communication deck where the one-point-one's were getting into action, I passed their gun crews working swiftly, mechanically in the darkness without a hitch, as their guns pumped out shell after shell. Momentarily I caught a glimpse of tracers hustling out into the night. They were beautiful.

Before I reached the bridge every gun on the ship was in action. The noise they made was magnificent. The *Houston* was throwing knockout punches. . . .

As I stepped on the bridge the *Houston* became enveloped in the blinding glare of searchlights. Behind the lights I could barely discern the outlines of Jap destroyers. They had come in close to illuminate for their heavy units which fired at us from the darkness. Battling desperately for existence, the *Houston's* guns trained on the lights, and as fast as they were turned on, just as fast were they blasted out.

Although the bridge was the *Houston's* nerve center, I was unable to find out what we were up against. . . . What we had actually run into was later estimated to be sixty fully loaded transports, twenty destroyers, and six cruisers. We were in the middle of this mass of ships before either side was aware of the other's presence.

Suddenly surrounded by ships, the *Perth* and *Houston* immediately opened fire and turned sharply to starboard in an effort to break free. However, the fury of the Japs was not to be denied and the *Perth* was mortally wounded by torpedoes. Lying dead in the water she continued to fire with everything she had until Jap shells blasted her to bits and she sank.

When Captain Rooks realized that the *Perth* was finished, he turned the *Houston* back into the heart of the Jap convoy, determined in the face of no escape to sell the *Houston* dearly.

At close range the *Houston* pounded the Jap transports with everything she had, and at the same time fought off the destroyers that were attacking with torpedoes and shell-fire. Jap cruisers remained in the background, throwing salvo after salvo aboard and around us. The *Houston* was taking terrible punishment. A torpedo penetrated our after engine room, where it exploded, killing every man there and reducing our speed to fifteen knots.

Thick smoke and hot steam venting on the gun deck from the after engine room temporarily drove men from their guns but they came back and stayed there in spite of it. Power went out of the shell hoists which stopped the flow of five-inch shells to the guns, from the almost empty magazines. Men attempted to go below and bring shells up by hand, but debris and fires from numerous hits blocked their way. In spite of this they continued to fire, using star shells which were stowed in the ready ammunition boxes by the guns.

Number Two turret, smashed by a direct hit, blew up, sending wild flames flashing up over the bridge. The heat, so intense that it drove everyone out of the conning tower, temporarily disrupted communications to other parts of the ship. The fire was soon extinguished, but when the sprinklers flooded the magazine our last remaining supply of eight-inch ammunition was ruined, which meant that the *Houston* was now without a main battery.

Numerous fires were breaking out all over the ship and it became increasingly difficult for the men to cope with them. Another torpedo plowed into the *Houston* somewhere forward of the quarterdeck. The force of the explosion made the ship tremble beneath us, and I realized then that we were done for.

Slowly we listed to starboard as the grand old ship gradually lost steerageway and stopped. The few guns still in commission continued to fire, although it was obvious that the end was near. It must have torn at the Captain's heart, but his voice was strong as he summoned the bugler and ordered him to sound "Abandon Ship."

When I heard the words "Abandon Ship" I did not wait to go down the ladder which already had a capacity crowd, with men waiting; instead I jumped over the railing to the deck below. That was probably a fortunate move, for just as I jumped a shell burst on the bridge, killing several men. I trotted out on the port catapult tower where the battered and unflyable hulk of our last airplane spread its useless wings in the darkness. It contained a rubber boat and a bottle of brandy, both of which I figured would come in handy, but I was not alone in this, for five people were there ahead of me.

Despite the fact that we were still the target for continuous shells and the ship was slowly sinking beneath us, there was no confusion. Men went quietly and quickly about the job of abandoning ship. Fear was nowhere apparent, due possibly to the fact that the one thing we feared most throughout the short space of the war had happened.

Captain Rooks had come down off the bridge and was saying goodbye to several of his officers and men outside his cabin, when a Jap shell exploded in a one-point-one gun mount, sending a piece of the breach crashing into his chest. Captain Rooks, beloved by officers and men, died in their arms.

When Buda, the Captain's Chinese cook, learned that the Captain had been killed, he refused to leave the ship. He simply sat cross-legged outside the Captain's cabin, rocking back and forth and moaning "Captain dead, *Houston* dead, Buda die too." He went down with the ship.

During this time I made my way to the quarterdeck. Dead men lay sprawled on the deck, but there was no time to find out who they were. Men from my division were busily engaged in the starboard hangar in an effort to bring out a seaplane pontoon and two wing-tip floats that we had filled with food and water in preparation for just such a time. If we could get them into the water and assemble them as we had so designed, they would make a fine floating structure around which we could gather and work from.

I hurried to the base of the catapult tower where I worked rapidly to release the life-lines in order that we could get the floats over the side and into the water. I uncoupled one line and was working on the second when a torpedo struck directly below us. I heard no explosion, but the deck buckled and jumped under me and I found myself suddenly engulfed in a deluge of fuel oil and salt water.

Up until that moment I must have been too fascinated with the unreality of the situation to truly think about it and become frightened, but when this sudden torrent of fuel oil and water poured over me, all I could think of was fire. It was the most helpless sensation I ever had experienced in my life. Somehow I hadn't figured on getting hit or killed, but now I was gripped with the sudden fear of blazing fuel oil on my person and covering the surface of the sea. I was panicked, for I could figure no escape from it. The same thought must have been in the minds of others, for we all raced from the starboard side to the shelter of the port hangar. No sooner had we cleared the quarterdeck than a salvo of shells plowed through it, exploding deep below decks.

Events were moving fast, and the *Houston* in her death throes was about to go down. There was only one idea left in my mind, and that was to join the others who were going over the side in increasing numbers. Quickly I made my way to the port side and climbed down the cargo nets that were hanging there. When I reached the water's edge I dropped off into the warm Java Sea. When my head came above the surface I was aware that in the darkness I was surrounded by many men, all swimming for their lives. Frantic screams for help from the wounded and drowning mixed with the shouts of others attempting to make contact with shipmates. The sea was an oily battleground of men pitted against the terrors of death. Desperately I swam to get beyond reach of the sinking ship's suction. As much as I loved the *Houston,* I had no desire to join her in a watery grave.

A few hundred yards away I turned, gasping for breath, to watch the death of my ship. She lay well over to starboard. Jap destroyers had come in close and illuminated her with searchlights as they raked her decks with machine-gun fire. Many men struggled in the water near the ship, others clung desperately to heavily loaded life rafts, and then to my horror, I realized that the Japs were coldly and deliberately firing on the men in the water. The concussions of shells bursting in the midst of swimming men sent shock waves through the water that slammed against my body with an evil force, making me wince with pain. Men closer to the exploding shells were killed by this concussion alone.

Dazed, unable to believe that all this was real, I floated there, watching as though bewitched. The end had come. By the glare of Japanese searchlights I saw the *Houston* roll slowly over to starboard, and then, with her yardarms almost dipping into the sea, she paused momentarily. Perhaps I only imagined it, but it seemed as though a sudden breeze picked up the Stars and Stripes still firmly two-blocked on the mainmast, and waved them in one last defiant gesture. Then with a tired shudder she vanished beneath the Java Sea. . . .[7]

VII

TAKE HER DOWN!

Before the United States wrested from the enemy island bases essential to the operation of land-based aircraft, American submarines carried the brunt of the attack against Japanese shipping. One of the epics of the silent service occurred on board the U.S.S. Growler *in February, 1943.*

Commander Task Force Forty-Two

File FF12–15(42)/P15/00–He   c/o Fleet Post Office,
San Francisco, California

Serial   0055   February 21, 1943

DECLASSIFIED

      S-E-C-R-E-T

From: The Commander Task Force FORTY-TWO.

To   :   The Secretary of the Navy.

Via   :   The Commander Southwest Pacific Force.

Subject: Commander Howard W. Gilmore, U. S. Navy, deceased; Medal of Honor—Recommendation for posthumous award of.

1.   Commander Howard W. Gilmore, U. S. Navy, deceased, assumed command of the U.S.S. GROWLER when she was commissioned on March 20, 1942, and remained in command until he heroically met his death on February 7, 1943, in an action with an enemy armed vessel during GROWLER's Fourth War Patrol. GROWLER inflicted heavy damage on the Japanese during her first three war patrols and, as a result of his successes, Commander Gilmore was awarded the Navy Cross and a Gold Star in lieu of a second Navy Cross. An outstanding highlight of GROWLER's earlier patrols and an incident illustrative of the daring, skill and intrepidity of her

captain, was an attack in Alaskan waters on three large enemy destroyers, two of which were sunk and the third heavily damaged.

2. GROWLER departed on her Fourth War Patrol on January 1, 1943, and arrived, on January 10, in her assigned patrol area off NEW BRITAIN, NEW IRELAND and NEW HANOVER Islands, covering the approaches to RABAUL and KAVIENG. The area patrolled was under almost continuous air patrol by the enemy and all vessels sighted were escorted by anti-submarine vessels. On January 16, GROWLER successfully penetrated a heavy screen and sank a 5425 ton freighter by torpedo fire, both torpedoes fired scoring hits. On January 30, a second freighter of about 6500 tons was damaged by torpedo fire, further attacks being frustrated by gun-fire from the target. Following each of these attacks GROWLER was severely depth charged but her Commanding Officer ably maneuvered his ship so as to avoid damage. On other occasions when enemy vessels were sighted, Commander Gilmore was most aggressive in his efforts to reach a firing position, but initial long ranges and large angles on the bow prevented additional successful attacks. On February 5 a dangerous leak developed in the forward torpedo room following a series of depth charge attacks by enemy patrol vessels, but flooding was controlled and depth control maintained as a result of the prodigious efforts of the well-trained and well-directed crew.

3. GROWLER was patrolling on the surface during the early morning of February 7 when, at 0110 (K), an enemy vessel was sighted close aboard. GROWLER turned away momentarily to prepare tubes for firing and then closed in to attack. The night was dark and visibility was very poor but when the range was reduced to about 2000 yards, the enemy vessel, a converted gunboat of about 2500 tons, sighted GROWLER and changed course to ram. No longer in a position to fire torpedoes, Commander Gilmore skillfully handled his ship to avoid the ramming attack of the enemy, and having done so, then courageously and daringly turned the tables on the enemy and rammed the gunboat with the GROWLER. GROWLER making seventeen knots, struck the enemy gunboat on her port side and ripped her side plating wide open. The gunboat apparently sank, but while doing so, opened fire on GROWLER's bridge and conning tower structure with heavy machine guns.

The GROWLER's Commanding Officer gave the order to clear the bridge. Although in a position near the hatch where he could quickly reach the comparative safety of the conning tower, Commander Gilmore, without regard for his own safety, bravely ordered the remainder of the bridge force to precede him. Four men, two of whom were wounded, reached the conning tower, but the heavy fusillade of .60 cal. bullets ripped through the thin side plating and mortally wounded the gallant captain and two others. As the captain fell dying to the deck his last words to the officer of the deck were "Take her down," knowing he would be left on the bridge. Thus, in his final living moments, having done his utmost against the enemy, the captain had thoughts only for the safety of his beloved GROWLER and for the preservation of her fine crew. His orders were carried out. The damaged GROWLER dived and her well-organized crew kept her under control in the face of dangerous leaks caused by enemy gunfire, with bow planes and vital auxiliaries inoperative. Motivated by the fighting spirit of their dead captain, they effected necessary repairs and brought their ship safely to port where she will be repaired and will fight again.

4. Our country has lost one of its most distinguished Submarine Captains, one whose dominating purpose was to inflict maximum damage on the enemy without regard for his own personal safety. His career will long serve as a shining example to the Submarine Service which claims him as one of the outstanding heroes of the war. It is considered that our nation can properly confer upon him only its highest award.

5. In view of the above, it is most strongly recommended that Commander Howard W. Gilmore, U. S. Navy, deceased, be posthumously awarded the Medal of Honor, with proposed citation as follows:

CITATION

For distinguishing yourself conspicuously by gallantry and intrepidity at the risk of your life above and beyond the call of duty and without detriment to the mission of your command, in an action with an armed enemy vessel.

During the Fourth War Patrol of the U.S.S. GROWLER, of which you were Commanding Officer, you adroitly and aggressively maneuvered your ship into positions from which to strike the enemy, and aggressively attacked, sinking one medium freighter and damaging another. On February 7, 1943, after an enemy gunboat had attempted to ram your ship, you, with great skill, avoided the enemy's maneuver and instead courageously rammed and sank the enemy gunboat. When the enemy opened fire at point blank range with heavy machine guns you ordered the bridge cleared, and without regard for your own life, heroically stood aside, braving the fusillade of bullets, while your men reached comparative safety below, as a result of which you were mortally wounded by the enemy gunfire. Furthermore, you then ordered your ship to submerge knowing you would be left on the bridge and would be lost. Your ship, though damaged, safely reached port and will fight again, but you gave your life in the service of your country.

Your actions were in accordance with the finest traditions of the Naval Service.

JAMES FIFE[8]

VIII

THROWING THE BIG STUFF

In June, 1944 Allied navies, armies, and air forces unleashed a gigantic offensive which penetrated the inner defenses of Germany and Japan. The invasion of Normandy preceded the assault against Saipan in the Pacific by nine days. Two months later, at dawn, 15 August, guns and bombs from 1,300 planes and fifty-three ships softened up the coast east of Toulon in southern France. Divisions stormed ashore.

During that vicious bombardment, Harold Clements was Turret Captain on the battleship Arkansas.

August 22, 1944
U. S. S. Arkansas

Dear Mom and Dad:

The Allies struck a heavy blow in the invasion of Southern France several days ago and the American warship, as in the Normandy invasion, was present at the initial assault helping to blast a path for the first landings. Not long after we left port the captain spoke to us describing the task which lay ahead. Meanwhile, we were joined by men-of-war of both our own and other nations. As we plowed onward I wondered if the enemy realized when or where we were about to strike and would he be ready to "take it" and "dish it out."

During the night many shapeless, obscure forms of transports and landing craft were overtaken and left behind in the darkness as we moved into our forward and final position. Angry rumblings of bomb bursts and flashes of fire came from the distant area as bombers unloaded their deadly cargo. Swarms of bombers, fighters and troop transport planes droned overhead passing to and from the engaged area.

When the skies began to glow just before dawn, we found ourselves surrounded with ships and landing craft of all descriptions while the shores of France loomed surprisingly near, shrouded with a haze of dust and smoke from the night bombing attack. We were then well within range of enemy coastal batteries and I for one hoped we would not long delay our opening fire. We had not long to wait, however, as the main battery was trained on an enemy installation of casemated guns and the sounding of the firing buzzer announced "standby for opening salvo." With a deafening roar we sent our salutation to Hitler's crowd on the beach. All around us ships of all nations were blasting away as we fired salvo after salvo while hundreds of landing craft moved shorewards.

As you know, the Army took the beach in stride and moved inland in high gear. We had a number of German prisoners aboard for a while. They didn't have the tough superman appearance the German propaganda experts would have us believe. A couple of nights we were sighted by JU-88 snoopers but a lusty barrage of A.A. fire drove them off.

The gun crews really enjoy throwing the big stuff over here at the Germans and are getting worried for fear the war will be over for the Navy and we will be left out at the finish. Anticipating this possible situation, the gunners are trying to have the engineers install wheels on our ships so we can catch up with the Army and help chase Heinies through the streets of Berlin. . . .

Yours,
Harold[9]

IX

THE DAMN SUBS HAD US SCREWY

In the Atlantic Theater, the United States Navy hunted German submarines which stalked merchant convoys. Seaman 1/c Morton Vicker on board a PC boat and Radioman 3/c Arnold McKee on a "tin-can" describe the battle to keep the shipping lanes open.

Submarine attack!

The long black pennant streaming from the yardarm of the pitching, plunging PC boat, a large submarine-chaser, shrieked this warning to the rest of the convoy. Battle stations were manned on the double. The hopes and prayers of the merchant crews rode with the tossing little craft. Not a very large ship, perhaps, but it was all that stood between them and a possible sudden watery death.

A few days before, the PC's, looking like small steel slivers in the gray haze of dawn, had lain at anchor, waiting for the convoy to form. Looking down from the superior height of their decks, the merchant sailors might have been inclined to laugh as they passed the puny-looking little vessels. It had seemed odd for these giant ships, huge British freighters with catapult-projected Spitfires mounted on their bows, American Liberty ships fresh from the shipyards, Norwegian tankers with the highly polished mahogany paneling of their bridges, ancient French hulks carrying tiny antiquated cannons on their poop decks, to be escorted by the Lilliputian PC's. Now, though, no one saw any humor in it.

From the moment the minefield had been passed the big French destroyer at the head of the formation and the PC's had set up an impenetrable ring of sensitve sound about the cargo ships. Zigzagging in and out, constantly on the alert for enemy U-boats, they constituted adequate submarine defense for the convoy.

The 1600 to 2000 sound machine operator had just relieved the watch. Sitting down and turning the knob that controlled the sound beam, he had jerked to attention at the first echo to come in. The unmistakable "ping" of a contact had been clearly audible.

Searching the area carefully with his apparatus, he had quickly noted the speed, distance, and bearing of the target. In a brief moment he had made every check and verification. "Sir," he had shouted to the Officer of the Deck, a lieutenant (junior grade), "I've a very strong contact at bearing two seven five, true, and about —— yards away."

The seaman at the wheel had peered over his shoulder, his face pale and grim.

The OOD had hurried over to the sound machine from the wing of the bridge where he had been taking a sight on the convoy. After listening to the echo for a moment he had dashed over to the phone and called the commanding officer's stateroom.

"Captain," he had reported hurriedly over the phone, "there's a strong contact at two seven five at about —— yards."

"Aye, aye, sir," he had answered a moment later. Running over to the general alarm he had rung it, snapping out orders.

"Steer two seven zero, both engines ahead full speed, hoist the sub attack pennant. . . ."

The captain, a lieutenant commander, a middle-aged veteran of World War I, stood on the bridge directing operations. The chief gunner's mate—he had been aboard a battleship at Pearl Harbor that fateful day in December, 1941—headphones on head crouched at his post between the stern depth charge racks. "Junior," a seventeen-year-old lad who had been in the Navy about four months and held the rank of seaman second class, stood by the after gun, pale as death but ready to pass a shell up to the first loader. "Stu," the Negro officer's cook third class, had scrambled down to his station in the magazine, and was shouting up in his rich baritone, "Just holler down, and I'll send up plenty of these pebbles to heave at Mr. Hitler's children." Everyone stood by, ready for anything that might come.

The little ship veered sharply away from the convoy. At full speed she bounced and pounded terrifically. At times it seemed as if the bottom must give away under the violent beating of the sea. Still, her decks awash and leaving a wake like that of a speedboat, she continued her charge out to the dangerous rendezvous. . . .

Back at his post "Guns" readjusted the phones so as to more clearly hear the orders. As the ship noticeably slackened speed everyone stared at him. He remained motionless and cool. At the sound of a bell he bent down and pulled a small lever. One of the depth charges rolled off the racks, dropping into the water with a splash. Very soon afterwards it exploded, making the ship tremble, and throwing a mountain of grayish water high into the air.

Turning in a sharp circle the PC was back over the same spot even before the disturbed water had had a chance to settle. Stopping her engines, she lay there for a moment, motionless, listening. . . .

Gathering about the sound gear, the captain, the executive officer, and the sound man tried to pick up the sub's motors. A sound came through the machine's amplifiers. Pausing for the smallest fraction of a second to look at the dial, the captain ordered, "Both engines ahead two thirds. Come left to one eight zero."

Back on the fantail "Guns" rapidly made the settings on the "ash cans" in the racks. When he finished these he ran a few feet forward to where the K-guns were mounted. He removed the safety forks from the charges in the guns, set them for the proper depth, attached an electric wire to the firing mechanism, and then hurried back to his original position. He had no sooner returned when two of the TNT containing cans, released by remote control from the bridge, fell into the water. A loud report and a blinding flash followed closely as the K-guns were fired. They hurled their missiles which traveled in a slow arc, landing about 150 feet on each side of the ship. Then two more cans dropped from the racks. The pattern was calculated to thoroughly cover the area.

As the last charge left the racks "Guns" reported the fact to the bridge. The ship immediately picked up speed. At the same time "Guns" yelled, "Reload K-guns, on the double."

Four men ran to the small boom mounted near the depth charge locker, and, attaching it to one of the spare charges, reloaded the empty port K-gun. Then they reloaded the starboard one.

The increased speed had carried them a scant 200 yards beyond the spot where the final charge had disappeared in the gray sea, when the "cans" which had been released began to go off. At each detonation the midships section of the PC seemed to rise out of the water, while the bow and stern showed a tendency to droop. For hundreds of yards around, after the huge spouts of water raised by the explosions had settled down, the ocean was a gray oily mass, its surface covered with dead fish. It looked like fish chowder coming to a boil.

In the wheelhouse the three men were once more gathered around the sound apparatus. Angrily the captain said, "The damn thing is still going. I can still hear the screw beats. Can't you?"

The others nodded in assent. Walking over to a chart hanging close by, he studied it for a second. Turning to the exec, he said, "We'll attack once more." At that he ordered the men at the wheel and at the annunciator, the instrument which is used to transmit orders from the bridge to the engine-room, "Both engines ahead standard speed. Right, fifteen degrees rudder."

The ship wheeled in a graceful curve. After circling in this manner for a short while, the speed was soon cut down again. More depth charges were dropped. Again, the ship shivered violently. Again, huge geysers of water were flung up.

There was a difference, though, in the color of the water. A great cheer arose from the men on the deck of the American patrol craft. The blackness of fuel oil was clearly visible. As the surface calmed down a spreading blot of oil about 50 feet wide remained.

"We got her, we got her," Junior yelled. Running to the side of the ship, he pointed at the black blob. "See the 'slick.' We got the damned thing, all right," he shouted hoarsely.

Other men ran over to the side to stare at the flowing lifeblood of the stricken sub.

"Where in the hell do you people think you are, Central Park lagoon? Get back to your stations and train those guns on the 'slick,' before you all go on report," the gunnery officer bellowed from the flying bridge. This put an instant stop to the rubber-necking.

Immediately every gun on the ship was pointed at the greasy spot. . . .

No more signs of the U-boat had been picked up, and at length the captain gave the order to return to the convoy. The signalman sent a message to the French destroyer to the effect that an enemy submarine had been contacted, damaged, and possibly destroyed. The attack pennant was hauled down, and "secure," was sounded. . . .[10]

April 25, 1945
New York, N. Y.

Dear Harry:

. . . We came in last Sunday for a few days of recreation. We can really appreciate it, too, after a winter in the North Atlantic. We stumbled on a poor old lonely sub about 400 miles off Cape Cod, and proceeded to sink same. Up around Halifax and Newfoundland all winter, where the subs are supposed to be thick as hell and no luck. They sent us home and on the way in we accidentally found this one—just like rabbit hunting all day without getting any, and then as you cross the back yard one jumps up.

The damn subs had us screwy up north all winter. They would sink a merchant ship, or occasionally, an escort, and by the time we arrived they would be to hell out, or safely bottomed among the wrecks and rocks. The "sound men" went nuts trying to distinguish sub echoes from bottom echoes.

This one by himself really didn't have much of a chance. The hedgehogs were fired, they exploded and about one-half minute later there was an underwater explosion that shook the hell out of us, and us on top, by that time 300 or so yards away. There was a lot of oil came to the surface, a lot of papers, plus a lot of other things—many of them with German markings. Most of the officers are under the impression that the navy will give it a Class B rating. For a Class A, I think you have to have the sub's skipper's autograph.

I noticed a headline in last night's paper that the army is to discharge all men over forty-two—so all I have to do is convince the navy to do the same—then serve ten more years and 'lo and behold I'm a civilian again. Simple. The forty-two ruling probably won't affect anyone from around home, but it is very cheerful news. Anyway, it's a step in the right direction. . . .

As always,
Arnold[11]

X

THERE WAS GLORY IN IT FOR ALL

In the Pacific the offensive gained momentum. On 20 October 1944, General Douglas MacArthur's forces supported by naval units swept ashore on Leyte in the Philippines against light opposition. The Japanese, in a desperate gamble, designated 25 October as the day for their ships to break through into Leyte Gulf.

Two United States Fleets operated in Philippine waters. The Seventh—six old battleships, sixteen escort carriers, four heavy cruis-

ers, four light cruisers, thirty destroyers, twelve destroyer escorts—was commanded by Vice Admiral Thomas Kinkaid. His superior was General MacArthur; the fleet's mission, defensive.

Admiral William F. Halsey, Jr. commanded the Third Fleet. His superior was Admiral Chester W. Nimitz; its mission, offensive. Halsey's Third Fleet was composed of Task Force 38 under Vice Admiral Marc A. Mitscher and was divided into four Task Groups: 38.1 commanded by Vice Admiral John S. McCain; 38.2, by Rear Admiral Gerald F. Bogan; 38.3, by Rear Admiral Frederick C. Sherman; 38.4, by Rear Admiral Ralph E. Davison. These Groups were not uniform in strength, but averaged a total of twenty-three ships: two large carriers, two light carriers, two new battleships, three cruisers, fourteen destroyers.

The battle for Leyte Gulf, lasting four days and covering nearly 30,000 square miles, is narrated by Lieutenant Commander R. C. Benitez, Executive Officer of the submarine Dace, and Admiral Halsey.

[Benitez]   The tomb-like silence that reigned in the conning tower was suddenly shattered by a series of explosions. "Depth Charges! Depth Charges!" exclaimed one of the quartermasters.

"Depth Charges, Hell," said the Captain. "Those are Darter torpedoes, and she is getting her licks into the Jap fleet."

It was 0532 the morning of October 23, 1944. The above was part of the conversation that took place in the conning tower of the U.S.S. Dace, Submarine 247, as the first shot in the Battle for Leyte Gulf was fired by her sistership in the wolfpack, the U.S.S. Darter.

The Dace and the Darter had left their forward base on October 3, 1944, on the second phase of a scheduled fifty-five day war patrol. Their destination was Palawan Passage, the body of water lying between the island of Palawan and that shoal-infested area of the South China Sea known as the Dangerous Ground. Their mission was to guard the passage; to report all contacts; and to attack enemy ships.

The mission of the two submarines represented part of the overall plan evolved to safeguard the landings to be made at Leyte. Our leaders felt that the Japanese Fleet, in an attempt to stem the tide of American island-hopping victories, would in all probability attack our

Leyte beachheads. The problem was to determine the origin of the attack and the day on which it would take place. As a partial solution to the problem a line of submarines was stretched from the island of Palawan to the China coast with the expectation that the Southern Japanese Fleet would pierce that line. A submarine contact report, if received in time, would give the necessary warning and provide the necessary time in which to integrate the American task forces then plying the waters of the Philippines. Once these mighty forces could be brought to bear against the Japanese Fleet, there could be no doubt as to the outcome, and even the most pessimistic could foresee a sweeping American victory. Submarines had proved their scouting value before. Would they be equal to the occasion once more? Our high command fervently hoped so.

Passage to the area was uneventful. Occasionally a Japanese patrol plane would force us down during the day, but the majority of the transit was made on the surface both day and night. We arrived in the Palawan area on October 10.

Endless days of routine patrol went by all too slowly. The *Darter* was usually to the south, the *Dace* to the north of the Passage. Those were interminable days of constant periscope and surface watch. Always waiting—waiting for the tip of a mast; for the smudge of smoke on the horizon; for the radar contact that heralded the arrival of a target. The days dragged on, their sameness only broken by the personal problems of eighty-five men imprisoned in a steel, cigar-shaped hull three hundred and eleven feet long. . . .

Submarine warfare, however, was not characterized by eternal dullness. During each war patrol something always happened to liven up the monotony, and this patrol was no exception. One morning we finally sighted a convoy. We were unable to close it during the day, but immediately after surfacing late the same afternoon we gave chase. We regained contact near the Borneo coast and that night delivered a torpedo attack. It was pitch black and the Japs never knew what hit them. We sank an oiler and a transport, and after lying low the next day we eventually returned to our patrol station in Palawan Passage. We resumed our incessant vigil.

The morning of October 19 found both submarines on the surface. Information was being exchanged between them when the tip of a mast was sighted by a *Dace* lookout. The *Darter* had at the same time become aware of the stranger. As if by a combined signal, but actually independent of each other, both ships submerged. The stranger soon identified herself—a *Fubuki* type destroyer—and she was accompanied by one of her sisters. Both submarines were apart from each other, yet we in the *Dace* knew that every one of our movements was being duplicated in the *Darter*.

"Battle stations submerged!" The persistent, frightening, yet challenging tone of the General Alarm brought men tumbling from their bunks. There were seconds of orderly confusion as the men hurriedly manned their battle stations. In a matter of seconds a slumbering ship became awake, alive, animated. Gone was the lethargy and the drowsiness, and in its stead there came into being an alertness and watchfulness that boded ill for the stranger who had dared intrude into our area.

"Make ready all torpedo tubes!" There was feverish activity in the torpedo rooms as the . . . crews readied their deadly missiles. Expert hands adeptly manipulated wrenches, levers, and valves to assure a run that would be straight, hot, and normal.

"Stand by for a set-up!" The conning tower was a beehive of activity as the fire control problem was plotted, developed, solved.

The contact was made at 1010; we dove seconds later; we fired at 1045. As the third torpedo left its tube, the Captain at the periscope observed the target make a radical change of course away from us. We checked fire. It was useless to fire on a target that had taken evasive action. The Captain noticed a signal being hoisted on the leading destroyer as a few depth charges were heard to explode nearby. The Japs had become aware of our presence; the game of the mouse and the cat was about to start.

It started in the usual manner with the mouse on the run and the cat in hot pursuit; but—almost immediately he lost us. For the next twenty minutes we flirted with him, but it gradually became apparent that we were losing ground. Finally, with the destroyer at a range of two thousand yards and with a target angle of zero, we decided that we did not want to play any more. We went deep and managed to avoid them at deep submergence. The mouse was in its hole safe and unobserved, but he was not content. He wanted to see what was happening so he came back up to periscope depth. There was nothing in sight; the game was over. We had tracked them out on a southerly course so of course we headed *north*.

Later on that night the *Darter* and the *Dace* rendezvoused and exchanged information. The *Darter,* as we well expected, had also fired at the Jap but she had fired seconds before we did. The radical change of course that had spoiled our fire control problem had taken place when the Jap turned towards the *Darter* to comb her torpedo wakes. . . .

October 21 was just another routine day for us in the *Dace*—another day like so many others that we had spent on this and other patrols. The eternal vigilance was maintained, but we were beginning to grow weary and tired of our task. Thoughts turned to the return trip, which according to our orders was to start in two days. Australia was a very popular base of operations, and our thoughts were more on that island, on fresh food, mail from home, and the two weeks of shore leave than on the war. We surfaced at dusk and commenced another surface patrol in the Passage. All was serene until shortly after midnight, at which time the Executive Officer was summoned to the conning tower by the Captain. Without a word of comment he was handed a despatch from the *Darter.* It said, "Fast ships on northeasterly course."

The curtain had risen on the part we were to play in the life and death drama that was to have its finale in the Battle for Leyte Gulf.

The despatch had said *fast* ships so there was no time to lose. At full speed we set a northwesterly course to intercept. Amplifying reports soon came in. They informed us that the contact was a task force; that the *Darter* was trailing but could not overtake; that the enemy base course was 020 T, his speed 20 knots. Those reports represented an excellent solution to a problem in wolf-pack tactics. Our long arduous days of pre-patrol training were paying off. To the south there was the *Darter* in contact, trailing, supplying vital information. To the north there was the *Dace* interpreting that information to gain an attack position. The *Darter's* solution to the problem was more than excellent; it was perfect. Before long we had even been supplied with the Japanese zigzag plan. We could not miss. All we had to do was intercept at dawn.

Intercept at dawn! That was all we had to do, but as the hours passed the navigational problem before us loomed larger and larger. Our calculations gave us an intercept point on the eastern half of an area that up to this time we had gladly avoided. That area was the Dangerous Ground, and our incomplete foreign charts, populated as they were with countless reefs, shoals, and rocks, were mute evidence of the appropriateness of the name which the area bore. Using maximum speed through those treacherous waters we could arrive at the Japanese 0500 position at 0430. The time element was perfect; we could make a dawn attack. But before we could attack we first had to arrive at the proper intercept point. To reach that point we had to travel about four and one-half hours, in waters where we had found the current unpredictable. At the end of that time we had to be at the intercept point; near to it would not do. We had to hit it right on the nose.

The thrill of the chase had gripped the boat. "Hell, man, this is a task force and we got them cold." "Here is where we pick up our citation. . . ." "We will hold reveille on them. . . ." "We will murder those bums. This happens only once in a lifetime." The men were right; it was the chance of a lifetime, and we in the conning tower echoed their thoughts as we kept going forward at full speed while leaving a phosphorescent trail on the black waters of Palawan Passage.

To the Navigator, however, the night seemed interminable. There was no moon so he was denied the consolation of star sights by moonlight. "What if I don't make contact? What if I foul this one up?" he asked himself. For the nth time since midnight he looked at the chart; he checked the courses, the speeds, the times. The Captain came down from the bridge and asked, "How are we doing?"

"Right on schedule. We will hit the intercept point right on the nose—" was the reply. The Captain, busy with his own thoughts, turned away and did not hear the Navigator's low but fervent "—I hope. . . ."

Time, however, was not standing still. It was still dark when at 0430 the *Dace* was slowed and the Captain notified that the ship was in position. At slow speed we began to patrol back and forth along an east-west line. If all went according to plan we would be in contact in less than thirty minutes. Once more we went to battle stations.

Minutes passed—the ship moved back and forth slowly along the scouting line. Minutes passed—the radar operators eagerly scanned the radar scope for signs of the target. Minutes passed—the bridge watch, their eyes glued to their binoculars, tensely strained to make out dim shapes in the half darkness that enveloped us. Minutes passed—and it was suddenly 0500. It was 0500, and we wanted to believe that we were on station. But—where were the Japs? It was all too soon 0505; then 0510; then 0515. Still no contact. The realization that perhaps we had made a fatal error began to grip us. . . .

Our fears, however, had no factual basis. Seconds later we received a message from the *Darter* which said "Enemy changed course to left at dawn."

We had been outmaneuvered: we were hopelessly out of position. The *Darter,* because of her slower speed, had slowly fallen astern during the night. Her fire control party became aware of the unusual change in course at dawn, but they could not immediately assume a change in base course by the enemy. They knew that we were in position and that false information would draw us out; that change in course had to be positively verified. Verification came too late for us to take any action. It had been a gamble and we had lost. With the change in base course the Japs had also increased speed and the *Darter* soon lost contact. The *Dace* immediately started a sweep to the westward in the Dangerous Ground. It was to no avail. The Japs had disappeared as effectively as if they had been swallowed by the sea. Near noon we dismally secured the search. It is true that we had succeeded in sending a warning, and that our high command had become aware that the Japs had begun to move north. But our role had been a negative, unsatisfying one. We had wanted to hit that Jap task force awfully bad.

We began to move south. This was our last day on station and that night we were to start our trip back to the base. Charts for the trip were broken out; the fuel and the lubricating oil were closely checked; another count was made on the provisions. We could have saved ourselves all this trouble, for at noon we received a despatch that a Jap convoy had been sighted heading south in the area. We immediately changed our plans and decided to postpone the return trip until we had worked on this convoy. We arranged a rendezvous with the *Darter* to coordinate a search and attack plan.

At midnight we met as per schedule. Messages were exchanged by line-throwing guns, and both Captains went below to read over the communications. The bridge watches were talking to each other through megaphones when their conversation was cut short by a report from the *Darter* radar operator: "Radar contact—maximum range. It looks like rain," he said.

The information was immediately relayed to us on the *Dace*. "An overeager operator," we said at first. But upon checking ourselves we not only confirmed the contact but identified it as ships. There was no doubt that they *were* ships and that we had made contact at maximum range. Only by the grace of God were we in contact, but this was no time to think of what might have been. Both ships were ordered to close the enemy. Minutes later the radar scope gave us a beautiful picture of many ships, and once again we knew that this was no ordinary convoy. Once again we were in contact with a Japanese task force.

The Captain and the Executive Officer were admiring the radar scope, exclaiming over the beauty of the picture, when with dramatic suddenness the picture disappeared from the screen.

"Now what the hell!" said the Captain. "What is this, a game?"

"Not quite, Captain," answered the unperturbed radar operator. "The radar has conked out!"

This is just fine, we all thought. Here we are in contact with a task force, and our radar decides to take a rest five minutes after we make contact. It just had to be fixed, that is all there was to it. And although it had been a major breakdown, in an hour and a half the radar was back in commission. With a great sigh of relief we saw the Japs appear on the radar scope once more.

We tracked the remainder of the night. The *Darter,* being the senior ship, began making contact reports shortly after the contact was identified. The flow of information was maintained throughout the night, and thus our high command received vital information on the movements of the Japanese fleet. There was no doubt that this was the "A" squad, and it was so reported. The plan had worked. The Japanese had crossed the submarine line; the subs had made contact. From here on it was only a question of maintaining contact as the Japs moved northward, and of eventually bringing to bear our forces at the right time and at the right place. The day had arrived when we could predict the total destruction of Japanese sea power.

We in the *Dace,* although somewhat aware of the tactical situation, were not too concerned with the over-all picture. Our main thought was to hit the task force, and consequently we were very pleased to receive a foolproof plan of attack from the Commanding Officer of the *Darter.* His plan was simple. We had determined the enemy fleet to be in two columns, with the left column slightly ahead of the right column. He proposed to have the *Darter* dive ahead of the left column and the *Dace* dive five miles bearing 045 T from the *Darter*. The attack was to take place at dawn. By this arrangement he placed both submarines in a position of maximum effectiveness. . . . This time a change in the base course at dawn would find us ready. We had profited from our lesson of the day before. This time we knew that one of us was sure to hit at least one ship out of that Japanese fleet that consisted of five battleships, ten heavy cruisers, two light cruisers, and fifteen destroyers.

. . . At 0500 the word was passed to man battle stations. It was a useless command. The men during the night had slowly gravitated towards their stations, and in a matter of seconds each man was reported at his appointed place.

A faint glow to the east heralded the approach of dawn as the radar man at 0510 reported the *Darter* disappearing from the radar scope. She had submerged. We continued northward, feeling alone and naked in the wide expanse of Palawan Passage. Minutes later the diving alarm broke the stillness of the tropical dawn. The *Dace* slid beneath the sea in the most fateful dive of her career.

Neither the *Darter* nor the *Dace* had long to wait. The Japanese, as unwilling and unsuspecting participants, propelled themselves on the stage and were promptly greeted by a salvo of torpedoes from the *Darter*. A series of rapid explosions indicated to all in the *Dace* that the *Darter* had made a successful attack.

"It looks like the Fourth of July out there!" exclaimed the Captain. "One is burning," he continued. "The Japs are milling and firing all over the place. What a show! What a show!"

It must have been a grand show. Those of use unable to see what was happening on the surface hung on to the Captain's words as he continued to describe what he saw. . . .

"Here they come," said the Old Man. "Stand by for a set-up! Bearing, mark! Range, mark! Down scope! Angle on the bow, ten port. . . ."

. . . with the Captain's words, "Let the first two go by, they are only heavy cruisers," we began to fire. We fired six torpedoes from the forward tubes. Almost immediately they began to strike home— one—two—three—four explosions. Four hits out of six torpedoes fired!

The offensive phase was over. Now it was time to start running, and we wasted no time in doing so. Hardly had the sixth torpedo left its tube when we ordered deep submergence. On our way down, a crackling noise that started very faintly but which rapidly reached staggering proportions soon enveloped us. It was akin to the noise made by cellophane when it is crumpled. Those of us experienced in submarine warfare knew that a ship was breaking up, but the noise was so close, so loud, so gruesome that we came to believe that it was not the Jap but the *Dace* that was doomed.

Anxious, agonizing seconds elapsed as we awaited the reports from the compartments that all was secure. They finally came. We were all right. But then a new, terrifying thought gripped us—could the Jap be breaking up on top of us? We were making full speed in an attempt to clear the vicinity of the attack, but that crackling noise was still all around us; it was perfectly audible to every man on board; we could not escape it. Then relief came with a rush. We were leaving the noise astern. We not only had hit but had sunk a major Japanese warship. The crackling and crumbling noises as she broke up were unmistakable.

Our elation was shortlived, for hardly had we settled down at our running depth when a string of depth charges exploding close aboard announced the arrival of the Jap destroyers. At first we thought they had made a mistake, for this attack was contrary to our expectations. We had fully expected that the destroyers would concentrate on the *Darter* and leave us alone. Another string, just as loud as the first one, exploded close aboard. This time the doubt was dispelled. There was no mistake on their part. We were the target.

"Most inconsiderate of the *Darter*," said someone.

"The dirty stinkers!" exclaimed another.

"Hold your hats—here we go again!" came from still another.

"Wham!—Wham!—Wham!" said the Japs.

They were going off all around us, and they were close. The boat was being rocked considerably. Light bulbs were being shattered; locker doors were flying open; wrenches were falling from the manifolds.

The Japs were very mad and we were very scared. . . .

Finally they left us. We stayed deep for a while but later came up to periscope depth. We began to work our way back to the scene of the attack. At the time, of course, we did not know that the *Darter* had sunk an *Atago* class cruiser and damaged a second heavy cruiser, but as we continued northward we sighted masts. It was the Jap cruiser crippled by the *Darter*—lying dead in the water. She was being jealously guarded by two destroyers and two airplanes. We attempted to get in another attack during the day but were unsuccessful because of the effective screen provided by the destroyers and the airplanes. We were not too concerned, however, as we had the cruiser in view at all times and we knew that that night we could team up with the *Darter* to finish her off. We surfaced before the *Darter*. The Navigator got a fair fix. The *Darter* surfaced; we made contact and began to lay plans for finishing the cripple.

The Jap cruiser, however, still had some life in her. Accompanied by the two destroyers she got underway on a southwesterly course at a speed of six knots. We began our attempts to polish her off but soon realized that it was not going to be an easy task. The two destroyers were over officious, perhaps trying to atone for the lack of care they had given the big ships that morning. We went in and out, trying to draw them out, but all to no avail. We were beginning to come to the realization that the only hope of success was in a submerged attack and were discussing the possibility of such an attack when we received a despatch from the *Darter*. There were just three words but they were pregnant with meaning. They were: "We are aground."

The Captain of the *Dace* was faced with a grave decision; either to continue in his attempts to sink the cruiser or to go to the rescue of the *Darter*. His decision was not arrived at hastily, but when announced it had the approbation of every man on board. We were to go to the assistance of the *Darter*. It was hard to give up pursuing a ship that we knew would probably sink with one torpedo hit, and it was hard to give up what we had started so brilliantly the day before; but it would have been doubly hard to abandon our comrades to certain death on the shoals of Palawan Passage.

About an hour and a half later we were within stone's throw of the *Darter*. There was no doubt that she was aground. She was so high that even her screws were out of the water—she seemed like a ship in drydock. We soon realized that getting close to her would not be an easy task. We decided to approach from the stern, that is, to travel over the *Darter's* water. We took position astern and slowly began to close her. The current took charge and we had to make a second approach. The Captain of the *Darter* became quite concerned over the audacity of the Captain of the *Dace*. He kept telling him to stay out a bit; not to come so close; to beware of the reef. We paid no attention and continued to close until we could pass over our bow line. By the use of that line and by the use of the engines we were able to keep away from the reef that, only fifty yards away on our starboard side, exerted its utmost to draw us to it.

The fact that the *Darter* could never get off the reef was obvious from the outset. As soon as the bow line went over, the transfer of personnel began. In the darkness gnome-like figures on the deck of the *Darter* were seen to go down her side into the rubber boats awaiting them below. Minutes later they reappeared at the side of the *Dace* where willing hands hoisted them aboard. There was little conversation. It was a grim and distressing task. There were only two six-man rubber life boats available and it was slow work. We had started about 0200 and it was not until 0439 that the Captain of the *Darter,* the last man to leave the ship, appeared at the side of the *Dace*.

No time was lost in clearing the immediate vicinity, for not only were we in mortal fear of the reef, but upon reporting on board the Captain of the *Darter* informed us that he had set demolition charges on his ship. Upon hearing this report we set the annunciators at *full speed* and never changed them until we considered ourselves a safe distance away.

The allotted time for the charges to go off began to draw near. With bated breath and blinking eyes we saw the second hands of our watches draw nearer and nearer to the zero time. It finally got there. We braced ourselves, expecting the morning stillness to be shattered by a terrific explosion. But only a ridiculously low and inoffensive "pop" came from the *Darter*. . . .

What had happened? Something had obviously gone wrong, and the *Darter,* instead of exploding before our eyes, was very much in evidence on the reef. Some said that the charges were no good. Others that the ship was not ready to die. What difference did it make then? That was no time to philosophize nor to enter into the relative merits of our demolition charges. That was time for action. There was one possible answer—blow her up with our few remaining torpedoes.

We took position on her beam and fired two torpedoes, one at a time. Both torpedoes exploded on the reef without as much as rocking the *Darter*. This confirmed our unexpressed fears that she was too high on the reef.

We had two more torpedoes; we went directly astern of her and fired. The story was repeated. Both torpedoes went off against the reef. It was now 0530. The first streaks of light were beginning to appear in the eastern sky. What to do next? We had to destroy that ship, and there was only one thing to do—hit her with the gun.

"Gun crew, man the gun!" was passed over the General Announcing System. Almost immediately the previously deserted deck became alive with men as our gun crew expertly prepared the gun for action.

We were well aware of the dangerous situation in which we had placed ourselves. We were still in the vicinity of our attack the day before, and we were engaged in a gun action. It was not without some trepidation that we had ordered the gun manned, for now there were about twenty-five men on the topside. A crash dive would be a risky undertaking and might result in some of the men being left topside. It was a chance we had to take. The men had been warned to swim to the reef in case they found themselves in the water. It was a small consolation, but the rapidity of the fire and the percentage of hits scored on the target belied any misgivings that the men might have had.

We were scoring telling hits on the *Darter* and we were beginning to feel a bit easier in our minds about the whole undertaking when a much dreaded cry came from the conning tower, "Plane Contact—Six Miles!"

"Clear the deck—Diving alarm—Take her down!" was the immediate command.

The instinct of self preservation took charge of all of us. Our twenty-five inch conning tower hatch, the only means of ingress into the *Dace,* attracted every one topside as if it had been a magnet. Some walked down; others slid down; still others were pushed down. Some came down feet first; others head first; still others sideways. The Officer of the Deck managed to close the hatch bare seconds before the boat went under.

We all braced ourselves for the bomb explosion that we felt sure would follow. . . . We did not have long to wait, but for the second time that day an awaited loud explosion resolved itself into a distant "pop." We again wondered what had happened. Perhaps if we were to write a book on the subject we could not express it any better than that unknown enlisted man who at the time said, "That dumb ass of a Jap pilot! He made his drop on the *Darter!*"

He was correct. . . .

The Japanese pilot had sighted two submarines on the surface. He could not tell that the *Darter* was aground. He saw one of the submarines diving. Believing that his chance of success was greater with the slower boat, he had decided to bomb the *Darter* instead of the *Dace*. The consensus of opinion was that he had made an excellent choice and we hoped that he had been able to do what we had failed to do earlier that morning with our torpedoes and our gun.

Our troubles, however, were not yet over. There was still one big unanswered question in our minds. Was everyone on board, or was there at this time some poor soul thrashing in the waters above us? We took a quick count. Everyone was accounted for. We checked again and this time there was no doubt about it. We had all made it. . . .[12]

[*Halsey*] . . . On October 23 we learned from one of our submarines, U.S.S. *Darter,* that a sizeable portion of the Japanese Navy was proceeding northwestward in the China Sea and would undoubtedly attempt passage through one of the Straits to reach the Leyte Gulf Area. We had been at sea since October 6 and during the entire time had repeatedly struck air fields and enemy installations on Formosa, Okinawa and Luzon. We had been under severe enemy air attacks and had been most active throughout this period at sea. We planned to send each of the Groups in rotation into Ulithi for repairs and replenishment, and Task Group 38.1, on October 23rd, was enroute to Ulithi for this purpose. The other three Task Groups were standing eastward of the Philippines, awaiting their turn to retire, and meanwhile preparing further offensive strikes in support of MacArthur. On the basis of the *Darter's* report, I ordered them to close the islands and to launch search teams next morning in a fan that would cover the western sea approaches for the entire length of the chain.

Accordingly, by daylight on October 24, the three carrier groups were disposed off the east coast of the Philippines from Central Luzon to just north of Surigao Strait, from which points they could search and attack any shipping that entered either San Bernardino or Surigao Straits, or the waters immediately to the westward thereof.

Our early searches on the 24th of October found two Japanese

Forces: one apparently headed for Surigao Straits (this Force will be hereafter referred to as the Southern Force) and a second and stronger Force in the Sibuyan Sea (hereafter called the Central Force).

The Group on its way to Ulithi was ordered to reverse course and prepare to fuel at sea.

Our planes hit the Central Force repeatedly throughout the day and reported sinking the battleship *Musashi,* three cruisers, and a destroyer, and inflicting severe damage on many other units. These seemed to mill around aimlessly, then withdraw to the west. They were still in the Sibuyan Sea at 1600 on course 290, but later turned east again.

That they might attempt to transit San Bernardino Strait, despite their fearful mauling, was a possibility I had to recognize. Accordingly, at 1512 I sent a preparatory dispatch to all Task Force Commanders in the *Third* Fleet and all Task Force Commanders in Task Group 38, designating four of their fast battleships, with supporting units, and stating that these ships will be formed as Task Force 34 under Vice Admiral Lee, Commander Battle Line, with the mission of engaging decisively at long ranges.

This dispatch, which played a critical part in next day's battle, I intended merely as a warning to the ships concerned that, if a surface engagement offered, I would detach them from Task Force 38, form them into Task Force 34, and send them ahead as a battle line. It was definitely not an executive dispatch, but a battle plan, and was so marked. To make certain that none of my subordinate commanders misconstrued it, I told them later by voice radio: "IF THE ENEMY SORTIES, TASK FORCE 34 WILL BE FORMED WHEN DIRECTED BY ME."

Meanwhile, at 0943, we had intercepted a message from one of the Task Group 38.4's search teams, reporting that it had sighted the enemy's Southern Force—two old battleships, three heavy cruisers, one light cruiser, and eight destroyers, southwest of Negros island, course 060, speed 15 knots—and had scored several damaging hits with bombs and rockets. We did not send a strike against this comparatively weak force.

It was headed for Surigao Strait, where Kinkaid was waiting with approximately three times its weight of metal—six old battleships, four heavy cruisers, four light cruisers, and twenty-one destroyers, plus thirty-nine PT's. Our estimate, at the time, was that this

Force would be soundly defeated by Oldendorf's group of the 7th Fleet.

Task Group 38.3, the northernmost Group off Luzon, was under continuing violent attack by carrier planes. The Group shot down 110 of them, but they succeeded in bombing the light carrier *Princeton*, which later had to be abandoned and sunk. The *Birmingham* and three destroyers were damaged by the explosion of the *Princeton's* magazines and were sent to Ulithi with the *Princeton* survivors.

The discovery of the Southern Force buttressed my conviction that the Japs were committed to a supreme effort, but the final proof was still lacking. There was no naval carrier strength (CV's or CVL's) involved in these known forces converging on the Philippines. It did not seem probable that the Japanese would commit such a large portion of their naval strength without providing some measure of naval air support. The location of their carriers up to this point was a mystery. We believed that a strong carrier Task Force was probably also converging on the Leyte Gulf area from the north, probably having sailed directly from Empire ports. On this basis, orders were issued to the Northern Task Group to conduct an intensive air search to the north and east of their positions to attempt to locate the suspected enemy carrier force.

During the late afternoon reports were received from our Northern Carrier Group 38.3 and from land based air searches that the suspected Japanese Northern Force had actually been located. We had also received information indicating that Commander *Seventh* Fleet was prepared to meet any enemy force which might attempt the passage out of Surigao Strait. The enemy force to the north, as reported from our air searches, was shown to consist of practically all the remaining operative Japanese strength plus supporting surface ships, and was thought at the time to be the most formidable threat to our present and future operations in the Western Pacific.

We had all the pieces of the puzzle, and fitting them together, we noticed that the three Forces had a common factor: A speed of advance so leisurely—never more than 15 knots—that it implied a focus of time and place. The crippled Central Force's second approach to San Bernardino against overwhelming strength, after being heavily mauled, was comprehensible only if they were under adamant orders to rendezvous with the other forces off Samar next day, the 24th, for a combined attack on the transports at Leyte.

Three battles offered. The Southern Force I could afford to ignore: it was well within Kinkaid's compass. The Central Force, according to our pilots, had suffered so much topside damage, especially to its guns and fire-control instruments, that it could not win a decision. I believed it, too, could be left to Kinkaid. (The pilots' reports proved dangerously optimistic, but we had little reason to discredit them at the time.) On the other hand, not only was the Northern Force fresh and undamaged, but its carriers gave it a scope several hundred miles wider than the others. Moreover, if we destroyed those carriers, future operations need fear no major threat from the sea.

We had chosen our antagonist. It remained only to choose the best way to meet him. I had three alternatives.

1. I could guard San Bernardino with my whole fleet and wait for the Northern Force to strike me. Rejected. It yielded to the enemy the double initiative of his carriers and his fields on Luzon that would allow him to use them unmolested.

2. I could guard San Bernardino with Task Force 34 while I struck the Northern Force with my carriers. Rejected. The heavy air attacks on Task Group 38.3 which had resulted in the loss of the *Princeton* indicated that the enemy still had powerful air forces and forbade exposing our battleships without adequate air protection. It is a cardinal principle of naval warfare not to divide one's force to such extent as will permit it to be beaten in detail. If enemy shore based planes joined with his carrier planes, together they might inflict far more damage on my half-fleets separately than they could inflict upon my fleet intact. Furthermore I was confident from the reports of my aviators that Kurita's Force in the Sibuyan Sea had been damaged to such an extent that even if they sortied through San Bernardino Strait, Kinkaid had adequate strength to defend against them.

3. I could leave San Bernardino unguarded and strike the Northern Force with my whole fleet. Accepted. It preserved my Fleet's integrity, it left the initiative with me, and it promised the greatest possibility of surprise. Even if the Central Force meanwhile passed through San Bernardino and headed for Leyte Gulf, it could only hope to harry the landing operation. It could not consolidate any advantage, because of its reported damage. It could merely hit-and-run. I felt Kinkaid was amply strong to handle this situation if it should develop.

My decision was to strike the Northern Force. Given the same

410

'Murderer's Row'.—the *Wasp, Yorktown, Hornet, Hancock*, in Ulithi Atoll 2 December 1944.

circumstances and the same information as I had then, I would make it again.

About 1950 on the 24th, I informed Commander *Seventh* Fleet: CENTRAL FORCE HEAVILY DAMAGED ACCORDING TO STRIKE REPORTS. AM PROCEEDING NORTH WITH THREE GROUPS TO ATTACK CARRIER FORCE AT DAWN. At 2330, I ordered Mitscher: SLOW DOWN TO 16 KNOTS. HOLD PRESENT COURSE UNTIL 2400, THEN PROCEED TOWARD LAT 16 LONG 127 (northeastward). The purpose of this was to permit the three Groups to close up and to avoid over-running the Northern Force's "Daylight Circle," the limit which it could reach by dawn from its last known position. If the enemy slipped past my left flank, between me and Luzon, he would have a free crack at the transports. If he slipped past my right flank, he would be able to shuttle-bomb me—fly from his carriers, attack me, continue on to his fields on Luzon for more bombs and fuel, and attack me again on the way back. I had to meet him head-on. It was also essential to bring him under attack at dawn. Otherwise I would, at least partially, lose the advantage of initiative and surprise. I was trusting the *Independence's* night search planes to set my course.

They began to report and by daylight the composition of the Northern Force was established as one large carrier, three light carriers, two hermaphrodite battleships with flight decks aft, three light cruisers, and at least eight destroyers.

I ordered Task Force 34 to form and take station 10 miles in advance, and my Task Group Commanders to arm their first deck-load strike and launch it at earliest dawn, and launch a second strike as soon afterwards as possible. The first strike took off at 0630. At 0850, a flash report reached me: ONE CARRIER SUNK AFTER TREMENDOUS EXPLOSION. TWO CARRIERS, ONE LIGHT CRUISER HIT BADLY, OTHER CARRIER UNTOUCHED. FORCE COURSE 150 SPPED 17.

We had already increased our speed to 25 knots. If the enemy held his course and speed, he would be under our guns before noon.

At 0648, I had received a dispatch from Kinkaid: AM NOW ENGAGING ENEMY SURFACE FORCES SURIGAO STRAIT. QUESTION IS TASK FORCE 34 GUARDING SAN BERNAR-DINO STRAIT. To this I replied in some bewilderment: NEGA-TIVE. IT IS WITH OUR CARRIERS NOW ENGAGING

ENEMY CARRIERS. Here was my first intimation that Kinkaid had intercepted and misconstrued the preparatory dispatch I had sent to my Fleet the preceding day. I say "intercepted" because it was not addressed to him, which fact alone should have prevented his confusion. I was not alarmed, because at 0802 I learned from him: ENEMY VESSELS RETIRING SURIGAO STRAIT. OUR LIGHT FORCES IN PURSUIT.

When the Southern Force pushed into Surigao soon after midnight of the 24th, it pushed into one of the prettiest ambushes in naval history. Rear Admiral Jesse B. Oldendorf, Kinkaid's tactical commander, waited until the enemy line was well committed into the narrow waters, then struck from both flanks with his PT's and destroyers, and from dead ahead with his battleships and cruisers. Almost before the Japs could open fire, they lost both their battleships and three destroyers. The rest fled, but the heavy cruiser *Mogami* was badly damaged, later collided with the heavy cruiser *Nachi,* and was sunk by Japanese destroyers about noon. About 1000 on the 25th, Army B-24's sank the light cruiser *Abukuma,* which had been previously torpedoed by our PT's. One of Oldendorf's PT's was sunk, and one destroyer was damaged.

At 0822, twenty minutes after Kinkaid's second dispatch, I received his third: ENEMY BATTLESHIPS AND CRUISERS REPORTED FIRING ON TASK UNIT 77.4.3, FROM 15 MILES ASTERN. Task Unit 77.4.3, commanded by Rear Admiral Clifton A. F. Sprague and comprising six escort carriers, three destroyers, and four destroyer escorts, was the northernmost of the three similar Task Units in the *Seventh* Fleet's Task Force 77.4, assigned to guard the eastern approaches to Leyte. The enemy ships were evidently part of the Central Force, which had steamed through San Bernardino during the night. I wondered why search planes had not given warning of the enemy's approach, but I still was not alarmed. I figured that sixteen little carriers had enough planes to protect themselves until Oldendorf could bring up his heavy ships.

Eight minutes later, at 0830, Kinkaid's fourth dispatch reached me: URGENTLY NEED FAST BATTLESHIPS LEYTE GULF AT ONCE. That surprised me. I was not previously committed to protect the *Seventh* Fleet. My job was offensive, to strike with the *Third* Fleet, and we were even then rushing to intercept a force which gravely threatened not only Kinkaid and myself, but the whole Pacific strategy. However, I ordered McCain, who was fueling to the east: STRIKE VICINITY 11–20 N 127–00 E AT BEST POSSIBLE SPEED—and so notified Kinkaid.

At 0900 I received his fifth dispatch: OUR LIGHT CARRIERS BEING ATTACKED BY FOUR BATTLESHIPS, EIGHT CRUISERS PLUS OTHERS. REQUEST LEE (Commanding Task Force 34, and Battle Line) COVER LEYTE AT TOP SPEED. REQUEST FAST CARRIERS MAKE IMMEDIATE STRIKE. I had already sent McCain. There was nothing else I could do.

Then came the sixth dispatch, at 0922: COMMANDER TASK UNIT 77.4.3 (Rear Admiral "Ziggy" Sprague's Unit) UNDER ATTACK BY CRUISERS AND BATTLESHIPS 0700 11-40 N 126-25 E. REQUEST IMMEDIATE AIR STRIKE. ALSO REQUEST SUPPORT BY HEAVY SHIPS. MY OLD BATTLESHIPS LOW IN AMMUNITION.

This was a new factor, so astonishing that I could hardly accept it. Why hadn't Kinkaid let me know before? I looked at the date-time group of his dispatch. It was "242225" or 0725 local time, one hour and fifty-seven minutes ago, and when I compared it with the date-time groups of the others, I realized that this was actually his third dispatch, sent eighteen minutes after he had first informed me that Task Unit 77.4.3, was under attack.

My message was on its way to him in five minutes: I AM STILL ENGAGING ENEMY CARRIERS. MCCAIN WITH FIVE CARRIERS FOUR HEAVY CRUISERS HAS BEEN ORDERED ASSIST YOU IMMEDIATELY—and I gave him my position, to show him the impossibility of the fast battleships reaching him.

The next two dispatches arrived close to 1000, almost simultaneously. The first was from Kinkaid again: WHERE IS LEE. SEND LEE. I was impressed by the fact that it had been sent in plain language, not code. I was speculating on its effect. The second dispatch was from CinCPac and asked the location of Task Force 34.

At that moment the Northern Force, with its two remaining carriers crippled and dead in the water, was exactly 42 miles away. However, in view of the urgent request for assistance from Commander *Seventh* Fleet, I directed Task Force 34 and Task Group 38.2 to proceed south toward San Bernardino Strait, and directed Commander Task Force 38 with Task Groups 38.3 and 38.4 to continue attacks against the enemy carrier force.

I notified Kinkaid: TASK GROUP 38.2 PLUS SIX FAST BATTLESHIPS PROCEEDING LEYTE BUT UNABLE TO ARRIVE BEFORE 0800 TOMORROW.

While I rushed south, Task Groups 38.3 and 38.4 repeatedly struck the Northern Force and late that afternoon it retired in straggling disorder. When it was over the score for the Northern Force was:

Sunk—four carriers, one light cruiser, and two destroyers.

Slightly damaged—two battleships, one light cruiser, and two destroyers.

A curious feature of this engagement is that the air duel never came off. Our strikes found scarcely a handful of planes on the enemy carriers' decks and only fifteen on the wing. We assumed that the rest had ferried into Luzon, and that our attack had caught them by surprise, because during the morning our radars picked up large groups of bogeys approaching from the westward, but they presently reversed course and disappeared.

Meanwhile, Kinkaid had been sending me another series of dispatches: ENEMY RETIRING TO NORTHEASTWARD. Later: LIGHT CARRIERS AGAIN THREATENED BY ENEMY SURFACE FORCES. Still later: SITUATION AGAIN VERY SERIOUS. YOUR ASSISTANCE BADLY NEEDED. LIGHT CARRIERS RETIRING LEYTE GULF. Finally, at 1145: ENEMY FORCE OF THREE BATTLESHIPS, TWO HEAVY CRUISERS, NINE DESTROYERS, 11–43 N. 126–12 E., COURSE 225, SPEED 20.

This position was 55 miles northeast of Leyte Gulf, but the course was not toward the entrance. Moreover, the dispatch had been filed two hours before I received it, and I had no clue as to what had happened since then. The strongest probability was that the enemy would eventually retrace his course through San Bernardino Strait, and my best hope of intercepting him was to send my fastest ships in advance.

I threw a screen of light cruisers and destroyers around the battleships *New Jersey* and *Iowa* as Task Group 34.5, and told them on TBS: PREPARE FOR 30 KNOTS AND BE READY FOR NIGHT ACTION. I also notified Kinkaid that we would arrive off San Bernardino at 0100 next morning, seven hours earlier than my original schedule.

I was puzzled by the Central Force's hit-and-run tactics and still more puzzled when I learned the complete story. Four battleships, six heavy cruisers, two light cruisers, and eleven destroyers which had survived our air attacks on October 24th had transited San Bernardino that night, while two destroyers remained until the sinking of *Musashi* and the damaged *Myoko*. When they were sighted next, at 0631 on the 25th, they were only 20 miles northwest of Sprague's Task Unit.

The enemy continued to close, and presently his fire began to take toll. Sprague's losses to the guns were three ships from the screen, and one escort carrier.

At 1050 the enemy's shore-based air struck, but at 1310 planes from Task Group 38.1 arrived. In the emergency, McCain had launched them from far outside their range of return. After their attack, they had to land and rearm at Tacloban and Dulag fields on Leyte, which had fallen to MacArthur only a few days before. Together with planes from Task Group 77.4, they sank a light cruiser and a destroyer and damaged most of the other ships. Task Group 77.4 had lost 105 planes.

The Central Force was in full retreat by late afternoon, and by 2200 it was reentering San Bernardino, with my force still two hours away. However, shortly after midnight one of my van destroyers made contact with a straggler, and sank it. This was our last surface action.

Thus ended the major action of the threefold Battle for Leyte Gulf. Six of our ships had been sunk and thirteen damaged. In my official report, I was able to write with conviction that the results of the battle were:

"(1) The utter failure of the Japanese plan to prevent the reoccupation of the Philippines; (2) the crushing defeat of the Japanese Fleet; and (3) the elimination of serious naval threat to our operations for many months, if not forever." The Japanese had lost one large carrier, three light carriers, three battleships, six heavy cruisers, three light cruisers, and nine destroyers.

In all of the foregoing I have attempted to describe the battle as it unfolded before my eyes at the time, using only the information which was available then. No battle of such magnitude can be fought without great risks nor without someone getting hurt. The later established facts that no Japanese air attacks developed from Luzon on the 25th; that the Central Force suffered less damage due to air attacks on the 24th than originally reported; and that this force did finally make its sortie from San Bernardino Strait to surprise the *Seventh* Fleet Units could not be determined in advance. Only "Monday Morning Quarterbacks" can speak of such items with certainty. As seen on the afternoon of the 24th and as viewed in retrospect, a Japanese Carrier Force to the north, particularly if allowed the initiative, was the most urgent and serious threat to the final success of our forces.

After the surrender, the U. S. Strategic Bombing Survey learned, from the study of Japanese documents and the interrogation of Japanese naval officers, the Japanese plans for the Battle for Leyte Gulf.

The Japanese were divided into three forces, the Northern, designated Mobile Attack Force; the Central, designated Second Diversionary Attack Force; and the Southern, divided into two forces designated the First Diversionary Attack Force and "C" Force.

The plan called for two segments of the Southern Force to enter Leyte Gulf via Surigao Strait and attack the transports and supporting units off the Leyte beach-head. The Central Force was to arrive in Leyte Gulf via San Bernardino Strait two hours later and attack what remained of our forces after their engagement by the Southern Force. The planes from the carriers in the Northern Force had been launched on October 24, and had attacked Task Force 38.3 and then landed on Luzon, from which point they were to continue to attack our forces within range. Few planes remained aboard these carriers. The carriers were to permit themselves to be attacked by my Task Forces so that my Fleet would be pulled north and brought under attack by land based planes in Formosa and Luzon. The Japanese northern forces were expendable so long as they gave the southern forces the opportunity to destroy our forces lying off the beaches at Leyte.

The plan failed because the Southern Force never passed Admiral Oldendorf's Force and the Central Force was so badly damaged by air strikes on October 24 that it was retiring and had so advised CinC Combined Fleet. However, CinC Combined Fleet on receipt of this message sent the following dispatch: "With confidence in heavenly guidance the entire force will attack." The Central Force again changed its course toward San Bernardino Strait. The attack on Sprague's Forces were broken off and the enemy withdrew without

QUARTER-DECK AND FO'C'S'LE

pressing into the Gulf because the air and torpedo attack launched by Kinkaid's Forces had further damaged his communication and fire-control facilities, had resulted in severe damage to four of his cruisers, and had caused his force to fall into disorder. Furthermore he was far behind schedule and he was afraid of our air attacks. When he heard that the Northern Force was attacking my Fleet he decided to join this attack, but when no engagement offered in daylight he retired through San Bernardino. The Northern Force was disposed of by my Task Forces.

In conclusion I would like to emphasize certain principles and lessons which are illustrated by this action.

It had always been a cardinal principle of our naval tactics to bring all force of the opposing enemy under effective attack. In modern naval warfare there is no greater threat than that offered by an enemy carrier force. To leave such a force untouched and to attack it with anything less than overwhelming destructive force would not only violate this proven principle but in this instance would have been foolhardy in the extreme.

The battle also illustrates the necessity for a single naval command in a combat area responsible for and in full control of all combat units involved. Division of operational control in a combat area leads at least to confusion, lack of coordination, and over-loaded communications, and could result in disaster.

The two and a half days during the progress of this battle my communication officers decoded no dispatch on the circuit linking me with Commander *Seventh* Fleet that had a precedence lower than urgent. Much of this traffic consisted of intelligence summaries of previous unrelated action and other matters not directly related to the tactical situation of the battle.

I am certain there should always be a command circuit linking all commanders in a combat area which is kept clear of all traffic except that of an urgent tactical nature.

The Battle for Leyte Gulf stands as a tribute to the effective employment of sea-power and sea-air-power and of close mutual support. There was glory in it for all.

The credit for our overwhelming victory belongs in full measure to all who participated in its many phases and most particularly to those pilots and sailors who made the supreme sacrifice in order that our cause might prevail.[13]

XI

FATE? I GUESS SO!

In the battle for Okinawa, begun 1 April 1945, a million Americans and 1,500 ships struggled three months to take an island at Japan's doorstep. Enemy air attacks damaged 404 surface craft, half of which were seriously injured, including thirty-four sunk. Radio Technician 1/c Robert C. Barker, Jr., was on board the Indianapolis.

> 1945—*On U.S.S. Indianapolis,*
> *Flagship of the 5th Fleet—*

Dear Mother and Dad:

. . . left Ulithi March 14th and we didn't know to where. Well, March 18th, we were near South Japan. Had an air alert earlier this morning. We shot down 3 Japs—midmorning a carrier got a hit very near us. March 19th early A.M. saw "Franklin" receive several hits—about two miles from us. So many explosions and smoke we thought her gone—a few destroyers and a carrier stayed with her and we went on. Planes from our carriers attacked Kyushu early next morning, March 19th. Next few days we were up and down this one area and arrived in sight of Kerama Retto—off Okinawa 24th of March. Next few days we bombarded by day and patrolled by night till March 31st. We were approaching shore again for bombardment, we had another air raid—we had had the regular G.Q. alert and had secured supposedly with no enemy planes near, for breakfast. Being Saturday and beans for breakfast, I hit my sack.

A few minutes later the air alert was sounded (I have no A.A. station but thought to myself maybe I'd better get up and see what was cooking), but before I could really make up my mind our 20 mm. guns opened up—then I knew a plane must really be close, but before I could move we were hit. The ship shook and bounced and I found myself on the deck, covered up with bunk and mattresses and stuff. I was scared, of course, but determined to be calm, so calmly dug myself out—found my glasses hanging on my bunk unharmed, moved a few bunks and found my shoes. There were maybe six of us in my compartment and all ran up the ladder and out

419

immediately but me and one other guy. This other guy had been in an upper bunk and he bumped his head on the ceiling and knocked himself out—I didn't even know he was up there!

I tried to be so calm that later I realized how silly I was. I went over to my locker on the other side of the compartment from my bunk and got clean clothes, put them on—got out my toothbrush and put paste on it and then went topside to the "head" and washed my teeth. Then up to the radio shack where I looked myself over and found a nice cut on my left leg just above my knee, my elbow skinned up and 3 cuts on the bottom of my toes. I went to the first aid kit and painted them with iodine. I knew that the sick bay must be pretty busy. And it was, I later learned. Well, I went down then to look over the damage—even then we were under way as fast as we could go. Well, the plane had come in on the starboard quarter, went barely over and then smack down through the port quarter. Parts of the plane went through the main deck into one corner of the mess hall—some of it and the bomb on through the mess hall deck into a sleeping compartment and the bomb on through that, through the evaporator room (evaporator room pumps in salt water and makes fresh water) on through the hull of the ship and then exploded underneath the ship in the water and buckled the hole it had made upwards, knocking off two of our four screws (propellers) and the supporting yoke of one of the shafts. As soon as all the men that could got out of that living compartment it was dogged down and shut off to prevent flooding of the ship. Later learned that 8 men were trapped in that compartment—either instantly killed by the debris falling in there or drowned while unconscious in the oil that filled it. Oil tanks burst and flooded it and oil being heavier held the water out. . . .

Next day—Easter. . . . A salvage boat came alongside and divers welded a patch on the ship's bottom and we started pumping out the flooded compartments. Six of the trapped men were pulled out and we had burial services for them. They were taken by boat to land and buried. For lunch we had cold meats and Spam, salad and fruit juice. Still no fresh water for washing and rationed drinking water. Drinking fountains turned on for 15 minutes at the change of watches. . . . For supper we had ham sandwiches and ice cream. That night 0030 (thirty minutes past midnight) we had an air raid alert lasting till 0630. Fired at enemy planes at 0330. There we sat unable to move

Okinawa—1 April 1945.

—being repaired—but several fighting ships in same harbor. Breakfast this Monday morning—spam, gravy and baking powder biscuits. Two more of the missing men found and burial services for them in afternoon. That night—another air raid alert from 0130 to 0800. During the night we heard some Jap commandos boarded an LCM ship in our harbor and cut up four men before overcome. Think maybe they were trying to get to their radio transmitter to call the planes in this harbor!

Tuesday, April 3d (next morning), Admiral Spruance conducted a Purple Heart ceremony for 15 men on the quarter-deck and 7 men in sick bay—5 men had left our ship to go to hospital ships the day we were hit. One of them, an aviation radio man, was up in a plane on the catapult working on its radio when we got hit. The plane fell off its perch and this kid fell on his head. I had helped him the day before and was going to help him some more that morning, but since up all night on G.Q. I put it off for a little shut-eye till later in the morning. Fate? I guess so! . . . That night I was on watch and most of the R.T.'s sitting around the radio shack when an announcement at about 2030 came over the system for all hands to dog down all hatches, and turn on all lights below decks and set a watch on all compartments, as there was a possibility of a Jap being aboard. A Marine guard had been found at his outside guard post with his throat slit—he didn't die, however! Well, we about passed out but weren't worried about the Jap himself getting to us—too many guys on gun watches outside our shack and I put on a .45 pistol—but we worried about what the bastard might do—such as put a charge of dynamite in an ammunition "ready box" or something like that— so we stayed up all night and next morning but no Jap was found, he either got scared off or was never on and the Marine cut up by a personal enemy in the crew! This day—in the afternoon I was told I was to be transferred into the Flag Allowance and to move the next day (Thursday, April 5th) to the U.S.S. "New Mexico."

We moved early next morning. While transferring our gear to an LCI, I barely got my foot caught between a railing and the wooden plank we had across the two ships, when the LCI rolled a little; I jerked it out quickly and wasn't hurt! Two minutes later a kid of the crew of the LCI did the same thing only he didn't get his out and got a crushed foot out of it. Fate! I guess so.

Well, while transferring to the "New Mexico" it started to rain

Night bombardment—USS *New Mexico.*

a bit so we had a nice job moving all our stuff aboard. We worked like mad all day hooking up our receivers, but that night was the first really big air raid over Okinawa. The C.A.P. shot down over 100 enemy planes, a few got in to our part of the fleet just off shore of our landing place off Okinawa. The "New Mexico" shot one down. The next day Task Force 58 met a Jap force north of us and sank one of their battleships and two cruisers and others. Task Force 58 is the fast carrier force and their battleships (latest class), cruisers and destroyers that were on the Tokyo strikes and patrolled up and down north of Okinawa all the while protecting us. The next few days were spent working till late at night installing our equipment and some new stuff, with air alerts each night.

Roosevelt died, Ernie Pyle killed—but so were thousands of plain G.I.'s all around us! No mail received from March 26th till April 17th. All these days we were bombarding with our 14-inch guns most of the day each day and sometimes all night—then take a day off and go around to Kerra Merrato harbor for supplies and ammunition.

April 22d Admiral Nimitz came aboard to confer with Spruance, spent night aboard and we had a good air raid that night to show him. April 26th Admiral Halsey was aboard. Flew in from Guam. April 27th a Liberty ship sank about a mile from us from a suicide plane. And two tin cans sunk out on patrol by same. April 28th we were at G.Q.'s for five and one-half hours. . . .

. . . On May 12th a few enemy planes got through Task Force 58 and two came in at us—one port, one starboard; the starboard one was shot down but not before he strafed the quarter deck and hit some of the gunners back there. But the port one came right on in midship, mowed off the "Jap-Trap" (a tub containing 4–20mm. machine guns) and went on to the smokestack and then down. He, too, strafed all the way in—several men were lost due to this—which is unusual for suicide pilots to do.

Well, my G.Q. station on the "New Mex" was in the radio transmitter room—three decks down and center of ship—two-thirds way back. So we hardly felt the crash. But, of course, fires were started and some ammunition boxes went off. But we couldn't leave our post to go see. I did go to the "head" about one hour later—and to go there had to go through one of the mess halls and they had the injured on stretchers all over the place. It was terrible, most of these burned badly, some with shrapnel in them, some with limbs missing.

Post-World War II operations off the Hawaiian Islands.

One of the Flag R.T.'s was up on bridge and just started down—came down two decks and just started outside—and got blown back in, receiving a flash burn on face and one piece of shrapnel in his leg just above the knee. An LCM came alongside and took some of the most serious casualties to the hospital ship.

At 0030 next morning we had another raid lasting till 0110 A.M. and another from 0250 to 0432. At 1030 next morning—Mother's Day—we had burial services for 52 men. Later we knew that some men taken from the ship had died en route to or later on the hospital ship—making the total killed 67. All day, Mother's Day, salvage crews started cleaning up the mess and it was a mess but the ship had no holes in the bottom so no danger of sinking. All but one of our antennas were either down or their trunks flooded. The Flag radio intelligence shack was a wreck—we lost a radioman chief in there, shrapnel went through his radio and then into his heart. Another shack up higher, where we had two small transmitters, was riddled beyond repair. A salvage repair ship came alongside and started repairs. The rubble that went down the stack got into two of our boilers, damaging them badly. Two days later men had arrived by air from Pearl Harbor to repair the boilers—specialists on that type of work. The stack was patched with huge sheets of steel welded in place. A canvas hood put over it and the welders worked all night —but had to quit several times each night for more air raids.

We did receive mail the afternoon of Mother's Day which helped our morale until one stopped and thought of how many of those letters were not delivered—but marked, deceased. Next two weeks was same old stuff. . . . May 27th Halsey's flagship came within spitting distance and next morning at 0530 we were underway for Guam, even though we had a raid starting at 0510—lasting till 0900. Later heard a tin can sitting 100 yards aft of where we were anchored got sunk! Fate? I guess so! May 31st—we moored at Guam. Next morning the Flag left the "New Mex" to set up headquarters ashore at Guam.

The rest you know. . . .[14]

[*Radio Technician Robert C. Barker, Jr. of Lebanon, Indiana, assigned once again to the* Indianapolis, *lost his life when the ship was torpedoed on 30 July 1945. He received the Purple Heart and Victory Medals posthumously.*]

CHAPTER VI

Ahead Full

1960

F IVE years of uneasy peace followed World War II. The Communists invaded South Korea in June, 1950, and the air, sea, and ground forces of the United States fought to preserve that country from foreign domination. But the end of the "police action" brought no real peace to an apprehensive world.

During the 1950's, emphasis shifted from surface ships to aircraft, from piloted to guided missiles, from conventional explosives to atomic and thermonuclear weapons. The Navy speeded up the development of atomic power in submarines.[1] The first nuclear-powered submarine, the *Nautilus,* far exceeded the hopes of her supporters when, in August, 1958, she traveled from the Pacific to the Atlantic via the North Pole. Other nuclear submarines—the *Seawolf, Skate, Sargo*—pioneered new areas. The *Seawolf* remained submerged for sixty days completely independent of the earth's atmosphere; the *Skate* made two trips under the Arctic ice and, on 17 March 1959, surfaced at the North Pole; the *Sargo* on an exploratory mission spent thirty-one days beneath the polar ice. On 30 December the same year, the first Polaris-firing nuclear submarine, the *George Washington,* was commissioned.

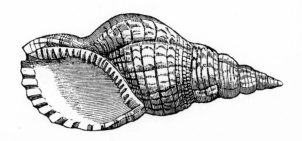

I

THE CRUISE OF THE *TRITON*

In 1522 the Vittoria *anchored in Cadiz, Spain and Ferdinand Magellan's men became the first to sail around the world. The passage lasted three years. In 1960, the nuclear submarine USS* Triton *surfaced after completing the first submerged circumnavigation of the globe. She retraced Magellan's track, "undetected by our own or other forces," in sixty days.[2] The skipper of the* Triton, *Captain Edward L. Beach, USN, logs this historic voyage.*

TRITON has been scheduled for shakedown cruise in northern European waters. Having suffered from frustrating delays during the building period, largely due to the over-riding Polaris priority, now that the ship was in commission there appeared, at any rate to *TRITON* people, to be some urgency in getting on with operations. Despite the concurrence of COMSUBLANT with this ambition, however, other considerations interfered.

TRITON consequently remained at Electric Boat from 1 December 1959 until 20 January, and the new installation looked more extensive with every passing day. Lay-over during Christmas was welcome, but with January we began chafing with the lengthening inactivity. On 20 January, finally, the ship got underway for tests at sea, determined to make up lost time to the best of our ability. A 24-hour per day schedule was set up.

1 February 1960, returned New London, tests completed. Received orders for the Commanding Officer to be in Washington on 4 February for an important conference.

In company with the Commander, Submarine Squadron Ten, the C.O. called at Headquarters, Commander Submarine Force, U.S. Atlantic Fleet. There, under the strictest secrecy, it was learned that a submerged world circumnavigation might be ordered.

At the appointed time, the conference met in the office of Vice Admiral Wallace M. Beakley, Deputy Chief of Naval Operations for Fleet Operations and Readiness. Also present was the Navy Hydrographer, Captain H. G. Munson; Rear Admiral L. P. Ramage, Director, Undersea Warfare Division; plus the head of OPNAV's Atomic Defense section, representatives from CINCLANTFLT and COMSUBLANT, and others. For purposes of geophysical and oceanographic research and to determine habitability, endurance and psychological stress—all extremely important to the Polaris program—it had been decided that a rapid round-the-world trip, touching the areas of interest, should be conducted. Maximum stability of the observing platform and unbroken continuity around the world were important. Additionally, for reasons of the national interest, it had been decided the voyage should be made entirely submerged, undetected by our own or other forces, and completed as soon as possible. *TRITON*, because of her size, speed and the extra dependability of her two-reactor plant, had been chosen for the mission.

I declared that *TRITON* could sail as soon as additional stores were loaded and the special equipment required for the voyage installed. The conference then resolved itself into smaller groups concerned with the several projects and problems.

Upon the Commanding Officer's return to New London, a period of strenuous activity ensued for all hands in the ship, but in view of the high classification imposed, only *TRITON's* officers could be made aware of the change in our shakedown cruise. The rest of the crew were told nothing. . . .

A ticklish administrative difficulty was how to advise as to the duration of financial arrangements for families left behind. The crew, of course, expected to be home, or at least to have access to the mails, by the end of March, whereas we knew not only that the voyage would actually last into May but also that there could be no mail either sent or received. This was solved by letting it become known that our northern cruise might be followed immediately by a series of Bureau of Ships trials in Caribbean waters, possibly without return to New London. And a completed check-off list prescribing

430

Edward L. Beach, (right) commander of the USS *Triton* (below) at the time of its submerged circumnavigation of the globe.

personal preparations lasting until mid-May was required of all hands. To the credit of the crew, not even this fictitious confidence was leaked.

Soon a great number of extra chart portfolios were delivered, followed by crates of special equipment. Much of the latter, dismantled and in boxes, was not to be set up until we were finally clear of land. There were a few curious looks, but no one asked embarrassing questions. . . .

Tuesday, 16 February 1960 All times Romeo (Zone +5 or EST)

1416R Underway from New London in accordance with COM-SUBLANT OpOrd 5–60, proceeding surfaced until clear of Block Island Sound.

1543R With Long Island abeam to starboard, entered International waters. Set course due south. In this area the Continental Shelf runs far out to sea and deepens very gradually. Our fathometer registers about 30 feet of water under the keel as we cross Endeavor Shoals bar.

1737R With soundings increasing to 30 fathoms, dived. Continuing on course 180° to clear submarine operating areas. We will be coming to periscope depth occasionally, but we shall not surface until May. Our running depth gradually increases as the ocean bottom slowly drops away.

2240R Changed course to 134° T, on the first leg of our voyage. We will follow this course for 3250 miles to St. Peter and St. Paul Rocks, a lonely spot a few miles north of the equator, lying off the bulge of Brazil. The "Rocks" will mark the beginning and completion of our circumnavigation of the world; but while we're at it, we intend to make the entire voyage in the submerged condition. The necessity of rounding the tips of Africa and South America and twice traversing virtually the length of Atlantic Ocean makes the total length of the trip some 34,000 miles.

Wednesday, 17 February. All times R (+5)

0540R Periscope depth for morning star sights and to ventilate the ship. Our #1 periscope, a brand-new design by the Kollmorgen Optical Company, features a device by which observations of celestial bodies can be made nearly as accurately as with the time-honored sextant. Until recent years submarines navigated in exactly the same way as any other ship, by using a navigator's sextant when on the surface. Required to remain surfaced for long periods for transit or battery charging, earlier submarine navigators experienced only those difficulties inherent in working from their tiny exposed bridges. The snorkel, while not emancipating the submarine from the surface, enabled it to stay under while running engines and thus focused attention upon the need to make observations through a periscope. Many were the stratagems tried, and many the special periscopes built (mainly by Kollmorgen) for the purpose. Our first checks with our new periscope are very pleasing, its only apparent drawbacks being that the submarine must be at periscope depth, with sun, moon or stars visible. Coming to periscope depth takes time, for one must first listen cautiously at slow speed.

With the high SOA (Speed of Advance) required to complete our trip within the time allotted, every minute spent at a reduced speed requires many times that minute for recovery of the distance thus lost. One of our objectives is to determine which are the limiting factors for *TRITON* and to minimize their effect as far as possible.

Two things now under development will help greatly in the future and are now almost operationally ready: a really effective oxygen generating system—which no submarine has as yet and on which major research effort is being expended—and a means of determining position by instruments, without celestial observations of any kind. Deep in *TRITON*'s belly we carry a complicated machine on which the Navy, MIT and the Sperry Gyroscope Company have worked for years. Called "Ship Inertial Navigation System," SINS for short, it measures earth rotation and other undetectable forces by means of extraordinarily precise gyroscopes; and from these measurements automatically calculates our latitude and longitude. . . . I venture the prediction that this device will one day spell the end of that time-honored professional—the Navigator of the Ocean Sea.

0640R On securing ventilation, the inboard induction valve would not close. Both the hydraulic outboard valve and the electric head valve had shut properly, however, and, the ship being tight, we went on down anyway. A check of the pipe through a removable inspection plate rewarded us with a smashed and rusted flashlight which had lodged across the induction valve seat, a legacy from some careless workman. In 1939, with a known defective inboard air-induction valve, the brand-new submarine *SQUALUS* dived on trials depending for her safety on the proper functioning of the outboard valve. It had worked properly on previous occasions, but this time, in some unaccountable fashion, the outboard valve also failed (some say it shut and then opened). With the other valve in the huge 36 inch pipe also open, *SQUALUS* sank instantly. Half of her crew was drowned in the flooded after compartments. This costly lesson we have well learned.

1200R Noon position—36–33N, 68–04W. Course 134°T. After some thought—now is the time to notify the crew as to our objective. As I reveal our intention over the general announcing system, there is a most attentive audience. The southerly course we have been making good, instead of the expected northeasterly course, has caused a lot of speculation. Some, accurately enough, suspect we might be heading for the Pacific. But now with the full knowledge of our final objective, the tremendous task ahead of us evokes much discussion. As we had anticipated, every man aboard is thrilled with the prospect, yet soberly mindful of the effort required.

Thursday, 18 February 1960. All times R (+5)

1345R Exercised the crew at general drills. Our routine for the trip will be to exercise daily at one or more of the many drills which we, like all naval vessels, must have letter-perfect. . . .

Friday, 19 February 1960 (All times Q, +4)

0235Q The "fix" just computed shows us to have fallen behind our

PIM (Position of Intended Movement). In preparation for the voyage, a detailed track chart with our exact routing and times to pass through each point had been left with COMSUBLANT, so that at all times he will know exactly where we are. The somewhat reduced speed necessary for recent repairs has caused us to fall farther behind than seems proper, and it is obviously time we drew upon some of *TRITON*'s tremendous reserve. With speed increased to flank, our submarine cruiser begins to tear through the water at a speed few ships can match on the surface. And yet, there is no sensation of speed at all. . . .

1300Q Released our first hydrographic bottle. This appears to be a good time to start one of the projects of the cruise, which is to release a bright orange-colored bottle once or twice a day, containing a printed Hydrographic Office form requesting the finder, in several languages, to note the time and place found in the blanks provided and forward the paper to the nearest U.S. Government authority. Concern over possible premature discovery of one of these bottles has prompted circumspection regarding the information we ourselves place in the blanks, and they are therefore made out in a simple code and serially numbered. The master—myself —is simply "CAPTAIN," (or sometimes CAPTAIN, USN). "Vessel," is filled in with the letter "T." The serial number, for which there is no provision, is hand-written in a convenient place and prefixed by the letters "MT" signifying "Magellan—*TRITON*." On the back we have written a short statement of the bottle's importance to the U.S. research. Carbon copies of each bottle-paper, with all blanks filled, are retained.

The Magellan idea arose when it was noted that with the exception of his famous Strait our track very closely approximated his. Minor adjustments of the routing occasioned no difficulty, and will add measurably to our sense of accomplishment after a long and tedious journey.

Putting a sealed bottle into the water has turned out to be no problem at all. A standard medical bottle answers the purpose admirably, fitting easily into our submerged signal ejector. . . .

Saturday, 20 February 1960 (All times Q, +4)

0336Q   Periscope depth for celestial observations, to listen on the radio for any possible message, to ventilate the ship, and to tune around for a news broadcast. This will be our procedure once a night, for approximately one hour.

We carry a large supply of stored oxygen and have the latest equipment to remove waste products from the atmosphere inside the ship. All nuclear submarines are fitted with a ventilation tube, identical in nearly every respect to a snorkel pipe except as to size, by which outside air can be drawn in and used air can, in effect, be exhaled. We intend to ventilate as necessary during the first part of the cruise and carry out an extensive "sealed-ship" test toward its conclusion.

While near the surface, of course, a radio antenna can also be raised clear of the water into reception position. We would stay at periscope depth longer, were it not necessary to make such a large reduction in speed at the same time, for already we are feeling out of touch with the rest of the world. For morale purposes alone, during the extremely long submergences now practicable, it appears desirable that daily digests of general news be transmitted over official circuits. We have started a ship's newspaper, but so far the editor has had to write almost everything in it himself. Even so, nearly everyone reads it from cover to cover. . . .

1340Q   Slowed to half power, our normal cruising speed, which is still much faster than most ships can go. . . .

Monday, 22 February 1960 (All times Papa, zone +3)

0034P   Garbage ejector out of commission with a jammed outer door. This prosaic gadget is a large potential hazard because of the frequency of its use and the low experience level of the individuals customarily handling trash and garbage. . . . Fortunately, we have an empty torpedo tube to eject from, if we have to; but Lt. George Sawyer, torpedo officer, has already begun an earnest campaign to rid me of this idea.

Meantime, with only the breech door shut and full sea-pressure on the other side of it, it is desirable temporarily to restrict our submergence depth.

0126P   Ejector door is shut, jam cleared. At least, we now have both muzzle and breech doors between us and the Atlantic Ocean and can resume normal cruising depth. The jam was most likely due to over-greasing the external mechanism, an excess of enthusiasm against which we shall hereafter guard ourselves.

Tuesday, 23 February 1960 (All times Papa, Zone +3)

During early morning, sudden and very rapid shoaling was recorded on the Precision Depth Recorder. Normal soundings have been more than 2,000 fathoms in this area. For fear the shoal might reach a depth dangerous to us, the Officer of the Deck immediately slowed to creeping speed. We passed very slowly over the area, recording a minimum sounding of 930 fathoms, then executed a Williamson turn in order to retrace exactly our track and passed again over the spot on the reverse course. Sounding, 1,011 fathoms. Passing over it again on a southerly heading, the reading was 1,061 fathoms. The profile of this sea mount shows nearly precipitous sides. Its height above the ocean floor is nearly 9,000 feet. . . .

Wednesday, 24 February 1960 (All times Papa, Time Zone Plus 3)

Today we expect to make our first landfall. This also will be the spot to which we shall return upon completion of our circumnavigation of the globe. Though the Sailing Directions describe St. Peter and St. Paul Rocks as bare and useless, interest has run high anyway. . . .

0845   At periscope depth, contact in sight. It is a motor-ship of about 8,000 tons. She has a white hull, buff stack, nice looking clipper bow, large deck house, many kingposts and apparently much deck machinery. Very modern in appearance. Nationality not determined. The ship was tracked on course 023°T at a speed of 18 knots, apparently on a normal shipping route between South America and Europe. Minimum range: 7,000 yards. . . .

1136   St. Peter and St. Paul Rocks should be about 10 miles ahead. Periscope depth for search. . . .

1206   Rocks in sight bearing 134°T. For "The Rocks" to show up so precisely on schedule and so precisely as predicted is a feather in the Navigator's cap. Everyone on board shares in appreciation of an unusually precise navigational accomplishment under sub-average conditions.

1243   Stationed photographic reconnaissance party. Lt. Richard Harris in charge with Chief William R. Hadley assisting. This is the first opportunity we have had to try periscope photography, and we plan to make the most of it. For the next three and one-half hours *TRITON* cruises slowly around the rocky island at various ranges, avoiding shallow spots and generally conforming to the bottom topography. Our fathometer and pinging sonar are both extremely valuable in detecting the shallow areas.

St. Paul Rocks . . . is merely a spot where the Atlantic Ridge happens to come above the surface in the form of a group of jagged peaks. This sub-surface ridge runs generally north and south and is the source of most of the shallow spots or "sea-mounts" in the Atlantic basin. . . . The whole islet, but a few hundred feet long, can with a little imagination be made to resemble a damaged ship laboriously proceeding at slow speed.

1605   Photo Reconnaissance completed. Enroute Cape Horn.

2004   *TRITON* crosses the equator for the first time. . . .

25 February—1 March

The psychologist assigned for the voyage from the Medical Research Laboratory in the Submarine Base, Dr. Benjamin Weybrew, is supposed to test our over-all reactions during the entire period of the trip. He has already assembled a group of volunteer guinea pigs and is commencing to chart such things as sleeping hours, smoking and coffee-drinking habits, general feeling of lassitude and the like. After he has studied the results and compared them with similar investiga-

tions conducted in Operation Hideout and in *SEAWOLF*, as
well as elsewhere, he hopes to make a contribution toward
solution of the problems to be faced by Polaris Missile submarines in a succession of similar long submergences. This
data it also expected to provide basic information for future
space travel.

Not all the effects are psychological, of course, for the inter-
relationship of physical environment to mental reaction, and
the reverse, is well known, if as yet imperfectly understood.
Concurrently, we are carefully recording the levels of carbon
dioxide, carbon monoxide, oil vapor concentrations, air pressure within the ship, and similar phenomena. One test we
will carry out toward the end of the cruise, total prohibition
of smoking for several days, has already caused a great deal
of divergent comment. Suppose it is provable that elimination of tobacco smoke has beneficial effects of great importance. What about the psychological results? How much
effort should be expended for a device to make such a prohibition unnecessary—or would extended prohibition of
smoke be more feasible? . . .

If all goes as we hope, we shall see St. Paul Rocks again on
the 26th of April. We have already traveled 3,000 nautical
miles, with 31,000 to go. Our trip is considerably longer
than the straight-line distance around the world, for both
Suez and Panama Canals are to be avoided; our total submerged voyage will cover 34,000 miles.

It is our "shakedown cruise," of course, in addition to all
the rest, and the Executive Officer has evolved a daily program of drills and instruction lasting from 1300 to 1600.
This, added to 8 hours of watch per day and necessary division work, makes for better than a 12-hour working day. We
have, however, neither reveille nor taps. Despite their latter-
day size, submarines are still so crammed full of equipment
that a man not on watch is less bother (and more comfortable) in his bunk than up and about—and more people
asleep means less oxygen consumed, less food eaten, more

room for watch-standers and men repairing or working on equipment. A number of men, as a matter of fact, skip meals by sleeping through them. To have all hands ready for the daily drill period, we need some kind of reveille, though it is carefully not referred to by this name. Therefore, we make it our custom to test all our alarm signals—the General Alarm, the Diving Alarm, the Collision Alarm—every day at 1245, just prior to the beginning of the day's schedule of drills and lectures. It is an effective alarm clock. . . .

There is a series of evolutions relating to the ship's own operational development which, because of her newness, we shall have to perform. We must know, for instance, for how many minutes we must suck air through our ventilation pipe in order completely to change the atmosphere of the ship. And naturally we have to know how long we can go before we need to do it again. Simultaneously with ventilating we can carry out numerous other processes, such as taking celestial observations through the periscopes, sending or receiving radio messages, ejecting the hydrographic bottles, blowing sanitary tanks and the like. Some of these evolutions can be carried out below periscope depth, sometimes at greater cost of a valuable commodity such as high pressure air. High pressure air itself must be conserved, and another of our problems is to see how well we can manage it. As *SEAWOLF* found during her long submergence, one cannot afford to expel it from the ship. If it must be used, it should be released within the ship after use and recharged back into the air banks via the air compressors.

Our weekly routine is as follows: Monday and Tuesday are regular days, with drills, lectures, school of the ship and classes during the noon to 1600 watch. Wednesday is a "Rope Yarn Sunday"—Navy traditional surcease from drills while at sea. During the sailing days this was the opportunity, if weather was good, to get up one's kit for mending or washing, generally to do odd jobs of one's own volition, or just to relax in the sun.

Thursday is a regular drill day.

Friday is "Field Day," and is the only day when reveille is held in the morning. After Field Day there is a formal inspection by the Commanding Officer. If you had the 4 to 8 watch in the morning, you also have the 16 to 20 watch that same evening with Field Day and Inspection in between. This makes a long day; but every two weeks we equalize things by shifting the watches.

Saturday is a regular work day with drills in the afternoon. As much as possible Sunday is observed as a day of rest, the only scheduled activities being Church and normal watches.

Friday, 26 February 1960 (All times Papa, Zone Time Plus 3)

Field day all day long. An amazing amount of trash and garbage has been collected out of the various recesses in the ship. She looks clean superficially, but deep in the corners there is a great deal of shipyard dirt. It is obvious that a single field day will not even come close to getting the ship into the condition we want her.

1600   Began Commanding Officer's below decks inspection. The ship looked pretty good, all in all, but after a thorough inspection a number of discrepancies were found. We shall do better next time.

At the conclusion of the inspection, despite the Gunnery Officer's protests, I directed that some of the trash be loaded into number six torpedo tube and ejected that way. Our garbage ejector will handle about ten bags at a time, and we had accumulated over one hundred. As an emergency garbage ejector, a torpedo tube looks like a practicable alternative. During the war this was so—but our torpedo tubes nowadays eject torpedoes by water instead of air, and the problems are different.

The experiment was successful in that a large amount of garbage was ejected; however, rags and other material were apparently sucked into the torpedo tube mechanism, fouling it. "Guns" has won his point, but I can be stubborn too and we have now evolved a system to prevent this from happening. Nevertheless, the sight of TM3 A.W. Steele crawling into the clammy interior of the torpedo tube to push the garbage down toward the end, with water squirting in under pressure all the while from a fouled valve, has convinced me we should not use the tubes for garbage ejection unless it is an absolute necessity. . . .

1 March 1960 (All times Papa, Zone Time Plus 3)

This morning Commander James E. Stark, Medical Corps, U.S. Navy, our Atmosphere Control Analyst as well as our ship's Medical Officer in charge of the health of the crew, asked to see me about a serious problem which has arisen. J. R. Poole, Chief Radarman, has been having excruciating abdominal pains for several hours and it is Jim Stark's conviction that he has a kidney stone. Apparently Poole had been suffering a milder ache for several days and had not reported it, hoping it would go away. This has not been the case, and he is now in serious pain.

My profession as an officer of the United States Navy has not heretofore required me to know much about kidney stones, but insistent questioning of Jim Stark and a few moments of quick research in an encyclopedia give me a pretty good idea of the problem. Poole may have had an unsuspected kidney stone for some time and never known it; but once it starts to pass it must either pass all the way through or else serious complications will result. The passage of the stone is usually accompanied by severe pains of exactly the type Poole is experiencing now, and the only thing to do is to ease his discomfort as much as possible, and wait. In the meantime I am faced with the problem of what to do in case Poole does not pass the stone. The equipment required is standard in any hospital but we do not have it on board ship. Where can we take Poole if he needs more attention than Jim Stark is equipped to give? And will we have to surface to get him there? Will our submerged record be ruined on this account?

1015   Troubles come in pairs. Our fathometer, which has been operating continuously since departure from the States, is suddenly out of commission. This equipment, perfected many years ago by our Navy, has been so dependable for so long as to be taken almost for granted by all ships. Our normal practice in making a transit (except when attempting to avoid sonar detection) is to take and record a sounding every 15 minutes. For this particular cruise a precision depth recorder, or PDR, has been installed which takes a sounding approximately 30 times a minute and records the same on a piece of specially prepared paper, thus producing a continuous record of the bottom profile along our course-line. It is the PDR which found the previously uncharted submerged sea mounts along our track.

Now, however, the fathometer is out of commission and my anxiety about Poole is compounded by worry over it. Fortunately at the present time we are in an area where the water is deeper than normal for the Atlantic and for a number of hours there is [no] worry about unexpectedly scraping the top of some unsuspected submerged peak. But we will want that fathometer badly as we approach Cape Horn. It is also apparent that submarines need fathometers more than other ships. . . .

1500   Progress report on Poole indicates no improvement yet. The trouble with the fathometer, however, has been localized as a transformer and two crystals blown in the receiver, most probably because of insufficient cooling.

1900   Poole has been "asymptomatic" for several hours now, and may have passed the stone. We won't know for some little time but it does look hopeful.

1915   . . . At this time good news is reported. Our fathometer is at last back in commission. . . . The precision depth recorder also is back in commission and we lay on a rigorous program . . . to watch both carefull from now on.

2200   The good news as well as the bad comes in batches it seems. All indications are that Poole has passed his kidney stone and will be restored to duty and full vigor in a matter of hours.

2 March 1960 (All times Papa, Zone Time plus 3)

0100   Poole is having another attack; more severe than the last one.

Maybe he did not pass the stone a few hours ago despite all indications to the contrary; or as Dr. Stark points out, there may be more than one kidney stone involved.

0232   Possible submarine contact. We are in fact within about 300 miles of Golfo Nuevo, where the press has recently reported unknown submarines under attack by the Argentine Navy. In their present state of mind the last thing we want to do is to make contact with a vessel of the Argentine Navy. Even though *TRITON* would most likely be able to show them her heels, the repercussions could not fail to create public notice. But, of course, there is always the possibility that this is indeed a submarine contact. Maybe the Argentines had something; we decided to investigate. . . .

0258   Periscope depth for further investigation. So far as we can tell, this is not a surface ship; and our contact definitely has movement. It is not on the bottom. As we slowly and cautiously draw closer, however, it commences to fade and change shape. Final evaluation; a close pack of fish moving around and feeding, and probably wishing this huge intruder would leave them alone. . . .

0420   Poole's second attack has progressed to an extremely painful and apparently serious condition. I visited him in his bunk but he is unable to talk coherently with me because of the severe cramping pains. Jim Stark explains that he has received the maximum amount of morphine. . . .

1500   Poole appears much better after having slept soundly for several hours. He feels so well that he has gotten up and gone back to work in the Radar Department where there has been a little difficulty in one of the pieces of equipment with which he is particularly familiar. . . .

2200   Periscope depth for navigation. We expect to make landfall on the Falkland Islands tomorrow and we will need an accurate position. No luck. The sky is completely overcast. . . .

3 March 1960: (All times Queen, Zone time plus 4)

0722   Hurray for the fathometer! It indicates that we have crossed the 100 fathom curve exactly on time.

0733   Periscope depth in attempt to obtain a sight of the sun. This combination with the fathometer indication might give us a fairly good position. No luck however. It is still overcast.

0800   Estimate we are 35 miles from the Falkland Islands. Will conduct a photo reconnaissance as before, on Port Stanley. . . .

0950   Radar contact on the Falkland Islands—another landfall on schedule. The photo reconnaissance party under Lt. Harris is standing by with their instruments at the ready. Although the pictures of St. Peter and St. Paul Rocks turned out fairly well, our prints look too much like HIJMS *Mikuma* shortly before she sank during the Battle of Midway. We hope to do better on the Falklands.

At this point Jim Stark reappears, his recent good cheer notably absent. Poole has suffered a third and by far the most violent attack of the entire series. In this instance in Jim's opinion, there is no doubt that either he is seriously in difficulty with the original stone, which may not have been passed after all, or else he is passing a series of them. In either case, there is no telling how long this will continue and to what condition he will ultimately be reduced. Nobody wants to turn back. Poole himself begs that we go on, says he is sure this will be the last time. Everyone in the ship seems to be staring at me. Their eyes are eloquent. It is reassuring to have a doctor on board to fall back on in these serious matters.

It isn't as though I have not had plenty of opportunity to think the situation over. We certainly cannot go on like this. It is my duty to get our shipmate to a place where he can receive x-rays and special studies, and as soon as possible. We dare not go farther. Since we were informed by dispatch several days ago that the USS *MACON* was in Montevideo Harbor, I made the decision to go in there.

1020   The decision made, it is simply done. I pick up the telephone, call the Officer of the Deck, order him to change course to head for Montevideo Harbor, increase speed to maximum, and secure the Photo Reconnaissance Party. In the meantime Will Adams, Bob Bulmer, Jim and I sit down to compose a message. . . .

1248   Periscope depth to transmit our message requesting assistance

445

from the *MACON*. There is just one way in which there may be a reasonable possibility of not aborting our unprecedented submerged voyage, and it is really entirely out of our hands. After a terse statement of the situation, we simply announce that we are heading at maximum speed to a point off Montevideo where we will arrive about midnight on the night of the 4th of March. "Can the *MACON* meet us there, receive Poole, and take him to where he can get the help he needs?" is the plea we compress into brief naval phraseology. This is a bad time to transmit messages, it being well known that you get much greater range at night. But we don't have that kind of time. We have no idea what sort of schedule the *MACON* is on.

1415   Our message has been delivered, not to the nearest U.S. Radio Station, but to Guam, 8300 miles away as the crow flies—straight across the South Pole and into the Pacific— if a crow could stand the temperature. . . .

Since turning back, except for the time spent transmitting our call for help, *TRITON* has been racing northward, deep beneath the sea, at the maximum speed that her two great propellers can drive her. There is no noticeable motion in the ship, not even vibration. All we note is a slight drumming of the superstructure from her swift passage through the water. Forward she is as steady as a church, as solid, and as quiet.

In the control and living spaces, the ship has quieted down, too. Orders are given in low voices; the men speak to each other, carry out their normal duties, in a repressed atmosphere. A regular pall has descended upon us. I know that all hands are aware of the decision and recognize the need for it. Perhaps they are relieved that they did not have to make it. But it is apparent that this unexpected illness, something that could neither have been foreseen nor prevented, may ruin our submergence record. If the *MACON* cannot meet us, if we have to go into the port of Montevideo to transfer Poole to medical authorities, we shall have to surface. We shall still, in that event, continue the cruise, for this would affect only our incentive factor. But that would be a big loss.

2300   Periscope depth. Maybe there will be a message for us—there could be, though it is probably too soon.

2325   There is, indeed, a message for us from Admiral Daspit. Admiral Stephan is getting underway in the *MACON* and will meet us at the time and place we have requested. The Navy can sure come through any place in the world! The news is immediately announced to the entire ship and at the same time we can now announce how we shall handle the rendezvous and transfer. We will not surface, at least, not fully. With Poole and the "topside party" in the conning tower, we will seal it off from the rest of the ship by dogging down the lower hatch. Then we'll "broach," that is, get the upper part of our sail out of water high enough to open the upper conning tower hatch. The broached condition will in fact make the transfer easier, since we'll not be so high above *MACON*'s boat. Poole will be all ready, all necessary papers strapped to his belt, and once he's in the boat we'll simply ease back down and be on our way.

4 March 1960 (All times Queen, zone plus 4)

Flank speed all day. One can almost become lyrical thinking of the tremendous drive of the dual power plant of this grand ship. Except in calm water, there are probably not more than a few dozen ships in the world which can go as fast as we are right now, and we are doing it deep beneath the surface where they can't go. Lt. Curt Shellman, Main Propulsion Officer, reports with delight that the engines seem to be running smoother and quieter at flank speed than they were at our normal cruising speed, in itself pretty fast. . . . Almost with disbelief, we note what speed we are registering. And, looking at the various gages of the propulsion equipment, we realize we have but scratched the surface of *TRITON*'s real potential. If we were really to let her out, as we might have to in war, she has even more under her belt.

5 March 1960 (All times Queen, zone plus 4)

Our rendezvous with *MACON* is for 2 A.M. At 0100 we

slowed and came to periscope depth. *MACON* is out there waiting for us.

The rendezvous is perfect. She is heading south, we north, and the two ships meet at the designated position.

0245   Approximately in position for the transfer.

0250   Broached on safety tank. Ship's draft reduces to 40 feet, indicating that the top of the conning tower is five feet out of water. All hands are ready; the lower conning tower hatch is shut. I hastily don a jacket and a cap and then direct Curtis K. Beacham, QM1(SS), to crack open the conning tower upper hatch very cautiously in case there is an inch or two of water above it—which indeed there is. A small cascade pours down through the barely opened hatch, and we jam it shut again. This is remedied by a short blast of high pressure air into our most forward tank, thus lifting the bow a foot or two above the swells and giving a better drainage angle to the bridge.

A second time I direct Beacham to open the hatch, and this time no water comes in. We are out of water. He holds it at a quarter-inch opening for a minute or two to be sure that water is not sweeping over it. None does. We are definitely out. "Open the hatch!" I tell him. He flips it open, jumps out. I am right behind him. As I swing up the ladder to the bridge, one deck above, by pre-arrangement Beacham jumps below again and slams the hatch nearly closed, ready to shut it instantly the rest of the way should it swamp.

It is a bit of a lonely feeling to be the only man topside in an 8000 ton ship which is 99% under water. We have been very careful with our computations, but there's always the possibility that some miscalculation somewhere, or a sudden change in water density, might send the whole thing back down again. There is however not much time to dwell upon this, and besides there's very little chance it will happen. *TRITON*'s crew is too well trained, too intent on doing this thing correctly. Will Adams, Bob Bulmer and Tom Thamm are down below watching over this operation like old mother hens, and nearly everyone else is standing by his station just in case. There won't be any mistakes down there. . . .

It is pretty dark but there seems to be fair visibility, despite a drizzle of rain. I fumble for the bridge command speaker, find the knob just where it is supposed to be. Pressing upon it, I call the conning tower and, to our mutual and infinite pleasure, Will Adams immediately answers from down below. We had pretty well expected this instrument to be grounded out from its prolonged submergence and it is a boon to find it in working order.

With communication once established, things are a great deal easier. I pick up the binoculars, scan the *MACON* and the water between us. We are lying to, stern into the wind, about five hundred yards downwind from her. She is broadside to us, her decks amidships ablaze with lights where her deck crew is hoisting out a motor whaleboat. All we have to do is receive their boat, when it comes, and keep a careful watch on the other ship to ensure that she does not drift down upon us. This will be easy, since our radar is constantly reporting ranges.

I reach forward, press the 7MC command communication button and call into it, just to make sure: "Control, Bridge, keep and log ranges to the *MACON* and report immediately when she commences to close."

The return from Bob Bulmer in the Control Room is immediate; "Range 600 yards, Bridge, and steady."—Then a minute later, "Bridge—From the *MACON*, their boat is in the water heading toward us."

I acknowledge over the 7MC and direct my next order to Will Adams in the conning tower. "Conn, Bridge—send George Sawyer and the topside line handling party to the bridge, through the conning tower hatch." We had already arranged that this group of people under our first lieutenant and gunnery officer would be standing by with all necessary equipment. Upon the order they would proceed up one by one to the bridge and prepare to receive the lines from the *MACON*'s boat when it comes alongside.

Will Adams' answer from Conning tower comes back immediately "Line handlers are standing by. We will open the lower conning tower hatch as soon as ready."

A few minutes later, "Bridge, Conn—request permission to open the bridge hatch and send line handling party topside." I press the speaker button and respond, "Bridge, aye, permission granted."
In a moment George Sawyer's determined voice resounds from the bridge, "Line handlers on the lower bridge, sir, Sawyer and three men."

I have been looking over the side and making up my mind as to which is the better angle for the boat to approach from; the starboard side looks a bit better; besides, the access door from our sail is on that side. "Standby to take them along the starboard side, George," I call down to him, "I'll signal the boat to make our starboard side." "Starboard side, aye aye," from Sawyer. The four people with him are Peter P. J. Kollar, Gunner's Mate first class; Wilmot A. Jones, Torpedoman's mate second class; Thomas J. Schwartz, torpedoman's mate third class; and David F. Boe, seaman.
The noises emanating from the lower bridge indicate that Lt. Sawyer and his men are breaking out the necessary gear, stored there in a watertight tank, to receive the boat alongside. Each man has on an inflatable life jacket with attached flashlight, and a safety belt with traveler.
The latter device is the result of an accident several years ago in northern latitudes, when the U.S. Submarine *TUSK* rescued the crew of the sinking submarine, *COCHINO*. In preparation for the rescue, *TUSK* rigged life lines on deck forward. Nevertheless, a huge sea came aboard, swept the people on deck off their feet against the lifeline and broke it, plunging them all into the sea. Herculean efforts on the part of the *TUSK* got most of them back aboard, but a number lost their lives in the freezing water.
As a result of this accident, a safety track similar to a railroad rail was installed on the decks of all submarines. Anyone going topside in bad weather or under hazardous conditions wears a strong canvas belt, with chain and traveler attached. The traveler clamps over and slides along the safety track, and may only be put on or removed from the track at certain places. This arrangement permits a man to move back and

forth on deck and still remain firmly attached to the ship by a short length of very strong chain (with a "quick release" hook in case of need). When two people want to pass each other, the technique is to seek a safe moment and quickly exchange travelers by unsnapping the chains from one's own belt and snapping the other man's into it.

I am well aware of all these historical matters as I look over the side and ponder the advisability of letting George and his people go down on deck. Seas are sweeping freely across our deck aft but that is of no particular importance at the moment. Our bow is staying about a foot out of water, but aft around the conning tower, where I am looking over the side, the deck is occasionally inundated with water.

The night is cold and dark, completely overcast, and a light drizzle is falling. The sea feels warm. With a little luck, George and his men will very likely have no difficulty under conditions as they are. But the risk looks a little too great. With a low freeboard the transfer is aided, provided it isn't so low that there is risk to your deck crew. Besides, even though Poole is at the moment having a remission, partly with the help of morphine, transferring him under any but the best conditions for his health and safety is out of the question. Again, there is really no decision to be made at all.

Technicalities about staying submerged have got to give way to the realities of the situation; the safety of the people involved in this operation is more important than anything else. We will have to come up a little higher. I push the button energizing the microphone to the Control Room, "Control, Bridge, blow forward group for one second."

"Forward group, one second, aye aye," from Control. Almost simultaneously, I hear air whistling into the tanks forward. It blows for a long second, stops abruptly. The effect is most apparent. The ship having previously been carefully brought to perfect trim, addition of a thousand pounds or so of buoyancy in the forward section lifts her until the displacement (not weight) of *TRITON*'s above-water volume equals that of the water displaced by the air in the tank. The superstructure, being entirely free to flood, displaces very little water, except for the conning tower itself, and the forward section rises about two feet. The main deck in the area of conning tower and sail is now fairly clear, only an occasional wave slapping over it. Sawyer's voice from below, "Permission to open the access door and go out on deck, Captain?"

"Open the door, but do not go out on deck until I give you permission." This is just to keep control to the last before letting him go. I can hear the sound of the fastenings being opened up and the door swinging wide.

George again: "Looks all clear topside, Captain, permission to go out on deck?"

"Affirmative!" I yelled back. In the distance, the lights of the approaching motor-boat are visible coming around our stern. Down below in the flickering semi-light cast by their flashlights, the men of the deck force reach through the open access door, affix their travelers to the track and then, holding their safety chains taut, step swiftly forward on the main deck. Two men quickly turn to on a collapsible cleat just forward of the sail and rotate it upward. This is the point from which we plan to take the boat's bow line.

Possibly some unknown vagary in water density or wave action has commenced to effect us as *MACON*'s boat approaches. Two or three seas roll over the foredeck. George has his men by this time arranged alongside the sail gripping the hand hold bars and of course holding on to their safety belts. As I watch them anxiously, a larger than average sea mounts up the side, and all of them are momentarily buried up to the neck. George shouts "hang on" as the water rises about them. All were already pretty well soaked and the danger is more apparent than real, but we can't let this continue. "Blow the forward group for one second," I again order the Control Room, and again there is the welcome blast of high pressure air into the tanks. This brings the deck up again and we motion the boat alongside.

In the meantime Jim Stark and John Poole have been waiting in the conning tower. We have used the last few hours, during which he has been free from discomfort, to brief Poole thoroughly on what he can say and not say once departed from *TRITON*. His transfer papers and other official documents are made up in waterproof bags and attached firmly to his person. He himself is so bundled up and swathed with protective clothing and life jackets that he can hardly get through the hatch. At the word from Stark that all is ready, I order the two men to the lower bridge. Our good-byes have already been said. There is no time for more than a last hasty "good luck" to Poole.

The boat is alongside, bow painter around the cleat and held by Wilmot Jones. Two men in the boat hold her off from our side with reversed boat hooks. Chief Fitzjarrald and Sawyer steady Poole and a couple of the men in the boat stand by to catch him. Seizing a moment when the gunwale of the boat is level with the edge of our deck, Poole steps easily and quickly into it. It is a standard navy motor-whaleboat, evidently *MACON*'s lifeboat, manned with a crew of about 5 people. It is a pleasure to watch the boat's coxswain maneuver his frail craft alongside. There is no doubt that he knows his business. Poole hasn't even got wet, and the boat's gunwale has only once touched our side. In a moment the riding line is cast off. The men with boat hooks push hard, the coxswain guns the engine, and they are away. Another moment suffices to get George and company back on the lower bridge. Then they are below, hatch shut behind them.

While waiting for further word from the *MACON*, Machinist's Mate Bob Carter is busy with a hack-saw taking off the loose bridge guard rail we had noticed. In a few minutes the welcome word comes from our Communications Officer, Lt. Bob Brodie, in Radio: "Bridge, Radio—from the *MACON*—Poole safely on board."

Among the papers Poole has with him are personal letters of appreciation to Admiral Stephan and Captain Reuben Whitaker. More than our thanks for their help, there is little information we can give them about our trip. They must be bursting with curiosity. We sent a final message of thanks and then, with topside clear and hatch shut, I order Dick Harris, Diving Officer of the Watch, to return to periscope depth. The air bubble in our tanks is released, and gently *TRITON* eases her sail into the warm sea. The total time with the bridge above water has been less than an hour. With a deep feeling of gratitude for the way the Navy has come through, we shape our course at maximum speed southward.

Now that we have successfully solved the difficult problem about Poole, the atmosphere in our ship lightens considerably. With everything wide open, *TRITON* is again heading for Cape Horn. This time we will pass to the west of the Falkland Islands and head for Estrecho de Le Maire, a small strait between Staten Island (familiar name) and the main part of Tierra del Fuego. We calculate that we will have gone 2,000 miles out of our way on this mercy mission, and it has cost several days. The distance is almost equal to an Atlantic transit. . . .

7 March 1960 (All times Romeo, Zone Time Plus 5)

1408 Upon reaching longitude 67°–00′ west we have officially passed from the Atlantic to the Pacific Ocean and from the control of ComSubLant to ComSubPac. We will, at last, carry out the photo reconnaissance practice which had been denied us at the Falkland Islands. Our photographers on photo reconnaissance party, Lt. Harris and CTC W. R. Hadley, are on the job and complete their assignment in good order. Photos of this famous Cape will shortly be posted.

It has additionally been announced that any sailor rounding Cape Horn must, if possible, get a look at it. This was considered bad luck in the days of sail, when the sight of Cape Horn was usually the result of either bad navigation or bad weather conditions and generally portended a serious accident. But deliberately sighting the Cape is a privilege—in fact, a duty—devolving on any seaman fortunate enough to round it under conditions permitting him to do so. It has consequently been directed that all men aboard, one by one, file

The *Triton's* cruise.

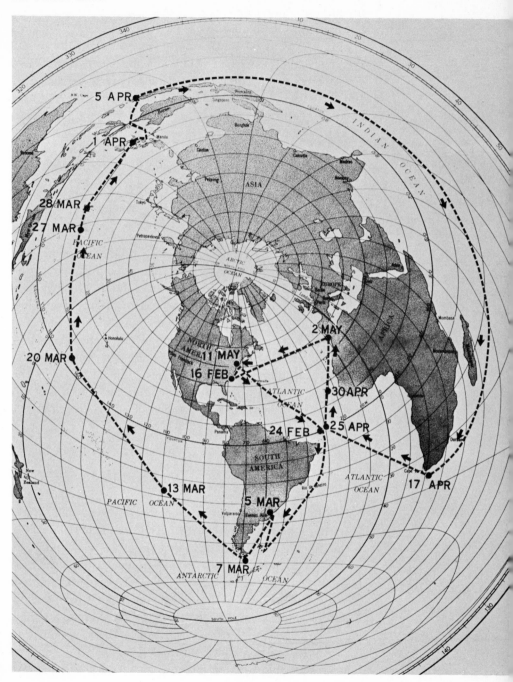

up into the conning tower and take a look at this Cape which has figured so in the history of our country. . . .

1705   We have had to go by the Cape twice in order to permit everyone to get a look at it. Technically speaking we have crossed from the Atlantic to the Pacific, back to the Atlantic, and then back to the Pacific. Now we set forth on the next leg of our journey. Our next stop is Easter Island. Magellan passed by just over the horizon and failed to see it. We have selected it, however, because it is on our track, and because it is about the only point of interest in the immediate vicinity. From Cape Horn to Easter Island the distance is 2,500 miles.

8 March 1960 (All times Romeo, Zone Plus 5)

1111   Passed over a sea mount registering minimum depth 350 fathoms. Total height of sea mount 7,000 feet above the ocean floor. The Pacific seems to have fewer of these than the Atlantic, probably because there is no sharply discernible mid-Pacific ridge corresponding to the mid-Atlantic ridge. . . .

1325   For the drill today, emergency shutdown of both reactors and loss of all power was simulated. In reality this double casualty is most unlikely; nevertheless it is one we should practice. The drill went very well, and we carried out the procedures laid down in the instructions on operation of nuclear reactors. . . .

12 March 1960 (All times Sierra, Zone Plus 6)

. . . Tomorrow we should reach Easter Island where we intend to conduct another photographic reconnaissance drill. Nick Mabry, who is aboard from the Hydrographic Office, happens to have a copy of AKU-AKU by Thor Heyerdahl, with him. This we should have thought of while planning our cruise. At any rate, Nick is having trouble reading his own book. It has had such a sudden vogue of popularity that we have to issue instructions that no one may take it from the Air Control Center. It must be left there so that all those attempting to read it simultaneously will at least have a chance to look at it for a few minutes now and then.

One of our objectives at Easter is to identify and perhaps

photograph one of the huge monolithic statues which some ancient tribe built there. Heyerdahl's expedition records the spot where they replaced one on its pedestal. Maybe we can spot it.

13 March 1960 (All times Tango, Time Zone Plus 7)

0706   Commenced photographic reconnaissance of northeastern coast of Easter Island. About 0930, after careful search of the area, Thor Heyerdahl's statue is located, right where he said it was. Several other old stone heads have been sighted, none clearly identifiable from a distance, but there is no doubt about this one. The word is passed throughout the ship that anyone wishing to see a stone statue had better come to the conning tower.

In no time at all there is a regular procession of men coming up for periscope liberty, as was the case off Cape Horn. The statue faces inland and not much can be made out of its features, but the morning sun glints in orange and crimson upon the angular granite—and many details are filled in by our imaginations, reinforced by Heyerdahl's book.

In the meantime we have been carefully searching the shore and slopes of Easter Island to detect any movement of personnel or any possibility of our periscope being spotted. The possibilities are remote; not many people spend much time gazing at the unchanging landscape of the South Pacific ocean. Nevertheless it is a possibility—but search as we may, not a single moving creature is seen on the island. A number of habitations are seen, one, not far from the statue, consisting of a small but attractive pink stucco house surrounded by well-tended foliage and an apparently nicely graded dirt road.

1116   Took departure from Easter Island enroute Guam, 6734 miles distant. . . .

14 to 16 March 1960

As we slowly approach the equator for the second time, we notice a continual rise in water injection temperature. Main condenser vacuum naturally reduces under these conditions and as we had expected there is a slight reduction in speed by consequence of the reduced thermal efficiency of the condensers. At 1500T on 14 March, we turned clocks back one hour to conform with zone time Uniform, plus 8; and at this time on 16 March we again turned clocks back one hour to conform to Victor (plus 9) zone time. . . .

19 March 1960 (All times William, Zone time plus 10)

As we approach the equator from Easter Island, on course approximately west by north, our track leads us clear of all land; but in some cases we pass not too many miles distant. There are indeed variations in depths of the water, according to the charts, though not as severe as those in the Atlantic. But should we be seriously off our course, we might find ourselves in rapidly shoaling water, perhaps on the approach to a coral atoll or even more possibly an uncharted growing atoll.

1210 Our sonar has detected a submerged peak with an estimated height above the ocean floor of some 12,000 feet. The highest point, as nearly as we can determine, may be in the neighborhood of 300 fathoms.

Sunday, 20 March 1960 (All times William, Zone Time plus 10)

0805 Another submerged ridge, dead ahead. Instead of changing course to go around as has been our practice to date, this time we watched carefully as *TRITON* approached the submerged ridge and noted all indications confirming its existence. Minimum depth was estimated at about 500 fathoms; and at the appropriate time as we approached and passed over it, indication was received on the gravity meter. . . .

1800 We are now at our closest point of approach to Pearl Harbor. In honor of the occasion a ship's party has been planned for this moment. Bob Fisher's commissary department, led by First Class Cook William ("Jim," naturally) Crow, has really outdone itself in preparing the traditional fixings for a fancy Hawaiian Luau. . . .

Many aloha shirts are in evidence, and a number of beachcomber outfits. Several of the crew have either found or in some manner manufactured straw hats, and despite the crowded conditions existing just before we shoved off from New London, to my amazement a king-size guitar and a set of bongo drums suddenly appear.

One or two hula dancers also have showed up, but somehow, it seems, our party goers would rather have their illusions than face the reality (i.e., the hairy-legged hula dancers which are the only ones we can provide).

Monday, 21 March 1960 (All times William Zone Time Plus 10)

Shortly after midnight, as we came to periscope depth for celestial observations, it was discovered that the sextant built into our new periscope had gone out of order. This will be a serious blow if we can't fix it, ameliorated only by the fact that running submerged as we are we find that our dead-reckoning is most phenomenally accurate. Rarely has our estimated position deviated from our actual observed position by more than a mile or two. It appears that currents and other forces affecting surface ships during transits are much less a factor during submerged runs. To paraphrase an aphorism, "deep waters run still."

0531   Periscope sextant is back in commission as the result of some rather inspired work by L.D. Garlock, FTCA(SS) and W. E. Constantine, FTL(SS).

Wednesday, 23 March 1960 (All times Xray, Zone time plus 11)

0834   Crossed International Date Line from west longitude to east longitude at latitude 10°–36′ North. . . .

Friday, 25 March 1960 (All times Mike, Zone Time minus 12)

. . . 24 March has been dropped from our calendar. This day—a full day from the lives of all hands—has this date been extracted in tribute for crossing the date-line (technically speaking we have advanced all clocks to Mike zone (Zone Time minus 12). We shall also have to do penance by working the ship for 24 full 25-hour days before we get home again, some of which has already been done. . . .

Sunday, 27 March 1960 (All times Lima, Zone Time Minus 11)

0840   Sonar reports an apparent distant echo ranging signal: 6 to 7 pings; then there is an interval of silence followed by another set of transmissions. This will bear a little investigation so the ship is slowed and maneuvered in an attempt to obtain better information on its characteristics. It seems to change from long scale to short scale and possibly very slightly in frequency.

0934   We deduce that a fishing vessel is using sonar in an attempt to locate or maintain contact on a school of fish. This is a known technique employed by the Japanese and others, and would explain the apparent erratic movements of the echo-ranging ship. Whoever it is, it is distant and obviously has no relation to us. Resumed course and speed.

1349   We will soon be passing through our nearest point of approach to the presumed location at which the first *TRITON* (SS-201) was lost in action during World War II. As a matter of interest, this took place almost exactly seventeen years ago, and by a strange coincidence the first *TRITON* departed on her last patrol from Brisbane, Australia, on the same day (16 February) as we . . . departed from New London. *TRITON I* is presumed to have been lost as a result of depth charge attack by three Japanese destroyers on 15 March 1943, in a position almost exactly 800 miles due south of where we are now. . . .

The services were announced at 1340, with directions that all hands not on watch assemble in the Crew's Mess, the Air Control Center or the Officer's Wardroom. At 1345 the services were broadcast throughout the ship, begun by rendition of Tattoo. This was followed by the National Anthem and a scripture reading from Psalms 107.

Following the scripture reading a short prayer similar to the committal service was read, followed by reading of the tribute, which could hardly be called an eulogy but which was an attempt to put the significance of the occasion into words for our own better inspiration and understanding: The sacrifice made by the first *TRITON* and all the sacrifices by all the people lost in all the wars of our country, sanctify the service of those who follow in their footsteps.

Rendering of proper honors gave considerable occasion for thought, and it finally was decided that the only salute a submarine can fire is actually the most appropriate one anyway. Upon command, *TRITON's* course was changed to due south and the officer of the deck was directed to stop all engines. The entire ship's company, was then brought to attention by order of the officer of the deck, all directed to face forward. This was, of course, possible even at their regular watch stations. Then, with the entire crew silently at attention, the forward torpedo tubes were fired three times in rapid succession.

We could hear the resounding echo of the water ram and feel the fluctuation of air pressure on our ear drums. Three times the harsh war-like note traveled through the ship and as the last air-fluctuation died away, the clear notes of Taps sounded in the distance.

The bell of the old *TRITON*, normally located on an overhead hanger in the Crew's Mess Hall, was taken down from its regular place and set on a table in front of the assembled crew and officers. Flanking it to the left were the National Colors, supported by Floyd W. Honeysette, QM2(SS). Alongside him stood Max L. Rose, SN, Color Guard.

The moment of reverence was a real one, truly caught. Everyone on board felt it; and though their response was by command, their personal participation sprang from deep within themselves and was given willingly.

1404   Memorial Services completed. Resumed base course and Speed.

Monday, 28 March 1960 (All times Kilo, Zone Minus 10)

0725   We should be within sight of both Guam and Rota, according to our calculations. Periscope depth to see.

0726   At periscope depth. Guam, bearing 268°True, is nearly dead ahead. Rota bears due north. Another perfect landfall to the credit of our Navigators, Will Adams and Bob Bulmer, and their very able assistants, Chief Quartermaster William J. Marshall and Curtis K. Beacham, QM1(SS). We intend to make another photographic reconnaissance of the island of Guam. It is good training, furnishes a welcome break in the monotony of the trip, and provides us with a record of what we have seen. . . .

As we prepare for our reconnaissance our vision is occasionally obscured by a succession of torrential downpours which come marching in from the north. At times the rain is so heavy that it is impossible to see more than a few hundred yards in any direction. Our photographic efforts therefore are under unusual difficulty—that of timing the showers so that part of the island we wish to photograph is for the time being clear. . . .

Today is a big day for Edward S. Carbullido, SD2(SS), USN. Carbullido was born on Guam and has youthful memories of the period of Japanese occupation during the war. Subsequently, when old enough, he enlisted in the U.S. Navy and has been in the Navy for 14 years during which he has never returned to his home island. Today is, in fact, the closest he has ever been. We wish it were possible to let him go ashore for a few days, and we shall do as much as we can for him.

Carbullido's father is a Chief Quartermaster in the Navy, now retired and living here. He has recently built a new home in the town of Agat, just to the southward of Orote peninsula, around the point of land from Apra Harbor and the main city in Guam, Agana. . . .

We spread a map of Guam on the Wardroom table and require of Carbullido that he pinpoint, as accurately as he can, exactly the spot where his parents' house is. In "The Skipper's Corner," a column which I write occasionally for the ship's newspaper, I have explained that today, after we have carried out our scheduled drill photographing the Island of·Guam, we shall expend a few hours giving Carbullido the best possible look we can through the periscope at his home town. This seems to suit everyone. . . .

462

Carbullido is ready a full hour ahead in the Conning Tower, wearing a clean suit of dungarees and grinning self-consciously. As we approach Agat, he gets his turn with the periscope alternately with the Executive Officer and myself. His eagerness is evident as we approach closer and closer, and the objects on shore become clearer to him. . . . As we draw closer, we insist upon Carbullido identifying his father's house, which he feels he can do from the descriptions and pictures he has received by mail. Finally, with a wide smile, he has it spotted, and we all eagerly take turns to look it over. . . . We stay a long time at slow speed in Agat Bay in order to give Carbullido the maximum periscope liberty possible. 1630 We have been in Agat Bay an hour and ten minutes; it is time to go. Carbullido's eyes are shining as he thanks everyone in the Conning Tower and starts down the ladder into the Control Room.

One of the things which has impressed me from the beginning of this episode is the consideration and kindness of the rest of the crew and the conning tower personnel for their shipmate. So far, at every landfall we have made, there has always been a number of men wanting to come up for a look; off Cape Horn and Easter Island there had been a determined effort to get as many people as possible to the periscope so that they could say that they had seen them. In this instance, not a soul has asked for permission to come up and take any of Carbullido's periscope time; and if he had been the Captain of the ship himself, he could not have received more attention or assistance from the quartermasters with regard to focusing the periscope, aiming it in the right direction, setting his bearings, etc. As Carbullido's grateful face vanishes below the conning tower hatch to the Control Room, Chief Quartermaster Bill Marshall puts into words the thought which has occurred to all of us; "Wouldn't it be great if we could figure out some way to get him to Guam for a real leave? Fourteen years away from home is a long time." We have already been gone a long time too; a month and a half. To Marshall's words there is general nodding assent.

Tuesday, 29 March 1960 (All times India, Zone Minus 9)

1946   Aircraft contact bearing 070°T. Flashing red and green lights. Two nights in succession; maybe we have been detected. Who could be so persistent? Has he figured out our routine? Only a submariner could do that—maybe ComSubPac, my ex-skipper, is playing games with us; or maybe the fliers in Guam have some extra gasoline to expend. Possibly they suspect a non-U.S. submarine.

1953   We are being very cautious with our periscopes, taking only short observations and spacing them fairly far apart, in case the plane has a hot radar. Again it is noted that the bearing of the aircraft is approximately constant. A few observations and we realize the range does not seem to have changed. "Let's check the star charts," someone mutters, and all at once I feel like a fool. I run the periscope all the way up and leave it there.

In a moment, sure enough, from Chief Quartermaster Marshall in the Chart Room below: "Arcturus bears 070 at this time of night and approximately the altitude we have sighted our aircraft." Furthermore Arcturus is known to have a red glow upon occasion. Our red and green lights are simply refraction through the spray and dampness on the lens at the top of the periscope—not at all an unusual occurrence. Undoubtedly, last night's "aircraft contact" was also our friend Arcturus.

Thursday, 31 March 1960 (All times Hotel, Zone Minus 8)

0213   Periscope depth to see if the Philippine Islands are in the location they should be. We are so confident now of our submerged navigation that failure to find Suluan Island where expected would put more doubt in our minds as to the precise charted location of the islands than in our navigation. Almost, that is.

0215   Sighted Suluan Island light bearing 285, exactly where expected.·

0545   As we cross the Philippine Trench, the bottom rises precipitously to the 100 fathom curve. Our echo-ranging sonar picks it out like a brick wall as we come up on it, and once again the gravity meter indicates a rapidly shoaling bottom.

0743   Passed Desolation Point on Dinagat Island, Philippines, abeam to port, distance 3 miles. Entered Surigao Strait. We have been taking water samples of the various bodies of water through which we have passed during this voyage. One of the things for which the water samples can be used is the Naval Academy's annual Ring Dance. Part of the ceremony for the Ring Dance is to christen the class rings of the new senior midshipmen in the waters of the seven seas. As can be appreciated, getting an authentic sample of water from a remote spot of the world is sometimes difficult. We may, at least, help them out. Additionally, the class of 1945, less than a year ago, donated a small-boat navigational light to the Academy and named it the *TRITON* Light, without realizing, apparently, that their light and our ship have something very much in common. So we shall also send USS *TRITON's* own unique tribute to the *TRITON* Light.

Here in Surigao Strait there is a special reason for collecting water, and a special sample of it is going to be sent to Admiral Jesse P. Oldendorf, USN, retired. Admiral Oldendorf had command of a squadron of cruisers, destroyers, and old U.S. battleships, which, it will be remembered, crossed-the-T at the Battle of Surigao Strait. It was here that the repaired and regenerated *CALIFORNIA, TENNESSEE, WEST VIRGINIA, MARYLAND, MISSISSIPPI* and *PENNSYLVANIA* gave back the wounds they had received at Pearl Harbor on the day the war began. It was probably the last time the T will be crossed in battle.

Whitey Rubb (additional duty as water collector) assures me that there are indeed great streaks of rust to be found in the Surigao Strait water—and that, upon close inspection, it is undubitably identified as rust from old and long-sunk Japanese warship hulls. We think Admiral Oldendorf will appreciate a sample of this body of water and though he may not have the precise instruments Whitey and I do for detection of the rust streaks, I am sure he can devise an adequate test of his own. . . .

Our track leads us down Surigao Strait, across the Mindanao Sea and around Bohol Island to the west and into Bohol

Strait; thence northward to Mactan Island. This is not the same track followed by Magellan, who went east of Bohol Island to the Camotes Sea and thence southward to Cebu. This route is much too shallow for us. Mactan is a very small island lying close to the much larger Cebu and terminating Bohol Strait. On the western side of Mactan is Cebu Harbor, with north and south approaches through the channel between Cebu and Mactan. To the east of Mactan lies deep and straight Hilutangan Channel, joining Bohol Strait and the Camotes Sea.

The place we have come to see is Magellan Bay, on the north shore of Mactan Island. We shall pass through Hilutangan Channel to get there. . . . The Sailing Directions and the chart of the area show a spot on the north shore of Mactan Island, in a small indentation labelled "Magellan Bay," which is marked "Magellan Monument." To traverse these historic waters and sight this monument constitutes a high point in our cruise, already 19,700 miles long. . . .

Friday, 1 April 1960 (All times Hotel, Zone Minus 8)

We have been slowly working up Bohol Strait toward Mactan Island all night long, occasionally coming to periscope depth where radar and the periscope observations have assured us as to our safe navigation. We have likewise seen, or heard on sonar, numerous small fishing vessels and a few coastal type freighters or passenger ships. All are brightly lighted.

0608   Ejected hydrographic bottle number MT-71. Like the others the paper inside is filled out in our code, except that now on the back is written in English, "Hail Noble Captain, It is Done Again," for which Mr. Charles Parr [author of a biography of Magellan, *So Noble a Captain*] can take most of the credit, if he desires it, though my guess is that he would want this to go to Don Antonio Pigafette, Magellan's scribe. It is, of course, the translation of the Latin inscription on the plaque Tom Thamm designed to commemorate our submerged circumnavigation. We have left the pattern with our Squadron organization in New London to be cast, and have requested permission to terminate our cruise at Cadiz. Maybe the finished plaque can be brought to us there. We should like to see it delivered to the starting point of Magellan's epochal voyage. . . .

0623   Sighted two small merchant ships at range of about 1 mile steaming in close contact and apparently headed for Cebu. As we cautiously dunked the periscope, they passed within about 1,000 yards and proceeded on their way.

0722   Heard the first of a series of explosions—7 in all during the forenoon—apparently coming from the vicinity of Mactan Island. No visual dust or smoke cloud to confirm the source of the explosions, but we assume it is blasting in connection with some harbor work. . . .

0800   Entering Hilutangan Channel. Speed, 4 knots, at periscope depth. Tide and current tables indicate that we should receive a pretty strong set to the northward, in the direction we want to go. This indeed proves to be the case, since our speed over the ground is about 3 knots faster than our speed through the water. As we enter the channel, we are much interested in the picture presented by our echo-ranging sonar. The sonar-repeater in the conning tower gives an actual picture of the shape of the channel. The depth of water is in many places greater than one-hundred fathoms and the shore is steep-to. As a result, the area of shallow water near the shore is very clearly outlined on the face of our conning tower repeater. With this kind of gear we could easily go deep and proceed at high speed. Not knowing, however, exactly what we will find at the other end, we shall go through at periscope depth; perhaps on the return trip we can transit the channel at deep depth. . . .

To ensure that all craft are avoided by a safe distance, our periscope observations are frequent and carefully timed. Upon one occasion as I raised the periscope (invariably first dead ahead) and swung it around, I caught a glimpse of a canoe with neither mast nor sail. It had two occupants; a small and elderly woman with her back to us, and at the other end of the boat, facing me as I looked at him with my solitary eye, a rather portly gentleman, bare to the waist and heavily tanned, even for a Filipino. As I looked, he lifted his hand and waved at me in a manner almost as if he were saying, to his companion, "Now as I was saying, that could almost be a periscope. It looks just like that and sticks up out of the water just like that thing over there."—at which point I quickly swung the periscope around for a swift check ahead and lowered it again.

The portly gentleman did not appear particularly disturbed at our periscope and in fact probably did not recognize what it was—unless, indeed, he is a retired U.S. Navy Steward.

1057 With the help of a strong current, we have made a remarkably fast passage through Hilutangan Channel.

1100 We are past the north end of Mactan Island and enter Magellan's Bay. This bay also has very deep water extending well inside the points of land which form its two extremities, though it is very shallow close inshore. (Magellan was killed here fighting in water up to his knees.)

The picture our sonar gives us of the bottom contour corresponds closely to the chart. *TRITON* is, however, a pretty big ship to take into this tiny bay, and our navigation is rapid. There are fortunately several clearly defined landmarks as well as a couple of lighthouses upon which to take bearings. In the distance, over the end of Mactan Island, can be seen the buildings of Cebu marching up into the hillside, with the dome of the Provincial Capitol, etched white against the verdant hillside. Near the waterfront several large modern structures can be described; one in particular, which would not be out of place in any modern city, is three to five stories high and approximately three hundred feet long.

Our foray into Magellan Bay is complicated somewhat by the discovery of three tall tree-trunks sticking out of the water. Apparently they are long timbers planted on some sort of bottom structures, since they have no supporting wires of any kind. Maybe they delimit fishing areas. At all events, we carefully avoid them and the rock piles they may mark.

1120 We have been carefully, without much luck, searching the south shores of the bay to determine for sure whether the

Magellan Monument can be seen. About this time, as I scrutinize the shore, it finally bursts into full view. Without any doubt whatever, I announce to the conning tower party, "there it is!" The water is too shallow for us to approach close enough to get a really good photograph, but we take many pictures of what we can see of it from as many angles as it is possible to get them. It can be seen clearly from only one bearing, probably straight front where trees and foliage have been cut away. . . . Apparently made of masonry, probably recently white-washed, it gleams white in the sun. There are dark objects in its center which might be one or more bronze tablets or possibly openings into the interior. It is a rectangular pedestal with long dimension vertical, straight sides and a slightly curved top, standing on a set of steps or a base. The impression is that it may at one time have supported a statue or been intended to, but what we see consists in that case only of the statue base. We shall make it our business, after we are again in position to send and receive mail, to obtain a photograph of this place to keep with our records of the voyage. . . .

1146   Upon raising the periscope I am looking right into the eyes of a young man in a small dugout, close alongside. Perhaps he has detected the dark bulk of our hull in the relatively clear waters of the bay, or he may have sighted our periscope earlier. He and I study each other gravely. His boat is a small dugout, perhaps 12 feet long, innocent of any paint and without mast or sail (which is why he got so close in on us). He has a paddle with which he easily maintains a position abeam of us·at our present slow speed. He looks ahead and looks behind, looks down in the water and maintains position about 50 yards abeam with occasional muscular sweeps of his paddle. Our friend is a dark complectioned moon-faced young man with a well-fed physique. His clothing is tattered and he wears some kind of a battered hat for protection from the sun. Our photographic party obtains several pictures of him which will be interesting to look over at greater leisure. "Down periscope!" The steel tube slithers down into its well as I describe the scene above to the people in the conning tower. They would all like to get a look at him. . . .

I motion for the scope to slide up once more. Sure enough, there is our friend impassively leaning on his gunwales and staring right at the periscope as we raise it barely two inches out of the water. "We've played with this gent long enough," I mumble inaudibly. Spinning the periscope around for one last cut on the now-familiar landmarks and to say aloha to Magellan and his intrepid spirit, I sight a fair course between the nearest set of poles, take a final look at our friend in the dugout canoe, and snap up the periscope handles as a signal for it to start down. "All ahead two-thirds . . . Right full rudder!" This is something our swarthy friend won't be able to handle. *TRITON* slips neatly ahead of him and away to the right. Upon slowing for a look a few minutes later I spot the dugout many hundreds of yards away, paddling rather strongly in the wrong direction.

In the conning tower, the irrepressible Bill Marshall says aloud, "Wonder what he is going to tell his friends in Cebu tonight." Quartermaster second class Russell K. Savage probably has the right answer: "They won't believe a word he says." As *TRITON* eases slowly out of the bay checking her position every two minutes or so because of the swift currents we have encountered, we are all aware that today will go down as one of the high points of our trip. Poetically speaking, we have come more than half way around the world to see this spot. . . .

2035   Entered Sulu Sea. Will spend the rest of the night and tomorrow morning crossing the Sulu Sea enroute to the Celebes Sea and departure from the waters of the Philippine Republic.

Saturday, 2 April 1960 (All times Hotel, Zone Minus 8)

0047   There is severe oscillation in our gyro repeaters probably caused by something wrong with one or more synchro amplifiers. Shifted to direct gyro input to the helmsman and began to check-out the synchro amplifiers. After some moments the oscillations ceased and the situation reverted to normal. This may be a warning of trouble to come.

With the trouble gone, we are for the moment unable to

470

determine what is the precise cause of the difficulty. . . .

0859   At periscope depth to fix our position prior to passing through the Pearl Bank Passage and then through Sibutu Passage into the Celebes Sea. Locating and passing through Pearl Bank Passage is somewhat like threading a needle. There is a difference, however. Should we miss the deep water hole between reefs, we have an excellent chance of digging a groove in the coral with our bow. The land is very low-lying hereabouts and it is difficult to detect by periscope or radar. A complication develops when a ship is sighted hull down on bearing 076°T, approximately 8 miles away. From course and speed it is quite possible that this fellow may be the one we detected on sonar seven hours ago. If so, we have run right past him. Very likely *TRITON* and he are trying to thread the same needle. Proximity of the ship prevents us from raising our periscope as high as we might like or using our retractable radar to fix our position accurately. The sea is nearly glassy; any unusual activity in the water would attract notice. Went deep, increased speed and headed for the presumed position of the Pearl Bank Passage.

1130   Periscope depth again, land in sight more clearly, and we are now obtaining a rough position. Changed course to head for the presumed location of Pearl Bank Passage when again we sight the same ship, range now only seven miles, bearing 030°T.

1245   This ship is going to give us trouble. He is much higher out of the water than we, therefore can see better, and very likely knows this area thoroughly. Although we have the speed on him, we must proceed slowly at periscope depth and with extreme caution to be sure of our position before we try to run through the narrow Pearl Bank Passage. With no such problems he has been overhauling us for the past several hours. We believe we have Pearl Bank Passage pretty well defined, now, bearing due south; and we have been steering south for about 45 minutes. We should, however, remain at periscope depth as we pass through the channel because of variable currents expected according to the Sailing Directions. Besides, Will says he still is not fully satisfied with the accuracy of our position. After thinking things over, it is

471

apparent that our best bet is to let the ship precede us. We reverse course to the north to let him go first, therefore, exercising extreme caution with our periscope and swinging wide. Commander Joe Roberts and photographer Ray Meadows are, of course, in the conning tower ready to take pictures should any opportunities develop. The merchantman, a victory type freighter of World War II with black hull, white superstructure and a black and red shape on his funnel goes by at range 3,300 yards. We are able to take a few pictures as she passes.

1310   Changed course to 180°T to follow behind the freighter. This makes it easy.

1417   Sighted Pearl Bank Light bearing 234°T and obtained the first really good fix of the day.

1436   Commenced transit of Pearl Bank Passage.

1517   Cleared Pearl Bank Passage heading for Sibutu Passage and entry into Celebes Sea. . . .

2036   Passed Sibutu Island abeam to starboard at about 7 miles.

2200   Passed into Celebes Sea, departed from waters of the Republic of the Philippines.

Sunday 3 April 1960 (All times Hotel, Zone Minus 8)

1147   Entered Makassar Strait. Departed Celebes Sea. . . .

1422   Crossed equator for the third time this voyage at longitude 119° − 05.1'E. . . .

Monday, 4 April 1960 (All times Hotel, Zone Minus 8)

0613   Sighted a sailing vessel to westward. Joe Roberts' eyes glisten as he evaluates the report. This is the kind of sailboat he has been hoping to photograph, a Makassar inter-island merchantman. As he passes nearby, Joe obtains what should prove to be excellent pictures.

0930   Completed photographing the Makassar merchantman. The vessel in many ways resembles a Chesapeake Bay schooner of the type I had seen many times from my room in Bancroft Hall at Annapolis. . . .

1700   Having come to periscope depth to get a fix on Balalohong Island Light, observed up ahead a great deal of splashing and frothing around in the water; thought for a moment that we might have found the mythical sea serpent. It next appears to be a tide rip similar to one observed earlier today, but upon closer inspection it is evident that these are big fish and little fish, and that the little fish are having a hard time. Maneuvering to close and take pictures of the operation. There are evidently at least three kinds of fish present. Nearest to us is a lazy group of porpoises swinging along and gamboling among themselves. Up ahead it is evident that the predatory fish are probably porpoises also, and we cannot understand why the band close aboard is so unconcerned with the battle-royal going on just ahead. Perhaps this is a different tribe. Try as we can to approach close enough to get a look at either group, however, we are unable to do so. Apparently they consider us an unwanted witness to whatever is going on. The lazy band of frisky porpoises avoids us by adroit maneuvers at the right time, while up ahead the fighting fish move steadily away and even the ones being eaten seem to co-operate in keeping us at a distance. It is a thrilling sight to see the sleek black bodies of the porpoises flashing around in the water. With their tremendously powerful tails working back and forth like pistons, they dash about at speeds reportedly between 20 and 30 knots. . . .

Tuesday, 5 April 1960 (All times Hotel, Zone Minus 8)

0650   Approaching Lombok Strait to enter the Indian Ocean. Lombok Strait was one of the principal submerged highways for submarines based in Australia. Situated between the islands of Bali and Lombok, it is one of the widest straits through the Malay Archipelago and is spectacular in that it has precipitous volcanic peaks on both sides. The water in the Strait is deep but treacherous because of strong currents. During the war there were reported cases of submarines spending hours at maximum sustained submerged speed only to surface at night to find that they had been going backwards. The Japanese knew that Lombok Strait was "Submarine Highway" and made efforts to close it. Generally you could depend upon at least two patrol vessels being somewhere in the area and frequently there were more than that. Toward the end of the war, before the Japanese were pushed out of this area, they took to flying patrol planes back and forth also. . . .

1030   . . . While transiting Lombok Strait we sighted several ships of various types. One was a small sailing ship similar to the one seen two days before in Makassar Strait except it had only a single mast. Later, at 0950, sighted 3 ships, apparently small Naval or Coast Guard craft, heading north up Lombok Strait. In attempting to determine the course and speed of these last sighted vessels we experienced considerable difficulty in fixing an accurate angle on the bow. Every time the periscope was raised for an observation they seemed to be heading in a different direction. There was no indication of a search pattern or deliberately erratic steering, but no two of them ever got together on a course, and they were never twice heading in the same direction. Finally, after some time, they steadied out and proceeded past us up Lombok Strait on a steady course and speed. We forgot the problem until later.

During a period while relatively free from near contacts, the opportunity was seized to inspect Bali carefully. Bali is a spectacular volcanic mountain, now extinct. Viewed from Lombok Strait it is perfectly symmetrical, in many ways similar to Mt. Fuji in Japan, the only difference being lack of a snow-cap. According to the chart, however, Bali Peak is not quite as symmetrical as Fuji for the northwestern side was blown off by an eruption a long time ago. . . .

1029   In connection with our hydrographic and oceanographic work, of which very little can be told in this report, we seized the opportunity while in Lombok Strait to obtain deep water samples, measure the general density, and observe temperature and other characteristics of the water. One of the simplest ways of measuring density is by behavior of the ship herself, since she will be considerably lighter in denser water and heavier in less dense water. Correlation with known constants can give us a very good measure of the actual water conditions. To this is added the careful analysis of the sample itself. Upon going deep in Lombok Strait there were two distinct layers found where the temperature changed rather rapidly, and at maximum submergence *TRITON* was some 20 tons lighter than at periscope depth. This was easily understood, for directly to the south were the waters of the Indian Ocean, while due north were the warmer waters of the Sunda Sea and Flores Sea.

The heavy currents reported as existing here at various depths we can also well believe, and we have measured them. The existence of these currents bears out theories regarding the meeting of the Indian Ocean and the Flores Sea, and the resulting water density changes.

1215   Sighted ship bearing 205°T, at 7,000 yards. Once again, in tracking the vessel it proved difficult at first to determine his angle on the bow because he was continually changing course. Finally he straightened out as the others did earlier today, and came by us at a reasonable range, steady course and speed. The vessel was a small but beautifully maintained trawler type. Probably a fisherman, possibly a government vessel or even a small yacht.

1300   Through the periscope sighted ahead a ridge of water several feet high, apparently caused by the confluence of the waters sweeping down from the north through Lombok Strait and those of the Indian Ocean coming up from the south. About this time the Diving Officer commenced to have difficulty in maintaining periscope depth at ⅓ speed, ⅔ speed was ordered to give him a little more control. In spite of this, and with a slight up-angle, the ship slowly drifted downward, thinking all the time this would shortly stop, when suddenly the depth gauges began to spin; depth increased to 125 feet in the space of 40 seconds. Standard speed was ordered to pull out of the involuntary dive, and we steadied out at 125 feet, shortly thereafter regaining periscope depth with an entirely new set of trim readings.

In reconstructing the incident, it would appear that a strong northerly current from the Indian Ocean had been setting in to Lombok Strait for some time, but that a current from the north had also commenced to make up. This would account for the apparent ridge or wall of water which we had seen ahead, for the variations of the water density as we went deep not long before, and for the erratic courses of the ships we had been watching.

At the point where we experienced the sudden change in depth it would appear that there must have been a swirling, perhaps a downward current of water as the Indian Ocean current met Lombok Strait current.

Nick Mabry, the Hydrographic Office representative for oceanography, confirms our hypothesis as being a probable one. It was as though we had hit a hole in the water—similar to an "air-pocket" in an aircraft—and had commenced to fall. Under the circumstances, *TRITON's* size, tremendously strong hull and great power pretty well eliminated any danger, especially since we had tight control of the ship at all times; but, the situation of a wartime submarine with a weaker hull and only battery power is less comfortable. I had experienced changes in water density many times before, but never one of this magnitude. . . .

1400   With all contacts pretty well out of sight, periscope liberty was announced for those who might be interested. Approximately 75 crew members came in to the conning tower to say a fond hello and sad farewell to Bali of the beauteous damsels. They will at least be able to say they have seen it—and incidentally, despite all argument, the song Bali Hi was not written about Bali. . . .

Sunday, 10 April 1960 (All times Foxtrot, Zone Minus 6)

0000   Ventilation secured after a thorough sweep-out of the atmosphere. . . . One of the requirements of the cruise is to conduct a sealed-ship test under controlled conditions for observation of certain phenomena. Our time with a sealed atmosphere will not approach that of *SEAWOLF* in 1958, mainly because of the expense of all that oxygen, nor does it need to, so far as this test is concerned. But since we are a brand new ship, this is one of the things we need to accomplish merely to develop our own techniques and limiting factors.

The Medical Research Laboratory in New London has been pursuing this particular project for a long time, the first announced test being Operation Hideout in the moth-balled submarine *HADDOCK* in 1953. In our case, probably the forerunner of a number of associated tests which will be required from time to time from various submarines, there are particular things that the Medical Research Laboratory wishes to investigate. Doctors Ben Weybrew and Jim Stark have been putting their heads together for several days and finally have come up with a proposed procedure. We will remain sealed for approximately 2 weeks, running various physical and psychological tests among selected volunteers from the crew. Somewhere during the mid-point of this period we will put out the smoking lamp for an extended time. Careful checking of all factors will continue for several more days before terminating the study. The non-smokers among our crew are lording it over the others, but there is a definite apprehension among the heavy smokers and I tell Dr. Weybrew, "The psychological reaction has already started." A quizzical grin is his only response (later I learned that in anticipation of this period he had placed his only pipe, purchased just before he came aboard, in the garbage ejection chute). . . .

1500   . . . We all realize that upon completion of the trip we will have counted one less day than our friends who remain behind, but we will not, as did Magellan's mariners and Phileas Phogg from Jules Verne's story, find ourselves at variance in reckoning the date. When we have girdled the globe at St. Peter and St. Paul Rocks on the 25th of April, it will be exactly 60 of our days since we last saw these same "Rocks." We will, however, have logged a number of 25-hour days as we followed the sun westward—a net total of twenty-four, to be exact. . . .

Friday, 15 April 1960 (All times Charlie, Zone Minus 3)

0000   Out goes the smoking lamp, eliciting many unfavorable comments by the smokers, a great air of superiority on the part of the non-smokers. All hands have been carefully briefed for some time as to the purpose of the test and how it is supposed to be run, but we have avoided giving any indication as to the intended length, stating only that the operation order prescribes it shall not exceed 10 days. Ben Weybrew tells me privately that it will not have to be nearly that long, but that he wishes to avoid any complications from anticipation of an early "relight." In preparation for it Lcdr. Bob Fisher (SC), USN, (the only supply corps officer attached to and serving on board a submarine) has laid in a stock of candy and chewing gum. It is shortly discovered that some of the men had apparently also brought along a supply of chewing tobacco, which introduces an unforeseen variable into Jim Stark's and Ben Weybrew's test. Some of their volunteer subjects had neglected to mention their intentions to chew tobacco in place of smoking during this period. It was noted too that cigars are at a premium since they can be cut into short lengths and chewed also.

Saturday, 16 April 1960 (All times Charlie, Zone Minus 3)

The smoking lamp is still out and the psychological reaction building up is surprising. Although I had not felt repressed by the atmosphere in any way previously, there is to me an indefinable but definite improvement to it. It feels cleaner, somehow better, and so do I. Will Adams agrees, being also a non-smoker, but nobody else does. Tom Thamm announces that the limits of human endurance had been reached in the first 3 hours, so far as the smokers of the ship were concerned, and the remaining time of the test is purely a sadistic torture invented by Weybrew and Stark. . . .

We have nearly crossed the Indian Ocean. Tomorrow we expect to arrive at the Cape of Good Hope. It has been a pleasant trip, unmarred by submerged peaks or other alarms. The water is as uniformly deep as anywhere we have seen, not too cold, but cool and beautiful through the periscope. It is one of the least known oceans, bounded on the north by the subcontinent of India, on the west by Africa and on the east by the Malay Archipelago and Australia. Its southern boundary is Antarctica. One of its noticeable characteristics, at least so far as we have observed, is a consistently heavy sea condition, and in this it resembles the Atlantic. Every time we are at periscope depth for observations it appears that a state 3 to 4 sea is running (corresponding to wave heights from 5 to 10 feet), enough to make surface ships uncomfortable. . . .

So far as the no-smoking test is concerned, Weybrew and Stark contend that they have enough now to fulfill the requirement laid upon them by Medical Research Laboratory. It is also apparent, according to them, and I must confess having noticed something of the same myself, that the test has gone on just about long enough. Overt feelings of hostility are coming to the fore, expressed in a number of small ways, and there have been instances of increasing irritability. Deprived of a normal intake of mild stimulant there obviously have been withdrawal symptoms among the heavier smokers in the crew.

The same is evident in the officers, whom I see more frequently and on informal terms. Most noticeable, to me, are signs of forced gaiety, frequently with a sharp edge to it. Jim Stark, himself a heavy smoker, enjoys egging his wardroom buddies on—and this, in my opinion, is his compensation.

These were expected manifestations of adjustment and are cause for no particular notice, but there are also one or two cases where evidence of heightened nervous reaction is accompanied with relatively poor adjustment. In a ship's company of 183 people, something of this sort is bound to turn up. But answering my question as to what the ultimate results might be in the most severe cases if the smoking lamp could not be relighted, the savants spread their hands expressively, "Who knows?" they say. Most likely, if the man recognizes that it is impossible to smoke he will psychologically adjust to it with relative ease. Symptoms will withdraw or maladjustments will work themselves out. The point is that here in *TRITON* the only reason for prohibiting smoking is for a test. Everyone knows it requires but one word, and the smoking lamp will be lighted. Were we in a dangerous situation where safety of the ship or life of personnel were involved, as for example in an explosive atmosphere, the entire situation would be different.

Easter Sunday, 17 April 1960 (All times Bravo, Zone minus 2)

We are commencing to approach the Cape of Good Hope. Many people will be surprised to learn that the Cape of Good Hope is not actually at the southernmost tip of Africa at all. This honor is reserved for Agulhas Point, but Agulhas is not a prominent landmark like the Cape of Good Hope. . . .

0600   Periscope depth to fix position with regard to Cape of Good Hope. The sky is overcast and weather not too favorable for the photo reconnaissance which we had planned. Went deep and continued running.

1136   At periscope depth with contact on Hangklip Point, South Africa. Resumed base course and speed heading for Cape of Good Hope. As we enter the Atlantic Ocean again, we observe a noticeable drop in the water temperature. At the same time we are most anxious to notice whether there is any definable current. Charts and Sailing Directions indicate that this is the case, probably setting us to the northeast. Without a fathometer we are staying well clear of possible shoal water in anticipation of this effect. . . .

1540   . . . Mt. Vasco de Gama on the Cape of Good Hope reminds me of Diamond Head, having somewhat the same shape and dimensions, though not quite the same rugged characteristics. Possibly Good Hope is a considerably older formation. Little foliage or natural growth is visible, something of a surprise for this temperate latitude (33°S). . . .

1721   With Cape of Good Hope bearing 117°T, distance 8 miles, took departure for St. Peter and St. Paul Rocks in the mid-Atlantic. We will arrive there on the 25th of April.

Monday, 18 April 1960 (All times Bravo, Zone minus 2)

0000   Smoking lamp is relighted. Maybe I am a bit sadistic; no one was expecting it, so instead of directing that the word be passed to relight the smoking lamp, I strolled about the ship smoking a cigar, blowing smoke in the faces of the various people and inquiring in a pleasant conversational tone, "Don't you wish you could do this?" It took some 37 seconds for the word to get around.

As in any group there were probably a few of our people who secretly welcomed the no-smoking edict as a crutch to help them make the break. By far the majority had no intention of stopping; and it is noticeable that few, if any, have continued their abstinence after the smoking lamp was once lighted. . . .

Wednesday, 20 April 1960 (All times Alfa, Zone minus 1)

0100   Crossed from east to west longitude.

           Today is my birthday and also, incidentally, Lt. Sawyer's. After dinner I repaired to my cabin to work this report.

2100   Chief of the Ship Fitzjarrald came knocking on my door saying "Something is wrong down in the Mess Hall, Captain; we need you down there right away." This is a strange message for the skipper of a ship to receive.

           "What's the matter, is there a fight?" I asked, starting up from my desk. It was only a jump down the ladder to the lower deck and forward one compartment into the Crew's Mess Hall where I was greeted by popping flash bulbs, a raucous rendition of "Happy Birthday to You" and a tremendous birthday cake. The cake, prepared by Ramon D. Baney, CS2(SS), was about 2 feet square and 2 inches thick, with great extravagant gobs of frosting all over it. . . . Earlier that afternoon there had been a cake and coffee ceremony for George Sawyer in the wardroom; and consequently, it has been a very pleasant day with much good cake eaten. . . .

Sunday, 24 April 1960 (All times Zulu)

0436   Completed sealed ship test, having run sealed for exactly two weeks. Remaining sealed is considerably less strenuous than ventilating once a day, and we are sorry to go back to the earlier routine. When you ventilate, you are attempting to conserve oxygen and at the same time trying to minimize time at periscope depth. It naturally develops that just before you ventilate the ship her internal atmosphere is at its lowest in oxygen, its highest in carbon monoxide and carbon dioxide. At this time cigarettes are difficult to light, a little exertion sets one to panting, and generally one does not feel in the best of form. On the other hand, with the ship sealed you maintain a steady atmosphere and set your equipment to keep it that way.

We have learned a lot about *TRITON* during two weeks of sealed ship operations and are extremely gratified with the results. Among other things, we have had no difficulty at all in retaining our precious air inside the ship. But it was a good thing that we recognized the problem, or we might have. . . .

2001 Casualty in the After Torpedo Room. The manner in which this develops is illustrative of a point many Naval Officers are fond of making—there is no sudden alarm, no quick scurry of many people carrying out an expected drill. By the time anyone in authority even knew what had happened, the need for alarm was past. There was left only the correction of the trouble and cleanup of the mess, which took some time. What took place is instructive: The torpedoman on Watch in the After Torpedo Room (Allen W. Steele, TM3(SS) who had only last night been notified of his prospective advancement to second class) heard a loud report, as he later described it nearly like an explosion, followed by a heavy spraying noise. Turning, he saw clouds of oil vapor issuing from beneath the deck plates on the starboard side. Instantly realizing that this was trouble, Steele called the control room and reported a heavy hydraulic oil leak in the stern plane mechanism; then he plunged into the stream of oil hoping to find the leak and isolate it. In the control room, LCDR Bulmer had just relieved Lt. Rubb of the Conn, preparatory to bringing the ship to periscope depth. Rubb's first indication of trouble came when Raymond J. Comeau, Electrician's Mate second class, at the stern plane controls, called out, "The stern planes are not working right, sir!" He had noticed a failure to respond to his control arm movement. At nearly the same moment, the report of a large hydraulic leak in the After Torpedo Room was received from Steele.

Whitey Rubb's action was the one for which we have trained many times: "Shift to Emergency!" Comeau threw a single switch, tested controls and reported them satisfactory. This restored control of the ship, but it did not solve the basic difficulty. In the After Torpedo Room, Steele determined the leak to be in the stern planes normal power hydraulic system, and diagnosed it as a hydraulic failure. His third immediate decision was also a correct one. Diving into the midst of the high pressure spray, he reached the two quick-closing valves to the supply and return pipes and shut them. One came shut easily but the other was very difficult to move. Desperately struggling with the valve, with assistance by Arlan F. Martin, Engineman third class, who ran to his aid, Steele finally got it also shut. By this time, fifteen to thirty seconds after the onset of the leak, the entire after part of the compartment was filled with oil vapor and visibility was reduced to only a few feet.

With the closing of the isolation valves, the oil flow stopped immediately. Steele's action was instantaneous and precisely correct.

Personnel who behaved with credit were Arlan F. Martin, Engineman third class who ran to Steele's assistance and participated with him in shutting the last and most difficult of the two hydraulic cutoff valves, and Ronald Dale Kettlehake, who had just entered the compartment in process of tracing some system required for submarine qualification. Realizing the possible danger, he showed presence of mind by waking the dozen or more sleepers and routing them forward into the after engine room.

2002   Things had been happening so swiftly that the first anyone other than those dealing with it knew of the casualty was when the OOD ordered "Smoking Lamp is out!" "Rig After Torpedo Room for Emergency Ventilation." There had been no confusion, no warning, not even any raised voices. Tom Thamm—our damage control officer—quickly got to his feet and strode purposefully aft, followed by Jim Hay, his assistant.

2030   Steele has been recommended for award of a Secretary of the

Navy Letter of Commendation with Commendation Ribbon for meritorious service. We are preparing the papers now.

2130   Everything is pretty much back to normal so far as the After Torpedo Room and the hydraulic system is concerned, except that we are still in emergency on the planes and shall have to remain so until a replacement is found for a fractured valve.

Monday, 25 April 1960 (All times Zulu, GMT Zero)

1200   Position 00°–53' North, 29°–01' West. We are within a few miles of St. Peter and St. Paul Rocks, at which point we will have completed the first submerged circumnavigation of the world. It has taken us exactly 60 days by our reckoning, though as previously stated a person marooned here would have counted 61. But the number of hours would have been the same.

1330   St. Peter and St. Paul Rocks in sight, bearing due west.

1500   First submerged circumnavigation of the world is now complete. We are circling and photographing the islet again, as we did just two months ago. The weather is nice and the sun is shining brightly. Our mileage (Rock to Rock) is 26,723 nautical miles and it has taken us 60 days and 21 hours (days calculated as 24 hours each). Dividing gives an average overall speed of just over 18 knots. No other ship—and no other crew could have done better. We are proud to have been selected to accomplish this undertaking for our Nation.

Our total mileage for the trip will be a little more than 36,000 nautical miles (including the 2,000-mile mercy mission for our ill crewman) and it now looks as though our over-all time since departure from New London will be 85 days (New London computation). We have been instructed to proceed to a rendezvous point off Cadiz, Spain where the destroyer *WEEKS* is to meet us. *WEEKS* will send aboard the completed bronze plaque we designed in tribute to Magellan, but it is our understanding it is to be presented at a later date, possibly by the U.S. Ambassador. For the time being we are still to avoid detection, making our rendezvous off Cadiz beyond sight of curious onlookers.

We earnestly hope *WEEKS* will bring mail for us, in addition

Cutaway drawing of the USS *Triton*.

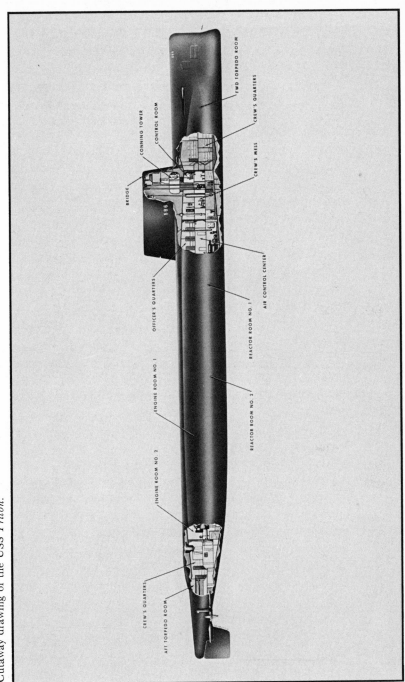

CREW'S QUARTERS

AFT TORPEDO ROOM

ENGINE ROOM NO. 2

ENGINE ROOM NO. 1

OFFICER'S QUARTERS

REACTOR ROOM NO. 2

REACTOR ROOM NO. 1

AIR CONTROL CENTER

CREW'S MESS

BRIDGE

CONNING TOWER

CONTROL ROOM

586

FWD TORPEDO ROOM

CREW'S QUARTERS

to the plaque. Even though we can depend upon our Squadron organization in New London doing everything in its power to insure our families are all right, and that it stands ready to assist them in problems large or small, there's nothing which can substitute for a letter from your loved ones (except seeing them). More than this we neither need nor want. Our provisions are still adequate, though non-scrambled eggs would certainly taste good, and our personal tobacco stocks have lasted surprisingly well despite demands placed upon them by people like Curtis Beacham, Quartermaster first class, who brought a dozen and a half boxes of cigars with him; then early in the cruise gave most of them away in an effort to break clean; and for weeks now has been abjectly relying on the occasional generosity of the friends to whom he gave them. We still do not know when or whether—knowledge of our submerged voyage will be made public. We therefore shall not surface, will only bring our high conning tower hatch clear of the sea to pass the plaque and its custodian through as we did our sick shipmate nearly two months before.

1645   A congratulatory message has arrived from our Force Commander. It is read to the crew as soon as decoded and everyone aboard very much appreciates his kind and encouraging words.

1700   Preparation of a suitable message on our part recommending Steele for official recognition, thanking Admiral Daspit for his thoughtful message and announcing a successful mission is not always so easy as the few words employed might indicate. Lt. Robert Brodie III our nearly professional communication officer, and I draft, encode, and destroy five different versions before we are finally satisfied. Whatever Bob may have thought at the extra work, he need not fear, for the time being anyway, that the expression on his face may give him away. It can't possibly. He has the most villainous-looking crop of steel wool on his face I have ever seen. Through this no "expression" could ever reach the surface.

1700   Set course for Tenerife in the Canary Islands. The city of Santa Cruz, which Parr describes as having in Magellan's day a cliff-sheltered harbor entered through a "cleft in the rocky wall" of the island of Tenerife, was the last city of the old world seen by Magellan. Provisions and supplies were cheaper there than in Spain, and it was therefore customary for voyagers of Castile to "top-off" there before making their final departure. We shall be coming at it from the other direction, but it nevertheless will make a good final "port of call." If we have time, we shall make our final photographic reconnaissance there. . . .

2145   We are not quite home, but we may be considered to have taken a long lead off third base. So, tonight, to celebrate completion of the first submerged circumnavigation and our looked-for homecoming, we hold a "third base party" for the crew and officers. . . .

Thursday and Friday, 28–29 April 1960. . . .

With a comfortable SOA (Speed of Advance) requirement and our circumnavigation complete, these two days were devoted to engineering drills. Like all nuclear ships, we have rigid qualification requirements for officers and men before they may stand certain main propulsion plant watches. . . .

0430   Periscope depth for approach on Tenerife, Canary Islands. The spectacle on raising the periscope is remarkable. Although we are still quite distant from land, the lights of the city of Santa Cruz are so high above the horizon as to give the appearance of stars, or would have were they not spaced in certain orderly patterns. Tenerife, according to the Sailing Directions, is an extremely high and mountainous island. The highest peak, Pico de Teyde, is more than 12,000 feet.

We shall make a photo reconnaissance and then proceed to our rendezvous point off Cadiz, Spain, where we are due on the 2nd of May. As stated elsewhere in this report, Tenerife was Magellan's last European port of call before he set forth on his round the world cruise, and the site of the first attempted mutiny by his captains. According to Parr, Santa Cruz harbor lay between nearly precipitous clefts in the hillside. The chart shows that modern Santa Cruz has a large and efficient-looking artificial harbor formed by a long breakwater. Try as we may, we are unable to locate where Magellan's precipitous cliff-walled harbor could have been. . . .

0830   We are now near enough to begin our "photo-recon" of the outskirts of the city of Santa Cruz on Tenerife Island. It is indeed an imposing skyline, though search as we may, we still find no evidence of the harbor supposedly used by Magellan. The scenery is most spectacular, however, far and away the most breathtaking of this cruise. Tenerife, like the other Canary Islands, is a huge mountain with many peaks and comes nearly vertically out of the sea. The water between islands is extremely deep until very close to shore. . . .

0933   Departed Tenerife for rendezvous off Cadiz the early morning of Monday, 2 May. . . .

Monday, 2 May 1960

Our waking hours for the past several weeks have been devoted almost exclusively to drills, conferences, and the preparation of this report. It is finished at last, a few hours before we rendezvous *WEEKS*. Only a short homeward-bound voyage across the Atlantic Ocean remains—a mere 3,000 miles.

It must be appreciated that more of the personal has been related in these pages than a regular naval voyage report requires. There have been several reasons for this, among them the belief that *TRITON's* undersea voyage has accomplished something of value for our country. The sea may yet hold the key to the salvation of man and his civilization. That the world may better understand this, the Navy directed a submerged retrace of Ferdinand Magellan's historic circumnavigation. The honor of doing it fell to *TRITON*, but it has been a national accomplishment; for the sinews and the power which make up our ship, the genius which designed her, the thousands and hundreds of thousands who labored, each at his own metier, in all parts of the country, to build her safe, strong, self-reliant, are America. *TRITON*, a unit of their Navy, pridefully and respectfully dedicates this voyage to the people of the United States.[3]

ACKNOWLEDGMENTS

I would like to thank the following persons for helping compile the bibliography and for making the illustrations available: Elbert Huber and staff, Navy Branch, National Archives; Ernest Dodge and Myron Brewington, Peabody Museum of Salem, Massachusetts; John Pomfret and staff, especially Miss Mary Isabel Fry, Henry E. Huntington Library; Admiral Ernest M. Eller, USN, ret., Commander D. V. Hickey, USN, and staff, Naval History Section, Navy Department; Lieutenant Commander F. A. Prehn, USN, Office of Information, Navy Department; Eugene Holtman, the Ohio State University Library; Wilbur Leech, Arthur Breton, Betty Ezequelle, and Arthur Carlson, New York Historical Society; Robert W. Hill and Jean McNiece, MS Division, New York Public Library; David Mearns and staff, MS Division, Library of Congress; Roger C. Taylor, Managing Editor, *United States Naval Institute Proceedings*.

SOURCES

For introductory notes, see Carroll Storrs Alden and Allan Wescott, *The United States Navy* (Chicago, 1943); Dudley W. Knox, *A History of the United States Navy* (New York, 1948); and E. B. Potter, *et al., The United States and World Sea Power* (Englewood Cliffs, 1955).

Abbreviations are used for the following: LC, Manuscript Division, Library of Congress; NA, National Archives; RG, Record Group; *USNIP, United States Naval Institute Proceedings.*

CHAPTER I

1. Original draft in John Paul Jones' letterbook, U.S. Naval Academy, reproduced in *John Paul Jones, Commemoration at Annapolis, April 24, 1906* (Washington, 1907).
2. "Narrative of John Kilby." Original MS narrative at the U.S. Naval Academy, reproduced in *Scribner's Magazine* (1905).
3. *The Magazine of History with Notes and Queries* (1913), extra number 21.
4. Courtesy of American Antiquarian Society.
5. *The Federalist,* No. XI.
6. Courtesy of American Antiquarian Society.
7. RG 45, NA.
8. *United States Naval Chronicle* (1824).
9. Elijah Shaw, *Narrative* (Rochester, 1845), courtesy of Henry E. Huntington Library.
10. Edward Preble Papers, LC.
11. U.S. Navy, Office of Naval Records and Library, *Naval Documents Related to the United States Wars with the Barbary Powers* (Washington, 1939–44).
12. Edward H. Tatum, Jr. & Marion Tinling, eds., "Letters of William Henry Allen, 1800–1813," *Huntington Library Quarterly* (1937–38).
13.–15. *Naval Monument* (Boston, 1840).
16. *Niles Register,* 30 October 1813.

17. Journal of Surgeon James Inderwick, MS Division, New York Public Library, reproduced in Victor Hugo Paltsits, ed., *Cruise of the U.S. Brig Argus in 1813* (New York Public Library, 1917).
18. Courtesy of American Antiquarian Society.
19. *Columbian Centinel*, 23 September 1812.
20. Samuel F. Holbrook, *Threescore Years* (Boston, 1857), courtesy of Henry E. Huntington Library.
21. David C. Bunnell, *Travels and Adventures* (Palmyra, 1831).
22. Copy, MS Division, New York Public Library.
23. *Naval Monument*.

CHAPTER II

1. *American Monthly Magazine* (1824).
2. W. F. Lynch, *Naval Life* (New York, 1851), courtesy of Henry E. Huntington Library.
3. Francis Warriner, *Cruise of the United States Frigate Potomac,* (New York, 1835); Edgar Stanton Maclay, "An Early 'Globe-Circling' Cruise," *USNIP* (1910).
4. Commander R. C. Parker, USN, ed., "A Personal Narrative of the Koszta Affair," *USNIP* (1927).
5. "Commodore Perry's Landing in Japan—1853. From the Journal of Commodore John Rodgers Goldsborough," *The American Neptune* (1947), courtesy of the Peabody Museum of Salem, Massachusetts.
6. Charles Nordhoff, *Man-of-War Life* (Cincinnati, 1856).
7. Holbrook, *Threescore Years*.
8. Nordhoff, *Life*.
9. Naval Courts, No. 844, RG 125, NA.
10. *Army and Navy Journal* (1878).
11–12. Naval Courts, Nos. 1237, 1016, RG 125, NA.
13. Fitch Taylor, *The Broad Pennant* (New York, 1848).
14. Joseph T. Downey, *The Cruise of the Portsmouth,* ed. by Howard Lamar (New Haven, 1958), courtesy of Yale University Library.
15. *Report of the Secretary of the Navy 1848*.
16. Charles Erskine, *Twenty Years before the Mast* (Boston, 1890).

CHAPTER III

1. John Rodgers Papers, LC.
2. Charles A. Post, "A Diary on the Blockade," *USNIP* (1918).

3. *Harper's Magazine* (1864).
4. Arthur M. Schlesinger, ed., "A Bluejacket's Letters Home," *The New England Quarterly* (1928).
5. MS letter, Peabody Museum of Salem, Massachusetts.
6. *Atlantic Monthly* (1863).
7. "Recollections of Bartholmew Diggins," MS Division, New York Public Library.
8. "Outline Story of the War Experiences of William B. Cushing as Told by Himself," *USNIP* (1912).
9. *Report of the Secretary of the Navy 1871.*
10. Hanson W. Baldwin, ed., "Narrative of William Halford, Only Survivor of the Cruise of the Gig of the Saginaw," *USNIP* (1935).
11. Emma DeLong, ed., *The Voyage of the Jeannette, the Ship and Ice Journals of George W. DeLong* (Boston, 1884), II.
12. E. B. Potter, ed., *The United States and World Sea Power* (Englewood Cliffs, 1955).
13. Alfred Thayer Mahan, *The Influence of Sea Power upon History, 1660–1783* (Boston, 1890).

CHAPTER IV

1. Charles D. Sigsbee, *The "Maine" An Account of Her Destruction* (New York, 1899).
2. *Century Magazine,* (1898).
3. *The Voyage of the Oregon from San Francisco to Santiago* (Boston, 1898).
4. Captain J. K. Taussig, USN, "Experiences during the Boxer Rebellion," *USNIP* (1927).
5. *North American Review* (1900).
6. Frank T. Cable, "The Strange Cruise of the 'Octopus,'" *Cosmopolitan Magazine* (1907).
7. Captain W. Irving Chambers, USN, "Aviation and Aeroplanes," *USNIP* (1911).
8. "A Destroyer in Active Service," *Atlantic Monthly* (1918).
9. Captain J. K. Taussig, USN, "Destroyer Experiences During the Great War," *USNIP* (1922–23).
10. "Naval Notes—Lieutenant Gresham's Account of the Sinking of the 'Aztec,'" *USNIP* (1917).
11. "A Destroyer in Active Service."
12. Taussig, "Destroyer Experiences."
13. Ralph D. Paine, *The First Yale Unit* (1925), II.

CHAPTER V

1. Commander John H. Towers, USN, "The Great Hop, the Story of the American Navy's Transatlantic Flight," *Everybody's Magazine* (1919).
2. A Junior Officer's Widow, "Even the Birds," *USNIP* (1934); Lieutenant Commander Herbert V. Wiley in *Literary Digest* (1933).
3. Lieutenant Commander Edward Ellsberg, USN, ret., "Inside the S-4," *Collier's* (1928).
4. Jack O'Donnell, "How Men Act in a Sunken Submarine," *Collier's* (1926).
5. Communications, testimonies of Lieutenant Commander Samuel Glenn Fuqua & Ensign Nathan Frederick Asher, *Hearings Before the Joint Committee on the Investigation of the Pearl Harbor Attack,* 79 Cong., 1 sess. (Washington, 1946), pts. 23, 24.
6. Fleet Admiral Ernest J. King, *Official Reports to the Secretary of the Navy* (Washington, 1946).
7. Commander Walter G. Winslow, USN, "The 'Galloping Ghost,'" *USNIP* (1949).
8. Copied in Naval History Division, Navy Department, *The Submarine in the United States Navy* (Washington, 1960).
9. Howard H. Peckham & Shirley A. Snyder, eds., *Letters from Fighting Hoosiers* (Indiana War History Commission, Bloomington, 1948).
10. Morton Vicker, "A PC Attacks," *USNIP* (1944).
11. *Fighting Hoosiers.*
12. Lieutenant Commander R. C. Benitez, USN, "Battle Stations Submerged," *USNIP* (1948).
13. Fleet Admiral William F. Halsey, Jr., USN, ret., "The Battle for Leyte Gulf," *USNIP* (1952).
14. *Fighting Hoosiers.*

CHAPTER VI

1. Potter, *World Sea Power.*
2. Naval History Division, *The Submarine.*
3. USS *Triton, SSRN 586. First Submerged Circumnavigation, 1960.* (Washington, 1960).

INDEX

501

PRINTED IN U.S.A.

DRAWN BY WADE